iry
tive
rch

Systemic Inquiry

Innovations in Reflexive Practice Research

Edited by

Gail Simon and Alex Chard

First published 2014 by
Everything is Connected Press
9-11 Main Street, Farnhill, UK, BD20 9BJ

British Library Cataloguing in Publication Data
A.C.I.P. for this book is available from the British Library

ISBN 978-0-9930723-0-7 (pbk)
ISBN 978-0-9930723-1-4 (ebk)

Systemic Inquiry: Innovations in Reflexive Practice Research
Edited by Gail Simon and Alex Chard
Cover image based on a photograph by Janine Lees
Design and formatting by Kate Kirkwood

www.eicpress.com

Contents

Foreword
Mary Gergen

This book is exciting in its revolutionary twist of putting the practitioner in the driver's seat when it comes to formulating ways of doing research in practice settings while collaborating on the research design with those the inquiry involves. The turn to collaborative research is an invitation to novelty. Of course, there is a certain messiness – often the bane of more traditional research approaches – yet, while chaos and disorder are the enemies of traditional research, in this case they are hallmarks of significant, humane, and relevant outcomes. This work privileges an ethics of openness, the creation of collaborative relationships, and the space for new and unanticipated stories to emerge. As Gail Simon proposes, it is possible to "move away from a notion of choosing a research method to engaging with and shaping a research process." The editors and contributors for this book have gone to wonderful lengths to make this possibility a reality.

The book contains a moving chorus of voices. Overall, there is a strong sense of harmony among the authors, each of them drawing from a pool of concepts, themes, approaches and theories that have melded together over the past fifty years. Beginning with the systemic moves of the 1960's, including the work of Bateson and the cybernetic movement, the Milan school of therapy, discourse process, early social constructionist ideas, and the literary turn, more generally, the music is lush, tonal, and exotic. As in a symphony, different sections function as movements with their own specific tones and unexpected melodies.

The major theme of the book is that it is possible *and* desirable to engage in research practices as a part of the daily engagement with others in the work setting. The book serves as a textbook for those teaching courses in qualitative methods with new and fresh materials obtained in commonplace settings. It is wonderfully accessible and practical in terms of providing resources for research-based practices. This is also a book that might encourage seasoned practitioners to explore their long-held hunches about what is taking place in their worlds of practice. I can imagine the book being especially helpful to post-graduate practitioners who want to inquire into their own practice. There is no need, according to these writings, to see the road diverging, with only a few taking the path to research.

Although there has been progress on the academic front in the acceptance of qualitative research, the tendency has been for theorists to lead the way. Following a longstanding but flawed tradition, practitioners should follow in the wake of the academic captains, and devise, as best they can, the practices that might follow from the abstract and erudite wordsmithing of these leaders. Professors in the academic world are supposed to do the research and create the theories. Practitioners are not expected to be researchers. Researchers are expected to be neutral in terms of their personal values and to position themselves as external to the methods and findings of the research itself. The idea of doing research "with" a group of participants, or of sharing research findings with a population that contributed to the study is either non-existent or quite peripheral to the goals of the research itself. For many committed to doing qualitative research from a systemic, constructionist bent, these criteria are not only irrelevant, but undesirable. The present volume reverses the pattern. The challenge put forth by this volume is to create a space for practitioners to conduct research derived from their own practices.

Each of the chapters offers a unique approach to research, yet each resonates with elements suggested by others. Among the various contributions, we can find practitioner-researchers who work in organizational consulting, community organizing, coaching, and therapy. Their chapters suggest inventive activities and notions of doing research. A strong motif throughout is answering the question of how a systemic approach, within a constructionist framework, enhances ways of going on together within the practitioner setting. There is an emphasis on innovation suited to the circumstances, a daring to do, a disregard for ordinary limits, and the integration of unfamiliar ideas. There is much that is fresh to discover. Always in the background is the notion of reflexivity, a continuous consciousness of the valuational or ideological consequences of their actions. This heightened awareness is a major factor in keeping ethical concerns at the forefront of the researcher's interests.

I was enchanted to read philosopher Richard Rorty's words, that the aim of the researcher-practitioner is to keep reinvigorating the conversation by finding new descriptions capable of forever restoring freshness in our engagement with the world, to elicit a "sense of wonder that there is something new under the sun" (Rorty 1980 p. 370). What a challenge to make this so.

Alongside the emphasis on practice led research, this volume brings together two important traditions that have been kissing kin, but seldom acknowledged as such. On the one hand, there is the tradition of systemic work especially connected to the Kensington Consultation Centre and now, the University of Bedfordshire. On the other hand, we have social construction developed through my own practice home with colleagues at the Taos Institute. All too often books written out of one theoretical community fail to acknowledge the other. I congratulate these editors for finding ways of combining the voices from both of these fields. The combination of systemic-constructionist research inevitably creates a generative and complimentary contribution to the fields of relationally sensitive practice based inquiry.

Mary Gergen

Preface

This is the book we looked for but didn't find many years ago when we were novice researchers during a doctorate in systemic practice. Instead we relied on John Shotter plying us with papers and we followed trails of other people's references in search of key texts. But there was no one collection which brought together contributions from people in the systemic field. So, whilst the idea for this book originated in meeting the needs of doctoral and masters students, the texts are written for anyone wanting inspiration about systemic approaches to research or who are planning to undertake systemic inquiry into human systems practice. We are excited that this book brings together 'old' and 'new' voices from practice research creating a book specifically for systemic and relationally reflexive practitioner researchers.

Systemic practice research is an exciting proposition. It builds on our creative practices and rigorous theories. This book acts as a joining edge between the everyday practice of consultants, therapists, leaders and activists and encourages novel and reflexive ways of inquiring into that practice. This is *not* a book on how to produce a certain kind of evidence or leave behind everything you have ever learned! The writers in this book show how you can stay living in the first language of your professional practice *and* make an inquiry into that professional practice. It is an invitation to critical reflexive thinking about *what counts* as research and as knowledge.

Professional practice is challenging and changing the academy with knowledge arising out of lived experience, out of professional practice and with its critical thinking about scientific method. The academy is gradually reviewing its premise that has separated knowledge from professional knowing. This is a false distinction and one which is being deconstructed across the academic field especially helped by the flourishing of professional doctorates. The academy is recognising that professional knowledge has equivalent status to academic knowledge *and* that professional practice generates academic knowledge from practice based evidence.

Systemic practitioners bring important insights and knowledge to the academic playing fields. We understand systems, relational being and the complexity involved in human communications. We have theories of change which reach beyond dominant stories of a single unit and can engage people in reflexive inquiry about the systems within which they live and work. This book encourages systemic researchers to foreground systemic knowledge, relational know-how, ethical concerns and develop a way of inquiring into one's own or other people's practice using the discursive tools we learned in our training and with our practice partners.

Reflexivity runs through all of these chapters like a red thread, creating ethical validity and enhancing our abilities to be accountable. It has emerged as a main theme in the book and is a good demonstration of what systemic practice has to add to the broader field of professional practice and to the field of qualitative research where reflexivity is understood often in quite limited ways to mean self-reflection or awareness.

It is no coincidence that organisational practice and therapeutic practice find a common home in systemic theory. They are both practices that take place within continually emergent and evolving human systems. The contributions in this book address a range of practice contexts with highly practical and transferable theory. The book deals with methodological challenges, ethical issues and practical matters.

The first part of the book addresses methodological matters.

Gail Simon opens this collection with an essay on the connections between systemic inquiry and qualitative inquiry. Gail draws out a history of the systemic practice of inquiry and shows how we can use our existing systemic ways of being and speaking to inquire from within our professional roles and employ all that we already know, use and value. Systemic irreverence, positive delinquency, curiosity and reflexive positioning coupled with theoretical rigour make for productive and ethical methods of inquiry. Gail suggests how we can benefit from the work of our postmodern qualitative inquiry cousins but also identifies some of the unique systemic offerings which systemic researchers can bring to the research community.

Alex Chard lays out a historical and philosophical context for systemic practitioner research. Alex demonstrates how the influence of Cartesian dualism undermines recognition of complexity in systems. Tracking some of the great contributions of systems thinking, Alex invites us to adopt a cybernetic stance and resituate the self of the researcher as an active participant in the system one is researching. Knowledge arising out of systemic inquiry is not intended as reproducible so much as a product of mutual inquiry in helping people go on together with an increased understanding.

Harlene Anderson invites us into a reflexive consideration of collaborative dialogue as a form of inquiry. Harlene situates these ideas in stimulating critique of what counts as knowledge and how "knowledge" is transmitted, deconstructing taken-for-granted scientific assumptions. Harlene reminds us of Maturana and Varela whose important work on information systems influenced systemic thinking in being more conscious about our intentions and understanding. Harlene emphasizes the importance for research of getting into everyday relational etiquette, an alongside position of joint attempts to understand and go on together. "Dialogue," says Harlene, "is a relational generative pathway to newness and possibilities in which each participant contributes to what is created through dialogue and not a unilateral monovocal content search for facts of details. It cannot be otherwise."

Sheila McNamee offers an eloquent framing of research as an act of social construction and highlights the centrality of relational processes in the creation of knowledge. Sheila draws some useful distinctions between types of qualitative research but also shows where there are points of connection and offers bridging language to maintain relationships of value with other approaches while retaining a systemic orientation. Sheila raises important questions about what counts as evidence and issues some bold encouragement "to continually remind ourselves that *we* make choices about inquiry – *we* decide what to study and how".

John Shotter challenges scientific practice explaining why it is flawed and why the human arts need to prepare for inquiry by entering into practices of relational orientation. John suggests "we have ignored too much of what is readily available to us"and invites us to consider how we deal with the stuff of life, how we make sense of things. He challenges the about-ness position expected of traditional researchers and explains the importance of with-ness thinking and knowing as something contextual to relational surroundings. John proposes a two stage process of "moving from a bewildering, confusing, indeterminate situation towards its gradual clarification ... a process that we can perhaps liken to bringing a severely blurred scene into focus. We can then outline a set of possible next steps to do with noticing openings and incipient beginnings within it that might afford its innovative development, the emergence of new inner articulations".

In the second part, we have an inspiring collection of systemic inquiry approaches.

Vikki Reynolds offers an exciting chapter on research as a social justice intervention using the metaphor of rhizome to understand movement and connection in community and personal change processes. Vikki describes the solidarity approach to inquiry guided by relational ethics in a collaborative inquiry in learning more about differences in identity and lived experience and through foregrounding a critical awareness of power relations in both practice, community and research relationships.

Saliha Bava takes a holistic systemic view of research situating it in a community practice and in a methodological free-for-all. She discusses how professional practice, research, research supervision and research writing are all forms of performance and need to be understood as performative and relational acts.

Jacob Storch and Karina Solsø have given us a useful bridging chapter in exploring the differences and connections between practice and research. Their dialogical writing offers the reader an invitation to listen in to their conversation with each other while they reflect on their own dilemmas and distinctions. Their chapter is a collage of talk with each other, an exploration of their own stories about practice and research and methodological contextualising.

Lisen Kebbe writes an eloquent and encouraging chapter on essay writing as a form of inquiry set in a story of her journey into research. It is an engaging tale with many opportunities for reflection on what undertaking research at doctoral level can involve. She offers a history of essay writing and explains how writing is a form of inquiry using examples from her own research into facilitating family business succession.

Kevin Barge, Carsten Hornstrup and Rebecca Gill invite us to consider the place of reflexivity in conversation through their description of Practice-Based Systemic Constructionist Research. They offer a clear and comprehensive exposition of how they understand reflexivity operating between people, with texts, and suggest how and why research conversations should be different from other kinds of conversations. "Conversational reflexivity", they propose, "is associated with a number of core animating values including playfulness, generativity, experimental attitude, curiosity, co-creation, and increasing the possibility space for alternative forms of meaning making and action." The concept of animating is important in systemic inquiry as we work in lively – alive environments and part of our job as practitioner researchers is to ensure people can breathe, develop and move around in the world with ease and safety.

Ann-Margreth Olsson cycles, often in a peloton and she uses this metaphor to inform her inquiry into complex and evolving systems of movement, coordination and leadership when trying to introduce client-led change in dialogical practice. She proposes a philosophical and practical development to participatory action research by emphasising the centrality of dialogue in professional relationships. As part of Dialogical Participatory Action Research, she introduces the practice and theory of Delta Reflecting Teams, an innovative development on ideas from Andersen, Shotter and Bakhtin.

Andreas Juhl offers a thorough exposition of pragmatic inquiry. Andreas offers a clear and detailed model for conducting an inquiry into one's professional practice drawing on the work of Brinkmann, Dewey, Lyotard, Rorty, Cronen and Bateson. We are invited to reflect on how organisations often have particular ideas about knowledge and how it can be used. Andreas describes a research process which opens up contextualising choices for the practitioner researcher with a series of guiding questions followed by theoretical and practice based responses. He opens up an important discussion about validity which he breaks down into communicative validity and pragmatic validity.

Chris Oliver uses Co-ordinated Management of Meaning theory to explore how change happens in linguistic systems. She re-visits the history of systems through a detailed description of systemic reflexivity and shows how using CMM as a form of inquiry can enable "reflexive exploration of the meaning and impact of cyclical patterns in our co-construction of communicative contexts". Chris uses an example of conversation from work with a couple to show complexity and discuss the relationship between insight, understanding and transformation.

Sally St George and Dan Wulff end this first collection by inviting us to reflect on the place of inquiry in everyday professional practice. They offer a helpful model of understanding the parallel and reflexive relationships between research and practice using key systemic principles while connecting with qualitative research theory and situating action in community contexts.

The rich legacy of the Kensington Consultation Centre in London included a systemic research degree, the Professional Doctorate in Systemic Practice which continues at the University of Bedfordshire. Six of the chapters in this book are written by doctoral graduates from this programme. We recall KCC Director, Peter Lang saying "We don't yet know what a systemic practice doctorate can look like, what systemic research can be and do." This was an exciting invitation and it is one this book also issues – to do and see what emerges as a useful form of inquiry and what is co-created in your practice.

When one produces a book like this, it feels a bit like tossing a message in a bottle into the sea and wondering where it will end up and whether it will connect with someone in a far off land or a few miles down the coast to where it started off. So feel free to communicate with us and we look forward to hearing how you develop the ideas and practices in the book. Talk to us!

Gail and Alex

Systemic Methodology

Systemic Inquiry as a form of Qualitative Inquiry

1

Gail Simon

Introduction

There are some striking 'family resemblances' between Systemic Inquiry and research methodologies gathering under the umbrella of Qualitative Inquiry (Denzin & Lincoln 2005, 2011). In this chapter I draw out areas of commonality in qualitative and systemic inquiry in practice research and propose Systemic Inquiry as a form of Qualitative Inquiry.

Common interests include:

- a reflexive and emergent shaping of methodology, focus and participation
- a relational emphasis
- a critique of power in the social world
- a social justice agenda
- ethics-led practice
- fluidity
- asking what counts as 'knowledge', with whose authority and with what consequences for others
- a concern with the politics of description and with the creation of narratives
- relationships in inner dialogue and outer talk
- social accountability: speaking from within the first person, transparency, showing context
- reflexivity
- a critical approach to 'professionalism' and 'methods'
- collaborative participation
- irreverence and respect
- practice as an art

In this opening chapter, I invite you to consider two main areas which I see as challenging to systemic practitioner researchers. Firstly, there is the debate of what counts as method in practice and in research. Postmodern systemic practitioner researchers have treated method as a fluid development in response to context. In other words, methodology evolves, inspired by a reflexive movement between emergent theory and practice. Secondly, in practitioner research, *relationality* is foregrounded. Ethics, know-how and reflexivity are not seen as stand-alone things. Instead we tend to speak of relational ethics, relational know-how, and relational reflexivity. After exploring connections between the postmodern movements of Qualitative Inquiry and Systemic Practice, I show how Systemic Inquiry is a form of Qualitative Inquiry in which methodology is treated as an emergent and ethical activity. This ethics-led, relational model of practice research incorporates room for spontaneous, emergent and collaborative responses to power and decision making in research practices.

The Evolution of Systemic Methodology

> *"... there is always a kind of developmental continuity involved in the unfolding of all living activities."* (Shotter 2005, p.26).

As a systemic practitioner researcher, I have been concerned to find ways of creating accounts of my practice which reflect and respect the collaborative, conversational relationships of systemic-social constructionist practice. Finding or developing a model and a language for research which can be woven into the careful co-ordinations of therapeutic, consultancy, supervisory and learning conversations is not just a practical decision but an ethical one too.

In this chapter, I invite systemic practitioner-researchers to approach the problem of choosing a research methodology with some degree of irreverence and with a social constructionist critique to ensure that we initiate an ethical and an ideological fit with our practice. Markovic has spoken of the rule creating culture of systemic practice and encouraged a stance of *positive delinquency* to our theoretical heritage in the interest of usefulness in practice relationships (Markovic, then Radovanovic 1993). Harlene Anderson invites practitioners to question the relevance of inherited rules created by our profession (Anderson 2007, cited in Simon 2010) and Betty St Pierre comments, "I'm tired of old research designs being repeated so many times that we think they are real – we forget we made them up!" (St Pierre 2010). Sheila McNamee extends Cecchin's concern with *irreverence* (Cecchin 1987) in showing how *promiscuity* in systemic practice allows practitioners to treat theories as discursive options which open up or close down relational possibilities (McNamee 2004).

We are reminded that, like all theories, research methodologies are products of time, place and culture. Research methodologies are not items on a shelf which one takes down and uses as ready-made products. It can be more useful and in keeping with a systemic approach to think about research as a process of mutual shaping in which researchers and co-researchers are changed by each other and by the activities; in turn, the research methods and activities also evolve through the influence of researchers and co-researchers. By accepting the inevitable mutual shaping in practice and research relationships, by fostering space for new and unanticipated stories to emerge, we privilege the ethics of methodological openness and move away from a notion of *choosing a research method* to *engaging with and shaping a research process.*

> *"when someone acts, their activity cannot be accounted as wholly their own activity – for a person's acts are inevitably 'shaped' in the course of their performance partly by the acts of the others around them, i.e., each individual's action is a joint creation, not the product of a sole author – this is where all the seeming strangeness of the dialogical begins."* (Shotter 2011, p.32)

The Development of Systemic Inquiry

Types and Uses of Questions
The early Milan School developed a method of inquiry as a response to a finding: they noticed that people did not maintain any improvements gained in psychiatric hospital when discharged to their family (Boscolo et al 1987). This observation formed a premise for their work and, inspired by the work of Gregory Bateson (1972, 1979), Maturana & Varela (1980, 1987, 1988) and others, they developed a theory of family systems which developed innovative questioning techniques to explore how a family system organised itself in response to actual or imagined change, and how information could be obtained and used by the therapy team. The international systems community soon realised that the Milan approach was not simply a matter of using questions to understand the workings of a particular human system and explore a hypothesis; they recognised that their questions also had an impact on parts of the family system and that the relational act of asking questions of people is inevitably an intervention on the system (Selvini Palazzoli et al. 1980; Tomm 1987a).

This inspired a blossoming of interest in inquiry and in theorising what inquiry does. Systemic questions were developed to create opportunities for new tellings of old stories, for imagining alternative futures and for reconfigurations in relationships between people, their narratives and actions. Karl Tomm developed a range of practical interventive questions in his collection of papers on interventive interviewing (Tomm 1987a, 1987b, 1987c). Peggy Penn emphasised a need for a temporal dimension by introducing future oriented questions (Penn 1985). Insoo Kim Berg and Steve de Shazer proposed questions within a brief solution focused model (de Shazer 1985, 1988). Later, through a postmodern lens, John Burnham introduced questions which invited self reflexivity and relational reflexivity (Burnham 1992, 1993, 2005). Michael White and David Epston developed questions to identify problematic dominant narratives and inquire into their influence. They showed how questions could uncover and strengthen alternative, preferred narratives which created opportunities for overturning an unhappy status quo (White 1988; White & Epston 1990).

The concern in systemic practice to re-evaluate power in therapeutic and management relationships and in the storying of management and therapeutic practices, led to questions which enquired into the clients' strengths, abilities, dreams and hopes (Combs & Freedman 1990; Flaskas et al 2007; O'Hanlon et al 1998; Cooperrider and Srivastva 1987). The recognition of wider systems in which people were living influenced the development of questions which reframed the individual as members of different community groups (for example, McCarthy & Byrne, 1988; Burnham & Harris 1996; Simon 1998). These power and culture sensitive questions reframed the professional relationship so that knowledge of the systemic practitioner shifted from 'conductor' (Selvini Palazzoli et al. 1980) or expert knower (Anderson & Goolishian 1992) to curious respondent which foregrounded the expertise of the people with whom they are working.

Theorising practices of inquiry and the influence of context

Vernon Cronen's and Barnett Pearce's Coordinated Management of Meaning theory (CMM) invited us to question how the different contexts we are acting out of and into influence the direction, content and shaping of meaning in the professional relationship (Pearce 1989; Oliver 1996). The model of CMM invites us to question the range of narratives, theories and practices which influence a person's or team's systemic practice through the centring of *reflexivity* as an ethical response. This continuous reflexive influence between theory and practice makes for a continual methodological evolution of *and as* systemic practice (Leppington 1991; Burnham 1992; Simon 2012a).

The Milan team's advice not to marry one's hypothesis was further developed by Cecchin by encouraging curiosity and irreverence in systemic practice (Cecchin 1987). John Burnham demonstrated the art of irreverence despite and, perhaps, because of the constant movement between creativity and respectful co-ordination in his work (Burnham 1992, 1993, 2005). In mapping out the relationships between approach, method and techniques Burnham used the model of interlinked levels of context from CMM to upturn and re-contextualise stories of power and influence (Burnham 1992, 1993, 2011). He suggests practical ways in which ideas can influence and re-shape systemic practice.

In both Leppington's (1991) and Burnham's (1992) descriptions of reflexive practice cycles, practitioners are invited to question their ideological influences: their most deeply held beliefs, their most cherished assumptions, cultural stories operating at a less mindful level but having an impact on practice choices and findings. The shift in postmodern systemic practice away from a model based on a one-sided embodiment of professional expertise to a model of collaborative inquiry (Anderson & Goolishian 1992), a shared process of reflection (Andersen 1987) invited systemic practitioners into a reflexive process in which all theories, personal, professional, cultural beliefs etc. are open to review. To actively engage in critical reflexivity about practices and the theories supporting them, to be aware of one's preferences and how they can serve to turn away countering voices and alternative narratives (White & Epston 1990) opens up possibilities for ethical consideration of the relationships between theory, practice and ideology (Leppington 1991).

By including ideology within methodology, Leppington advocates for the socio-political-philosophical contextualising of method and theory. This requires us to transparently reveal and own the ideological influences at work in our choice of any one research 'method'. By asking not only *'What counts as data?'* but the ethics-led question of *'What can data count as?'* Leppington proposes that we allow ourselves to be changed by what we find – our methods, theories and most deeply held beliefs - and not simply impose our own meaning on material with the risk of reproducing existing values and power relations. For these reasons, I suggest the term *research methodology*, as opposed to research method, is more coherent with an ethics-led approach to systemic practice.

Systemic practice has gone through many significant theoretical shifts – some in the name of a scientific attempt to perfect an approach, others arising out of ethical concerns. Emphasis has turned away from how we can 'really' understand systems to how we generate useful stories about people and relationships (Hoffman 1993; White & Epston

1990). This move away from generalising theory to contextually specific knowing is a more ethically comfortable fit with relationships involved in collaborative inquiry (Anderson 1997). In recognising that theory almost never works as a one-size-fits-all without exclusionary and dangerous consequences (Lather 1994), systemic practice has gone on to encourage dialogue about the differences in knowledge and knowing and know-how (Andersen 1997; Anderson & Goolishian 1992; Seikkula 2002). This ethical shift invited systemic pracitioners to consider how to work collaboratively with people (Anderson & Gerhart 2006). Anne Hedvig Vedeler builds on Cecchin's idea of curiosity (Cecchin 1987) preferring the term *benevolent curiosity* which she feels better reflects a respectful dialogical and collaborative approach in consultation, teaching, supervision and therapy. Vedeler reinterprets fellow Norwegian, Tom Andersen's reflecting team as Resonance Groups and frames them as a means of embodied dialogical inquiry (Vedeler 2010).

Systemic practice has foregrounded the place of *inquiry* in a number of ways. In addition to our vast and extraordinary library of questions, systemic inquiry can be understood as technique, as method, as ethical, reflexive and collaborative ways of being with people, as reflexive inner and outer dialogue, as reflexive writing in training contexts. So why, when we have developed such rich and sophisticated theory about the emergent and co-constructionist nature of inquiry, would we look to a positivist research model advocating a prescribed model with one person extracting information from another or interpreting material without involving our co-researchers?

Certainly, the trend in economy-led public and private services encourages practitioners to employ positivist ways of measuring decon-textualised improvement and overlook relational consequences of change and the meaningfulness of professional interaction. Practitioners are often bullied into stepping into a different language to co-ordinate with positivist discourses at the expense of developing professional knowledge and know-how. Opportunities need to be created for inquiry which is coherent with, for example, the coordination with micro-movements at bodily and emotional and temporal levels in the improvisational practice of systemic dialogue, practices which do not necessarily lend themselves, nor should they, to any form of categorisation or results tables.

Systemic inquiry is not intended to be a reproducible solution so much as a stance of methodological irreverence which abandons any modernist attempt to achieve and impose a streamlined scientific method. Instead, it advocates a form of inquiry which emphasises a shift from knowledge to ethics (Leppington 1991), in which we have a loose attachment to precious, hard come by theories and practices and one which is powered by self and relational reflexivity. Systemic inquiry is a form of research and professional practice which will always evolve as a reflexive response to news of difference (Bateson 1979).

A short story from practice

After a conversation with a supervisee, I feel a residue of conflicting feelings: an attachment to an idea and some discomfort about the degree of that attachment. I use reflexive writing as a form of inquiry (Richardson 1994) to create opportunities for further stories to emerge from my inner dialogue about the conversation with the supervisee. After a while of writing, I feel I am missing the voice of the supervisee. I share my writings with the supervisee and in the spirit of collaboration, I invite her responses. At our next meeting, she brings a lengthy written response and reads it aloud to me. As I listen, I am shocked by my mis-understanding of something she has said. I hear her voice and what she is saying in quite a different way. I hear my own listening and talking differently too. How I listen and what I hear, have been changed by this experience. I listen with a broader range of conversing voices in my mind akin to bringing the reflecting team into the room (Andersen 1997) and with more attempts at resonance (Vedeler 2010). The talk between us changes and my listening starts to feel more alongside her than about her.

This story demonstrates how the constant acting on one's noticings in an attempt to co-ordinate with the interests of the other, describes a model of practice which is not working towards refining a theoretical model with a static, scientifically 'accurate' body of knowledge to compete in acquiring academic and professional status and a secure identity. Instead, it is characterised by an ethics-led agenda which decentres the practitioner / researcher (Lather 2007; Tootell 2004) and, in improvisational reflexive inquiry, weaves narratives and relational responses.

Our attempts to communicate are inevitably not only flawed but messy. We ask, and expect to be asked, questions which help us know how to go in conversation with writers, colleagues, clients, research participants and so on. As we leave a fixed way of talking behind, our communications spring from spontaneous responsiveness (Shotter & Katz 1998), improvisation (Burnham 1992; Keeney 1990) and emotional openness (Anderson & Jensen 2007) which, as often seen and heard through video reviews or through transcriptions, appear chaotic and unpredictable. The *apparently* disorderly passages of interaction between people or within our inner dialogue may not require or lend themselves to examination through a methodology with a repeatable, re-describable method – something you learn to roll out and find ways of teaching to others for them to perform. Research with people, as with most relationships, professional or otherwise, can be an unpredictable process generating what some describe as 'messy texts' (Clifford & Marcus 1986; Lather 2007; Law 2007; Marcus 2007). Most forms of text analysis (for example, grounded theory, Charmaz 2012; Interpretive Phenomenological Analysis, Smith et al 2009; conversational analysis, Woolfitt 2005; discourse analysis, Woolfitt 2005) exclude opportunities to enter into learning from within the hub of systemic activity and have not addressed the complex inner and outer workings of *relational processes* (and the relationship between inner and outer).

Additionally, there are ethical dilemmas for systemic researchers concerned with the practice of co-creating of meaning. Despite an increasing interest in relational ethics, such methods still position the researcher in an about-ness position (Shotter 2011) in relation to 'the material' as if it is a thing in itself apart from the relational processes. This attempt at objectivity counters the situated collaborative and reflexive inquiry at the heart of systemic practice and often promotes a confused assumption that objectivity coupled with a prescribed method is synonymous with rigour.

Accounting Practices and Legitimacy

Michael White encourages an exploration of relationships between stories, storytellers and audience and he situates narratives in the relational context of texts. He says the *"text analogy introduces us to an intertextual world. In the first sense, it proposes that persons' lives are situated in texts within texts. In the second sense, every telling or retelling of a story, through its performance, is a new telling that encapsulates, and expands upon the previous telling"* (White & Epston 1990, p.13). White's suggestion that there is no ultimate truth to be told corresponds with Barnett Pearce's advice that we should *"treat all stories, your own as well as others, as incomplete, unfinished, biased and inconsistent."* (Pearce 2004, p.50). Their ideas help us understand why systemic inquiry needs to challenge 'research' as an attempt to make objective, decontextualised knowledge claims and offer instead a relational and reflexive understanding of research as producing of narratives-in-progress. White (1992) invited us to be curious about which narratives dominate people, families and the communities in which they live, to understand the contexts in which these narratives have established their dominance and he invites practitioners to look at how other accounts or descriptions of people or events have been lost or silenced. White draws on Foucault's idea of *subjugated knowledges* *"that survive only at the margins of society and are lowly ranked- considered insufficient and exiled from the legitimate domain of the formal knowledges and the accepted sciences"* and goes on to quote Foucault as saying these knowledges are the "naïve knowledges, located low down on the hierarchy, beneath the required level of cognition or scientificity" (White & Epston 1990, p.26).

Denzin and Lincoln point to the political backdrop for this method- ologically dilemmic era as a climate which is dominated by narrow ideas about what counts as 'evidence' and research projects struggling to influence policies driven by economics over social need. They describe this time as the *"methodologically contested present"* and how it is *"a time of great tension, substantial conflict, methodological retrenchment in some quarters ... and the disciplining and regulation of inquiry practices to conform with conservative, neoliberal programs and regimes that make claims regarding Truth."* (Lincoln & Denzin 2005, p.1116).

The Narrative of Method

If we understand social constructionism as treating all theories as stories, we can also recognise methods as narrative products and as producing of narratives. The narratives people bring to their workplace or social life are co-constructed, shaped between people and subject to interpretation (Anderson & Goolishian 1988; Burr 1995). Our theoretical narratives arise out of our ideological beliefs, values and most taken for granted deeply held assumptions. Methods and techniques sit more or less neatly on the back of these ideologically influenced narrative structures but can easily appear as stand-alone entities without prejudice, without social underpinnings.

The more dominant stories of professional practice and research about methods suggest a clearly signposted order of events to be carried out by a trained individual or team who 'knows' what they are doing. This 'knowing' mostly corresponds to a learned technique or process. Case examples from many recent leaders in narrative and systemic practice often perpetuate an idea of a clean, reproducible method in their writings or presentations with an emphasis on what was *said*. There is little attention in most professional texts to the times between the sparkling moments which is probably 99% of time. In amongst the gems are messy, clumsy attempts to co-ordinate, half-finished sentences and retracted questions, mm's and aha's and a range of physical responses such as nods, eyebrow movements, outer and inner twitches. I have noticed through my work as a systemic therapist and as a supervisor that when a practitioner isn't using a particular technique, she or he is trying to co-ordinate with the client(s). Is this time wasted or does it set a context for the moments identified as important by the practitioner or their conversational partners?

We are hoping our attempts to communicate and understand the communications of the other will count as something important to participants in the conversation. We know, for example, that just coming up with a miracle question (de Shazer 1988) at any moment will not have as much impact as if the client feels the practitioner has been paying attention to what they have been saying and responding empathically. The human element in the work may count for more than we realise and this is supported by much research (Sexton & Whiston 1994) and more is being written about the relational activities in the professional relationship (Anderson & Gehart 2007; Flaskas 2002; Flaskas et al 2004).

The shift in systemic practice towards the dialogical and the collaborative brings an expectation of improvisational coordination between participants. John Burnham (Burnham 1993) has embraced the inevitability of chaos and confusion arising in conversation and taken an approach to not-knowing (Anderson & Goolishian 1992) how to go on with people as part of the negotiation about how to go on. He has given many examples of his practice in which he demonstrates meaningfulness arising out of the random. He advocates a model of therapy, supervision or consultation in which any governing level of context can be upturned and reviewed at any moment in time (Burnham 1992, 1993, 2005). This approach is not led by some theory about the importance of the random (though random choices can be very generative of useful connections) so much as by an ethical concern to be client-led or supervisee-led and by a pragmatic approach to find a way forward. Burnham tries to co-ordinate with people in recognising any meaningful elements in exchanges however bizarre or unexpected they may be. This model of ethics-led systemic practice involves a negotiation with the people with whom one is working throughout the process otherwise the practitioner stance is that of imposing a method on others. In engaging in a practice-research process, it is often important and fruitful to mirror this commitment to spontaneous, relational co-ordination.

A Relational Focus

Social Justice: Inspiration for Practices of Inquiry

> *Critical researchers start from an ethical principle and do research designed to emancipate people from patterns of social relations prejudged to be oppressive, to expose patterns of exploitation, or to subvert structures of power that allow some people to be dominated by others.* (Pearce and Walters 1996, p.10).

An overarching link between Systemic Inquiry with Qualitative Inquiry is the commitment to open up space for a multiverse with polyvocal participation across all parts of a research process concerned with beneficial consequences for participants of research intervention (Denzin & Lincoln 2005, 2011; Lather 1994; Parker 2005; Pearce and Walters 1996; Tuhiwai Smith 2005; Visweswaran 1994; Reynolds 2010, 2013 and elsewhere in this book).

Social constructionist-systemic-collaborative-dialogical therapy has moved away from normative and pathologising discourses. Narrative therapy invites therapists and community workers to allow themselves to be moved to action by the stories they hear, become activists in trying to overturn injustices and experiment with creative, socially inclusive, relational practices. (White & Denborough 2005). Sheila McNamee shows the significance of women taking hold of research and responding in a way which privileges finding their own ways of researching (McNamee 1994). Tom Andersen encouraged practitioners to be moved by the circumstances of the people whose story one was hearing (Shotter 2007). Jaakko Seikkula suggests that if a person is drowning, one has to jump in the water too in order to try and save them even if that puts the practitioner in some degree of risk (Seikkula 2002). Reynolds speaks of the practitioner researcher as a "fluid, imperfect ally" in describing the importance of ethics led alliances in getting beyond the constraints of colonial professional positioning (Reynolds 2013).

We can frame the practice of systemic inquiry as caring, as involvement in the lives and communities of others, as an openness to be changed by the words and feelings of others, as a preparedness to be moved to action in and beyond the consulting room or classroom. Both Systemic Inquiry and Qualitative Inquiry encourage experimentation with useful and user-friendly ways of inquiring into the lives of people and communities. Qualitative Inquiry methodologies try to amplify the voices of research participants over those of researchers (for example, Lather & Smithies 1997) and position the researcher as a reflexive research participant (Etherington 2004). There are many echoes some of the understanding in postmodern systemic therapies about the reflexive positioning of the practitioner (Amundson et al 1993; Andersen 1987; Anderson and Goolishian 1988, 1992; Anderson 1997; Burnham 2011; Reynolds 2013; Rober 2005; Shotter & Katz 1998; Seikkula & Arnkil 2006).

Working the Prejudicial Turn

> *Producing 'things' always involves value—what to produce, what to name the productions, and what the relationship between the producers and the named things will be. Writing 'things' is no exception. No textual staging is ever innocent (including this one). Styles of writing are neither fixed nor neutral but reflect the historically shifting domination of particular schools or paradigms.* (Richardson 1994, p.518).

Systemic practitioners drawing on a postmodern critique recognise that it is impossible to be value free and that we work with our prejudice in a mindful manner through reflexive inner and outer dialogue. When it comes to *researching* our work, we may feel the pull of 'objectivity' to depict process and outcomes 'fairly'.

It is, in this moment, that the language of systemic practice is often assumed by systemic practitioners to be redundant. There is a strong story of expertise from other professional academic discourses which teach us to evaluate our work 'fairly' or 'accurately' and without prejudice. We are keen to be fair and rigorous but we are already trained in methods of inquiry. And we are prejudiced because we value the stories people tell us, we recognise their uniqueness, we want to be moved by people and perhaps show people how we are moved – and we want this movement between us to count as something. We hear stories which many people do not get to hear but which are worth hearing; stories which will have taken their time to choose a suitable platform to speak from and audience to speak with. We use selective hearing to influence our ways forward because we allow ourselves to be moved by our conversational partners. We work with people so they can hear what it is they want to say and find ways of saying it to themselves, to us and to others who matter. Systemic practitioners have dialogical, communicating abilities which help to create the circumstances for the performances of other selves, alternative narratives and we want to be supportive of those preferred stories or more useful ideas and life choices. We are far from neutral in our work and the intricacies of our co-ordinations do not lend themselves to a system of measurement.

> *Value-neutrality elaborates the disinterested aspect of objectivity: the conviction that knowers have no vested interest in the objects of their knowledge; that they have no reasons other than the pursuit of 'pure' inquiry to seek knowledge. These ideals are best suited to regulate the knowledge making of people who believe in the possibility of achieving a 'view from nowhere' – of performing what Donna Harway calls 'the god trick'.* (Code 1995, p.15)

And then there is the question of whether just anyone or any systemic practitioner or researcher can ask and get the same answer. We know that not to be true. Why? Because the systemic community has reclaimed the importance of the working relationship and we have recognised how different relationships and contexts bring out different parts of us, different stories resulting in different tellings, hearings and meanings. Lorraine Code challenges the idea that:

> *"knowers are substitutable for one another in the sense that they can act as 'surrogate knowers' who can put themselves in anyone's place and know exactly what she or he would know." (Code 1995, p.16)*

Cronen makes a suggestion for systemic inquiry:

> *"It would be better to say that in the process of inquiry we make determinations of what related elements need to be included for any purpose of inquiry and call that the 'situation-in-view'. Identifying the situation-in-view is a provisional judgment. Further inquiry may lead to including new elements and disregarding others. [.....] Situations-in-view must be understood to include the inquirer. The inquirer cannot be outside the system. **The only choice to make is what kind(s) of relationship(s) one chooses for the purposes of inquiry.**"* (Cronen 2000) [my emboldening of last sentence.]

Leppington emphasised the importance of *relational know-how* and provided a way of contextualising which stories and which voices had more prominence (Leppington 1991). In proposing a move away from a method-led model of systemic practice which advocated training therapists and consultants to learn the theory and the application of techniques, Leppington described systemic practice as 'discursive practice'. She emphasised a significant paradigmatic movement which she referred to as the shift *'from knowledge to ethics'*.

These methodological differences link qualitative inquiry with postmodern systemic practice in confronting the ethics of method-led versus client-led or research participant-led practice. In a systemic practice context, theory and ethics merge to suggest the word ***theorethical*** which may be useful in highlighting the integrated and reflexive relationship between theory and ethics.

Both systemic practice and qualitative inquiry have adopted social constructionism as a *theorethical* context of influence. My intention is to see theory and ethics as one in order to highlight the ethics-led choices we make about selecting which practices to employ and how.

Relational Ethics

Relational ethics has been at the heart of systemic practice since the linguistic turn in the late nineteen eighties (Anderson and Goolishian 1988; Andersen 1987; Goldner et al 1990; Lang et al 1990; McCarthy & Byrne 1988; White 1992).

It is not uncommon in quantitative research and positivist qualitative research for the area of ethics to constitute a task which is *additional* to the research. Applications to research ethics committees or research advisory boards are often experienced by researchers as an irritating but necessary authoritative hurdle to overcome in order for the real thing – the research activity - to commence. Like systemic practice, qualitative inquiry is an ethics led activity. The research design has participants in mind and involved in consultation from the start. 'Warming the context' activities (Burnham 2005) make it comfortable for people to participate in research but are not simply a prelude to the 'real' research so much as an opportunity to create a culture of collaborative inquiry, exploring and generating practices together.

Systemic practice is an ethics-led way of being and doing with others. Ethics is not an add-on: it is our guiding light, whatever the area of relational practice. As such, systemic inquiry is an ethics-led practice and can proudly offer this approach to the broader field of qualitative research.

A systemic approach to research brings something unique and useful to the qualitative inquiry movement. Our preoccupation with *relational ethics* requires us to address:

- how we coordinate fairly in conversation with each other

- how we critically approach, acknowledge or challenge power in the relationship or in broader socio-political contexts

- how we manage the relationship between the polyvocality of our inner dialogue with the polyvocality in our outer dialogue

- which of our many selves we use and how

- how we reflexively question our attachments with theories, hypotheses, methods and other taken-for-granted values

- how we offer transparent accounts to others as to which stories we privilege and which we discard

- how we re-view what we have done together, what it means for now and what else we might have done

- how we acknowledge the value of the exchange between us and co-researchers

The reflections of qualitative researchers Ellis (2008), Bochner (2000), Richardson (1994, 1997), Gergen & Gergen (2002) include criteria for qualitative inquiry which address relational ethics. Mary and Kenneth Gergen remind us of how modernist research has positioned researcher and researched: *"the traditional treatment of research 'subjects' was inclined to be alienating, demeaning, exploitative...... We are now highly sensitized to the 'politics of representation', the ways in which we as researchers construct – for good or ill – those whose lives we attempt to illuminate. A new array of collaborative, polyvocal, and self-reflexive methodologies has thus been given birth (see, for example, Denzin and Lincoln 2005)."* (Gergen & Gergen 2002, p.13).

In reviewing her work as an autoethnographer, Carolyn Ellis addresses relationships with research participants:

> *"Relational ethics recognizes and values mutual respect, dignity, and connectedness between researcher and researched, and between researchers and the communities in which they live and work focuses on the changing relationship between researcher and research participants."* (Ellis 2008, p.308)

> *"Relational ethics draws attention to how our relationships with our research participants can change over time........ How can we act in a humane, nonexploitative way while being mindful of our role as researchers?"* (Ellis 2008, p.308)

> *"Relational ethics requires us as researchers to act from our hearts and minds, to acknowledge our interpersonal bonds to others, and to initiate and maintain conversations (Bergum, 1998; Slattery & Rapp, 2003). The concept of relational ethics is closely related to*

an ethics of care (Gilligan, 1982; Noddings, 1984), communication ethics (Arnett, 2002), feminist and feminist communitarian ethics (see Christians, 2000; Denzin, 1997, 2003; Dougherty & Atkinson, 2006; Olesen, 2000; Punch, 1994)" (Ellis 2008, p.308)

The points Ellis raises and the questions she encourages researchers to ask themselves and discuss with their co-researchers and colleagues, bear a strong linguistic and ethical resemblance to the in-the-moment-of-the-relationship questions systemic practitioners might ask themselves.

There is also another research relationship to take into account with regard to ethics – the relationship between writer and reader. Researchers are expected to produce research in a format designed to be accessible to an audience, and more, meaningful. A challenge inherent in critical reflexive practice is to make transparent to the reader the range and extent of inner dialogue in either the application of method or in the apparently spontaneous responses between people. Bochner's vision of poetic social science and alternative ethnography requires that research should allow space for interpretation and use language in a way that allows readers (and writers) to extract meaning from experience, *"rather than depict experience exactly as it was lived"* (Bochner 2000, p.270).

Mary and Kenneth Gergen draw attention to the researcher-audience relationship:

"Yet, there is one relational domain that has received little attention to date, that is, the relationship between the rhetor and reader, researcher and audience. As deeply engaged social scientists, the way we represent the world to our colleagues and related audiences contributes to our ongoing relationships within these life worlds (see Shotter 1997). Our words constitute forms of action that invite others into certain forms of relationships as opposed to others. Thus our manner of writing and speaking contributes to life forms that may be extended throughout the educational sphere and into public modes of existence." (Gergen & Gergen 2002, p.13)

The Place of the Researcher in the Research: the Question of Transparency

"The writer has a theory about how the world works, and this theory is never far from the surface of the text." (Denzin 2003, p.117)

One of the main principles in qualitative inquiry is to render oneself visible as the researcher – both in the doing of research with participants *and* in the writing of the research for the reader - to make some sense of who is doing the inquiry and the reporting. In the same way that participants can decide how to participate in the research, readers can make choices about how to engage with the text.

This challenge has been taken up in different ways within qualitative inquiry where, to a large extent, the choices have been influenced by the researcher's story of the 'self': single, contextually varied, or polyvocal. Qualitative researchers are interested in establishing a 'real' relationship with co-researchers so they become relaxed and give fuller responses. A woman researcher hoped that using an interpreter in interviews would strengthen her understanding of what research participants were saying. However, she noticed that they were more engaged with the interpreter than with her. So she decided to stop using the interpreter and privilege connection over accuracy. This generated an unexpected richness which she had not been able to access using an interpreter (Quiros 2010).

I was struck by a story told by an African American man who was conducting research interviews with women who had had breast cancer in the southern states of the USA. He described how one research participant, an African American woman, told him that she was alienated by his professional veneer at a research interview. She advised him to act and sound like the southern African American man he was so that she and other women would find it easier to open up to him about quite personal experiences. He reflected that while he was trying to fade himself out to foreground the research questions and be a 'good' (meaning unobtrusive) researcher, he wasn't allowing for how others saw him. (Gregg 2010)

> *"A crucial first step in developing an adequately sensitive feminist methodology is learning to see what is not there and hear what is not being said. Donna Harway urges feminists to 'become answerable for what we learn how to see'. To be thus accountable, feminists have to see what is systematically and systemically screened from view by the most basic assumptions about how people know the world; and they have to understand the power structures that effect these erasures."* (Code 1995, p.19)

In ethnography, sharing stories about their own experience is something researchers are expected to be open to; to be themselves in the research as a context for the conversation so as to level the conversational playing field. In the case of autoethnography or performance ethnography, there is an expectation of extended openness to make space for any difficult, unlikely, taken for granted, unthinkable, normally unsayable things which are around in our lives and which could go unnoticed unless described against a backdrop which render them visible. This involves 'relational risk-taking' (Mason 2005) as part of an ethical attempt to connect with readers and audience as well as with research participants. In systemic practice, we have learned to become the kind of conversational partner who is not only emotionally present but also, where useful, with intentionally visible life experience (Roberts 2005).

Some things touch us more than others and it is perhaps rarely a coincidence that we choose to work with a particular client group or do research on a particular subject or find some theoretical ideas more attractive than others. In a traditional research context, there is little expectation of the researcher 'outing' themselves as having an investment in the subject under investigation. In qualitative inquiry, there is an ethics-led expectation that the researcher will express their interest - not to counter any idea of bias but to illuminate the inevitability of prejudice and minimise any power imbalance in *knowing* between researcher and research participant (Etherington 2004) and to lend weight to one's conviction that something is worthy of investigation and public sharing.

In systemic practice, we also recognise the impossibility of neutrality and objectivity. We own our prejudices and work with them. How we use our own experiences, how we share them and discuss them with people with whom we work, varies. We are careful not to burden people with whom we are working with what might be experienced as troublesome information, particularly vulnerable clients. On the other hand, perhaps we have something to learn from practitioners whose starting point can involve some personal disclosure to conversational partners, research participants. This would make an interesting area to research.

Relational Reflexivity in Relational Know-How

Visweswaran criticises the normative ethnographic approach that presumes an observer and a subject with stable identities. She contrasts this stance with deconstructive ethnography, where the observer refuses to presume a stable identity for self or other (Visweswaran 1994). Denzin suggests *"Deconstructive reflexivity is post-modern, confessional, critical, and intertextual."* (Denzin 2003, p.236). In the field of qualitative inquiry tends to treat reflexivity as a form of *self-reflexivity* for the researcher.

Through a social constructionist-systemic-collaborative-dialogical lens, reflexivity is an ethical processing in and of research or practice activities. Reflexivity is always relational in that there is polyphonic responsivity in both inner dialogue and outer dialogue, be it of a cognitive, emotional, neurological or environmental source (Simon 2012b).

The actions arising out of continual relational reflexivity in our practice as consultants, leaders, therapists, supervisors, trainers, researchers and writers might be described as a dance which requires attention to certain themes: a sensibility to any externally imposed tempo and other environmental demands and influences; a sensibility to a relational tempo in which dancers respectfully share the directorship of pace, challenge and movement; a responsivity to the invitations of other(s) and a selectivity about the choices offered and taken up. Relational reflexivity is not only something which can be observed with the eye. To observe only visible movements would overlook the drama of the inner movements of self and partners in the dance: emotional, embodied, cognitive and theoretical responses, fluent and jerky. We negotiate context, agenda, roles, language and a moment to moment focus. We exercise reflexivity in our co-ordinations with the other; we ask, check levels of comfort, understanding and meaning.

Reflexivity is also a form of self-supervision driven by a desire to coordinate with others in an ethical manner:

- What choices I am making and with what possible consequences for me, for them, for others not present?

- What is informing those choices?

- What other choices am I overlooking?

- Where are those guiding values/prejudices coming from?

We find ways of creating space to recognise the less mindful processes at work: embodied, emotional, cognitive, normative discourses, desire, personal gain, for example. A significant offering from systemic practitioners to the field of qualitative inquiry is a sophisticated understanding and articulation of relationally reflexive activities in researching practice.

Emergent Collaborations

The social sciences have been engaging in a paradigm shift which is being hailed as *the relational turn*. It invites an interest into ethics-led co-ordinations of co-researchers and into the micro-detail of how those co-ordinations take place.

In discussing possible directions for qualitative inquiry, Betty St

Pierre's reluctance "to accept the 'I' in Qualitative Inquiry" could be understood as a signpost indicating a need for more of a relational emphasis in research (St Pierre 2010). The field of qualitative research has embraced the concept of reflexivity with a significant contribution by practitioners within the field of counselling. The field of systemic practice has something to contribute to the place of *relationality* in research, research relationships, writing research for a readership and specifically on the subject of relational reflexivity. This is perhaps the area where systemic practice has most to bring to the field of qualitative research. Much has been written about Self and Other but there appears, to my systemic eye, to be some space in the research field to explore the dynamic elements in relationships between researcher and research participants. Descriptions of this relationship are either minimal, or sound as if participants are separate static entities. So whilst there is acknowledgement of social constructionism and the power of language and narratives, there is room for more understanding of co-creative activity in the development of those narratives.

Diane Gehart, Margarita Tarragona and Saliha Bava promote a model of research based on collaborative practices:

> *"Collaborative inquiry is a way of practising a philosophical stance of respect, curiosity, polyphony and social meaning making. More than the methods used, it is the intentions and the assumptions that inform the research process that constitute the collaborative nature of inquiries."* (Gehart et al 2007, p.385).

Mary and Kenneth Gergen open an invitation to experiment with relational space:

> *"Alternative ethnographers break away from the conventions of social science inscription to experiment with polyvocality, poetry, pastiche, performance, and more. These experiments open new territories of expression; they also offer new spaces of relationship. They take different stances toward readers, describing them in new ways, calling into being alternative possibilities for going on together."* (Gergen & Gergen 2002, p.14)

In this suggestion, Mary and Kenneth Gergen are suggesting a means of doing research more akin to the improvisational response to not-knowing (Anderson & Goolishian 1992; Anderson 1997) that we come up with in the doing of systemic practice. Shotter and Katz describe the interactions between participants involved in any human interaction, be it professional practice or research, as involving spontaneous attempts at responding and coordinating with another (Shotter & Katz 1998). This attention to improvisational and relational know-how casts ethical doubt on a stance of technological 'knowledge' and the rolling out of predictable practice or research method. All research constitutes an intervention in the lives of the researcher, the research participants and the audiences or witnesses to this research. Each act of inquiry invites, mindfully or otherwise, the possibility of an implicative force which changes lives.

Summary

In this opening chapter, I hope to have shown how much systemic practice research has in common with our cousins in qualitative inquiry. This familial culture provides an existing and sympathetic *theorethical* context for the systemic practice communities to develop ways of inquiring into our practice which are coherent with systemic values, ethics and theory. By engaging in a collaborative and reflexive process of inquiry with relational ethics to guide our movements in inner and outer conversation, we are inviting change for ourselves and others and creating new relational spaces and know-how through which we can inquire into the movements of practice/research relationships.

Qualitative inquiry has much to support a systemic model of practice research but systemic inquiry also has many useful offerings to bring to qualitative inquiry including:

- a rich seam of theories and stories about relational practice

- a critical history of diverse methods of inquiry and the place of the inquirer in a system

- a critique of power and culture in relationships

- in-depth studies of reflexivity in relationships

- access to many styles of inquiry

- attention to relational ethics

Systemic inquiry is already an integral part of social constructionist systemic practice in therapy, organisational consultancy, education, leadership and community work. It informs and shapes the activities of a reflexive research process which comfortably overlap with key features of qualitative inquiry. Systemic Inquiry finds an ethical, theoretical and practical home in the playing fields of Qualitative Inquiry.

References

Amundson, Jon; Stewart, Kenneth & Valentine, LaNae (1993). Temptations of Power and Certainty. *Journal of Marital & Family Therapy,* 19(2), pp 111–123.

Andersen, Tom (1987). The Reflective team: dialogue and meta-dialogue in clinical work. *Family Process,* 26, pp.415 – 427.

Anderson, Harlene (1997). *Conversation, Language and Possibilities: A Postmodern Approach to Therapy.* New York: Basic Books.

Anderson, Harlene & Gehart, Diane (2007). *Collaborative Therapy: Relationships and Conversations that make A Difference.* London: Routledge.

Anderson, Harlene & Goolishian, Harold (1988). Human Systems as Linguistic Systems: Preliminary and evolving ideas about the implications for clinical theory. *Family Process,* 27, pp.371-393.

Anderson, Harlene & Goolishian, Harold (1992). The client is the expert: a not-knowing approach to therapy. In: Sheila McNamee and Kenneth Gergen (Eds.), *Therapy as Social Construction.* London: Sage.

Anderson, Harlene & Jensen, Per (2007). *Innovations in the Reflecting Process.* London: Karnac.

Bateson, Gregory (1972). *Steps to an Ecology of Mind.* London: Paladin.

Bateson, Gregory (1979). *Mind and Nature.* New York: E.P. Dutton.

Bochner, Arthur P. (2000). Criteria Against Ourselves. *Qualitative Inquiry,* 6, pp.266-272.

Boscolo, Luigi; Cecchin, Gianfranco; Hoffman, Lynn & Penn, Peggy (1987). *Milan Systemic Family Therapy: Conversations in Theory and Practice.* New York: Basic Books.

Burnham, John (2011 [1992]). Approach, Method, Technique: Making Distinctions and Creating Connections. *Human Systems: Journal of Systemic Consultation and Management,* 3(1), pp.3-26.

Burnham, John (1993). Systemic Supervision: The evolution of reflexivity in the context of the supervisory relationship. *Human Systems Journal of Systemic Consultation and Management,* 4(3-4), pp.349-381.

Burnham, John (2005). Relational reflexivity: a tool for socially constructing therapeutic relationships In: Flaskas, C. et al. *The space between: experience, context and process in the therapeutic relationship.* London: Karnac

Burnham, John (2011). Developments in Social GRRAAACCEEESS: Visible and Invisible, Voiced and Unvoiced. In Britt Krause (ed.), *Mutual Perspectives: Culture & Reflexivity in Systemic Psychotherapy.* London: Karnac Books.

Burnham, John & Harris, Queenie (1996). Emerging Ethnicity: A Tale of Three Cultures. In *Meeting the Needs of Ethnic Minority Children. A Handbook for Professionals.* Ed. Dwivedi, Kedar N. London: Jessica Kingsley Publishers.

Burr, Vivien (1995). *An Introduction to Social Constructionism.* Routledge.

Cecchin, Gianfranco (1987). Hypothesising, circularity and neutrality revisited: an invitation to curiosity. *Family Process* 26 pp 405-413.

Charmaz, Kathy (2008). *Constructing Grounded Theory.* Second Edition. London: Sage Publications.

Clifford, James & Marcus, George E. (Eds.) (1986). *Writing Culture: the poetics and politics of ethnography.* Berkley: University of California Press.

Code, Lorraine (1995). Questions of method in feminist practice. In *Changing*

Methods: Feminists Transforming Practice. Eds. Burt, S. & Code, L. Ontario: Broadview.

Combs, Gene & Freedman, Jill (1990). *Symbol, Story, and Ceremony: Using Metaphor in Individual and Family Therapy*. London: W.W.Norton.

Cooperrider, David L. & Srivastva, Suresh (1987). Appreciative Inquiry In Organizational Life. In W. Pasmore & R. Woodman (Eds.), *Research In Organization Change and Development* (Vol. 1, pp.129-169). Greenwich, CT: JAI Press.

Cronen, Vernon E. (2000). *Practical Theory and a Naturalistic Account of Inquiry*. Draft paper.

Denzin, Norman K. (2003). *Performance Ethnography : critical pedagogy and the politics of culture*. London: Sage Publications.

Denzin, Norman K. and Lincoln, Yvonna S. (2005). *The SAGE Handbook of Qualitative Research*. 3rd Edition. London: Sage Publications.

Denzin, Norman K. and Lincoln, Yvonna S. (2011). *The SAGE Handbook of Qualitative Research*. 4th Edition. London: Sage Publications.

Ellis, Carolyn (2008). *Revision: Autoethnographic Reflections on Life and Work*. Walnut Creek: Left Coast Press.

Etherington, Kim (2004). *Becoming a Reflexive Researcher: Using Our Selves in Research*. London: Jessica Kingsley Publishers.

Flaskas, Carmel (2002). *Family Therapy Beyond Postmodernism: Practice Challenges Theory*. London: Routledge.

Flaskas, Carmel; Barry Mason & Perlesz, Amaryll (2004). *The Space Between: Experience, Context and the Process in the Therapeutic Relationship*. London: Karnac.

Flaskas, Carmel; McCarthy, Imelda & Sheehan, Jim (Eds.) (2007). *Hope and Despair in Narrative and Family Therapy: Adversity, Forgiveness and Reconciliation*. London: Routledge.

Foucault, Michel (1980). *language, counter-memory, practice*. Ed. D. Bouchard. Ithaca, New York: Cornell University Press.

Gehart, Diane; Tarragona, Margarita & Bava, Saliha (2007). A Collaborative Approach to Research and Inquiry. In Anderson, H. & Gehart, D. (Eds.), *Collaborative Therapy: Relationships and Conversations that make A Difference*. London: Routledge.

Gergen, Kenneth J. & Gergen, Mary (2002). Ethnography as Relationship. In Bochner, Art and Ellis, Carolyn Eds. (2002). *Ethnographically Speaking. Autoethnography, Literature, and Aesthetics*. Walnut Creek: AltaMira Press.

Goldner, Virginia; Penn, Peggy; Scheinberg, Marcia & Walker, Gillian (1990). Love and Violence: Gender Paradoxes in Volatile Attachments. *Family Process*. 29(4), pp 343–364.

Gregg, Godfrey (2010). *Keeping and crossing boundaries: Negotiating identities in qualitative research*. Paper presented on 29th May 2011 at 6th International Congress of Qualitative Inquiry 2011. University of Illinois.

Hoffman, Lynn (1993). *Exchanging Voices: Collaborative Approach to Family Therapy*. London: Karnac.

Keeney, Bradford P. (1990). *Improvisational therapy: Evolving one's own clinical style*. Contemporary Family Therapy 12(4) pp 271-277.

Lang, Peter W., Little, Martin & Cronen, Vernon (1990). The systemic professional domains of action and the question of neutrality. *Human Systems: Journal of Systemic Consultation and Management.* 1, pp 39-55.

Lather, Patti (1994). *Getting Smart: Feminist Research and Pedagogy within/ in the Postmodern.* London Routledge.

Lather, Patti (2007). *Getting Lost: Feminist Efforts Towards a Double(d). Science.* State University of New York Press.

Lather, Patti & Smithies, Christine S. (1997). *Troubling the Angels: Women Living with HIV/AIDS.* New York: Perseus.

Law, John (2007). *After Method: Mess in Social Science Research.* Abingdon: Routledge.

Leppington, Rozanne (2011[1991]). From Constructivism to Social Constructionism and Doing Critical Therapy. *Human Systems: Journal of Systemic Consultation and Management.* 2(2), pp 217-31.

Lincoln, Yvonna S. & Denzin, Norman K. (2005). The Eighth and Ninth Moments – Qualitative Research in/and the Fractured Future. In *The SAGE Handbook of Qualitative Research.* 3rd Edition. London: Sage Publications.

Marcus George E. (2007). Ethnography two decades after writing culture: from the experimental to the baroque. *Anthropological Quarterly.* Downloaded from http://findarticles.com/p/articles/mi_6913/is_4_80/ai_n28477877 on 07 Feb, 2011.

Markovic (then Radovanovic), Desa (1993). Knowing Systemic Rules: From Stages of Disorder to Second Order Towards Positive Delinquency. *Human Systems: Journal of Systemic Consultation and Management.* 4(3), pp.235-258.

Mason, Barry (2005). Relational risk-taking and the therapeutic relationship. In: Flaskas, C. et al. (Eds.) *The space between: experience, context and process in the therapeutic relationship.* London: Karnac.

Maturana, Humberto & Varela, Francisco (1980), *Autopoiesis and Cognition: The Realization of the Living,* Boston. Studies in the Philosophy of Science, Vol. 42 (Dordrecht: D. Reidel).

Maturana, Humberto & Varela, Francisco (1987). *The tree of knowledge. Biological basis of human understanding.* London: Shambhala.

Maturana, Humberto (1988). Reality: The search for objectivity or the quest for a compelling argument. *The Irish Journal of Psychology,* 9(1), pp.25-82.

McCarthy, Imelda Colgan & Byrne, Nollaig O'Reilly (1988). 'Mistaken-Love: Conversations on the problem of incest in an Irish context'. *Family Process,* 27, pp.181–199.

McNamee, Sheila (1994). [Draft] Research as Relationally Situated Activity: Ethical Implications. *Journal of Feminist Family Therapy* 6(3), pp.69-83. Available at: <http://pubpages.unh.edu/~smcnamee/research/Research_as_Relationally_Situated_Activity.pdf > [Accessed 3rd January 2011].

McNamee, Sheila (2004). Promiscuity in the practice of family therapy. *Journal of Family Therapy,* 26, pp.224–244.

O'Hanlon, Bill and Bertolino, Bob (1998). *Even from a Broken Web: Brief, Respectful Solution-oriented Therapy for Sexual Abuse and Trauma.* Chichester: John Wiley.

Oliver, Christine (1996). 'Systemic Eloquence.' *Human Systems: the Journal of Systemic Consultation and management,* 7, pp.247-264.

Parker, Ian (2005). *Qualitative Psychology: Introducing Radical Research.* Open University Press.

Pearce, W. Barnett (1989). *Communication and the human condition.* Carbondale, Illinois: Illinois University Press.

Pearce, W. Barnett & Walters, Kimberly A., (1996). *Research Methods: A Systemic Communications Approach.* Draft. Pearce Walters Inc. Pearce Associates (2004 [1999]). *Using CMM.* Available at: <http://www.pearceassociates.com/essays/cmm_seminar.pdf > [Accessed 12th May 2007].

Penn, Peggy (1985). Feed forward: future questions, future maps. *Family Process,* 24(3), pp 299-310.

Quiros, Laura (2010). *Keeping and crossing boundaries: Negotiating identities in qualitative research.* Paper presented on 29th May 2011 at 6th International Congress of Qualitative Inquiry 2011. University of Illinois.

Reynolds, Vikki (2010). Doing Justice: A Witnessing Stance in Therapeutic Work Alongside Survivors of Torture and Political Violence , in J. Raskin, S. Bridges, & R. Neimeyer (Eds.), *Studies in meaning 4: Constructivist perspectives on theory, practice, and social justice.* New York: Pace University Press.

Reynolds, Vikki (2013). "Leaning in" as imperfect allies in community work. *Narrative and Conflict: Explorations in theory and practice,* 1(1), pp.53-75.

Richardson, Laurel (1994). Writing: A Method of Inquiry. In Denzin, Norman K. and Lincoln, Yvonna S. (Eds.),*The SAGE Handbook of Qualitative Research.* London: Sage Publications.

Richardson, Laurel (1997). *Fields of Play: Constructing an Academic Life.* New Brunswick: Rutgers University Press.

Rober, Peter (2005). The Therapist's Self in Dialogical Family Therapy: Some Ideas About Not-Knowing and the Therapist's Inner Conversation. *Family Process,* 44(4), pp.477–495.

Roberts, Janine (2005). Transparency and Self-Disclosure in Family Therapy: Dangers and Possibilities. *Family Process,* 44(1), pp.45–63.

St Pierre, Elizabeth (2010). Presentation. International Congress of Qualitative Inquiry, University of Illinois. May 2010.

Seikkula, Jaakko (2002). Monologue is the crisis - dialogue becomes the aim of therapy. *Journal of Marital and Family Therapy,* 28(3), pp.283-284.

Seikkula, Jaakko & Arnkil, Tom Erik (2006). *Dialogical meetings in social networks.* London: Karnac.

Selvini Palazzoli, Mara; Boscolo, Luigi; Cecchin, Gianfranco & Prata, Giuliana (1980). Hypothesising – circularity – neutrality: Three guidelines for the conductor of the session. *Family Process* 19(1), pp.3-12.

Sexton, Thomas L. & Whiston, Susan C. (1994). The Status of the Counseling Relationship: An Empirical Review, Theoretical Implications, and Research Directions. *The Counseling Psychologist.* 22(1), pp.6-78.

de Shazer, Steve (1985). *Keys to solution in brief therapy.* New York: W.W. Norton.

de Shazer, Steve (1988). *Clues: Investigating Solutions in Brief Therapy.* New York: W.W. Norton.

Shotter, John (2005). *The Short Book of 'Withness'-Thinking.* London: KCCF Pre-Book.

Shotter, John (2007). Not to forget Tom Andersen's way of being Tom Andersen: the importance of what 'just happens' to us. *Human Systems: Journal of Systemic Consultation and Management,* 18, pp.15-28.

Shotter, John (2011). *Getting It: With-ness Thinking and the Dialogical.... In Practice.* The Hampton Press Communication Series.

Shotter , John & Katz, Arlene (1998). 'Living moments' in dialogical exchanges. *Human Systems: Journal of Systemic Consultation and Management,* 9, pp.81-93.

Simon, Gail (1998). Incitement to Riot? Individual Identity and Group Membership: Some Reflections on the Politics of a Post-Modernist Therapy. *Human Systems Journal of Systemic Consultation and Management.* Vol. 9:1, pp.33-50.

Simon, Gail (2010). Self Supervision, Surveillance and Transgression. *Journal of Family Therapy,* 32, pp.308–325.

Simon, Gail (2012a). Praction Research: A Model of Systemic Inquiry. *Human Systems Journal of Systemic Consultation and Management.* Vol. 23:1 pp. 103-124. Available at https://docs.google.com/file/d/0B5TWuG0JVPe_UDNYdGJ5NXl1dGs/edit?pli=1

Simon, Gail (2012b). Relational Ethnography: Writing and Reading in and about Research Relationships. *Forum Qualitative Sozialforschung / Forum: Qualitative Social Research,* North America, 2012. Available at < http://www.qualitative-research.net/index.php/fqs/article/view/1735>

Smith, Jonathan; Flowers, Paul & Larkin, Michael (2009). *Interpretive Phenomenological Analysis.* London: Sage Publications.

Tomm, Karl (1987a). Interventive Interviewing: Part I. Strategizing as fourth guideline for the therapist. *Family Process,* 26, pp.3-13.

Tomm, Karl (1987b). Interventive Interviewing: Part II. Reflexive Questioning as a Means to Enable Self Healing. *Family Process,* 26, pp.153-183.

Tomm, Karl (1987c). Interventive Interviewing: Part III. Intending to Ask Lineal, Circular, Reflexive or Strategic Questions? *Family Process,* 27, pp.1-15.

Tootell, Andrew (2004). Decentring research practice. *The International Journal of Narrative Therapy and Community Work* No.3. Adelaide: Dulwich Centre Publications.

Vedeler, Anne Hedvig (2010). *Six Tales From My Practice on the Theme of Resonance.* Paper presented at the Systemic Cafe, Farnhill, Yorkshire, UK, 25th June 2010.

Visweswaran, Kamala (1994). *Fictions of Feminist Ethnography.* University of Minnesota Press.

White, Cheryl & Denborough, David (2005). *A Community of Ideas: Behind the Scenes.* Adelaide: Dulwich Centre Publications.

White, Michael (1988). The process of questioning: A therapy of literary merit? *Dulwich Centre Newsletter,* Winter 1988, pp.8-14.

White, Michael & Epston, David (1990). *Narrative Means to Therapeutic Ends.* New York: Norton.

White, Michael (1992). Deconstruction and therapy. In *Experience, contradiction, narrative, & imagination: Selected papers of David Epston and Michael White, 1989-1991.* Adelaide, Australia: Dulwich Centre Publications.

Woolfitt, Robin (2005). *Conversation Analysis and Discourse Analysis. A Comparative and Critical Introduction*. London: Sage Publications.

2 Orientations: Systemic Approaches to Research Practices

Alex Chard

Truth is not born nor is it to be found inside the head of an individual person, it is born between people collectively searching for truth, in the process of their dialogic interaction. (Mikhail Bakhtin 1984 cited by Shotter 1994)

Science sometimes improves hypothesis and sometimes disproves them. But proof would be another matter and perhaps never occurs except in the realms of totally abstract tautology. We can sometimes say that if such and such abstract suppositions or postulates are given, then such and such must follow absolutely. But the truth about what can be perceived or arrived at by induction from perception is something else again. Let us say that truth would mean a precise correspondence between our description and what we describe or between our total network of abstractions and deductions and some total understanding of the outside world. Truth in this sense is not obtainable. (Gregory Bateson 1979, p.27)

Whoever undertakes to set himself up as a judge of Truth and Knowledge is shipwrecked by the laughter of the gods. (Attributed to Albert Einstein)

My own practice and learning journey within the art of systemic approaches to organisational development and inquiry began in 2001. I enrolled on a programme at the Kensington Consultation Centre (KCC) which somewhat strangely was in Vauxhall, a quite different part of London. In the first few months of a Certificate in Systemic Management I experienced confusion and uncertainty. I struggled with the language used at KCC, which for me created a dense and unapproachable subject and indeed contributed to or created a culture that to me seemed strange and inaccessible. I was on the point of giving up when a conversation with one of my tutors helped to reframe my confusion and to recognise confusion as a point of transition. This was an important early lesson in systemic approaches and understandings.

Over the years at KCC, I completed an M.Sc. in Systemic Management and Consultancy and then the Professional Doctorate in Systemic Practice. I was in the first cohort of students to enter the doctorate, as it transpired we were the only cohort that completed the taught part of the Professional Doctorate in Systemic Practice at KCC which went into liquidation in early 2010. Some key KKC courses including the doctorate and the M.Sc. programme are now taught at the University of Bedfordshire where I work as a visiting lecturer.

The experience of so nearly stopping on the first rung of systemic practice continues to speak to me of the need to make systemic practice more open and accessible. Systemic practice has built up a rich but often seemingly impenetrable grammar of practice as well as a culture and ways of behaving and being that I think are not always easily understood by outsiders or novices. I also found that within KCC that there was significant assumed knowledge of a range of influences on what I now refer to as the KCC School of Systemic Practice.

In this chapter I am seeking to orient those who are new to a systemic approach to practice and inquiry into some of the underlying influences on such an approach and how I have subsequently built on that in my own practice and research. For those who are more familiar with systemic practice, I hope that the chapter will help to reveal coherence from across a range of related thinking. As with all things that fall within what I call a systemic practice tradition, the following should be viewed as an ongoing process of understanding being created with the reader, with knowledge always being treated as partial and situated. What I am describing here should be seen as creating theoretical context for an overall approach rather than any form of method, indeed it is something that I continually form, perform and re-perform in my day to day practice and in my ongoing inquiries.

In Brief

For me systemic practice is underpinned by a systemic, dialogical, social constructionist perspective on life and organisations. I suspect this is not an easy sentence for an uninitiated reader to follow. *A systemic, dialogical, social constructionist perspective.* What do I mean by that? Regarding a systemic approach Robert Flood argues that:

> *We can only meaningfully understand ourselves by understanding the whole of which we are an integral part. Systemic thinking is the discipline which makes visible that our actions are inter-related to*

other people's actions in patterns of behaviour and are not merely isolated events (Flood 1999, p.2).

An important insight from second order cybernetics is that when we observe systems we become part of those systems and those systems act on us and affect us and in a reflexive manner we act on them (von Foerster 1992).

Social construction as theory holds that our understandings of the world are constructed through language and within our interactions with others (Burr 1995). Mary Gergen and Ken Gergen observe that:

> *The foundational idea of social construction seems simple enough, but it is also profound. Everything we consider to be real is socially constructed. Or more dramatically, Nothing is real unless we agree that it is.* (Gergen and Gergen 2004, p.10).

A significance for me of taking a social constructionist orientation is the possibility it creates for change. Working from the view point that reality is constructed by people in relation, means that I can influence the way organisations work and help individuals to change their reality by influencing the way, on a moment by moment basis, they have their conversations.

A key understanding from within certain traditions of social construction (e.g. Barnett Pearce 1998; Cunliffe 2008; Shotter 2011) is also that interpersonal communication is the principal medium through which reality is relationally constructed. Consequently how people have conversations is significant to systemic practice. Bohm (1996) recognised the need to create dialogue distinguishing between dialogue which has linguistic roots in the Greek word dialogos or searching for meaning and discussion which shares linguistic roots with percussion and indeed concussion.

Hence a systemic, dialogical, social constructionist perspective which is detailed further below.

A Little Philosophy of Science

It is important I think to distinguish systemic practice and thinking from what is sometimes referred to as reductionist thinking which can be seen to have its roots in the philosophical traditions of René Descartes. Fritjof Capra (1996) provides a detailed account of the impact of Cartesian dualism where he includes Copernicus, Galileo, Bacon and Newton along with Descartes with the responsibility of moving western thinking from a medieval worldview which was based on Aristotelian philosophy and Christian theology (Capra 1996, p.19/20):

The notion of an organic, living, and spiritual universe was replaced by that of the world as a machine, and the world-machine became the dominant metaphor of the modern era.

René Descartes created the method of analytic thinking, which consists in breaking up complex phenomena into pieces to understand the behaviour of the whole from the properties of its parts. Descartes based his view of nature on the fundamental division between two independent and separate realms - that of mind and that of matter.

The conceptual framework created by Galileo and Descartes - the world as perfect machine governed by exact mathematical laws - was completed triumphantly by Isaac Newton, whose grande synthesis, Newtonian Mechanics was the crowning achievement of seventeenth century science.

As a wide range of commentators have noted, for example Bateson (1979), Capra (1996), Montuori (2003), Raine (1998), the impact of Descartes' thinking was also to objectify the natural world and create the dualism of subject and object and in turn the observed and the scientific observer. Whilst there have been a range of challenges to this position it is a position which has been the dominant story with Western scientific thinking for over 300 years.

However, an understanding of the limitations of such reduction-ist thinking is not new. In 1790, in the *Marriage of Heaven and Hell*, William Blake wrote in a way that can be viewed as a direct counter to Cartesian Dualism: *Man has no Body distinct from his Soul for that call'd Body is a portion of the Soul discern'd by the five Senses, the chief inlets of Soul in this age.* Writing on vision in 1802 Blake is also often quoted for his view on Newtonian science when he implores:

May God us keep
From Single vision & Newton's Sleep!

W. Barnett Pearce in an essay which recounts the schools of thought on systemic thinking also provides a historical analysis of Cartesian dualism and Newtonian science citing amongst those who challenged this perspective, Giambattista Vico, Karl Marx and Charles Darwin. Pearce sees that:

... the worldview of mechanistic materialism was struck a last, most damaging blow by a historian of science. Thomas Kuhn's The Structure of Scientific Revolutions, published in 1962, made two claims, both of which struck deeply at the worldview of mechanistic materialism. First, he claimed that science is "paradigmatic." That is, rather than being an unobstructed view of the universe, it consists of a set of disciplinary assumptions and research exemplars. Second, he claimed that there have been changes in paradigms, and that these changes occur by the means of persuasion, not (only) reason. (Pearce 2002, p.20).

At its simplest the most significant difference between Newtonian science and systems thinking is that Newtonian science seeks to break things down into parts in order to try to understand the whole. Whereas a systems perspective looks at wholes rather than parts. It is not that one is wrong and the other is right, indeed (at least within the Western world) we have reaped significant societal benefits from Newtonian science and it would be foolish not to recognise this. However, these are very different viewpoints as Pearce (2002) drawing on Laszlo (1996, p23) points out:

The classical worldview was atomistic and individualistic; it viewed objects as separate from their environments and people as separate from each other and from their surroundings. The systems view perceives connections and communications between people, and between people and nature, and emphasizes community and integrity in both the natural and the human world.

Here we also see a perspective on how a reductionist Newtonian viewpoint runs counter to the idea of a systemic relationally constructed world. Understanding the dominance of the voice of Cartesian philosophy and Newtonian science in natural and social science and management has been central to my understanding of how the KCC School of Systemic Practice is located differently. As Sheila McNamee and Dian Marie Hosking (2012, p.33) comment, "the modernist discourse ... is only one possible discourse". For me much that the KCC School of Systemic Practice represents can be understood as being from within a postmodernist tradition. Examples include the self as socially or indeed relationally constructed, reflexivity, knowledge as culturally located and co-constructed and the reconstructing of scientific social constructions such as researcher and research subject (Butler 2002; Cahoone 1996). In consequence, this thinking fundamentally impinges on how we view knowledge and how knowledge is created through research or, as I prefer to term it, inquiry.

Flyvbjerg argues that rather than trying to emulate the natural sciences which he sees as having focussed on Aristotle's concepts of *episteme* (epistemology) and *techne* (technology), social science needs to reorientate itself by building on Aristotle's concept of *phronesis* (practical knowledge and practical ethics):

> *The goal is to help restore social science to its classical position as a practical, intellectual activity aimed at clarifying the problems, risks and possibilities we face as humans and societies, and at contributing to social and political praxis* (Flyvbjerg 2001, p.4).

Central to his reasoning are that context and judgement are critical aspects of human action. He uses as one of his key sources the work of Dreyfus and Dreyfus (1986) and their model of learning. When experts act they act beyond rule-bound behaviour using embedded tacit knowledge applying judgement within a context. In developing guidelines for such practice based research Flyvbjerg suggests that:

> *Phronetic research focusses on practical activity and practical knowledge in everyday situations. ... What it **always** means, however, is a focus on the actual daily practices which constitute a given field of interest* (Flyvbjerg 2001, p.134). (Original emphasis).

Drawing on the above and other influences leads me to use the term systemic practice which for me also encapsulates ongoing reflexive inquiry into that practice.

Systems Thinking

In keeping with the position outlined above, Robert Flood (2006, p.118) sees the development of systems thinking in the twentieth century as being a response to reductionism and the *understanding of phenomena by breaking them down into constituent parts* rather than phenomena understood *to be an emergent property of an interrelated whole*. Systems thinking recognises that the whole is greater than the sum of the parts. Moving from simplistic understandings of pieces of systems, looking much more widely, recognising how we are affected by wider forces and looking for unforeseen consequences are some of the important aspects that thinking systemically brings.

Within this section, rather than try to provide a summary of systems thinking, I will identify and locate the aspects of systems thinking that I think are important within the particular context of systemic inquiry. One of the founding systems approaches developed in the 1940s following the Second World War and usually attributed to von Bertalanfy (e.g. Pearce 2002; Armson 2011) is General Systems Theory. Armson (2011) comments that:

> *The wartime experience of scientists, mathematicians and others of working on multi-disciplinary projects in US universities and government-funded enterprises such as the Manhattan Project, met with the emerging technologies of computing, control systems and management to create fertile ground for new ways of thinking about human concerns. From this ground sprang the Macy conferences and the Society for General Systems Research, founding cybernetics and GST respectively.*

General Systems Theory was an attempt to provide a systems model applicable to all systems. Pearce (2002) details some of the important insights of General Systems Theory. Those that Pearce identifies which I apply within with my practice and which are carried through into my inquiry are that:

- *Organisations are systems in which all the essential parts are interrelated.* This is a fundamental underpinning for systemic practice. Recognising that the areas in which we work are connected to and affected by the broader organisation and the wider context.

- *Rather than try to understand a particular phenomenon in isolation systemic thinkers look for the pattern of which it is a part.* Seeing the patterns that connect (or at least seeing some of them) and understanding the context from which people are acting is significant in appreciating what is taking place.

- *All systems are both comprised of organised components and a component of yet larger systems.* This reflects the fact that organisational practice and therapeutic practice are often located within structured, and usually bureaucratised institutions.

- *Emergence is a key feature of complex systems.* Change can be viewed as a socially constructed process of coming into being, human systems are surprising and often unpredictable.

From within this school of thinking Koestler developed the concept of Holons, a semiautonomous unit independent yet interdependent on a larger system. Holons are Janus faced and look both internally and externally (Koestler 1971). Koestler's model is something we can draw upon when considering for example how teams fit within a larger organisational system or families within a cultural and social milieu.

Cybernetics and Second Order Cybernetics

The term cybernetics is derived from the Greek *kybernetes*, or "steersman". Norbert Wiener is credited with developing the idea of cybernetics. The title of Norbert Wieners' 1948 book was *Cybernetics: Or Control and Communication in the Animal and the Machine*. The title defines the term. The key focus of first order cybernetics is on control and communication in both artificial systems and natural systems. Second order cybernetics or the cybernetics of cybernetics recognises the position of the observer in the system being observed. As von Foerster (1975) notes:

> *First Order Cybernetics is the Cybernetics of observed systems*
> *Second Order Cybernetics is the Cybernetics of observing systems.*

As is also alluded to in the quote from Armson above, the Macy conferences on cybernetics held between 1944 and 1953 brought together leading intellectuals including importantly in this context Gregory Bateson. Bateson worked with Paul Watzlawick at the Mental Research Institute in Palo Alto, California and used cybernetic theory in therapeutic work, in particular using the idea of paradoxical intervention. Bateson's work was then used by what has become known as the Milan Group in the development of systemic family therapy (Palazzoli et al 1978; Pearce 2002).

Peter Lang, Martin Little and John Shotter in conversation at KCC (2006) outlined that the significance of Bateson was the influence that Bateson had on the Milan School of Family Therapy and through that subsequent practice within KCC. So from this we can see that one of the roots of systemic family therapy and the development of organisational practice at KCC lay within cybernetics. Bateson (2000 p484) speaking on the importance of cybernetics comments, *I think that cybernetics is the biggest bite out of the fruit of the Tree of Knowledge for 2000 years.* Capra (undated) comments on Bateson:

> *As we replace the Newtonian metaphor of the world as a machine by the metaphor of the network, and as complexity becomes a principal focus in science, the kind of systemic thinking that Bateson advocated is becoming crucial. ...Bateson showed us how to connect the dots ...*

Systemically based practice continually helps me to help others as we join up the dots hopefully creating more cohesive, effective and fulfilling human organisations.

Humberto Maturana is attributed with describing second order cybernetics as *The science and art of human understanding* (Pangaro, P, Henry S, 2013). Maturana and Francisco Varela developed the theory of Autopoiesis; *discrete, autonomous entities that live their life as independent unities* Maturana (2011). Consequently despite the fact that we may attempt to view the world objectively our perception is almost always based on what we have previously experienced Korn (2011). Maturana was another key figure who was influential in the development of the KCC School of Systemic Practice. Korn comments that:

> *Maturana talks about how all our human acts take place in language. He distinguishes these acts as taking place in three different domains, and he calls these the Domain of Aesthetics, the Domain of Production and the Domain of Explanations. Maturana continues to explain that we exist in all three domains simultaneously, and that there are even more domains than these three.*
>
> *By 1990, the theories on the three action domains developed further through an interaction between Maturana, theologian Peter Lang, sociologist Martin Little and psychologist Vernon Cronen. Lang, Little and Cronen wrote an article on the three action domains that have been the written basis for the practical use of domain thinking. The article is primarily aimed at therapeutic practice, but the thinking has for many years had a spillover effect on those who work with leadership, management and organisational development from different positions.*

The article being referred to above is The Systemic Professional - *Domains of Action and the Question of Neutrality in Human Systems* Lang, Little and Cronen (1990), which provides a significant understanding of the key influence of second order cybernetics on systemic thinking and practice.

Second order cybernetics or the cybernetics of cybernetics importantly recognises that any observed system includes the observer. Humberto Maturana is credited with coining the phrase that "Everything said is said **by** an observer" which was then subtly re-phrased by von Foerster to "Everything said is said **to** an observer" Glanville (2002). Thus a key challenge to the alleged objective position of the researcher comes from within second order cybernetics. Von Foerster (1992) one of the leading cyberneticians made this point when he commented in a speech that:

What appears to us today most natural to see and to think, was then not only hard to see, it was even not allowed to think! Why? Because it would violate the basic principle of scientific discourse which demands the separation of the observer from the observed. It is the principle of objectivity: the properties of the observer shall not enter the description of his observations. I gave this principle here in its most brutal form, to demonstrate its nonsensicality: if the properties of the observer, namely, to observe and to describe, are eliminated, there is nothing left: no observation, no description. However, there was a justification for adhering to this principle, and this justification was fear. Fear that paradoxes would arise when the observers were allowed to enter the universe of their observations. And you know the threat of paradoxes: to steal their way into a theory is like having the cloven-hoofed foot of the Devil stuck in the door of orthodoxy.

Ranulph Glanville (2002) develops this position declaring that:

Second order Cybernetics presents a (new) paradigm in which the observer is circularly (and intimately) involved with/connected to the observed. The observer is no longer neutral and detached, and what is considered is not the observed (as in the classical paradigm), but the observing system. The aim of attaining traditional objectivity is either abandoned/passed over, or what objectivity is and how we might obtain (and value) it is reconsidered. In this sense, every observation is autobiographical. Therefore, second order Cybernetics must primarily be considered through the first person and with active verbs: the observers inevitable presence acknowledged, and should be written about in the first person, not the third, giving us an insight into who these observers are.

Within my inquiries I have accepted von Foerster's (1992) invitation to step *into the land where it is not forbidden, but where one is even encouraged to speak about oneself (what else can one do anyway?).* This understanding also means that my preferred approach to writing is to adopt a first person position.

Thinking Systemically

W. Barnett Pearce importantly distinguishes between *thinking about systems* and *thinking systemically* arguing that they produce different kinds of knowledge. Again, this is not about saying that one form of knowledge is better than the other but recognising that they are different, hence:

> *The distinction between thinking about systems and thinking systemically hinges on the perspective of the person doing the thinking. One can and usually does think "about" systems from outside the system. That is, whether we might describe the thinking as ontologically a part of the system or separate from it, in this instance the thinker takes the observer-perspective. When thinking systemically, on the other hand, the thinker is self-reflexively a part of the system and takes the perspective of a participant or component of the system* (p2).

After listing what he viewed as key literature on thinking systemically Pearce suggests that:

> *It is no accident that these books all emerge from a tradition of applied practice such as consulting or therapy rather than one of the "basic" sciences and that their knowledge claims are very different .... Instead of a representation "over here" of the structure and/or function of a system "over there," the kind of knowledge claimed in these books consists of advice about how to think and act into situations.* (Pearce 1998, p.3)

This is, I believe, a significant distinction. Viewing knowledge generated through systemic inquiry in this way invites the reader as inquirer to view knowledge as generated from within a tradition of thinking systemically from within a practice with the intent of assisting others (and the inquirer) to act more effectively into new and emerging contexts. Later in the same essay and reflecting on cybernetic thinking, Pearce argues that:

> *If we are part of a system, then our knowledge of the system affects (because it is itself a component) the system. But what is knowledge if the thing known is changed by the act of knowing itself? And who are we who know ourselves if we are part of a system? These questions emerge from the idea that our knowledge is not so much a reflection of reality (in the sense that Rorty would call the "Mirror of Nature") but has a reflexive relationship to reality (in the sense of reflexive verbs in grammar – that which acts is simultaneously and inexorably acted on). Many people think that this is one of the BIG IDEAS in the 20th century.* (Pearce 1998, p.7) (Emphasis in the original.)

I think that what we see brought together within this quotation is the powerful linking of systemic thinking with how reality is systemically socially constructed. This for me creates a useful bridge between systemic thinking and social construction; within human systems it reveals the relational nature of systemic processes.

Social Construction

In 1966 Peter Berger's and Thomas Luckman's (1966) *The Social Construction of Reality: a Treatise in the Sociology of Knowledge* was published. This is acknowledged by many writers to be the origin of the term social construction (e.g, Hacking 1999; Cunliffe 2008). Whilst Berger and Luckman acknowledged the potential affect on other disciplines including building a theoretical bridge to the problems of social psychology, *The Social Construction of Reality* (1967) was written from a sociological perspective; arguing that there was a need for the discipline of sociology to rethink how knowledge was created in society. Outlined below are some of the central propositions that Berger and Luckman made:

- *The reality of everyday life is organized around the 'here' of my body and the 'now' of my present.*

- *The reality of everyday life further presents itself to me as an inter-subjective world, a world that I share with others.*

- *I know that the world of everyday life is as real to me as it to others. Indeed I cannot exist in everyday life without continually interacting and communicating with others.*

- *My projects differ from and may even conflict with theirs. All the same, I know that I live with them in a common world. Most importantly, I know that there is an ongoing correspondence between my meanings and their meanings in this world, that we share a common sense about its reality.*

- *Not only is the survival of the human infant dependent upon certain social arrangements, the direction of his organismic development is socially determined. From the moment of birth, man's organismic development, and indeed a large part of his biological being as such, are subjected to continuing socially determined interference.*

- *The common objectivations of everyday life are maintained primar-*

ily by linguistic signification. Everyday life is, above all life with and by means of the language I share with my fellowmen.

- *This means that the institutions that have now been crystallized (for instance, the institution of paternity as it is encountered by the children) are experienced as existing over and beyond the individuals who 'happen to' embody them at the moment. In other words, the institutions are now experienced as possessing a reality of their own, a reality that confronts the individual as an external and coercive fact.*

- *The primary knowledge about the institutional order is knowledge on the pre theoretical level. It is the sum total of 'what everybody knows' about a social world, an assemblage of maxims, morals, proverbial nuggets of wisdom, values and beliefs, myths, and so forth, ... On the pre-theoretical level, however, every institution has a body of transmitted recipe knowledge, that is, knowledge that supplies the institutionally appropriate rules of conduct.*

In one of the closing paragraphs they state that:

Man is biologically predestined to construct and to inhabit a world with others. This world becomes for him the dominant and definite reality. Its limits are set by nature, but, once constructed, this world acts back upon nature. In the dialectic between nature and the socially constructed world the human organism itself is transformed. In this same dialectic man produces reality and thereby produces himself. (Berger and Luckman 1967, p.204)

This has particular significance in that it has a strong resonance with systemic thinking and particular with second order cybernetics and the concept of feedback loops. It is also inherently reflexive. Represented within it is the recognition of the individual or micro application of social construction and the macro and meta levels at which social construction can be applied. It also resonates with the position that our lives and relationships are socially constructed. Another of the central themes that Berger and Luckman contended was the role of institutionalisation (in its broadest sense) in how knowledge and the individual is created. Importantly they also recognise the *here* of the body.

During the early 1980s, links were being made between systemic practice and the theory of social construction (referred to as The Linguistic Turn). Sheila McNamee sees the coming together of systemic family therapy and social construction as being marked by the publication in 1982 of *Paradoxes, Double Binds, and Reflexive Loops: An Alternative*

Theoretical Perspective (Cronen, Johnson, and Lannamann 1982). McNamee comments:

> *This article was significant as a bridge between the coordinated management of meaning theory we were developing in Communication and Systemic Family Therapy. The authors of that article (one of whom is my husband, John Lannamann) and I had been working with the ideas of reflexivity, paradox and meaning making for several years. It all came together in that moment. I wrote my dissertation (McNamee, 1983) on the process of Family Therapy from a communication perspective, integrating the Milan Model with the coordinated management of meaning theory.* (McNamee 2006, p.128)

The Coordinated Management of Meaning is a communication theory developed by W. Barnett Pearce that is rooted within social construction. Nevertheless, as Ann Cunliffe comments:

> *... if we wish to take a social constructionist approach to research and teaching, it is important to think about our underlying assumptions regarding the nature and processes of socially constructing reality, the impact of these assumptions on how we think about the knowledge and how these then play through our research and our approach to management learning.* (Cunliffe 2008, p.125)

Consequently it is important to consider how we use and apply the term social construction. One of the challenges of delineating a specific model of social construction is that this assumes that social construction has been refined to this extent. It also runs the risk of attempting to solidify something that I see as fluid, dynamic, and changing. Rather than attempting to narrowly define the term, I outline below some of the important theoretical understandings that a social constructionist position offers both in practice and in understanding, inquiring into and in reconstruction of that practice.

Cunliffe details some of the *"interpretive tensions and choices faced by scholars taking a social constructionist orientation to research"* (2008, p.125) and then details *"critical choices that result in very different orientations to social constructionism ... those between the notions of subjective or intersubjective realities, and between an objectified reality and always emerging in-the-moment realities"*. (2008, p.127)

An objective approach to social construction can be seen to be aligned with Newtonian science and observable phenomena. One effect of which is to separate the observer from the observed. In contrast subjective approaches recognise the need to examine people's individual experiences. Intersubjective approaches take this further and recognise that experience and knowledge do not simply reside in the individual but are shaped between people (Fullbrook 2004). The distinctions made by Cunliffe illustrate how our own orientation or approach to social construction profoundly affects both how we use and apply the term and how it affects our approach to research and, critically, I would also add *practice*. A key feature of the argument lies in whether we see knowledge as being something that is individualised and objectified or whether we see knowledge as something that is fluid, contextualised and created by people in relationship. This understanding, to my mind, connects closely with the conception of social construction that Berger and Luckman originally envisaged. Meaning (or reality) is not fixed, it is created by people in relation. Cunliffe further asserts that:

> *Scholars taking the view of intersubjective social realities believe that our sense of our social world emerges continually as we interact with others. From this perspective, there is no 'I' without 'you' (Shotter, 1989) because we are always in relation to others whether they are present or not. ... The focus is not on what that social reality is—because there is no fixed, universally shared understanding of reality—but how people shape meaning between themselves in responsive dialogue.* (Cunliffe 2008, p.128)

This also helpfully provides a concise summary of John Shotter's perspective. John has had a significant influence on the development of the KCC School of Systemic Practice. Before turning his attention to communication John was a psychologist, his theoretical position has been significantly influenced by amongst others the philosophers Bakhtin, Vygotsky and Wittgenstein and Bateson. His version of social constructionism has been described as a *dialogical, rhetorical-responsive, embodied* version of social construction (Hibberd 2005). For me some of the most important aspects of the theoretical position that Shotter proposes are represented in the quotes below:

• *What is special about the rhetorical-responsive version of social constructionism that I want to offer, however, is its focus on our embodied practices, and our immediate, spontaneous ways of responding to each other's speech intertwined activities.* (Shotter 1997, p.3)

• *... something very special happens when living bodies interact with their surroundings, and that we have not (explicitly) taken this into* *account in our current forms of thought or institutional practices. The resulting relations have not just a dialogically structured character, as I once thought, but a chiasmic (or dynamically intertwined) structure.* (Shotter 2003, p.8)

- *If we are to understand how we can create a sense of our inner lives in our speakings, it is both our embodied, responsive nature that we must understand, and, its existence within 'forms of life'.* (Shotter 1997, p.7)

- *... when we talk to each other about our 'thoughts' and 'feelings', our 'motives' and 'desires', etc., we do not continually confuse and bewilder each other. How do we do this, how can we make sense of it as a possibility? It is the recognition of our embodied, socially responsive nature, that is the key.* (Shotter 1997, p.8)

- *If we are ever to study ourselves without emasculating ourselves in the process - without destroying our own ability to transform ourselves - it is Descartes's account of our being in the world (his ontology) and the accounts of how we came to know its nature (his epistemology) that we must replace.* (Shotter 2003, p.16)

Of particular importance to me is the philosophical position that Shotter adopts with regard to body and mind and what I see as our intuitive responsive bodily processes. Importantly what he also clearly identifies is the limits that have been placed on our thinking through Cartesian dualism as is discussed above. This is further illustrated in the quote below:

Descartes sets out here, not a living world, not a growing or developing world, existing in the cosmos as a complex, internally interrelated, indivisible unity with continuously emergent, uniquely new aspects and characteristics, but a world made up of a fixed number of separately existing particles of matter in motion, which, at any chosen instant in time, can simply take on a new configuration. (Shotter 2003)

This philosophical position Shotter argues is not reflected by many of those who adopt what he describes as an *unexamined Cartesianism* social constructionist position. Importantly, what we also see in the quotation above is seeing how this philosophical position links intrinsically to recognising the systemic nature of our world.

Creating a Fusion between Action Research, Social Construction and Systemic Thinking

Kurt Lewin who is credited by many with coining the term action research stated that:

> *The research needed for social practice can best be characterised as research for social management or social engineering. It is a type of action-research, a comparative research on the conditions and effects of various forms of social action, and research leading to social action. Research that produces nothing but books will not suffic.e* (Lewin 1946, p.35)

Here we see Lewin creating a shift from research to produce academic knowledge towards practice based research that could promote change. Since Lewin first promoted the idea more than half a century ago there have been a range of developments around the original concept. However at the heart of the process Lewin described there is a cycle of having an idea, exploring the idea, planning an action, taking action, evaluating the action, amending the plan and so on (Chard 2011).

Robert Flood (2006) provides an extensive analysis of *The Relationship of 'systems thinking' to action research*. He also distinguishes between systems thinking and systemic thinking, arguing that systems thinking *advocates thinking about real social systems as if they exist in the world.* Whilst systemic thinking *assumes only that the social construction of the world is systemic.* This can be seen as a second order cybernetic position. Heinz von Foerster (1992) expresses something similar when he asks, *"Am I apart from the universe? That is, whenever I look am I looking through a peephole upon an unfolding universe. Or: Am I part of the universe? That is, whenever I act, I am changing myself and the universe as well".* The significance of this for systemic research is that I am not an observer on a system, I am part of a system influencing it and in turn being influenced by it.

Flood further asserts that *the human mind is both the creator and the subject of complexity, not an externally created master over it and all its parts. That is why it makes no sense to separate action from research in our minds or in our practice.* Building on this argument he concludes that:

> *... I finally locate what I believe to be the conceptual convergence of systemic thinking and action research. It is through systemic thinking that we know of the unknowable. It is with action research*

that we learn and may act meaningfully within the unknowable.
Where these two arcs of reasoning converge, we witness the
incredible genesis of a conceptual universe that opens up otherwise
unimaginable ways in which people may live their lives in a more
meaningful and fulfilling manner. (Flood 2006, p.127)

So for me Flood creates an important fusion bringing together systemic
thinking, which he sees as being underpinned by a socially constructed
world, using systemic thinking to reveal that there is more than we
can know, whilst using action research to navigate that world. This
convergence can help to reveal implicit and tacit aspects of knowing
about practice and create new possibilities for acting *meaningfully* into
the emerging future.

Reflective and Reflexive Practice

There is I believe a very important connection between adopting a
systemic position and recognising as I detail above, that one of the main
roots of such an approach lies in cybernetics and that feedback loops
are an inherent feature within complex systems (Beer 2009). Frederick
Steier in a research context identifies the importance of second order
cybernetics, with *circularity as a central concept* requiring the observer
to accept responsibility for their own actions. This can be seen as an
ethical perspective. Steier also maintains that undertaking inquiry from
a social constructionist position is inherently relational and reflexive:

Constructionist inquiry, as a human activity, must concern itself
with a knowing process as embedded in a reflexive loop that
includes the inquirer who is at once an active observer. Reflexivity,
or a turning back onto a self, is a way in which circularity and self-
reference appear in inquiry, as we continually recognize the various
mutual relationships in which our knowing activities are embedded.
(Steier 1991, p.163)

If we accept Steier's viewpoint, then both adopting a social constructionist viewpoint and a systemic viewpoint are inherently reflexive and
relational. Within the research context, Rosanna Hertz sees reflexivity
as operating on several levels, to *"be reflexive is to have an ongoing*
conversation about experience while simultaneously living in the
moment...." (Hertz 1997, p.vii).
  Steier (1991) introduces the idea of *small circuit reflexivity* which he
sees as being in the moment of action and *long circuit reflexivity* which

he sees as being contemplative. This is I think closely allied to Schön's (1987) ideas of reflecting-in-action and reflecting-on-action. There is I think a very close similarity between reflexive practice and reflective practice both of which are important aspects of systemic practice and inquiry.

Qualitative Inquiry and Autoethnography

Earlier in this book, Gail Simon has argued that there are strong parallels between systemic inquiry and the field of qualitative inquiry. Arthur Bochner believes that Gregory Bateson was *"the person who first championed the importance of qualitative inquiry, at least the first one who got through to me"* (2009, p.340). This statement is important in that it recognises the influence that Bateson has had on the field of qualitative inquiry and particularly the field of autoethnography in which Bochner has been a key figure. Bateson's work (as noted above) was highly influential within the Milan School of systemic therapy (Palazzoli et al, 1978) and subsequently the KCC School of Systemic Practice (Lang et al 2006). From this it can be seen that autoethnography and systemic inquiry, which are forms of qualitative inquiry, share a common epistemological root within the work of Bateson. Bochner (2009) also recognises both the relational and social constructionist influences on qualitative inquiry which have also been fundamental within the KCC School of thinking.

Carolyn Ellis with Bochner (2000) are leading exponents of a key qualitative approach, autoethnography. The title of their paper 'Auto-ethnography, Personal Narrative Reflexivity; Researcher as Subject' begins to capture the flavour of the approach. The first part of the paper immediately steps out of the usual form of academic discourse by recounting a telephone call where they debate their thoughts on approach and how to recount it, they also reveal their personal relationship as a married couple. The paper goes on to outline the approach through stories of practice including supervising and guiding a student in the approach. Through a narrative form the fundamentals of autoethnography are elegantly told. The paper is juxtaposed with more traditional forms of academic writing and they give the following description:

Autoethnography is an autobiographical genre of writing and research that displays multiple layers of consciousness, connecting the personal to the cultural. Back and forth autoethnographers gaze, first through an ethnographic wide-angle lens, focussing outward on social and cultural aspects of their personal experience; then they look inward, exposing a vulnerable self that is moved by and may move through, and may refract, and resist cultural interpretations. (Ellis and Bochner 2000, p.739)

Ellis and Bochner (2000) nevertheless acknowledge the diversity of approaches that are encapsulated by the term autoethnography and consequently the difficulty of a precise definition. A little later they observe that:

In these texts, concrete action, dialogue, emotion, embodiment, spirituality, and self-consciousness are featured appearing as relational and institutional stories affected by history, social structure, and culture, which themselves are dialectically revealed through action, feeling, thought and language. (p739)

In traditional forms of research the researcher appears to be written out of the script by becoming the third person scriptwriter whereas within a qualitative approach the inquirers role and voice can be seen to be an integral part of the story. Returning to the work of Bent Flyvbjerg (2001) and phronetic research. Within the chapter of his book that discusses method, he relies on Cheryl Mattingly (1991) who observes that:

... narratives not only give meaningful form to experiences we have already lived through, they also provide us a forward glance, helping us to anticipate situations even before we encounter them, allowing us to envision alternative futures. Narrative inquiries do not - indeed, cannot - start from explicit theoretical assumptions. Instead, they begin with an interest in a particular phenomenon that is best understood narratively. (p137)

An inquiry which emanates from a desire to explore practice, to understand it better and develop it further does not in my experience start from a set of clear assumptions about that practice, rather it starts from a position of curiousness about aspects of that practice. It is also not intended to reify a practice, rather it is intended to further develop that practice and in that sense it is future facing.

Embodiment

Maurice Merleau-Ponty introduced into French philosophy the methods of the German phenomenological philosophers Husserl and Heidegger. An important aspect of phenomenology is the focus on processes within conscious life or human existence and their reliance on bodily processes and experience. They also implicitly reject the Cartesian view of a separate mind and body (Concise, Routledge Encyclopaedia of Philosophy (2000)).

> *The body is our general medium for having a world. Sometimes it is restricted to the actions necessary for the conservation of life, and accordingly it posits around us a biological world; at other times, elaborating upon these primary actions and moving from their literal to a figurative meaning, it manifests through them a core of new significance: this is true of motor habits such as dancing. Sometimes, finally, the meaning aimed at cannot be achieved by the body's natural means; it must then build itself an instrument, and it projects thereby around itself a cultural world. (Merleau-Ponty 1962, p.146)*

We can see from the quote above that not only does Merleau-Ponty argue for the recognition of the inherent link between mind-body and action, but also he recognises the way our bodies reach out into the cultural world. The concept of embodiment is no longer limited to the philosophical arena, there is increasing evidence that supports the view that the mind and body are intrinsically bound together as mind-body. In Minding the Body, Damasio and Damasio further argue not only the indivisibility of mind and body but the representation of the body within the brain and the implications of that:

> *The fact that the body of a given organism can be fully represented in the brain of that organism opens important possibilities. The first relates to consciousness, specifically with the part of the process called the self. Elsewhere we have argued that the construction of the self would simply not be possible if the brain did not have available a dynamic representation of its body. Consciousness is about the relation between a given organism and the objects perceived in its mind. In the mental process depicting the self, the integrated body representation serves as a stand-in for the organism. There is an invariant aspect to the body representation--its components and the schema according to which they are interconnected--and a variable aspect--the dynamic changes the components constantly undergo. Eventually the body representation behaves as an anchor for the construction of the self- a mental stand-in for the individual, for his or her personhood and identity.*

> *These body representations have another major implication: after allowing us to represent our own actions and emotional states, actual or simulated, they allow us to simulate the equivalent states of others. And because we have established a prior connection between our own body states and their significance, we can subsequently attribute the same significance to the states of others that we come to simulate. The body in mind helps us construct our selves and then allows us to understand others, which is nothing short of astounding.* (Damasio and Damasio 2006, p.22)

Neuroscience is now adding significantly to our understanding of how as human beings we interact with and understand each other at an emotional and physiological level with the ability to resonate with one-another. The description above by Damasio and Damasio of *simulated states* and *body in mind* constructing our selves and others has strong resonance for me with Shotter's (2003) description of chiasmic intertwined relationships where we co-construct our realities and co-ordinate our going on together.

The implication in the context of inquiry into human relations and human systems are profound. These include that if mind body are indivisible, as I believe they are, then our minds and our bodies and our physical and emotional responses as well as our intellectual understandings are an intrinsic part of our response to whatever we are enquiring into. Furthermore if we resonate on a physical and emotional level with others then attempting to detach ourselves from those who are the participants or subjects of our enquiry is impossible. This again fundamentally undermines the belief that in enquiry or research we can somehow separate our intellect from our emotions and ourselves from the issue or interest we are inquiring into.

We Don't Always Know What We Know?

> *The intuitive mind is a sacred gift and the rational mind is a faithful servant. We have created a society that honors the servant and has forgotten the gift.* (Albert Einstein - quoted in Klein 2004)

Michael Polanyi developed the concept of Tacit Knowing which has been described as a heuristic philosophy (Gelwick 1977). Polanyi's first major book on philosophy was Personal Knowledge (1958). A central concept in Polanyi's work was the distinction between subsidiary awareness and focal awareness:

I regard knowing as an active comprehension of the things known,
an action that requires skill. Skilful knowing and doing is performed
by subordinating a set of particulars, as clues or tools, to the shaping
of skilful achievement, whether practical or theoretical. We may
then be said to become "subsidiarily aware" of these particulars
within our "focal awareness" of the coherent entity that we achieve.
… Such is the personal participation of the knower in all acts of
understanding. (Polanyi 1958, p.vii)

Within Polanyi's work, Gelwick (a friend and student of Polanyi)
identifies the synthesis with the views of Wittgenstein and Merleau-
Ponty with emphasis on action, body and tacit knowledge. Making
further links between Wittgenstein and Polanyi, Gelwick comments
that:

The most striking similarity between Wittgenstein and Polanyi is
that they "both see language as meaningful only within the wider
context of culture, tradition, and ways of human living." … Wittgen-
stein used the Gestalt expression of "perceptual shift" to describe the
noticing of a new aspect, which is similar to Polanyi's notion that a
new way of perceiving a group of clues may enable us to grasp new
areas of reality. (Gelwick 1997, p.116)

Again we see the importance of the interaction between the self and
the outside world in developing knowledge and the important implicit
understanding that knowledge is socially constructed. This is consistent
with a relational social constructionist position that we create meaning
and our understandings in our everyday responsive processes (Cunliffe
2008), indeed Cunliffe contends that *"knowing lies within action, and*
action also lies within knowing" in a recursive relationship.

Perhaps the most quoted expression used by Polanyi is *"we can*
know more than we can tell" (1996, p.4). To illustrate his point he gives
examples. We can recognise a person's face in a crowd of thousands
but we cannot easily say how. However, through applying identikit
techniques the police have found ways of helping witnesses to identify
a face. This process Polanyi argues moves tacit knowledge to explicit
knowledge, helping us to tell what we know. He also identifies how
we often use tacit knowledge of human expressions to help us identify
another person's mood.

Polanyi (1966) discusses an experiment by psychologists Lazarus and
McCleary (1949). They presented subjects with a variety of nonsense
syllables and after specific combinations of nonsense syllables they

administered an electric shock. Presently the person showed symptoms of anticipating the shock, yet could not identify why. In a similar experiment which Polanyi also notes, Eriksen and Kuethe (1958), electrically shocked someone whenever they expressed certain words. Subjects learned to forestall the shock by avoiding those words; again on questioning, the subject seemed unaware they were doing this: *In both cases the shock producing particulars remained tacit. The subject could not identify them, yet he relied on his awareness of them for anticipating the electric shock* (p9). Hence Polanyi's assertion that we can *know more than we can tell*. Polanyi argues that this knowledge remained tacit because the subject's attention was focussed on the electric shock. As is noted above, Polanyi distinguishes between two kinds of awareness, *focal awareness* (in these examples the focus on the electric shock) and *subsidiary awareness* (in these examples the nonsense syllables or words that triggered the shock).

Intuition, in many contexts, can be seen as the everyday word for tacit knowing, for many writers the terms certainly seem to have very similar meaning. Usage is highly context dependent, so if the discussion is within a medical or scientific context we are more likely to come across the term tacit knowledge than within everyday conversation or popular media. However to try and distinguish between the two terms I would suggest that *intuition is tacit knowing that has been surfaced;* by the time we say that we have an intuitive feeling it has moved from the level of tacit knowing (which Polanyi established is beneath the level of conscious thought), to something that we are able to state, even if we don't know exactly why we know or think it. Intuition is therefore one aspect of a process in which we make cognitive sense of the world we encounter.

Our ability to discern patterns from fragments of information and use these as a way to go on, is described by Shotter (1984) as practical hermeneutics. One of the key issues here is when and how we use intuition in decision making. When decision making is required in the moment we don't have time to undertake a detailed analysis and we instinctively rely on intuition (or tacit knowing).

Khatri and Alvin (2000) argue that:

The process of intuition is very quick (Seebo, 1993). It is the smooth automatic performance of learned behavior sequences and often can short-circuit a step-wise decision- making, thus, allowing an individual to know almost instantly what the best course of action is. It compresses years of experience and learning into split seconds

(Isenberg, 1984). Intuitive synthesis allows calling a number of related problems or issues at the same time.

One of the key lessons from the literature on intuition is knowing when to rely on intuition and when to rely on deliberate decision making. *When we talk about analytical versus intuitive decision making neither is good or bad. What is bad if you use either of them in an inappropriate circumstance* (Gladwell 2005, p.143/4) quoting Paul Van Ripper.

Clearly then we can see that it is quite possible for us to have a greater level of knowledge than we can consciously realise or articulate. As is outlined above Polanyi (1966) identifies this as tacit knowledge. At the higher levels of skill, (proficient and expert) it is argued that there is a move beyond rule-bound behaviour. That knowledge has become embodied and the practitioner is able to act beyond what we might call logical thought (Dreyfus and Dreyfus 1986) and act intuitively. It is intrinsic to acting in this way that we do not always know why we have done what we have done, consequently it can be very hard for experts to describe retrospectively why they have acted in a particular way.

Understanding how a professional practice works can be seen as trying to reveal tacit and implicit knowing, the taken for granted knowledge we have and apply in undertaking our day-to-day practice and our linked intuitive action. Capturing such tacit knowing is I think a challenge within enquiries into professional practice; however I believe such inquiries have a key role in capturing the embedded professional knowledge of experts. Given that those who enquire into such practice are often experts in such practice it seems entirely possible that they will also be acting intuitively as they enquire into that practice. This requires that we use and develop reflexive methods of enquiry that help to reveal this tacit and intuitive knowing. Linking back to an earlier part of this chapter, one way of surfacing implicit and tacit knowledge lies in co-creating reflective dialogical processes (Nonaka and Tacheuchi 1995, Polanyi 1958, Benner 2001) which to my mind lie at the centre of systemic inquiry.

Aesthetics and Ethics

When we undertake an inquiry I believe that we have a moral (and often academic) obligation to ensure that such an inquiry is undertaken ethically. From a systemic position I believe that this obligation runs much more deeply than satisfying an ethics committee and I am reminded of the need to inhabit the domain of aesthetics:

The domain of aesthetics refers to "the emotion in the happening of living you recognise as aesthetics" (Maturana 1985). Thus this refers to such notions as elegance, beauty, harmony, desirability, consistency, morality, ethics. The aesthetic domain is a frame which relates both to the domain of production and to the domain of explanations. (Lang, Little and Cronen 1990)

Consequently aesthetics must inform both how our inquiries are lived and how they are subsequently told. From a perspective of relational social construction and learning and also creating an important link with reflexivity I am reminded of Anne Cunliffe's comments:

Relationally responsive knowing and learning means thinking more reflexively about how we construct multiple and emerging 'realities' and selves with others, through our dialogue. I suggest that it involves both self- and critical-reflexivity. Self-reflexivity goes deeper than reflecting on an event or a situation; it involves recognizing we are in-relation-to-others, that we 'summon each other in responsibility' (Levinas, cited by Ricoeur, 1992) and thus need to examine our fundamental assumptions, values, ways of interacting and how these affect other people. (Cunliffe 2008)

If we accept the position that within human systems our inquiries are tacit and intuitive and that we are feeling our way forward in gaining understanding through hearing views on the human system and the stories of the participants; then through much of our practice and inquiry we are making in the moment ethical judgements. Here I am reminded of Varela's writings on ethical know-how where he expresses the view that ethics *"is closer to wisdom than to reason, closer to understanding what is good than to correctly adjudicating situations ...* and he goes on later to state *... a wise (or virtuous person) is **one who knows what is good and spontaneously does it"**.* (Varela 1999, p.3/4 with emphasis in original). Consequently, our ethical judgements are made in the moment and in the moves of the conversational turn of inquiry, in making these judgements we are applying tacit practice wisdom.

In Conclusion

What I have attempted to do in this chapter is to illustrate the links that I see between systemic thinking and practice and how for me this is embedded within a world of inquiry that is dialogically co-constructed in relation with others.

When we move beyond a Cartesian world view we are able to recognise the indivisibility of our mind and body and when we think systemically we can see that as humans we are inherently part of the social world we inhabit. This has the implication that when we observe it we are intrinsically part of a system. Consequently, we are unable to separate ourselves in an abstract way from whatever human system we are inquiring into. In consequence we have to find ways of inquiry that not only recognise how we are systemically linked to our practice and inquiry but which also open up the future facing opportunities that this offers.

We also need to recognise that our understandings are not only generated by analytical processes but also through our abilities to think intuitively and our inherent capacity to act expertly based on tacit knowledge. This means that we also have to develop processes of inquiry that are able to reveal how as expert practitioners we and others act. This leads me to recognise the significance of reflective, reflexive based approaches to inquiry and that these are inherently dialogical in their approach.

Ultimately, I am not concerned by generating provable or replicable knowledge. The issue for me is whether the theoretical perspectives and understanding we generate from inquiry are helpful for ourselves and others in going forward through understanding and developing useful and aesthetic practice.

References

Armson, Rosalind. (2011), *Growing Wings on the Way: Thinking Systems for Messy Situations*, Axminster: Triarchy Press.

Bateson, Gregory (1979), *Mind and Nature: A Necessary Unity*. E. P. Dutton. New York.

Bateson, Gregory. (2000), *Steps to an Ecology of Mind*, University of Chicago Press. (online) available at; http://www.anecologyofmind.com/bateson/ Accessed 24/5/2012

Beer, Stafford., Whittaker, D. (ed) (2009), *Think Before You Think: Social Complexity and Knowledge of Knowing*, Waverstone Press.

Benner, Patricia. (2001), *From Novice to Expert*, Prentice Hall Health.

Berger, Peter., and Luckman, Thomas. (1967), *The Social Construction of Reality: A Treatise in the Sociology of Knowledge*, Penguin Books.

Blake, William. (1709), *The Marriage of Heaven and Hell* (online) Available at: http:// www.blakearchive.org/exist/blake/archive/work.xq?workid=mhh Accessed on 27/8/2012.

Bochner, Arthur. (2009), *Warm Ideas and Chilling Consequences, International Review of Qualitative Research* 3.3: 357-70.

Bohm, David., Nichol, Lee. (ed) (1996), *On Dialogue*, Routledge, London.

Burr, Vivien. (1995), *An Introduction to Social Constructionism*, Sage Publications.

Butler, Christopher. (2002), *Postmodernism; A Very Short Introduction*, Oxford UP.

Cahoone, Lawrence E. (1996), *From Modernism to Postmodernism an Anthology*, Blackwell.

Capra, Fritjof. (1996), *The Web of Life; A New Synthesis of Mind and Matter*, Flamingo Harper Collins.

Capra, Fritjof. (undated), Homage to Gregory Bateson (online) available at; http://www.anecologyofmind.com/gregorybateson.html, Accessed 14/09/2014

Chard, Alex. (2011), Guide to Monitoring and Evaluation of Services for Frontline Managers (online) Available at: www.ccinform.co.uk

Concise Routledge Encyclopedia of Philosophy (2000). Routledge.

Cunliffe, Alex. (2008), *Orientations to Social Constructionism: Relationally Responsive Social Constructionism and its Implications for Knowledge and Learning, Management Learning*, 2008 39: 123.

Damasio, Antonio., Damasio, Hanna. (2006), "Minding the Body," *Daedalus* 135.3 Questia (online) Available at: <http://www.questia.com/ PM.qst?a=o&d=5017452795>. Accessed 17/8/2008

Dreyfus, Hubert L, and Dreyfus, Stuart E. (1986), *Mind Over Machine, The Power of Human Intuition and Expertise in the Era of the Computer*, The Free Press, New York.

Ellis, Carolyn S., Bochner, Arthur. (2000), "Autoethnography, Personal Narrative, Reflexivity: Researcher as Subject", in Denzin, N., Lincoln, Y., Handbook of Qualitative Research, 2nd Edition, Sage Publications.

Flood, Robert (1999), *Rethinking the Fifth Discipline, Learning Within the Unknowable*, Routledge.

Flood, Robert. (2006), "The Relationship of 'Systems Thinking' to Action Research". In Reason, P, Bradbury H, *The Handbook of Action Research*, Sage.

Flyvbjerg, Bent. (2001), *Making Social Science Matter, Why Social Inquiry Fails and How It Can Succeed Again*, Cambridge UP.

Fullbrook, Edward. (2004), "Descartes' Legacy: Intersubjective Reality, Intrasubjective Theory", in Davix, J et al, eds (2004) *Elgar Companion to Economics and Philosophy*, Elgar.

Gelwick, Richard. (1977), *The Way of Discovery*, Oxford UP.

Gergen, Mary, and Gergen, Kenneth. (2004), *Social Construction: Entering the Dialogue*, Taos Institute.

Gladwell, Malcom. (2005), *Blink*, Little, Brown and Company

Glanville, Ranulph. (2002), Second Order Cybernetics, in Encyclopedia of Life Support Systems, EoLSS Publishers, Oxford, available at: http://www.eolss. net/sample-chapters/c02/e6-46-03-03.pdf

Hacking, Ian. (1999), *The Social Construction of What?* Harvard UP

Hertz, Rosanna. (1997), *Reflexivity & Voice*, Sage.

Hibberd, Fiona, J. (2005), *Unfolding Social Constructionism*, Springer.

Khatri, Naresh., and Ng Lai Oon, Alvin. (2000), *The Role of Intuition in Strategic Decision Making*. (online) Available at: www3.ntu.edu.sg/nbs/

sabre/working_papers/01-97.pdf Accessed 2/7/2013.

Klein, Gary. (2004), *The Power of Intuition*, Currency Doubelday.

Koestler, Arthur. (1971), "The Concept of the Holon", in Koestler, A., Smythies, J., *The Alpbach Symposium Beyond Reductionism New Perspectives in Life Sciences*. Houghton Mifflin Co.

Korn, Harald. (2011), *An Introduction to Context, Resonance and Domains*.

Lang, Peter., Little, Martin., Cronen, Vernon. (1990), "The Systemic Professional Domains of Action and the Question of Neutrality", *Human Systems*, 1:39-55.

Lang, Peter., Little, Martin., Shotter, John. (2006), Conversation on Origins of KCC, the Professional Doctorate in Systemic Practice, Recorded 13th July 2006.

Laszlo, Ervin. (1996), *The Systems View of the World: A Holistic Vision for Our Time*, Cresskill NJ: Hampton Press.

Lewin, Kurt. (1946), "Action Research and Minority Problems", *Journal of Social Issues* 2.

Mattingly, Cheryl. (1991) "Narrative Reflections on Practical Actions", in Schön, Donald. (Ed.), *The Reflective Turn: Case Studies in and on Educational Practice*.

Maturana Humberto. R., Paucar-Caceres Alberto. & Harnden Roger. (2011) Origins and Implications of Autopoiesis. Preface to the Second Edition of De Máquinas y Seres Vivos. Constructivist Foundations 6(3): 293–306. Available at http://www.univie.ac.at/constructivism/journal/6/3/293.maturana

McNamee, Sheila., Guanaes, Carla., Rasera, Emerson F., Therapy as Social Construction: An Interview with Sheila McName, Revista Interamericana de Psicología/Interamerican *Journal of Psychology* - 2006, Vol. 40, Num. 1 pp. 127-136.

McNamee, Sheila., Hosking, Dian. (2012), *Research and Social Change A Relational Constructionist Approach*, Routledge.

Merleau-Ponty, Maurice. (1962), *Phenomenology of Perception*, Routledge & Kegan Paul.

Montuori, Alfonso. (2003), "The Complexity of Improvisation and the Improvisation of Complexity: Social Science, Art and Creativity", *Human Relations*, vol. 56 no. 2 237-255

Nonaka, Ikujiro., Takeuchi, Hirotaka.,((1995), *The Knowledge-Creating Company: How Japanese Companies Create the Dynamics of Innovation*, Oxford UP.

Pallazzoli, Mara S., Boscolo, Luigi., Cecchin, Gianfranco., Prata, Giuliana. (1978), *Paradox and Counter Paradox; A New Model in the Therapy of the Family in Schizophrenic Transition*, Jason Aronson.

Pangaro, Paul., Henry, Sarah. (2013), interaction cybernetics design. (online) available at; http://www.pangaro.com/ecole-des-mines.html, Accessed 14/09/2014.

Polanyi, Michael. (1958) (Corrected edition 1962), *Personal Knowledge, Towards a Post- Critical Philosophy,* University of Chicago Press, Chicago.

Polanyi, Michael. (1966), *The Tacit Dimension*, Doubleday and Company.

Raine, Peter. (1998), *Who Guards the Guardians? The Practical and Theoretical Criteria for Environmental Guardianship*, Massey University.

Schön, Donald. (1987), *Educating the Reflective Practitioner*. San Fransisco: Jossey Bass.

Shotter, John (1994), 'Now I Can Go On': Wittgenstein and Communication. Paper given at University of Calgary, Department of Communication. (Given to me by the author).

Shotter, John. (1984), *Social Accountability and Selfhood*. Blackwell, Oxford.

Shotter, John. (1997) "The Social Construction of our 'Inner' Lives". *Journal of Constructivist Psychology*, *10*, pp.7-24.

Shotter, John. (2003)" Cartesian Change, Chiasmic Change – The Power of Living Expression". Janus Head: *Journal of Interdisciplinary Studies in Literature, Continental Philosophy, Phenomenological Psychology and the Arts*.

Shotter, John. (2011), *Getting It: Withness-Thinking and the Dialogical in Practice*, Hampton Press.

Steier, Frederick. (1991) "Reflexivity and Methodology: An Ecological Constructionism, in Steier, F., *Research and Reflexivity*, Sage Publications.

Varela, Francisco, J. (1999), *Ethical Know-How*, Stanford UP

Vernon E. Cronen., Kenneth M. Johnson. and John W. Lannamann., "Paradoxes, Double Binds, and Reflexive Loops: An Alternative Theoretical Perspective", *Family Process,* Volume 21, Issue 1, pages 91–112, March 1982

von Foerster, Heinz. (1975), *The Cybernetics of Cybernetics, Biological Computer Laboratory*, Champaign/Urbana, republished (1995), Future Systems Inc., Minneapolis, MN.

von Foerster, Heinz. (1992), Ethics and Second-order Cybernetics, Cybernetics and Human Knowing. (online) Available at: http://www.stanford.edu/group/SHR/4-2/text/ foerster.html Accessed 7/7/2012.

W. Barnett Pearce. (1998), *Thinking About Systems and Thinking Systemically*, Pearce Associates.

W. Barnett Pearce. (2002), *Systems: Schools of Thought and Traditions of Practice*, Pearce Associates.

Weiner, Norbert. (1948), *Cybernetics: All Control and Communication in the Animal or Machine*, MIT Press.

3 Collaborative-Dialogue Based Research as Everyday Practice: Questioning our Myths

Harlene Anderson

> *"Didn't you follow that exiled Austrian*
> *Who stood on my murky lane with a walking-stick*
> *Drawing diagrams for the birds to explain?*
> *Sea-urchins mocked him with folkloric tricks.*
> *He left, in my turf-shed rafters, a small sign*
> *To question all our myths.... Dear Wittgenstein."*
>
> from "Killary Hostel" by Richard Murphy

People around the world increasingly want to have a voice and input into decisions that affect their lives: what kinds of services they need, the kinds of services offered, and how the services are provided. They call for a more egalitarian world in which they are respected as persons who know themselves--their lives, circumstances, and requirements--better than a stranger: a person often experienced as an interloper. In other words, as Wittgenstein suggests, people challenge us to question the institutionalized myths on which we base our practices.

Collaborative-dialogue practice joins an effort to question the myths—the established conventions--of our social science research practices, not as an alternative practice methodology but as a different way of conceptualizing research and knowledge. These conventions include: research is scientific inquiry, only researchers execute research, performing research takes professional training, research is carried out by an objective outsider, the researcher must be objective and neutral, research is best conducted after the fact, research tells us what is, methods must be validated and reliable, methods must be repeatable, and results must be generalizable. If we take an incredulous stance toward these conventions from a collaborative-dialogue perspective we are challenged to rethink the traditions of research and the distinctions between research and other practices and the distinctions between so-called subjects and researchers

For the collaborative-dialogic practitioner the same assumptions orient practice regardless of the practice domain. In other words maintaining congruence between one's practices is important. Performing consistently within our practices, i.e., consultation and research, requires among other things what learning systems theorist Donald Schön (1983, 1987) describes as being a reflective practitioner. Schön refers to the practitioner's reflecting-in-action: reflecting, pausing and inquiring into to understand one's theoretical underpinnings and to describe one's practice as one does it. The practitioner not only becomes more thoughtful and accountable, but in doing so, theorizing and practicing are reciprocally influenced as the practitioner makes new sense of ideas and experiences and thus continues to generate new learning. Based on his research about how professionals learn, Schön suggests that incorporating reflective practice in education leads to learning that is more profound. To paraphrase Schön, self-discovered, self-appropriated learning or learning that belongs to the learner is the only learning that significantly influences behavior. I would add, the way that one lives in both one's professional and personal worlds. Taking a slightly different perspective that is based largely in the works of Bakhtin and Wittgenstein, John Shotter refers to such learning-in-action and learning-by-doing as "performative understanding" or "performative knowing" as described by Shotter in his chapter in this book.

Research as Discovering or Generating Knowledge

I recently heard a talk by an expert in the internet technology industry on what is called "customer or user experience design". He stressed the importance of "collaborative design" which requires research to create an internet product that is meaningful and useful for the customer. To reassure the small business owners in the audience who expressed great apprehension, he said "anybody can be a researcher" and gave examples of how we research in our daily lives. Engaging the audience in the familiar piqued their curiosity as to how they could think of research as a necessary component of their businesses and something they could do. In hearing this I reflected on writing this chapter and wondered how I might engage the practitioner-reader to consider research with fresh eyes and to think of it as part of their everyday practice and themselves as researchers? I kept returning to the notion of understanding and doing professional practice dialogically and the inherent challenge to rethink the "role" of the professional and to maintain congruence between all our practices: if professional practice is considered as dialogic then the professional is a researcher.

Practitioners like business owners often turn away from anything associated with research. For many research is a daunting specialized activity that others do and its reporting is often experienced as a dry foreign language that is difficult to understand. We pigeonhole ourselves and others into culturally and professionally designated roles and practices, and fit ourselves into the expectations prescribed by the associated discourses. Said differently, we fold ourselves into the familiar.

A collaborative-dialogue discourse offers an invitation into the unfamiliar. In other words, it calls us to notice and experience the uniqueness and nuance of the presumably known and to encounter it as if it is the first time. But before we turn to this discussion, let's step back a moment and look more closely at the etymology of the word research and its various meanings.

The Word 'Research' and Scientific Method

Some date the development of research or the scientific method back to Aristotle in the 300's BCE though the word research did not appear in the English dictionary until about 1577. The word

> *"comes from Middle French recerche, which itself comes from Old French recercher [meaning to] 'seek out, search closely' (re- 'intensive' + cercher `to seek out'. Cercher comes ultimately from Latin circare `go about, wander,' from circus 'circle.' The meaning 'a careful search for facts' first appears in English in the first half of the 17th century"* (http://laser.physics.sunysb.edu/~wise/wise187/2002/weblinks/theword_research.txt).

This latter reference to research soon became the language and center point of scientific method. Though the meaning of research and particularly the questions "what is research" and "is it a discovery or generative method" are still under consideration in scientific debate (http://telescoper.wordpress.com/2012/03/08/the-meaning-of-research/) as evidenced by cell biologist Frederick Grinnell (2009) in his *Everyday Practice of Science: Where Intuition and Passion Meet Objectivity and Logic*. He comments that Claude Bernard, a founder of modern biomedical research, "...warned that inability to put aside previously accepted beliefs, at least temporarily, interferes with the ability of the researcher to notice anything more than the expected." Quoting Bernard,

> *Men who have excessive faith in their theories or ideas are not only ill prepared for making discoveries; they also make very poor observations. Of necessity, they observe with a preconceived idea,*

and when they devise an experiment, they can see, in its results, only
a confirmation of their theory. In this way they distort observations
and often neglect very important facts because they do not further
their aim (p.55).

Grinnell (2009) concludes from Bernard's words that "there may not be
a method of discovery, but there is a clear strategy—be prepared to notice
the unexpected. Nothing noticed—novelty lost. . ." He challenges a myth
of scientific discourse: that science, whether discovery or generative and
from observing scientists at work in their laboratories, is not linear and
concludes that thinking of science as linear significantly distorts the
everyday practice of science. We might infer then that Grinnell speaks
to the risk of generalizing knowledge--knowing ahead of time. Grinnell's
challenges and similar ones call into question the predictability or
comprehension of the complexities, ambiguities and uncertainties of
everyday life and practice by so-called academic or scientific research.
Certainty in science and in everyday life as an illusion is echoed in the
words of professor and theoretical physicist S. J. Gates (2012): "Science
in my experience does not permit us the illusion of certainty."

The aforementioned challenges regarding conceptualizing and doing
research are compatible with the alternative ideas about knowledge and
its creation that weave through postmodern and rhizome philosophies
and dialogue and social construction theories. We participate in
constructing the world we live in. Though this is often thought to be
a recent perspective, it dates back at least to the seventeen hundreds
when Italian philosopher Giambattista Vico (1999) denounced the
Cartesian method that truth can be verified through observation. He
alternatively suggested that the observer participates in the construction
of what he observes, attributes their descriptions to it and wears
multiple interpretive lenses regarding the same. More contemporarily,
constructivists such as Heinz von Foerster (1982) called attention to the
notion of observing systems saying "believing is seeing" and Humberto
Maturana (1978) suggested that "Everything said is said by an observer
to another observer."

Put differently, embedded as it is in culture, history and language,
knowledge is a product of social discourse. Its creation (e.g., theories,
ideas, truths, beliefs, realities or how to) is an interactive interpretive
dialogic process that occurs within the discourses of knowledge communities in which all parties contribute to its development, sustainability
and transformation. As such it is not fundamental or definitive, it
is not fixed or discovered and it is not a product of an individual or

collective mind. In such a dialogic activity there is not a dichotomy between "knower" and "not-knower". As Maturana and Varela (1987) suggested there is no such thing as instructive interaction in which pre-existing knowledge (including meanings, understandings, etcetera) can be transferred from the head of one person (be it a teacher in person or the voice of an author on the pages of a book) and placed into the head of another (e.g., a student in a classroom or a reader). Knowledge acquisition by one person is not/cannot be determined by another person; for instance, a teacher cannot determine what a student will learn. Knowledge creation is relational, and it is fluid and changeable in its making. Yet personalized: when we share our knowledge with one another, we cannot know what each brings, we cannot pre-determine how each will interact with the shared knowledge and we cannot predict what each will create with what is offered and emerges in a dialogic process. The learning outcome will be something different than either started with, something more than either could have created alone, something socially constructed. This leads us to a review of some of the basic assumptions of collaborative-dialogue practice.

Basic Orienting Assumptions of Collaborative Practice

Collaborative-dialogic practice is largely informed by a set of abstract assumptions that weave through hermeneutic, postmodern and rhizome philosophies and dialogue and social construction theories exemplified by writers such as Mikhail Bakhtin, Gilles Deleuze, Felix Guattari, Hans-George Gadamer, Kenneth Gergen, Rom Harré, John Shotter and Ludwig Wittgenstein. These assumptions mainly signify alternative ways to consider language and knowledge, and thus our practice and the people we meet in it and ourselves in relation to each of these. As Wittgenstein suggests, it is within our relationships that language gains its significance. Orienting assumptions relevant to this chapter and the generation of knowledge in particular include:

Grand knowledge, and the meta-narratives and dominant discourses on which it is based, is best held in doubt and questioned as fundamental, universal and definitive.
Such knowledge is mostly invisible and taken-for-granted and makes up the contexts and conditions that have become a monopolizing influence on our practices. The authority and conventions of these seduce us into practices that are dualistic and hierarchical and to place ourselves in the role of the knowledge expert. Interestingly, Noah Richards

(2007) suggests that "any universal concept is unknowable or not understandable, since the act of knowing it would mean that it is not universal." This is not to suggest that we abandon these truths. Instead we are urged to conduct our daily practice with a certain amount of skepticism and reflection regarding their value, what they permit us to do and not do (including thought and action) and our reasons for doing and not doing, and in doing so as Richards suggests develop our local understanding.

Dominant discourses, meta-narratives and universal truths create pre-knowing that risks generalizing.

Pre-knowing has several risks: One, we tend to perceive similarities, to find what we think we know and are looking for, to fill in the gaps and then proceed based on these. Two, we are led to see the familiar and in so doing we close ourselves and miss the uniqueness of each person, situation and circumstance. Three, we consequently synthesize, thematize and summarize what we think we have learned and in so doing reduce personal distinctiveness to non-personal facts or figures. Four, we also distill the special and intimate into themes which then can quickly become fixed truths and future practice maps. This increases the probability that we classify people, cultures, and problems and so forth into categories, groups and kinds and in so doing we depersonalize them or worse yet we stereotype them. The ultimate risk of generalizing is that we can limit the potentials and possibilities both for us and the people we work with.

Local knowledge has advantages over universal knowledge.

Local knowledge is the indigenous narratives--the unique wisdom, expertise, competencies, truths, values, customs and language--created and used within a community of persons (e.g., people in a family, classroom, board room, factory team or neighborhood). The community of persons can be thought of as a knowledge system that has its own history and meaning-making practices. The unique nuanced meanings and understandings of the community members' first-person experiences bring a wealth of resources for the creation of practical, customized, useful and sustainable knowledge for its members. Privileging local knowledge inherently challenges and transforms the relationship between knowledge, expertise and power. We must, however, keep in mind that the local knowledge system is always context bound-developed and influenced by the background of universal narratives and dominant systems of discourses in which it is embedded.

Knowledge creation is a relational-dialogic social process that minimizes the dichotomy between "knower" and "not-knower".

In dialogue participants join in a shared or mutual inquiry in which they jointly examine, question, ponder, wonder and reflect on the topic to be addressed. Through their joint engagement of back-and-forth exchanges of asking questions and making comments they are, as best they can, involved in a process of meaning-making. That is, shared inquiry is meaning-making: trying to learn and understand the uniqueness of the other's language and sensing its uniqueness from the other's perspective, not theirs. Shotter refers to this process as relational-responsiveness: "A 'good' conversation is dynamic and opinions and feelings are woven across the 'gap' between us [i.e., the dichotomy between knower and not-knower], bridging us through responses that are 'crafted' and 'tailored' that particular instance..." (Shotter 2006, p.53). One must exercise caution, however, in reading the words crafted and tailored. These words do not refer to strategic means but rather to a 'know-how' (Anderson 2009): being careful to maintain coherence with the other person's language, and distinctive characteristics such as manner of expression and acting.

In summary, these orienting assumptions are not posed as a knowledge meta-narrative and do not call for the abandonment of any knowledge tradition. They simply suggest an alternative language and perspective for thought and action that provides a seemingly simple yet not-so-simple orientation to practice and how we educate practitioners and even approach life itself. In other words, relative to this chapter is an inherent appeal for a habit of continual consideration and re-consideration of how we think about research, and how we think of ourselves as practitioners and where our knowledge comes from.

Brief Thoughts on Inquiry as Collaborative-Dialogue

Collaborative-dialogue is a meaning-making process with language as its medium. Language refers to any means by which we express, articulate and communicate with others and ourselves. This would include the spoken word, and any conveyance such as written words, sighs and emotions and the multitude of bodily actions such eye movements, and gestures. We are, however, prisoners of our language: as we try to understand and make sense of our experiences, ourselves and others through our familiar language, we mostly do so within an inherited framework of language as representational rather than language as gaining its meaning in its use (Wittgenstein 1953).

Participants in collaborative-dialogue are always on the way to learning and understanding and being careful to not assume or fill in the meaning and information gaps. In other words participants mutually 'inquire into' something that has relevance for them. This learning, understanding and carefulness requires a responsiveness in which a listener (who is also a speaker) is fully attentive and present for the other person and their utterances whether expressed orally or otherwise. This also requires being aware of, showing acknowledgment of and taking seriously what the other person has said and the importance of it. In other words, a listener-speaker not only listens attentively but also responds so as to make sure that they have heard the other person as best they can. Such responsive understanding as Bakhtin (1986) refers to it tends to help clarify and "check-out" understandings and misunderstandings which in turn is part of the meaning-creating process, making responsive understanding is a generative process. This aim to learn and understand does not refer to asking questions to gather or verify information, facts or data. Questions, as is any utterance, instead are posed as part of the conversational-dialogical process: to learn and understand as best one can what the other person is expressing and hopes will be heard. It is a responsive interactive process rather than a passive one of surmising and knowing the other and their words based on pre-understanding such as a theory, hypothesis or experience. It is this kind of responsiveness to the other that invites them into collaborative-dialogue (see Anderson 1997). In other words, people are considered as naturally relational-dialogical social beings as suggested by Bakhtin (1986), Buber (1970) and Wittgenstein (1953) and by Shotter's interpretations' and extensions of Bakhtin's and Wittgenstein's perspectives.

I use the word dialogue to refer to a particular kind and quality of conversation: talking in which meaning-making is its essence-as previously discussed in Anderson, 1997. Dialogue according to Bakhtin (1984) is polyphonic: multiple voices and authors are always present, not just the spoken and silent ones of the in-person participants but others as well. Each person, present or not, has multiple voices, sometimes in harmony with each other though not necessarily so. Though humans are dialogical beings who are always in the process of meaning-making, sometimes we are more or less so, we oscillate on what can be thought of as a dialogical-monological continuum (Anderson 1997). In other words, sometimes we slip from multivocality into univocality. Monological refers to one idea or thought dominating to the exclusion of others and curiosity as well. Though this is not to suggest that is bad; it is a natural part of conversation. When monologue dominates, the opportunity for newness is diminished. Relating this to research as inquiry, the so-called researcher needs to be open to the newness of the other and their experience. If the researcher cannot maintain curiosity, the risk becomes that the researcher may only find what they are looking for and potentially does not learn anything new.

Our inner dialogue is a critical component in engaging another into dialogue with us and themselves, and sustaining it. In other words, to be in dialogue with another person requires first being in dialogue with one's self. This entails being able to suspend our pre-understandings, to be aware of when our pre-understandings are leading, and to open ourselves to the other and their otherness and let it enter us. What dialogue is and how to engage in it are not easy questions to respond to and are unanswerable if the questioner is seeking a structured map or step-by-step instructions. These questions though important are difficult to address because dialogue and collaborative-dialogic practice are based in a particular philosophy of *ways of being 'with'* others: a philosophical stance (Anderson 1997, 2012; Anderson & Gehart 2007) or as Bakhtin (1986) suggests, a way of being human. 'With' is a basic characteristic of the stance and the features of dialogue: talking with, thinking with, acting with and responding with. The stance can be expressed in many ways as dialogue is specific to the participants, relationships, contexts, circumstances, agendas and so forth. It is situational and depends on these specificities including the participants' styles, tones, mannerisms and so forth. In other words, the stance allows adaptability. Dialogue thus is a spontaneous activity and not a step-by-step one. As such it cannot be implemented, managed, predicted or guaranteed. Though dialogue can be invited and encouraged (e.g. by a consultant, coach, manager, and members of organizations[1].) it cannot be prescribed, scripted, or demanded. The invitation to engage in and the encouragement to sustain dialogue take continuous awareness, effort, flexibility and carefulness on the part of the inviter. Some features of this invitation and encouragement include: expression of sincere attentiveness to the other person, openness to and learning about their differences whether in values, opinions, language, etc., viewing dialogue as necessarily filled with the challenges and opportunities of tension, unclarity, ambiguity and incoherency as well as harmony, intelligibility, synchronicity and agreement.

In dialogue, each participant brings their local knowledge to the process; it is through the sharing and exploring of what each person offers that newly created understandings, meanings and actions relevant to the intent or agenda of the dialogue emerge. As a relational-dialogic process knowledge, therefore, is not viewed as something that already exists and lies in wait for discovery by the consultant or researcher.

Instead, knowledge is viewed as an interactive social activity that people do with each other. New knowledge is created through the mutual inquiry, through the joint exploring and looking into the focus of the conversation and the various paths it takes. As mentioned above this requires, however, that we remain willing and able to put aside what we think is there and what we want to find. In failing to do so we are apt to find what we look for and justify our finding. In other words, the production of knowledge-the result of inquiry-is considered a generative and not a discovery activity. This is a shift from what might be thought of as retrospective knowledge that is objectively established from a neutral outsider's perspective who then privately determines what is learned and the conclusions of the learning. Important here is to keep in mind that knowledge is used in its broadest sense: expertise, wisdom, truth, beliefs, and so forth.

Dialogue therefore is a relational generative pathway to newness and possibilities in which each participant contributes to what is created through dialogue and not a unilateral monovocal content search for facts of details. It cannot be otherwise.

Returning to Schön's (1983, 1987) notion of a reflective practitioner in-action and Shotter's notion of performative understanding, this rethinking requires a practitioner to pause and inquire into their practice to try to understand its theoretical underpinnings and to describe their practice as they do it. This becomes especially challenging if we think that most of what practitioners do is not only invisible but most likely involves tacit knowledge that one might not be aware of at the time. Often it is only in retrospect that one describes and interprets it. For instance, how would you describe or make sense of your choice when you took a particular fork on a conversational path instead of others? It's all after-the-moment.

Theory and practice reciprocally influence each other and co-evolve as the practitioner becomes more thoughtful and accountable, makes new sense of each, and invites their clients to join them in this. The consequence of this mutual inquiry perspective is that the separation between research and other practices, or between the learning (the doing) and the knowing (the outcome), is dissolved. This is contrary to the accustomed ways in which we separate practices.

Collaborative-Dialogue Practice-Based Research

Research from a collaborative-dialogue practice orientation as described above steps outside our familiar frameworks of understanding. Research becomes like other practices a subject-subject 'withness' shared inquiry. Research as shared inquiry is distinct from the more usual researcher-subject or researcher-object dichotomous form of inquiry in which the researcher is an external observer who looks backwards from outside and then describes, analyzes and explains (we might say partly determines) what *was* there. Importantly, shared inquiry focuses on the means of the dialogic process as relationally reciprocal. Each participant is influenced by the other, and each contributes to what is produced; it cannot be otherwise.

Research becomes a decentralized process of learning and knowing that brings in the voices of the people--the so-called subjects that the so-called researchers want to learn from—as active participants in learning with each other. It flips learning *about* to learning *with*. Each participant contributes to the determination of what is inquired into and how. This is in contrast to the one initiating dialogue-e.g., consultant or researcher-being in control of the direction of the talk or authoring its outcome. We might think of research from this perspective as social inquiry instead of scientific inquiry. In suggesting this I do not refer to the debate regarding qualitative versus quantitative social inquiry. My intent is to call attention to the relational "engagement" and mutually beneficial aspect of the knowledge that is created in the inquiry process.

Characteristic then of shared inquiry is that each participant has the opportunity to contribute their voice and viewpoint to the determination of what is inquired into, who is invited into the inquiry, what is learned—the interpretation or assignment of meaning—and how what is learned is used. The inquiry process, and its ensuing direction, is an iterative, emergent and fluid process in which each step informs the next. The destination that participants first agreed upon can change as the inquiry proceeds. For instance, the initial question(s), goals and "method" often change as the research proceeds.

In considering research as part of everyday practice, the consultant and client become co-researchers. Though what is it that they are researching? Interestingly, we could consider that the entire consultation is a process of researching the topic of inquiry: that is, the reason for the client seeking consultation. Likewise, we could consider that client and practitioner are researching the usefulness of the consultation and determining its future direction. Regarding the former, if the collaborative-dialogue relationship and process is similar regardless of the context and the agenda, then from this perspective there is not much difference between the process of consultation and research, or distance between the academic ivory tower and the everyday practice room.[2]

With the former the focus is to look at what the client and consultant are doing together: for instance, is it useful, how is it useful, is there something that could be accomplished differently, what suggestions do the client and consultant have for doing-the-doing differently? Any focus of inquiry or questions would be jointly created by a client and consultant, learner and teacher or members of an organization and leader and would be specific to the local organization culture, specific context, and agenda of the task as well as the relationship and other considerations particular to the task. As well, the inquiry would be part of the ongoing process of the task instead of something only conducted at its conclusion. This is similar to the idea of the reflective practitioner: researching or inquiring so as to extend, elaborate and refine what you do. In other words, understanding what we are doing, learning what we might do differently from within, and using what is learned by the insiders in the here-and-now.

Pausing my thoughts, consistent with the notion of knowledge creation discussed in above, what is learned—what is created in the meaning-making process of shared inquiry—in collaborative-dialogic research is practical knowledge that has local relevancy and usefulness for the participants. In other words there must be context specificity. This is the case whether the inquiry is centered on the topic of the client's agenda or on the "evaluation" of what the client and consultant are doing together: client and consultant are therefore co-researchers or co-inquirers. In conclusion, a collaborative-dialogue approach to research becomes more prospective than retrospective. Like any collaborative-dialogic practice it is characterized by dynamic sustainability. What is produced is not a fixed duplicable result. The process of the production becomes a springboard for the many other possibilities that can emerge in the outside-the-consultation-life of each participant. They carry with them *their* new means for navigating challenges and generating ways forward that have specific personal, relational and contextual relevance.

Notes

1 In the remainder of the chapter I mostly use the terms consultant and researcher, though I invite the reader the insert the word that best fits their practice: teacher, leader, manager, etc.
2 Discussion of education as mutual or shared inquiry is beyond the scope of this chapter (see Anderson, 2013).

References

Anderson, Harlene (1997). *Conversation, language and possibilities: A post-modern approach to therapy.* New York: Basic Books.

Anderson, Harlene (2009). Collaborative practice: Relationships and conversations that make a difference. In J. Bray & M. Stanton (Eds.). *The Wiley handbook of family psychology.* (pp. 300-313). New York, NY: Wiley.

Anderson, Harlene (2012). Collaborative practice: A way of being 'with'. *Psychotherapy and Politics International.* 10, 1002.

Anderson, Harlene (2013). Collaborative learning communities: Toward a postmodern perspective on teaching and learning. *Handbook of educational theories.* B. J. Irvy & G. Brown (Eds.). Charlotte, North Carolina: Information Age Publishing.

Anderson, H Harlene & Gehart, Diane (Eds.) (2007). *Collaborative therapy: Relationships and conversations that make a difference.* New York, NY: Taylor & Francis Group.

Bakhtin, Mikhail M. (1981). *The dialogical imagination.* Edited by M. Holquist, trans. by C. Emerson and M. Holquist. Austin, Tx: University of Texas Press.

Bogue, R. (1989). *Deleuze and Guittari.* Routledge: New York, NY.

Buber, Martin (1970). I and thou. Trans. W. Kaufman, Edinburgh: T. and T. Clark.

Deleuze, Gilles & Guattari, Félix (1987). *A thousand plateaus: Capitalism and schizophrenia.* Minneapolis, MN: University of Minnesota Press.

Gadamer, Hans-Georg (1989). *Truth and method.* 2nd revised edition. Trans. J.Weinsheimer & D.G. Marshall. New York: Continuum.

Gates, S. J. (2012). Retrieved August 12, 2012 from https://twitter.com/Beingtweets/status/162266096001486849.

Gergen, Kenneth J. (1985). *The social constructionist movement in modern psychology.* American Psychologist, 40, 255-275.

Gergen, Kenneth J. (1999). *An invitation to social construction* (2nd ed.). Thousand Oaks, CA: Sage Publications Ltd.

Gergen, Kenneth J. (2009). *Relational being: Beyond self and community.* New York, NY: Oxford University Press.

Grinnell, Frederick (2009). *Everyday practice of science: Where intuition and passion meet objectivity and logic.* New York, NY: Oxford University Press.

Harré, Rom (1983). *Personal being: A theory for individual psychology.* Oxford: Blackwell.

In the Dark: A Blog about the universe and all that surrounds it. The Meaning of Research. Retrieved August 12, 2013 from http://telescoper.wordpress.com/2012/03/08/the-meaning-of-research/

Maturana, Humberto (1978). *Biology of language: Epistemology of reality.* In G. Miller & E. Lenneberg (Eds.). Psychology and biology of language and thought. (pp. 27-63). New York, NY: Academic Press.

Maturana, Humberto & Varela, Francisco (1987). *The Tree of Knowledge.* Boston, MA: New Science Library, Shambhala.

Melanie & Mike. *Etymology of the word research. Take our word for it.* March 8, 2012. Retrieved August 6, 2013 from http://laser.physics.sunysb.edu/~wise/wise187/2002/weblinks/theword_research.txt)

Murphy, Richard (2001). *Collected poems 1952-2000*. Wake Forest University Press: Winston-Salem, North Carolina .

Richards, Noah (2007). *Wittgenstein and the language of Zen*. March 1, 2007. Retrieved August 12, 2013 from http://noahsmark.com/wp-content/uploads/2007/03/wittgenstein-and-the-language-of-zen.pdf

Schön, Donald (1983). *The reflective practitioner: How professionals think in action*. London: Temple Smith, 1983.

Schön, Donald (1987). *Educating the reflective practitioner*. San Francisco: Jossey-Bass, 1987.

Shotter, John (2004). *On the Edge of Social Constructionism: "Withness"-Thinking versus "Aboutness"-Thinking*. London: KCC Foundation.

Shotter, John (2005). *Wittgenstein in practice: His philosophy of beginnings, and beginnings, and beginnings*. London: KCC Foundation.

von Foerster, Heinz. (1982). *Observing systems*. Seaside, CA: Intersystems Publication.

Vico, Giambattista (1999). *New science*. (D. Marsh, Translator). Penguin Books: London, England.

Wittgenstein, Ludvig (1953). Philosophical investigations. G.E.M. Anscombe, Trans. New York: Macmillan.

4 Research as Relational Practice. Exploring Modes of Inquiry

Sheila McNamee

This chapter is an invitation to view research as a relational process. The focus on relational processes is the hallmark of a constructionist orientation where there is a shift from examining entities (whether they be individuals, groups, organizations or matter) to attending to what we refer to as language or language processes. To the constructionist, language is not simply a tool or vehicle used to transmit or exchange information about reality (often referred to as a representational view of language). Rather, language is seen as constructing reality. What we do together actually *makes* our social worlds. This is an important distinction for many reasons but, in light of the present chapter, this distinction is significant because it invites a deconstruction of our accepted, dominant view of research.

The dominant research tradition has emerged within a modernist worldview. Modernism assumes that, with the proper tools and techniques, we will be able to discover reality. Of course, part and parcel of this assumption is the belief that there is a reality to be discovered. Science and the scientific method serve as cornerstones of modernist thinking and thus the belief that research should follow accepted scientific methods remains a hallmark of modernism. Postmodernism, on the other hand, challenges the notion that there is one reality to be discovered. Instead, postmodern theorists propose that our ways of talking and relating to each other and the world should be the focus of study and therefore, the idea of multiple truths, multiple realities, and multiple methods for exploring such realities is paramount.

Research that is associated with discovery is situated within a modernist worldview. Traditional researchers are curious to *discover* how to understand the world "as it really is" and how to discover "new knowledge" about that world. Yet, if our view is a relational constructionist view, the "thing" (or entity) we are examining is the interactive processes of people in relation with each other and their environments. We are curious about what sorts of worlds can be made possible through particular forms of interaction, particular ways of talking and acting. Thus, the focus on relational processes that *construct* our worlds is understood as something very different from the focus *on discovering* how the world is.

In this chapter, I attempt to illustrate how the constitutive nature of language infuses the research endeavor with new possibilities. When we assume that our knowledge of the world is constructed in social processes (a postmodern assumption), we are invited to consider two important issues. First, we are invited to question our taken-for-granted ways of understanding research. Second, new ways of engaging in research are opened and thus knowledge production, itself, is reframed. Since constructionists give precedence to the constitutive nature of all inquiry, we are invited to explore what sorts of worlds we are generating as well as what sorts of knowledge and understandings are being crafted when we engage in any inquiry process.

There has been a great deal of debate (Holstein and Gubrium 2008; Woolgar 1996) concerning what constructionist research looks like, how constructionist research is conducted, what methods can be employed, and what analysis implies for social interaction. My hope is to illustrate that the divisive arguments that have emerged around these topics are not coherent within a constructionist orientation. Instead, I hope to offer alternative, relational understandings of research and the implications of this understanding for relational practitioners.

The Divisive Issues

Our understanding of what counts as research is most often couched within the discourse of science. What is known as the scientific method is borne out of what is believed to be objective, controlled observations by skilled researchers who employ reliable and verifiable methods to explore some phenomenon and reveal new knowledge about that phenomenon. On the basis of this new knowledge, progress is achieved. The traditional assumption is that research produces knowledge, facts, and evidence about the world *as it is*. This view of research (as a scientific endeavor) is referred to as the Received View of Science (RVS) by Woolgar (1996). This is the view of research that people commonly adopt despite the fact that it is not the view commonly shared by scientists (Latour and Woolgar 1979).

Scientists admit to the messy nature of life in the lab or in the field. They acknowledge the ways in which their research emerges within specific scientific communities, or what others have referred to as communities of practice (Lave and Wenger 1991). In this regard, the general view of what constitutes science, and therefore research (what

I am referring to here as the received view of science), is at odds with the actual practice of scientists and their description of what they do. Within the scientific community, there is acknowledgement that what one comes to call research depends upon the relational nexus within which one operates.

This notion fits well with constructionist notions where research is seen as a "form of life" practiced within different "language games" (Wittgenstein 1953). Thus what we commonly understand as the research tradition (i.e., post-positivist social science) is, indeed, a valuable form of research – *but it is not the only form*. There are other language games to be explored. Social construction is one.

The Language of Research: What Counts?

In an attempt to forge connections among different conceptualizations and understandings of research, Raboin, Uhlig, and McNamee (2012) suggest examining what we call "research worlds." A research world involves "the complex interdependencies that support and give scholarly rigor to particular approaches to research" (2012, p.1). Research worlds are constituted by

> *any distinct way of understanding and conducting research, including its unique purposes, practices, and conventions of rigor—together with the beliefs, assumptions and standards of the professions and communities of scholarship within which it is situated . . . A research world is a comprehensive context that guides, supports, funds, conducts and evaluates research in certain ways. A research world holds and maintains a particular approach to research based on core assumptions about the nature of reality (ontology), ways of knowing (epistemology), and ways of conducting research based on these understandings (methodology). What is acceptable in each world is constructed and held in place by many stakeholders. (Ibid p. 1)*

We might usefully understand differences in what counts as research by understanding these different worlds. Raboin, Uhlig, and McNamee propose three different research worlds: the diagnostic (quantitative), the interpretive (qualitative), and the relational (process oriented).

Significant in this conceptualization of research worlds is the understanding that *each one is constructed*. That is, each one of these research worlds is the byproduct of historically and communally situated negotiations. Each research world is internally coherent while potentially (and most often) incoherent from within any other research world.

Table 1. Understanding Consistency and Inconsistency across Research Worlds

SCIENTIFIC METHOD Traditional Quantitative Diagnostic Evidence Based Practice	LET'S UNDERSTAND Traditional Qualitative Interpretive	LET'S CHANGE IT TOGETHER Relational Constructionist
Prove	Understand	Change
Observe	Describe/Interpret	Co-Create
Researcher/Subject	Research/Participants	Co-Researchers
True or False	Situated Meanings	Generate New Meaning
Discoverable Truth and Cause/Effect Mechanisms	Contextualized Knowledge and Multiple Realities	Generate New Realities
Statistically Valid	Authentic to Participants	Locally Useful/Generative
Generalizable & Repeatable	Possibly Transferable	Local and Historical, Co-Evolving
Discover Truth	Expand Insight	Generating Possibilities

Within a relational constructionist stance, we recognize that people coordinate their activities with others and the environment – research worlds are also worlds of coordinated actions. The simple coordinations (e.g., observing and measuring in the traditional research world, interpreting in the qualitative research world, and collaborating in the construction of understanding in the relational research world) quickly emerge into patterned forms of action within a research community. For example, the importance of controlled environments and the means by which such control is ensured is a taken-for-granted pattern in the quantitative research world. These patterns, in turn, generate standards and expectations that participants use to assess their own actions and the actions of others. So, for example, researchers who inhabit the traditional quantitative research world are not expected to report the results of their research in emotional terms. Rather, they are expected to present their data and results as objective measures of "what is there." These evaluating and standardizing practices are carried into future interactions, where they will be confirmed and sustained, challenged, or transformed. Thus, from the very simple process of coordinating, we develop local-cultural norms and values and patterns of influence that, in turn, serve as "common sense" justification for future coordinations. This process can be summarized in Figure 1 following.

Figure 1. The Construction of Worldviews

Coordination

Rituals & Patterns

Realities - Moral Orders

Standards & Expectations

It is important to note here that this process is happening every time researchers engage with each other and the world. Thus, the potential to construct a multiplicity of worldviews is vast. And, with each construction of a worldview, we are constructing a local ontology (what is) and a local epistemology (how we can know what exists). Thus, we are also constructing a moral order that implies what is good and what is not. Consequently, there is a challenge in coordinating among these different research worlds. As we can see, it is impossible given this orientation, to expect that there could be one unified way of understanding and conducting research. Within a research world, patterns of action are sensible; attempting to understand another research world using the criteria for sense making in a different research world yields debate about what is right or wrong at best and disqualification of entire forms of practice at worst.

Figure 2. Quantitative and Qualitative Research Worlds

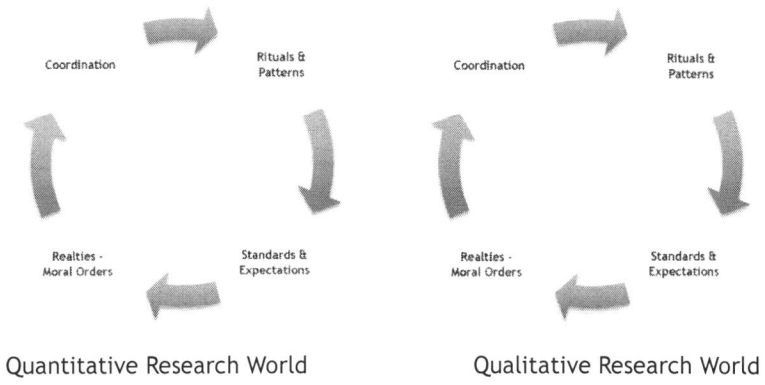

Quantitative Research World   Qualitative Research World

To the social constructionist however, there is a pivotal assumption that provides some nuanced understandings of how we might begin to coordinate diverse and competing research worlds. In the diagram above we can see that both the quantitative and the qualitative research worlds are completely coherent internally and yet there is no point of connection between them. This, of course, is not exactly the case. In fact, much qualitative research shares many of the same assumptions concerning objectivity, validity, and reliability as the quantitative research world. However, for purposes of illustration, I have positioned these two research worlds at odds with one another – and often they might be.

Within a social constructionist orientation, the possibility for constructing new understandings, new beliefs and values, new realities is always present. Each time we engage with others and our environment, the possibility of creating new meaning and thus new worldviews is present. What is interesting about this is that we are largely unaware of how persistently we work to maintain the sense of a solid, stable, and continuing worldview. Without our own participation, these worlds of research and the inevitable version of reality they produce would not endure. We are the ones who maintain these realities, these standards. Even as we resist, for example, traditional quantitative research, we maintain the hegemony of this research world in our very acts of resistance (Foucault 1972; 1976) – in our attempts to construct alternative research worlds. And, since the possibility to create alternative forms of action, alternative standards and expectations, and alternative belief and value systems is always present, the following illustration is a more useful representation of the diversity of world views (even in research) that are possible:

Figure 3. The Complexity and Diversity of Worldviews

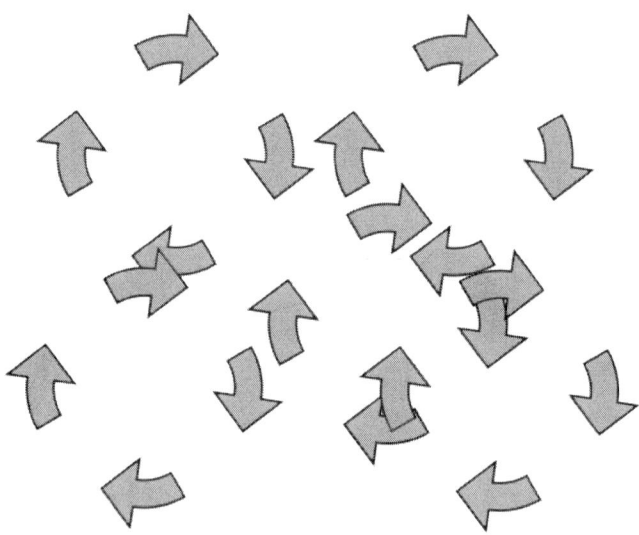

The relational constructionist research world appreciates this diversity and avoids attempts to adjudicate between one research world and another in any universal way. There may be, however, particular situated moments when one research world makes more sense than another.

As we can see, the constructionist orientation creates a research world where appreciation, curiosity, and acknowledgment of alternative research worlds (in this case, quantitative and qualitative research worlds) are centered.

That said, it might be more useful to adjust the description of research worlds above. Rather than see three distinct (and mutually exclusive) worldviews, the constructionist stance is positioned in an entirely different discursive plane, if you will. The relational orientation of constructionist research and practice (as each chapter in this book illustrates) invites one into an entirely different conversation. This conversation is not about right or wrong, good or bad, truth or falsity, evidence or opinion. It is a conversation centered on reflexive inquiry.

As such, it invites us to consider which languaging communities are speaking and which are silenced. It invites us to explore the central ways in which we are implicated in all aspects of the research process - or any practice. And the intriguing thing about this is that being implicated is also evident in our ability to construct the traditional, objective research process. With a very strong caveat acknowledging that any depiction of these complex ideas is potentially misleading, I offer the image in Figure 4 as a replacement for Table 1 (see above).

Figure 4. Intersecting Research Worlds

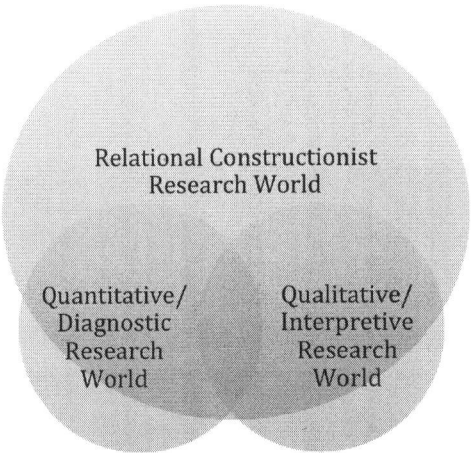

In the quantitative research world, the impetus is to learn what happens "to most of the people, most of the time" via aggregated data so that these results might inform practitioners' work with clients, educators' work with students, organizational leaders' work with constituents, and so forth. This is a practice aligned with the diagnostic research world to the extent that the search is for the "cause" of the problem so that "best practices" and "effective measures" can be put in place.

In the qualitative research world we confront an interesting confusion. Because qualitative research is not typically associated with the rigor and facticity of quantitative research (i.e., in quantitative research there is the oft quoted – and completely erroneous – saying, "the numbers never lie"), it is often associated with constructionist and other postmodern approaches to inquiry (cf, Iversen, 2000). This association might be captured in a comment such as, "Because interpretation and context are important, qualitative methods must be used by constructionist researchers." However, the act of *counting* – the use of quantitative data – is an interpretative act as well. There is nothing inherent in qualitative methods that would align them exclusively with constructionist inquiry. Furthermore, there are ample illustrations of qualitative research that is just as focused on "discovering truth" as quantitative data.

When qualitative methods are associated with constructionist forms of inquiry, we can surmise that the constructionist argument has not been understood since there is no constructionist method, *per se*. Social constructionism is a philosophical stance. As such, it marks a shift in orientation to the world. This shift can be summarized in many ways but suffice it to say that there is a shift in focus from self-contained, rational individuals to interactive processes (i.e., what people do together and what their doing makes). Thus, for the constructionist, the "doing" of research can take many forms. Each is, as mentioned earlier, a different language game. And, different language games construct different understandings of the world. Determining which is right and which is wrong (a modernist question) is replaced by which is most generative. We also become curious for whom it is most generative. This also invites the constructionist researcher to ask questions concerning whose voices are silenced, what practices are being privileged, and what moral orders we are creating in our research. In other words, the constructionist researcher is invited into a reflexive space where deliberation and curiosity are featured. We want to explore which inquiry process will help us know "how to go on together," to paraphrase Wittgenstein (1953).

For constructionist researchers and practitioners, research/inquiry is not an either/or issue. In other words, there is no way of talking about or conducting research that is off limits outside of any given languaging community. This is not to suggest that "anything goes." There are standards and collaboratively crafted realities within communities (see Figure 1 above). Identifying these locally crafted realities as moral orders helps us recognize the ways in which standards and expectations bind a discursive community together; one is not free to act in any way at all. However, once we step out of a given community, the same standards and beliefs might very well be challenged. And, it is important to note that we all inhabit multiple discursive communities. All the more reasons that the reflexive space constructionist research opens up is critical. Through constant reflexive inquiry, the constructionist researcher explores the ways in which certain research practices might marginalize some while elevating others. There is never a neutral research stance.

Shifting Discourses of Research

In order to more fully articulate the very different orientation of a constructionist philosophy, it is useful to understand three significant shifts between a modernist (scientific, quantitative/qualitative research world) and a constructionist research world. The first is a shift from individual to communal rationality. Rationality is no longer seen as a cognitive property of an individual but as a local-cultural performance. To be "rational" is to participate in the dominant discourses of some local tradition, re-constructing one's own identity as a member of a particular community as one does so. Rationality is a relational process. My hope is that Figures 1, 2, and 3 above help to make this process clear. My hope also is to underscore the continual reflexive dialogue that social construction invites; dialogues that acknowledge the ways in which some discourses grant power to certain groups while silencing others. Through this reflexive critique, researchers maintain an appreciation for difference and recognize how what counts as rational is communally constructed.

The second shift is a movement from empirical method to social construction. This shift reflects the wide recognition that we have no means by which to understand the world apart from our ways of talking, our theories, and the methods they both inform. Critical here is the notion that the questions we ask bring forth the answers we then receive. Methods and concepts, beliefs and understandings make sense in relation to some wider tradition (theory, perspective, or intelligibility). So, for example, the way we conduct our inquiry (methods, procedures, analysis), the way we talk and write about it (using, for example, the language of variables, observations, and data) both reflect a particular tradition and are constitutive of it (Woolgar 1996).

The third shift concerns our different view of language. Unlike the realist/modernist view of language as representational, the constructionist sees language as social action and therefore, as constituting our world. Language does not merely describe what is "already there" in the world, it is a form of action. Those who have access to certain, privileged (and communally constructed) discourses are afforded recognition as "rational," "correct," "normal," etc. Those who do not make use of the dominant discourse are then marginalized and pathologized. This also applies in the world of science; to engage in science is to participate in particular community-based practices. But, as I have argued, there are different ways of doing science and each is tied to a locally coordinated rationality.

Relational Research

A relational focus (as defined here) includes not only changed assumptions but also changed questions and interests. A key issue concerns the kinds of realities that wè are a part of and contribute to making in our research. What sort of world do we invite each other into when we act as if it is possible to represent the *one way* things really are? And, in contrast, what sort of world do we invite each other into when we assume realities are community-based local, historical, and cultural co-constructions? Both sorts of inquiry construct local-communal realities—but very different ones. One where there are experts and non-experts versus one where there are multiple and perhaps conflicting realms of expertize.

The relational shifts I have outlined provide the possibility to engage others (theorists, practitioners, researchers, as well as all social actors) in activities that broaden our resources for social life. The interest is in the very *practice* of a constructionist research world as it might open up different possibilities, as a *performance* that literally puts into action, and thus makes available, new relational resources.

In naming these different research worlds, the hope is to generate both curiosity and respect for the different understandings each world creates concerning what counts as research. This hope is distinct from the more common practice of debating which orientation to research is more accurate, more dependable, or more authentic. In addition, borrowing the idea of different research worlds might help dispel the myth many have about constructionist research; many (typically those new to a constructionist philosophical stance or those naively critiquing a constructionist stance) presume that embracing a relational constructionist orientation requires rejecting the standards of social science research (typified in both the traditional quantitative and qualitative research worlds). My hope is to encourage a more nuanced and complex understanding of how "data" and "evidence" produced in both quantitative and qualitative research worlds might be understood differently in a relational research world and vice versa.

Adopting the relational constructionist research world requires that we explore forms of "evidence" that are coherent within a postmodern sensibility. This is in line with recent calls to engage multiple forms of description (McNamee and Hosking 2012; McNamee 2010) where the diversity of moral orders can be explored. Others have argued for the need to create a "thick description" (Ryle 1949) that extends beyond observation of behavior to an understanding of research as a contextualized and situated practice that brings forward meaning and significance of what's described (Geertz 1973). Elsewhere (McNamee 2000), I have suggested that attention to not only what is described but also attention to *how* we describe raises the challenge that validity is an issue of the politics of research (of the rhetoric within which it is constructed). We must ask, by whose standards is validity determined? Who is awarded the right to name what is valid and what is not? Are research results valid when the researcher's theory and hypothesis are supported? When the results of the research "ring true" for professionals and their experience? Or when research participants (e.g., clients in therapy or consultation, students in educational contexts, patients in health care services) recognize the utility of certain forms of practice? We would not claim one of these options over others; rather, constructionists are interested in the collaborative construction of validity among all stakeholders.

To abandon the modernist approach (science) would be neither the constructionist nor the prudent thing to do. By rejecting empiricism in a totalizing fashion we would be rejecting one discursive frame in favor of another, which is akin to claiming that constructionism is the new "Truth" – a claim no constructionist would want to make. If we are to truly position social construction at the paradigmatic level of abstraction – a worldview defined in part by its embrace of multiplicity – then we would be failing to meet our own defining criteria. Why throw out one way of talking about the world, particularly when it is a way of talking with which so many people engage (here I am talking about modernism)? It is also not prudent to discard, out of hand, any particular discursive position. The challenge and the potential of social construction is its focus on coordinating the multiplicity of ways of being in—and speaking about—the world.

In the following section I offer a brief illustration of what I see as the current disconnect among the various research worlds described above. Specifically, the current domination of evidence-based practice in most professional fields (ranging from health care to education to organizational excellence) serves as a good example of how the problems that arise when research worlds are viewed as competitive, requiring a right/wrong determination. The constructionist (those operating within a relational research world) asks, *What counts as evidence and to whom and how might that be useful to practitioners and, similarly, how might practitioners' case studies inform future empirical research?*

Ideally, as practitioners are guided by the results of scientific studies about what works and what does not, they learn in nuanced ways, on a case-by-case basis, how the application of certain practices helps or hinders social life. These "data," in turn, are fed back to researchers for further exploration of the large-scale effect of alternative forms of practice and/or of the anomalies that have arisen in specific cases. This focus on the circular and mutual relationship between "large N" studies and single cases highlights the constructionist focus on relational processes. Unfortunately, in practice, our understanding of what constitutes research is largely focused on one side of this relationship: how "large N" studies determine local practices so that they can be efficient and effective.

Moving Beyond an Either/Or World of Research: The Case of Evidence-Based Practice

Many careers have been built upon the debate concerning the distinction and significance of modernist vs. postmodern research, and how these traditions influence professional practice. Each approach has its merit but, as with all things, that merit is contextually defined. Within a modernist worldview, the attempt in professional practice is to objectively distinguish a problem and provide the "correct" solution or treatment, drawing on the tradition of positivist social science. Within a postmodern worldview, a professional examines how meaning and understanding are achieved in interaction with clients, hoping for the collaborative creation of an understanding that is more useful and generative for both client and professional.

The positions of modernist and postmodernist orientations are further complicated by the erroneous conflation of quantitative methods with modernism and qualitative methods with postmodernism, as mentioned earlier. Such a distinction is a gross oversimplification of postmodern philosophy and practice. As we know, postmodern approaches champion a shift in focus from the self-contained individual to the language practices (i.e., all embodied activities) of persons-in-relation. To that end, we acknowledge that quantitative and qualitative methods are nothing more than different "language games" (Wittgenstein) and neither is any more or less appropriate to any given analysis beyond a given context. In other words, numbers and aggregated data can be just as interesting and useful as can qualitative case studies. Thus, the common response by postmodernists against evidence-based practice (EBP) is not entirely warranted. What professionals react against is the idea that disembodied research about a specifically and uniquely embodied practice (e.g., therapy, health care treatment, education, effective leadership) should dictate how one engages with specific clients in contextually situated activity.

Montgomery (2006), talking about the use of Evidence Based Medicine, points out the mutually informing relationship intended between research and practice.

> . . . *the variation of the single case is the starting point for the EBM project. Valuable though epidemiological studies are, aggregated information constitutes generalized knowledge that must be applied to a particular patient. She may be younger than the groups studied – or more athletic or a vegetarian; she may be from a different ethnic group or have a late onset or a parent with the same condition. How and to what degree the studies apply in different circumstances is itself an occasion for comparative clinical storytelling, even among clinicians who know the prior probabilities for the Bayesian analysis of every malady in their specialty. The authors of Evidence Based Medicine know this. They advise clinicians to start with a question about one of their patients, research it as well as current studies allow, not only as a way of deciding what should be recommended to the patient but also to test and improve their clinical judgment. From such particular cases will come the ideas for further epidemiological and clinical investigation. (Montgomery, 2006, pp. 129-130)*

The implications of the disparity between EBP as conceptualized and EBP as practiced has left many postmodern professionals in opposition to the world of research, numbers, and evidence. Rather than repel this community, the overall dominance of EBP should invite us to ask, *how might research be useful in my professional practice?* To pose this question is to embrace the mutually informing relationship between research and situated encounters. But first, we must turn our attention to evidence since it is the centerpiece of institutionally sanctioned professional practice and this centerpiece is most frequently viewed as emerging within traditional research worlds. To that end, those of us who position ourselves within a relational research world often feel invited into an either/or debate about the place of EBP and its institutional privilege.

What Counts as Evidence?

What counts as evidence in what circumstances is a topic to which constructionists are sensitive. Success in one professional relationship does not always offer useful practices in another. Do we want to engage in professional practices simply because "studies have shown," for example, that cognitive-behavior therapy (CBT) is more effective than depth psychology when working with individuals? Or, would we rather explore how the use of different discourses (i.e., models) might create the possibility for therapeutic transformation? The shift here is from granting the stamp of approval (i.e., funding in the form of insurance coverage, governmental subsidies, institutional vouchers, etc.) to one brand of practice to granting the stamp of approval toward opening the possibility of collaborative conversations with clients about what is and is not working in their engagements with professionals.

What counts as evidence of successful practice will vary, depending upon the research world one inhabits. In the diagnostic research world, statistical significance of tested practices serves as evidence. In the interpretive research world, the self-reports of clients/participants serve as evidence. Yet in the relational constructionist research world, the creation of new forms of understanding that allow people (clients/participants) to move beyond identified problems serves as evidence. Here, it is not enough to report that the professional's practice is working (interpretive research world). Rather, *it is the recognition and creation of new forms of practice for clients, community members, researchers/practitioners, and all participants that signals effective practice.*

Since researchers and research participants (practitioners and clients) inhabit different research worlds, re-visioning research as a process of social construction demands that we find ways to enter into curious conversation with those who inhabit different research worlds. If those who inhabit the quantitative research world of diagnosis and discovery view evidence as fact rather than one alternative for practice, then our attempts to coordinate divergent research worlds require respect and curiosity for this sense-making. Sometimes, those who purport to inhabit a relational constructionist research world deny the fact-based understanding of research results embraced by those who live in a traditional research. When they do so, they have (unfortunately) stepped into the traditional, quantitative research world view of right/wrong, truth/falsity.

Dispelling Common Myths about Research

I would like to close this chapter by highlighting what I refer to as common myths about research, each discussed in this chapter. First, is the myth that research is about discovery. As we have seen, the very idea of discovery is shaped by one's research world. If a researcher adopts a distancing, diagnostic stance, the language of discovery is plausible. If, however, a researcher adopts a collaborative, participatory stance, the language of discovery is incoherent. The construction of action possibilities and of new forms of understanding are byproducts of the mutuality of the inquiry process.

The second myth focuses on the suggestion that, with the right methods, we can discover the nature of the social world. Of course, this myth is not entirely distinct from the first; it simply extends the idea of discovery to the selection of the proper method. The Received View of Science (quantitative and much of qualitative research worlds) presumes just this (i.e., that the nature of the social world is discoverable with the right methods) and that discovery yields knowledge, advancement, and solutions to problems. However, when we inhabit the relational research world, we start with the presumption that the nature of the social world can be multiply defined and understood. Each understanding offers alternative forms of knowing and acting. In other words, while *one* answer/result might be most acceptable or appealing to one group situated in a particular context, that same answer/result might *not* be acceptable or appealing (or even feasible) to another group that is differently located.

The third myth suggests that practitioners are not researchers and researchers are not practitioners. This is probably the most significant myth for readers of this chapter simply because it allows any reader to recognize his or her practice as a legitimate and potentially useful research project. When we think of a harsh divide between research and practice, there is a tendency to avoid employing the resources for action that are most useful and familiar to us. Specifically, the RVS leaves us imagining tightly controlled environments, highly designed research instruments, and – probably most unfortunately – sterile, distant relations between the researcher and those who participate in the research process. Yet when we envision this view of research, we miss the very possibilities that could likely generate some significant human transformation.

Emergent Methods and Relational Responsibility

One of my former Ph.D. students, Murilo Moscheta, wrote about the debilitating effects of these myths. Murilo was interested in understanding how healthcare professionals understand and work with GLBT (gay, lesbian, bisexual, transgender) patients. He carefully designed his research to include (1) an open invitation to professionals to participate in his project, (2) one-on-one interviews with those who volunteered for participation so that he might gain a sense of their challenges in working with GBLT patients prior to gathering the group together, and (3) a series of open dialogues with all participants.

All was going quite smoothly in his research; he had a good number of volunteers and completed his one-on-one interviews. He carefully prepared for his first dialogue session with the health professionals by summarizing the questions and concerns voiced in the interviews. He decided to open his first dialogue session with these summaries as a way to create an open and welcoming atmosphere within the group. On the day of the group dialogue, a nurse assistant who had not previously volunteered for the project (and thus had not participated in a one-on-one pre-dialogue interview with Murilo) asked if she could join the project. In the spirit of open collaboration, Murilo said, "of course!" He was attempting to be sensitive to the local practices of the healthcare professionals. However, he was shocked and dismayed (to say the least) when the newly joining nurse assistant abruptly left the dialogue session when she realized that everyone else present had participated in a personal interview. She felt marginalized.

Murilo felt that his research was a disaster at this point until he made the decision to seek out the nurse assistant to talk with her about her experience in the opening of that first dialogue and invite her to re-join the group. His decision to have this conversation with the nurse assistant opened a new horizon of possibilities in his research. The group used the "unfortunate" event as a model to think about the challenges in the inclusion of GLBT clients in healthcare settings. The nurse assistant had felt excluded; how might this incident inform them all in their challenges working with GLBT clients? Not only did Murilo achieve an emergent quality to his research design and method but also he was able to see the implications of the research process itself for the topic of his research (inclusion in healthcare professionals' work with GLBT clients). Later he reflected on this research experience and highlighted the transformative potential of, as he described it, his encounter with "the unexpected:"

> *I believe that, until that time, a great part of my training as a researcher had been based on a clear right/wrong division. The tradition in which I was trained emphasized that a good researcher would be able to carefully plan how the research should go and to anticipate possible problems in order to take suitable precautions. For omniscient pursuers like me, doubts and surprises were problems to avoid, solve or fix. Method was a way of ensuring that everything would flow as planned. Above all, researching was about controlling. And, as daunting as this god-like position could be, it was also seductive once it waved to the possibility of joining a selected and socially appreciated group.*

So it is not surprising that I would feel devastated when something unexpected happened during my research. I was striving to do everything right and, since this perspective on research is so widely acknowledged, participants were also expecting me to make "all the 'right' decisions." Therefore, I first understood the unexpected as a sign of personal failure. In my efforts for perfection, my failure was later transformed into the nursing assistant's failure, as I tried to justify myself by accusing her of disturbing my research. So my first lesson in this experience was to realize that blame is the standard game in a right/wrong model of individual responsibility. Unfortunately, that is the game that so commonly prevented me from generously understanding the unexpected and learning from it. Once I did so, the possibility of escaping the blame game allowed me to reconsider research in two important aspects.

First, I reconnected with the basic element of research. For some researchers, research is about discovering what is new, while for some others it may be more like creating something new. However, in any case, it seems that research is a process by which we somehow create the conditions where we can be in relation with novelty. So what is the point of anticipating and controlling everything? How much space is left for "the original" if I am obsessed with predictions? I've realized that welcoming the unexpected can be a way of learning about what I was looking for without knowing I was looking for it. Paraphrasing T.S.Eliot, research can be about finding what I was looking for, and knowing it for the first time. Most important, this perspective liberated me from knowing everything and encouraged a lot of exploration. The Blame Game gave way to playful curiosity, generous questioning and exciting cooperation. Researching was elevated back to what it was when I first became interested in it: an adventure full of surprises for a boy playing with bugs and lenses in the backyard.

Second, I've learned that method is a compass, not a map. I was accustomed to the commonly accepted idea that relates to method as a process. However, the way I was embracing this process was transforming it into a product. I had planned interviews, I had prepared participants, and I had designed a group dialogue. And all this was a tool I wanted to apply in my research context. However, if method is truly a process, it is always in response to whatever is emerging in the research. So the most important aspect of method for me is not what I plan to do or the tools I want to use but how I respond to whatever emerges from them. Like a traveler with a compass, I can move toward one direction. But to get there, I need to be attentive and responsive to the signs I find in my way. How I get to my goal is more a matter of how I interact with both compass and signs than a matter of following the right track. Obviously that does not exclude preparation and planning, for I still do a lot of it before entering any research field or starting any trip. However, it allows me to be responsive to the unfolding nature of researching. Besides that, I consider the ethical importance of inviting participants not only to collaborate with what I propose but also to engage in the collective construction of the research process. I had heard social researchers frequently say that they were open to learn from the participants. So was I as I started my research. However, the collaboration I was expecting was restricted to the content of my research. I assumed that it was up to me, the researcher, to decide about the process and to demonstrate mastery of methodological and analytical strategies. The event was embarrassing because it suggested that I could not know how to conduct the research process. However, it was exactly because I didn't know that participants could feel invited to collaborate. Power relations were transformed and authorship could be democratized. (Moscheta 2011)

In Murilo's compelling story we see his metamorphosis from practitioner trying to become a "legitimate" researcher to practitioner trusting his familiar mode of practice (i.e., being attentive to the unfolding, emergent nature of interaction) as a legitimate form of research.

It is important to continually remind ourselves that *we* make choices about inquiry – *we* decide what to study and how. These choices can certainly be considered "right" or "wrong" within particular contexts. However, within a relational constructionist research world, no choice is ultimately right or wrong in a universal sense. Each choice invites different consequences. To that end, research practices, analyses, and results within any research world can be useful. The critical questions pose concern about *what communities we are talking to and from and whose values do we want to apply*.

This raises the question of objectivity – a sacred cow in the traditional quantitative and qualitative research worlds. Objectivity is a rhetorical construction. Gergen (1994) points out that the use of "*distention devices*, linguistics means of placing the object at a distance from our private experience . . . *the, that, those,* or *this* . . . [as] contrasted with *personalized descriptors* . . . 'My view,' 'my perception, 'my sense of . . .'" (p.173-4) serve to rhetorically create the sense of objectivity. Thus we must ask, *whose values are being promoted as "no value?"*

Rather than operate in controlled conditions, the constructionist embraces the relational quality of the research context, giving rise to practices such as collaborative inquiry (Lather and Smithies 1997; Holstein and Gubrium 2008; Gehart, Tarragona and Bava 2007), action research (Reason 1998; Reason and Bradbury 2001; McNiff and Whitehead 2006), and dialogue processes (Chasin and Herzig 1992; Gergen, McNamee and Barrett 2001; Seikkula and Arnkil 2006).

In viewing research as a relational process of crafting meaning and understanding collaboratively, we become mindful that all accounts are simultaneously descriptions of events *and* part of the event itself, due to the co-constructive nature of talk, of interaction. As mentioned earlier, the questions we ask bring forth their answers. We can choose to step into the language of objectivity – that is always an option. And once we do so, we must ask what values, what political stances, what relations are (silently) being granted authority and which ones are muted. I am not suggesting that this is an issue of right or wrong; I am simply urging that we ask the question. No research will or can provide the definitive result. All knowledge is provisional and contestable (from some other languaging community). All accounts are locally, historically, and culturally specific. The most important questions within all research worlds are: *In what ways is this inquiry useful? Does it generate new forms of understanding and thus new ways of 'going on together?'* And most important, we must remember that research itself is a practice – a form of professional practice, if you will. Thus, the research/practitioner divide is not a divide at all but a matter of stepping into diverse discourse communities. Any form of practice (e.g., education, psychotherapy, organizational development, community building, etc.) is a form of inquiry.

References

Chasin, Richard and Herzig, Margaret (1992). Creating systemic interventions for the sociopolitical arena. In B. Berger-Could and D. H. DeMuth (Eds.), *The global family therapist: Integrating the personal, professional, and political*. Needham, MA: Allyn and Bacon.

Foucault, Michel (1972). *The archaeology of knowledge*. London: Tavistock.

Foucault, Michel (1978). *The history of sexuality: An introduction* (vol. 1) (trans. R. Hurley). New York: Pantheon.

Geertz, Clifford (1973). *The interpretation of cultures*. New York: Basic Books.

Gergen, Kenneth J. (1994). *Realities and Relationships: Soundings in Social Construction*. Cambridge, MA: Harvard University Press.

Gergen, Kenneth J., McNamee, Sheila, and Barrett, Frank J. (2001). Toward transformative dialogue. *International Journal of Public Administration*, 24 (7/8), 679-707.

Gehart, Diane, Tarragona, Margarita and Bava, Saliha (2007). A collaborative approach to research and inquiry. In H. Anderson and D. Gehart (Eds.), *Collaborative therapy: Relationships and conversations that make a difference*. New York: Routledge.

Holstein, James A. and Gubrium, Jaber F. (Eds.)(2008). *Handbook of constructionist research*. New York: Guilford Press.

Iversen, Gudmund R. (2003). Knowledge as a Numbers Game. In M. Gergen and K. J. Gergen (Eds). *Social Construction: A Reader*. London: Sage.

Lather, Patti and Smithies, Chris (1997). *Troubling the angels: Women living with HIV/AIDS*. Boulder, CO: Westview Press.

Latour, Bruno and Woolgar, Steven (1979). *Laboratory life: The social construction of scientific facts*. London: Sage.

Lave, Jean and Wenger, Etienne (1991). *Situated learning: Legitimate peripheral participation*. Cambridge: Cambridge University Press.

McNamee, Sheila and Hosking, Dian Marie (2012). *Research and social change: A relational constructionist approach*. New York: Routledge.

McNamee, Sheila (2010). Research as social construction: Transformative inquiry. *Health and Social Change*, 1(1), 9-19.

McNamee, Sheila (2000). Dichotomies, Discourses, and Transformative Practices. In L. Holzman, Lois and Morss, John (Eds.), *Postmodern Psychologies, Societal Practice and Political Life*. New York: Routledge, 179-189.

McNiff, Jean and Whitehead, Jack (2006). *All you need to know about action research*. London: Sage.

Montgomery, Kathryn (2006), *How doctors think: Clinical judgment and the practice of medicine*. Oxford: Oxford University Press.

Moscheta, Murilo (2011). *Responsividade: Como recurso relacional para a qualificacao da assistencia a suade de lesbicas, gays, bissexuais, travesties e transexuais*. (Doctoral Dissertation) Riberao Preto, Sao Paulo, Brazil: University of Sao Paulo.

Raboin, Ellen; Uhlig, Paul and McNamee, Sheila (2012, unpublished manuscript). Research worlds in healthcare.

Reason, Peter. (1998). *Human inquiry in action: Developments in new paradigm research*. London: Sage.

Reason, Peter and Bradbury, Hilary (Eds.)(2001). *Handbook of action research: Participative inquiry and practice*. London: Sage.

Ryle, Gilbert (1949). *The concept of mind*. London: Hutchinson.

Seikkula, Jaakko and Arnkil, Tom E. (2006). *Dialogic meetings in social networks*. London: Karnac.

Wittgenstein, Ludwig (1953). *Philosophical investigations*. Oxford: Blackwell.

Woolgar, Steven (Ed.) (1996). *Psychology, qualitative methods and the ideas of science*. Leicester: BPS Publications.

Methods for Practitioners in Inquiring into "the Stuff" of Everyday Life and its Continuous Co-Emergent Development

5

John Shotter

"The child begins to perceive the world not only through his eyes but also through his speech" (Vygotsky 1978, p.32).

"What makes a subject hard to understand – if it's something significant and important – is not that before you can understand it you need to be specially trained in abstruse matters, but the contrast between understanding the subject and what most people want to see. Because of this the very things which are most obvious may become the hardest of all to understand. What has to be overcome is a difficulty having to do with the will, rather than with the intellect" (Wittgenstein 1980, p.17).

"And here we come on the difficulty of 'all is in flux'. Perhaps that is the very point at which to start" (Wittgenstein 1980, p.8).

Scientific inquiries are *deliberately conducted inquiries*, inquiries in which we intentionally set out to explain something, some 'thing' we think of as being already in existence[1] awaiting our discovery of it. And in such inquiries, we make certain *observations* on the basis of what our prior theories predict we should expect to see – where our theories work in terms of *idealizations*[2], that is, in terms of events that are brought into being only in the specially prepared conditions of the experimental laboratory, conditions which are hardly ever realized in the hurly-burly of everyday life. In other words, we have far too readily assumed the separateness, and thus already determinate nature of reality: that it already consists of separate, nameable, elemental things in motion according to pre-established laws.

Things in our everyday lives, however, are much more indeterminate, and a lot of our learning is much less deliberate: the development of our sensitivities to thing-like structures in our surroundings; the way our utterances within our mother tongue are intra-related with them; and many other features to do with *being-like* the others in our immediate surroundings, all just seem to *happen* to us. They *emerge* in the course of our practical involvements with the others around us. We do not, and cannot as infants (*infans* ~ without speech), set out deliberately to become *this* or *that kind* of person, as if the possibilities for what we can become already exist. We gradually become a unique, autonomous individual of a certain kind by *showing in our behaviour* as we grow up, that we know *what* matters to those around us: that we know *what* play is; *what* toys *are*, and what are not things to play with; *what it is* to be rude and what is 'proper' behaviour; *what* emotionally hurts another and *what is* being kind to them; what it is to assume that one has been *born to rule* (or not, as the case may be); and so on, and so on. We find ourselves making a certain kind of sense of, mostly *relational*, things without our ever having explicitly set out to do so.

Indeed, one of the very first things we learn (or can[3] learn) is how to take turns: *to be* a looker and listener; to *point* at things[4] and *to be* attentive to what is 'pointed out' to us, as well as also being ourselves a *doer* and a *communicator*. Thus in our first-language learning, we are not simply learning to 'put our thoughts into words', nor are we merely learning to link our practical activities in with those of the others around us, thus to coordinate our activities in with theirs in *accountable* ways (Mills 1940; Scott & Lyman 1968). We are learning something else much more basic: we are learning what elsewhere I have called "ontological skills" (Shotter 1984) – skills at *being* certain *kinds* of human beings, able to adopt appropriate *ways* of relating ourselves to the requirements of the situations within which we find ourselves. And this task – of developing a *way* or *ways* of relating ourselves to a *situation* in which we are involved – continues with us even as adults as we enter each uniquely new situation afresh.

Thus our talk is not just a matter of 'putting into words' what we individually see or think. As Winch (1958) puts it: "our idea of what belongs to the realm of reality is given to us in the language that we use" (p.15), thus what we are *doing* in *our uses* of language is showing the others around us what *counts as* an aspect fo reality for us. And as we grow up, we learn to live within many different realms of reality. So that later, in going on to train as a painter, a builder, a carpenter, a gardener, a farmer, a musician, a mathematician, an academic, a management consultant, the CEO of an organization, and so on, we come to learn specialist ways of 'seeing' the world, e.g., in learning arithmetic, we come to know that 1+1=2 and 5+1=1+5 (and that the order of the numbers doesn't matter), and so on. In other words, in learning to do arithmetic we do not learn just a set of facts that can be represented symbolically, or a matter of learning do something in the same way as our teachers; we learn something much more complicated. We learn to do many different things that can be *judged*[5] by them *as acting in the same way* – a never ending task in the still emerging, turbulent, indeterminate world of everyday life.

Indeed, in learning to speak, more amazing than the fact that we can use so many different words with a fair degree of accuracy in describing the world around us, is that fact that we can express ourselves and bring off an uncountable number of different practical consequences with such a limited number of words.

Thus before we can conduct anything like *scientific* inquiries, we face the preliminary task of coming to *a sense of*, a *feel for*, "the world or worlds" which we want to explore. Prior to our more intellectual inquiries, we need answers to questions such as: What are the 'things' I perceive within it; what are the relations I perceive between them; the values I attach to them; the opportunities for action and understanding my 'world' afford me; the nature of my rights, duties, privileges and obligations in relation to the significant others around me in my 'world'; the 'grounds' to which I appeal for the power and the authority of these rights and duties (do I find them 'in' myself or 'in' my community of which I am a part, or for some, in both places?); its 'horizon', i.e., what is not actually at the moment 'visible' to me in my situation but to what I can point to as being reasonable for me to expect in the future; plus the fact that at any one moment, my 'world' is ordered *perspectivally* in accord with what I take to be the 'point' (on the horizon of my current landscape of action) constituting the 'end in view' of my current action (intention, aim)[6].

Thus a good deal of what I will call *orientational* learning, or *orientational* work, is required before we can turn to deliberate, theory-driven inquiries into our everyday lives. For our later ability to say explicitly, "This is an X (but not a Y)," requires our already having come to know, *implicitly in our bodily activities*, what X-ness and Y-ness *is like*. And this capacity to orient towards the 'what-ness of things' in our surroundings as those around us do, and to *judge* that this is indeed an X and not a Y, is not something we acquire though explicit teaching. We learn it spontaneously, in the course of our extensive involvements with those others. It is something a 'good enough' mother (Winnicott 1988) teaches us, spontaneously, in the course of her being attentive to what she notices in our movements, in many different particular situations, as our indicative of our 'needs'. She thus acts to satisfy the unsatisfied tensions she can perceive us as feeling in the incipient intentions she can see us as *trying* to execute – as she feeds, comforts, plays, and otherwise actively involves herself in our activities[7]. It is our 'tryings' (and our 'failings') that are important to her at this stage in our development, not our actual achievements. And is precisely in moving away from what is thought to be *ideal* to what can be called 'good enough' ways in which to conduct our research practices – good enough in the sense of meeting practical needs – that I want to explore further below.

To assume, as many theorists do, that *ideally* we should proceed in our everyday affairs as professional scientists do in theirs, is, to my mind at least, to (mis)describe a co-emergent, back-and-forth, essentially hermeneutical process – in which 'I' as a *Subject* experiencing a certain kind of 'thing' in the world, and an *Object* experienced *as* that 'thing', arise together in the act of experience – as a cognitive and epistemological process, concerned merely with our thinking 'about' our bewilderment in a linear, rational manner. Only people who act as if they already know of the basic things making up their world can act in it on the basis of theory-confirming observations; but they cannot gain their knowledge of how *to be* and to act effectively *in the unique situations of everyday life* in the ways required of them by their society, in that manner. The fact is, in our everyday affairs, we simply cannot assume that we already know the 'things' to which to attend in taking effective steps towards a current, particular "end in view" (Dewey 1910; Wittgenstein 1953).

Making sense from within the flowing, turbulent "stuff" of everyday life

I have started the discussion of *methods* in this way – with a focus on what it is like for us in learning our first language, rather than assuming that we start our more professional forms of inquiry at a much later point in time, when we are all already linguistically competent – because I think it is much more in line with the everyday realities within which we actually live our lives, and must conduct our inquiries, particularly within our currently much more turbulent times. The dream of the ancient Greeks – that the task of Reason (rationality) is the unveiling of the *ideal forms* hidden behind appearances – which has shaped Western thought for the last 2500 years, is at last being relinquished. We are beginning to take appearances, the particular situations themselves that we now find ourselves inhabiting, seriously. Thus currently, from within the midst of experiencing the turmoil of a political (and physical) *weather-world* seemingly out of our control, we seem to be involved in a slow but inexorable shift away from a focus on forms and structures, away from 'seeing' finished patterns existing objectively out in the world, and to be moving towards a focus on the bodily 'sensing of similarities', towards a focus on unfinished processes still open to many different kinds of *expressive* realization.

Whilst the interest in flowing processes is not new (James 1890, 1912; Bergson 1922, 1974), interest in them is now acquiring momentum, a distinct presence as more and more voices are joining in (e.g., Gibson 1979; Law & Mol 1994; Barad 2007; Gergen 2009). But what we will find it hard to do, in turning in this new (or not so new) direction, is to give up a deeply rooted urge in our Western *uses* of language: to give a *name* or *names* to "the stuff" we continually deal with in our everyday affairs. But give it up we must. As Lao Tzu (1967), who lived in the 6th century BCE in China, suggested: "The way that can be named/ Is not the constant name;/ The nameless was the beginning of heaven and earth" (p.57). For clearly, as is obvious, the very search for "nameable things" commits us to finding *only* what is in some sense we already have names for, what is already familiar to us. To avoid the continual rediscovery of sameness and to turn to the task of bringing to light genuine innovations, previously unexpected, novel steps forward, we need another mode of inquiry.

So, although we cannot easily give proper names to what we are dealing with, this does not mean that what we need to deal with is forever inexpressible. Far from it. For as we shall find – and come to deal with in terms of what I will call "Performative Understandings" or "Performative Knowing"[8] (in contrast to the "Objective" or "Propositional Understandings" we usually seek) – giving expression to their nature is not in fact at all difficult. We can enact such understandings in our 'doings' out in the world[9], and we can begin to say what such doings *are like* by the use of what Wittgenstein (1953) calls "objects of comparison" (no.130)[10] – where, by their use, as he remarked, we can "establish an order in our knowledge of the use of language: an order with a particular end in view; one out of many possible orders; not the order" (no.132).

In other words, we can begin to say *what it is like*[11] to have a particular experience, to be involved in an activity of a certain kind. So, although our use of this method – the method of showing the nature of the influences at work in shaping our behaviour in our descriptions of them, what we might call "showing in our sayings" – may not help us achieve a final solution to the many *general* problems bothering us, e.g., the problem of what meaning *is*, or of what the mind *is* – and a whole crowd of other such general problems of the form "What *is* X?" It is a method, as we shall see, that can nonetheless lead us to a whole lot of particular, i.e., limited and partial, results that are in fact related to the situation of our concern, results related to a particular end in view. For the *performative* understandings we can express in such "showing sayings" can *move* the others around us towards re-relating or re-orienting themselves to their surroundings to 'see' in them possibilities previously unnoticed.

Withness-thinking

What, then, is it like in this manner, to think from within a kind of inner dialogue *with* a felt sense, the presence of a yet unknown something being there in one's surroundings which has not yet been given adequate linguistic expression? Elsewhere (Shotter 2005, 2006), I have described such *withness* (dialogical)-thinking, as I have called it, experientially as follows: The back-and-forth interplay involved gives rise, not to a visible seeing, for what is 'sensed' is invisible; nor does it give rise to an interpretation (to a representation), for our responses occur spontaneously and directly in our living encounters with an other's expressions. Neither is it merely a feeling, for it carries with it as it unfolds a bodily sense of the possibilities for responsive action in relation to one's momentary placement, position, or orientation in the present interaction. Instead, it gives rise to a *shaped* and *vectored* sense of our moment-by-moment changing involvement in our current surroundings – engendering in us both unique "transitory understandings" as to 'where' we are within the landscape of possibilties open to us in our acting, along with "action guiding anticipations" as to what-next we might expect *in relation to* the actions we might take. In short, we can be spontaneously 'moved' toward specific possibilities for action in such thinking. It is a knowing to do with one's participation within a situation, with one's 'place' within it, and with how one might 'go on' playing one's part within it – a knowing in which one is as much affected by one's surroundings, perhaps, even more than one affects them.

We can contrast it, strongly, with what I have called *aboutness* (monological)-thinking: such thinking works in terms of a thinker's 'theoretical pictures' (mental represeantations), but, even when we 'get the picture', we still have to interpret it, and to decide, intellectually, on a right course of action; thus in aboutness-thinking, "(in its extreme pure form) another person remains wholly and merely an object of consciousness, and not another consciousness... Monologue is finalized and deaf to the other's response, does not expect it and does not acknowledge in it any *decisive* force" (Bakhtin 1984, p.293). In other words, in working simply in terms of forms of 'pictures', it is unresponsive to another's expressions.

In more homely terms, we might express the contrast between to two by saying: In aboutness-thinking, we live, so to speak, *inside* our theories, and look out at the world with the expectation of seeing only the shapes and forms they make available to us. Whereas, in witness-thinking, we are living in the world *alongside* a set of 'good enough' friends, who like our 'good enough' mothers, draw our attention to noticeable features in our surroundings that might be of concern to us, and introduce us to bits of vocabulary that might useful in giving linguistic expression to them.

Knowing 'from-within'

In witness-thinking, then, we are not thinking *about* things *from the outside*, the 'thinking' involved is not solely, or even primarily, a cognitive process; it inevitably involves our *acting into situations*, and as we do so, developing our thinking – in a back-and-forth, from part-to-whole and from whole-to-part, hermeneutical process – as our acting unfolds. Thus, ontologically, we become a 'participant-part' of the very situation that we are inquiring into, and we need to teach ourselves how to think *from within* that involvement.

To those of us taught that theory-driven modes of inquiry are basic, this, at first, may seem a disorienting thought. As Richard Bernstein (1983) notes, it might arouse in us what he calls "the Cartesian anxiety" (p.16), the fear that if we do not have *certain*, i.e., *proven*, knowledge, we have no knowledge at all. But, to repeat, this is how, as children, we learn both our first-language, and how to be autonomous members of our local community able to account for ourselves in *its* terms (Shotter 1984). Recognizing that there is this other kind of knowledge, what we might call "insider's knowledge," "agent's knowledge" – or what above I have called *performative* knowing, the knowing that makes what we call "objective knowledge" possible – is crucial to our conducting our inquiries from within our own everyday involvements out in the world.

Scientific inquiries, as I noted above, are deliberately conducted, theory-driven inquiries in which we set out to explain something we think of as being already in existence 'over there' awaiting our discovery of it. But to assume that this is the case in our everyday lives, that our bewilderments are merely a matter of our ignorance as to the *real*, the already determined but hidden nature of the circumstances facing us, is to make, as Ryle (1949) calls it, a serious "category mistake." In describing our efforts at *making sense* of what is before us, we continually use "achievement-verbs," he points out, when we should provide an 'orchestrated' sequence of "task-verbs," along with their criteria of satisfaction[12]. In other words, in talking of *hearing* such and such, or *seeing* this rather than that – instead of talking of *listening* or *looking* with certain expectations in mind – we are continually talking of 'arrivals' and/or 'achievements' when really we should be speaking, not only of the 'journeyings' and/or the 'tryings' (as well as of the satisfactions we achieve or not, as the case may be, by each step we take along the way), but also of the overall *guiding tension* initially aroused within us by each new bewildering situation that motivates our efforts at 'bringing it into focus', so to speak. We far too easily act as if the situation is of an already determinate kind of which we are merely ignorant, rather than it in fact being indeterminate and open to our efforts to determine it in one way or another. But how can we start our inquiries 'from within' our bewilderments if we don't begin with theories?

Below, I want to propose a two-stage process: A set of first steps to do with moving from a bewildering, confusing, indeterminate situation towards its gradual clarification or determination as the unique situation it in fact *is* – a process that we can perhaps liken to bringing a severely blurred scene into focus. We can then outline a set of possible next steps to do with *noticing* openings and incipient beginnings within it that might afford its innovative development, the emergence of new inner articulations within it – a process that we might liken, say, to the development of a cultivated olive tree from a wild tree, by selective pruning, to poroduce an abundance of fruit.

Investigations into how we do in fact relate or orient ourselves toward the situation we find ourselves to be 'in', and *resolving* on a line of action to take within it, can be called, following Wittgenstein (1953) and Bateson (1979), 'grammatical' investigations. For, as Bateson (1979) says, all our understandings arise out of our relations to a context, and "without context, there is no meaning,... [and] contextual shaping is only another term for *grammar*" (p.27). Thus for Bateson, as also for Wittgenstein, a 'grammatical investigation' entails our imaginatively 'entering into', so to speak, the circumstances surrounding a person's actions to gain a sense of the way in which their surroundings (in an agential fashion) can influence the 'shape' of their utterances and other expressions. Thus rather than trying to analyze, i.e., break down, what is unknown to us into its elemental units, we can begin to move around within it, and by 'opening' ourselves to being spontaneously 'moved' by it, we can begin to 'enter into' an active, back and forth, dialogically-structured relationship with it – a relationship within which we can gain, if we go slowly and allow time for the imaginative work that each response can occasion in us to take place, a sense of the 'invisible landscape of possibilities' confronting us to become "visibly-rational" (Garfinkel 1967, p.vii) to us.

Resolving an unclarity

John Dewey (1910) describes the organizing role of having an *end in view* in relation to our thinking thus: "A question to be answered, an ambiguity to be resolved, sets up an end and holds the current of ideas to a definite channel. Every suggested conclusion is tested by its reference to this regulating end, by its pertinence to the problem in hand. This need of straightening out a perplexity also controls the kind of inquiry undertaken. A traveler whose end is the most beautiful path will look for other considerations and will test suggestions occurring to him on another principle than if he wishes to discover the way to a given city. The problem fixes the end of thought and the end controls the process of thinking" (p.12).

In other words, there is an overall pervasive quality to the *situations* within which we conduct our inquiries, a felt *tension* of a 'something' that we need to seek, which can act like a sensed 'compass' guiding our explorations into each bewildering situation we face – for the bewilderment we face is not any old bewilderment, but a unique bewilderment in relation not being able to even take a first step toward to a unique end in view, towards the needed resolution of our otherwise unclear situation. To illustrate what I mean here, I suggest that the next few statements are read very slowly, making use of a 'poetic' style of inner speech, with time taken at the end of each to imagine a particular, remembered, concrete situation :

- You enter a new situation;

- You are at first confused, bewildered, and don't know your way about;

- However, as you 'dwell in' it, as you 'move around' within the confusion, a 'something', an 'it' begins to emerge;

- It emerges in the 'time contours' or 'time shapes' that become apparent to you in the dynamic relations you can sense between your outgoing exploratory activities and their incoming results;

- An image comes to you, you find that you can express aspects of this 'something' in terms of this image;

- But not so fast, for you can find another, and another image, and another – Wittgenstein uses a city, a toolbox, the controls in the driving cab of a train, and many different types of games, all as metaphors[13] for different aspects of our experiences of the use of language;

- Having gone through a number of images, you can, perhaps, come to a more comprehensive sense of the landscape of possibilities giving rise to them.

Indeed, as we gain a sense of familiarity within such landscapes, we can come to feel confident of knowing our way around within them, and of being able to *resolve* on ways of *going on* within them. Thus the process of *resolving* on lines of action within such initially *unique* situations, cannot simply be a matter of calculation or decision making, to do with choosing among already existing possibilities. The situations would not be unique if such possible next steps already existed within them. They involve *judgments*; a need to move around within the landscape of possibilities; while being *spontaneously responsive* to the consequences of each move; and judging (valuing) which one (or combination of moves) best gives rise to an orientation that provides a way of resolving the tension aroused in one's initial confusion – for, to repeat, we are operating here, not in the realm of actualities but of possibilities.

And my purpose, of course, in asking you to speak to yourself slowly and expressively was both to arouse in your tone of voice more extreme responsive movements within you as readers than is usual in more intellectually oriented texts, as well as to allow time for the 'shape' of such movements to *resonate* within you, thus to "remind" you of something that might be already familiar to you (Wittgenstein 1953, no.89)[14] – to 'call up' one or two or more previous experienced concrete episodes whose 'time-contours' are similar to those traced out in the unfolding dynamics of my utterances – for the sensing of similarities within one's own experience is a very basic human capacity, and lies at the bottom of our seeing objective patterns out in the world.

Noticings

Once oriented, as 'participant parts' within the very situations we are investigating, rather than trying to begin with 'good ideas', or allowing ourselves to be *theory-driven*, we must begin our investigations with *noticings*, with *sensing* when a next step *different from an expected or wanted* next step might be taken. Let me list some 'noticings' in summary form:

- A first kind of noticing – 1) being 'struck by' an event or happening;

- A second kind of noticing – 'incipient forms': 2) "A community or a polis is not something that can be made or engineered by some form of techne or by the administration of society. There is something of a circle here, comparable to the hermeneutical circle. The coming into being of a type of public life that can strengthen solidarity, public freedom, a willingness to talk and to listen, mutual debate, and a commitment to rational persuasion presupposes the incipient forms of such communal life" (Bernstein 1983, p.266).

- A third kind – 'what is not being said' (the elephant in the room): As Billig (1999) points out in Freudian Repression – in relation to the case of Herr K. (an older man rejected by his wife) and Dora (the young daughter whose father was having an affair with Herr K's wife) – how people can use shared "dialogic routines" (p.101) to avoid raising those issues between them that would result I devastating conflicts – whereas, Freud had understood that "repression took place in the head [of individuals], not outwardly in conversation" (p.102).

- A fourth kind – 'telling moments': moments when 'collective narratives or ideologies' begin to be revealed, e.g., when people begin to say: 'This is how we do things around here'.

- A fifth kind – disquiets: a feeling that there is still a 'something more' that has not yet been captured in all the articulations of 'sensings' that we so far produced.

This last 'noticing' is a most important one, in at least the following three senses: (1) In one, it is central to Kuhn's (1962) account of scientific revolutions: "Discovery commences with the awareness of anomaly, i.e., with the recognition that nature has somehow violated the paradigm-induced expectations that govern normal action" (pp.52-53) – when something occurs that wasn't expected within the theory-shaped ways of sense-making adopted by inquirers, new steps have to be taken. (2) In another, as William James (1912) says: "Our fields of experience have no more definite boundaries than have our fields of view. Both are fringed forever by a *more* that continuously develops, and that continuously supersedes them as life proceeds. The relations, generally speaking, are as real here as the terms are..." (p.71). In other words, no matter where we draw the boundaries around a focal noticing, in relation to a particular end in view, we will not have exhausted all the possible influences at work in the situation of our concern; other ends in view will lead to us bring other influences to light. (3) But finally, ethically and politically, as we will see when I turn to Amartya Sen's (2009) work below, trying to work *from situated disquiets*, rather than *towards general ideals*, gives us a far more sure basis for our inquiries than we can ever arrive at from general, one-size-fits-all considerations.

Two kinds of inquiry aimed at overcoming two different kinds of difficulty: orientational difficulties and problem-solving

This need to contextualize – to situate the words we use, particularly those we try to use as the indicative names of basic 'things' – gives rise to a perhaps surprising consequence. It not only means that there are *two* kinds of difficulties we can face in our lives, not just one. Indeed, as Wittgenstein (1980) has made very clear to us, many of our difficulties in our practical lives are *not* of the form of *problems* that we can, by the application of a science-like methodology, solve by reasoning; nor are they are "empirical problems" that we can solve by discovering something already existing but currently unknown to us; they are difficulties of a quite another kind. They are *relational* or *orientational* difficulties, to do with discovering how to 'go out' towards an initially indeterminate state of affairs in our surroundings with certain expectations and anticipations at the ready, so to speak, appropriate to our finding our 'way about' and to 'going on' within them without (mis)leading ourselves into taking inappropriate next steps.

Grammatical investigations, 'philosophy' – the results of contextualized, practice-based inquiries

Indeed, as has now, perhaps, begun to be clear, the kinds of philosophical investigations Wittgenstein (1953) calls grammatical investigations – aimed at gaining a sense of the contextual influences at work in shaping our actions in this or that particular situation – are not merely *another* mode of investigation available to us, but are necessarily prior to all other kinds of inquiry. As Wittgenstein's (1953) put it in describing the nature of his own investigations: "Since everything lies open to view there is nothing to explain. For what is hidden, for example, is of no interest to us./ One might also give the name 'philosophy' to what is possible *before* all new discoveries and inventions" (no.126) – thus for him, the term 'philosophy' takes on here a very special kind of contextualized, practical meaning.

This because, for us, each new situation we face is initially indeterminate. Experientially, at least, we seem to find ourselves – especially in our visual fields, in our hearing, in our conscious experience – immersed in a continuous, irreversible, *flow* of activity, of ceaseless unfolding movement. Obsessed in the past with starting from already determined situations made up of configurations of already named entities, "it is just this free water of consciousness," says William James (1890), "that psychologists resolutely overlook. With it goes the sense of its relations, near and remote, the dying echo of whence it came to us, the dawning sense of whither it is to lead... We all of us have this permanent consciousness of whither our thought is going. It is a feeling like any other, a feeling of what thoughts are next to arise, before they have arisen" (pp.255-256).

Let me repeat those last two, seemingly paradoxical phrases: a feeling of what thoughts are next to arise, before they have arisen. In other words, such feelings are not bounded entities with a clear beginning and a clear end, but, as he put it earlier, they are "*feelings of tendency, often so vague that we are unable to name them at all*" (p.254), and as feelings *still in process*, so to speak, they can, as we shall see, serve the most important function of guiding us in our exploratory imaginings of the possible next steps we might take in our practical actions. They can function, James (1890) says, as "*signs of direction* in thought[15], of which we have an acutely discriminative sense, though no definite sensorial image plays any part in it whatsoever" (p.253). In other words, any aspect of it that we pick out as a figure against a background, is "fringed forever by a *more*" that, although perceptually invisible to us, is influential in determining the figure's performative meaning for us – how it can nonetheless motivate and guide us in our actions *in that situation*. Thus such *orientational* difficulties are *resolved* by the gradual emergence of a 'local best' action, a best way forward which develops, hermeneutically, within our tentative exploratory movements as we sense and evaluate the incipient "signs of directions in thought" that they give rise to within us.

This ignoring of the larger context within which the focal things of our attention have their being – James' "more" – is crucial. As Bateson (1979) noted, "without context, words and actions have no meaning at all" (p.24) – they exist simply as empty, meaningless forms. So, although we continually talk of *solving* problems by thinking about them within a well-defined, rational framework in order to arrive at a plan or strategy which we then try to put into action, such 'problems' can only be *solved* if the situations we face already consist in a set of determinate, separate entities awaiting our 'arrangement' or 're-arrangement' of them. This is precisely not the case with relational or orientational difficulties. Here, we cannot plan, we cannot by a cause-and-effect process bring an innovative circumstance into existence just when we want to. But what we can do, just as a 'good enough' (but not a perfect, *idealized*) mother can act at appropriate times to help her infant develop his or her *first* language, so can we can come to an understanding of the appropriate dialogic circumstances are in place (Shotter 2010b), to *occasion* or *circumstance* such innovative developments[16].

Thus rather than being aimed at reliable and repeatable results that can made accessible in some published form, so that they can be both publically criticized and tested, and thus generalized to apply in indefinitely many different contexts, the practitioner-relevant inquiries I want to outline here have a quite different aim. They are practice-oriented and practice-based. They are concerned with our gaining a sense of 'where we are' in relation to our immediate surroundings, and of the surrounding field or 'landscape' of real possibilities open to us for our next steps. Thus, unlike the idealized and de-contextualized nature of 'coolly rational' research, practitioner inquiry is concerned with *details* in our surroundings that are crucial to the performance of our actions. As Wittgenstein (1953) remarks, acting in idealized surroundings is like trying to walk on ice "where there is no friction and so in a certain sense the conditions are ideal, but also, just because of that, we are unable to walk. We want to walk: so we need friction. Back to the rough ground!" (no.107).

Rather than resulting in nameable, objective 'things' out in the world, in objective knowledge, the results of practice-situated inquiries come to be registered in, and to accumulate in, our embodied capacities and sensitivities. As Bateson (1979) puts it (see Shotter, 2010a), they contribute to a practitioner becoming better "calibrated" in "the *setting* of his nerves and muscles" (p.211) which, in practical terms, means that the practitioner can come to act automatically and spontaneously, i.e., without conscious deliberation by anticipating the direction of a client's next steps, i.e., the 'point' of their actions or utterances, before their actual expression of them.

On coming to think systemically – reversals in our expectations

Coming to think in this *relational, contextualizing,* or *ecological* manner – what we might call "thinking systemically" – entails abandoning many of the preoccupations of the Enlightenment, abandoning especially what we might call the 'coolly rational' approach to inquiry in which we take "analysis" – the breaking down of a whole (as a mechanism) into its cause-and-effect functioning parts, as a basic first step in our inquiries. At the heart of this approach is the aim, enunciated by Descartes in 1637, of putting certain aspects of what is natural available to us in our surroundings "to all the uses for which they are appropriate, and thereby make ourselves, as it were, masters and possessors of nature" (Descartes 1968, p.78) – a process in which even Darwin was led to assumed that human progress was a matter of humanity struggling to overcome the limitations of nature. Abandoning these presuppositions of inquiry is not easy.

Our assumed need to think rationally about the difficulties we face in our lives, to think almost in a linear fashion, almost mathematically, wholly within what we might call a single order of logical connectedness, makes the back-and-forth, hermeneutical task of thinking *systemically* or *ecologically* – doing *withness* rather than *aboutness*-thinking – hard to adopt. However, because it can lead us into many really quite surprising and disoriented situations and directions, we badly need to make ourselves a bit more aware of the easily unnoticed or ignored 'inner moves' we execute within ourselves and amongst us in arriving at a sense of something as being a 'thing' (Heidegger 1969) for us in our surroundings. Thus, before proceeding any further, I would just like to list in note form some of these 'surprises', some of the 'reversals' in our taken-for-granted ways of thinking about how our inquiries might best be conducted:

1) An important reversal: our bodily movements out in the world are more important to us than our thinkings[17].

2) Another important reversal: what just happens to us is much more important to us than what we achieve in our wanting and doing, it provides the 'background' from out of which our wantings and do-ings emerge and into which they return to exert their influence.

3) Another reversal: emotions as judgments (Nussbaum 2001)... be-ginning with *feelings* rather than calculations... the sense of a 'some-thing' of importance and value here...

4) *Yet another*: (Merleau-Ponty 1964)... it is as if *what* I as an agency thought *I* was 'bringing forth' begins to act in me as itself an agency to teach me a new 'way of looking', or a 'new way of thinking'... a new style of painting comes on the scene, we are at first disoriented, but later we find that *it* has taught us a new 'way of looking'[18].

5) *Yet another*: Mechanistically we talk of stimuli *causing* responses, yet it is the living responses of organisms that constitute, i.e., give not form but value to, the stimuli that they orient towards.

The temptation to move 'outside' and to talk 'about' self-contained systems 'over there' is pervasive in all 'coolly rational' approaches to scientific inquiries into social affairs. William James (1890) described the fallacy to which it gives rise as *'The Psychologist's Fallacy:'* "The *great* snare of the psychologist is *the confusion of his own standpoint with that of the mental fact* about which he is making his report. I shall hereafter call this the 'psychologist's fallacy' par excellence... The psychologist... stands outside of the mental state he speaks of. Both itself and its object are objects for him... The most fictitious puzzles have been introduced into our science by this means... Crude as such a confusion of standpoints seems to be when abstractly stated, it is nevertheless a snare into which no psychologist has kept himself at all times from falling, and which forms almost the entire stock-in-trade of certain schools. We cannot be too watchful against its subtly corrupting influence" (pp.196-197).

Bringing out the differences between the two forms of inquiry: thinking about systems and thinking systemically

1) Aboutness approaches

As qualitative forms of research develop, we can now begin to discern two kinds of what I will call aboutness-approaches: (1) more traditional theory-based approaches and (2) new methods-based approaches.

(1) Traditional theory-based approaches: In thinking *about systems*, as subjects, as agents, we actively attempt to characterize them within a system of logically interconnected theoretical propositions as objective things 'out there' or 'over there', in a part of the world separate from ourselves. Theory driven research is something we *do*, and it is the results of our 'doings' that matter; what just happens to us plays no part in the proceedings. And strictly, to count as a *scientific* theory, we should take care to ensure that each proposition in the theory should have:

(1) *Explicitness*: A theory should not be based on intuition and interpretation but should be spelled out so completely that it can be understood by any rational being.

(2) *Universality*: Theory should hold true for all places and all times.

(3) *Abstractedness*: A theory must not require reference to particular examples.

(4) *Discreteness*: A theory must be stated in terms of context-free elements - elements which make no reference to human interests, traditions, institutions, etc.

(5) *Systematicity*: A theory must be a whole in which decontextual-

ized elements, (properties, attributes, features, factors, etc.) are related to each other by rules or laws.

(6) *Closure and prediction*: The description of the domain investigated must be complete, i.e. it must specify all the influences that affect the elements in the domain and must specify their effects. Closure permits precise prediction.

In other words, our theories must stand before us as themselves objective entities. If these requirements are not met, if our theories cannot be publicly understood and criticized, then we have mere 'theoretical-talk', which is hardly different from the 'opinions- or good-ideas-talk' of specific individuals.

But the fact is, no so-called 'theories' in the social 'so-called sciences' come anywhere near to fulfilling these requirements. Further, the very requirements of explicitness, de-contextuality, and closure, etc., work to strip out the *relational* aspects of all living phenomena and as a consequence we 'lose the very phenomena' of our central concern: how our activities come to 'hang together' as meaningful wholes whose 'point' can be sensed by other in such a way that they can come to co-ordinate their activities with ours.

(2) Methods based approaches: In the turn away from theory-driven and theory-testing research, there is now a turn now towards a concern with *methods*, towards qualitative methods of inquiry. But does this turn work to move us from thinking *about* systems to thinking more systemically? I think not at all. For the organizing assumption, if I may call it that, of all these more methods-based approaches is still to think that there are definite processes already 'out there' in the world awaiting our discovery of their workings. In other words, they are again, implicitly, theory-driven. But what if, perhaps counter intuitively, specific, determinate realities as such do not exist without – or outside of – the sets of practices we use in our attempts to investigate them, including the inscription devices[19] and the larger networks within which think of them as being located?

But what if the 'systems' within which we think of ourselves as being embedded are not only still open to further development, but also multi-dimensional, so that it is only when we 'interrogate' phenomena occurring in our surroundings within the confines of, as Karen Barad (2007) calls them, a particular "material-discursive practice" – i.e., an intra-twined set of ways of talking and ways of acting that materially affect the world within which it takes place – that events occurring in the world around us come to take on a determinate form?[20] Indeed, what if much of the world in which we live is vague, fluid, unspecific, diffuse, slippery, ephemeral, elusive or indistinct, emotional, what if it changes like a kaleidoscope, or like the intra-mingling streams of hot and cold air in the atmosphere, or it doesn't really have much pattern at all, then where does this leave the social sciences, with their aim of 'discovering' the supposed already existing orders and patterns determining our behaviour? Chasing chimera in the realization of Theuseus' fear it would seem.

As Foucault (1972) put it in *The Archeology of Knowledge* quite a while ago: We face "a task that consists of not – of no longer treating discourses as groups of signs (signifying elements referring to contents or representations) but as practices that systematically form the objects of which they speak. Of course, discourses are composed of signs; but what they do is more than use these signs to designate things. It is this *more* that renders them irreducible to the language *(langue)* and to speech. It is this 'more' that we must reveal and describe" (p.49). It is this 'more' that we must try to bring to light and describe in a fashion that does justice to it.

Thus what can be called thinking in these two 'aboutness' approaches?: To grasp a bit more clearly what is involved here, let me examine the sequence of steps involved in both these two *problem-solving* approaches: 1) approaching a newness or strangeness as a problem to be solved requires us to first analyze it into a set of identifiable elements; 2) we must then find a pattern or order amongst them; and then 3) we *hypothesize* a hidden agency responsible for the order (call it, the working of certain rules, principles, or laws, or the working of a story or narrative, or the shaping of a practice by 'themes', or suchlike). We then seek further evidence for *its* influence, thus to enshrine its agency in a theoretical system or framework of thought. And we then go on to make use of such frameworks in our further actions.

As investigators, we ourselves remain unchanged in the process; we remain *outside* and *separate* from the other or otherness we are investigating; rather than being engaged or involved in with it we are 'set over against' it; in acquiring extra knowledge *about* it – in the form of facts or information – our aim is to gain *mastery* over it.

2) Systemic or withness thinking
At the heart of the difference between the two forms of inquiry, as two sides of the same coin, is on the one side, the Cartesian subject/

object spilt, and on the other, the peculiar nature (disparaged by rationalists) of *participative* thinking. In withness- thinking or thinking systemically, one functions as a participant within the very phenomena one is inquiring into. As a result, the placement of the subject/object split becomes highly variable, a matter of placing the divide within different regions of a phenomenon according to one's overall end in view. For, in deciding that we want to bring about a change in one aspect of our surroundings, we must leave ourselves open to being affected in an uncontrolled fashion by the rest of our surroundings, and as we turn to produce an intended effect elsewhere, we open ourselves to being affected by the very original aspect of our concern. Thus what we treat as being set over against us as an 'object' at one moment, becomes itself at the next an agency able to affect us.

Systemic thinking or thinking systemically: Thinking systemically is to think as a 'participant part' within the very systems we think of ourselves as investigating. But what is it to think "participatively" in this fashion? According to Bakhtin (1993), it can only be done by "those who know how not to detach their performed act from its product, but rather how to relate both of them [both the process and product of their thought] to the unitary and unique context of life and seek to determine them in that context as an indivisible unity" (p.19, footnote). In other words, understandings of this kind need to be lived within the context of a practice before they can be described, and their descriptions need to be voiced within that practice – as, in fact, a dynamic stability within that ongoing flow of activity – if they are to come to function as 'orienting landmarks', so to speak, in the landscapes of possibility we encounter in our relational practices.

   And we ourselves, as investigators, as we saw above, are changed in such encounters. For, in becoming involved with, immersed in, the 'inner life' of the others or othernesses around us, everything we do can be partly shaped by being in response to what *they might do*. Thus, rather than an objective *knowledge* of their nature, we gain an *orientation* toward them, we grasp how to 'go on' with them in terms of the *possible* ways they might respond to us. Although at first we can be wholly 'bewitched' (Wittgenstein 1953, no.109) by their 'voice', as our familiarity with them grows, their voice can become just one voice among the many other voices within us, and we can become 'disenchanted' with what they 'call' us upon us to do. However, we can never gain complete mastery over them – they can always surprise us, no matter how familiar to us they have become. Our constant vigilance is required; the precise words we use are important – for their *grammar* commits us *now* to what is expected of us in the future.

In other words, in more general terms, as we dwell in and move around in each new situation we face, a gradual growth of familiarity with *their* 'inner shape' can occur; we can then begin to gain a sense of the *value* of their *yet-to-be-achieved* aspects – the prospects they offer us for 'going on' within them. Thus, as we gain orientation, a sense of being 'at home' within them, we can come to find our 'footing', our placement or *who we can be* within such situations. And this, as was clear from your responses to my bulleted utterances above, can be done imaginatively, by undertaking appropriate imaginative work. And in so doing, make sense of our current circumstances by thinking *with*, or in relation to, certain of our past experiences. This is what I would like to call *systemic thinking* or *thinking systemtically* in such situations as these, and it is these situations – of initial disorientation or bewilderment – that we can sense (in Heidegger's 1979 terms) *what calls for systemic thinking*.

Relational stances and styles: to our 'subject matter' and to each other

> *"... philosophy ought really to be written only as a poetic composition"* *(Wittgenstein 1980, p.24).*

As we see it, there are two quite different styles of speaking and writing within which we, as academics, relate to the people around us:

i) *Professional*: one way is the supposedly 'objective', 'realistic', 'formal' or 'professional' style of speech or writing within which we currently present to our colleagues, the theories and the true facts our studies are meant to reveal;

ii) *Conversational*: the other is a more 'informal' or 'conversational' style that, traditionally, is thought to be in tension with it.

They each involve the adoption of a quite different *relational stance*, i.e., a different set of both methodological and ethical commitments, not only to those to whom we address ourselves, but also to the supposed subject matter of our talk.

i) *Cognitive*: While the former works in terms of us understanding them intellectually, as if from afar, in terms of representations, i.e., in terms of supposed similarities of form.

ii) *Intuitional*: The latter works in terms of us *sensing* in our living, embodied relations with them, up close, differences, differences that arise as they respond to our actions with actions of their own, differences that, initially at least, we can only voice poetically and metaphorically.

In other words, in the second, our understanding of other people comes about through a quite different route than that through which we understand them in the first: it comes about *dialogically*, in a way which we are all responsive in a living, embodied way to each other, and in which the others can respond back to us in way denied them in the first.

i) *Closed*: While the first way of talking, in which people relate themselves to each other cognitively and intellectually, can be thought of as a closed, finalized, monologic way of talking, functioning in an already existing and sustained 'disciplinary space', making use of fixed and finalized concepts.

ii) *Open*: The other, in which people are in a more sensuous contact with each other, is an open, unfinalized, responsive form of talk in which new 'spaces' may be opened up, and others closed down, freely, moment by moment.

Until recently, this second, nonconceptual, nonrepresentational, nondisciplinary, everyday form of talk has been very unfamiliar to us. We have been captivated by the picture of ourselves as isolated individuals, inhabiting an otherwise inert, mechanical body that, as a 'mind' we, so to speak, 'animate'.

But let us turn now to how our methodological and ethical involvements with each other, both with those we study as well as our professional colleagues, are played out in these two different styles of writing and talking:

i) *Monological-retrospective-objective writing*: In our official, academic style, we would be talking/writing to you as fellow professional academics, about what happened earlier, when we were involved with those whose activity is now the topic of our talk. We would provide you with a linguistic representation of the nature of that activity, but now *from outside* that involvement, looking back upon it as a completed process. In separating the activity from the people whose activity it was, and from its surrounding circumstances, we would be separating it from the practical part it played in their lives, its point from them. But this is not our concern. *Our* concern is with what logically 'can be said' about the patterning or form of that activity, an *order* that we can claim to have 'discovered' in it. We shall call this kind of writing, *monological-retrospective-objective* writing. Here, what we say or write is located in our professional relationship and is directed toward identifying that to which, as professional observers with a certain set of professional methodological commitments, we should attend. It is aimed at producing *explanatory theories*, i.e., representations of states of affairs that enable those in possession of them to predict and control the events they represent.

ii) *Dialogical-prospective-relational writing*: In the other style, we would be talking/writing to you of the character of our ongoing involvements with certain other people, *from within* that involvement - while both looking back on what had been achieved so far, and forward prospectively, toward the possibilities open to us for our next 'steps'. Our concern in such talk/writing would be with attempting to 'show' or 'make manifest' to you (metaphorically) how you might, *justifiably* be able to make sense of the character of such involvements. I shall call it *dialogical-prospective-relational* writing. What I say originates in the interactive relationships from within which I speak, and is directed toward instructing you, as ordinary everyday persons now involved in the relationship in some way (perhaps watching a videotape of it, or reading a transcript, or whatever), in noticing and making within in similar such connections and distinctions.

To contrast with the aim of the previous style, we might say that it is not aimed at explanatory theory, but at providing *practical theory*, or, at giving what are best called *avowal-accounts*: account-talk is talk that is useful in a tool-like way to those involved in a situation; it enables those involved to make and to notice differences in their activities, thus affording them with opportunities to coordinate their activities in with each other in an intelligible way.

Thus in these two styles, although you as the addressee of our writing might seem to be the same you, our 'positioning' of you would be different; and our 'ethical stance' toward those who are the 'subject matter' of our talk/writing is quite different too:

i) *Uninvolved writing*: In monological-retrospective-objective writing, we would have no need (at least, not immediately) to be accountable or responsive to the absent others of whom we speak. Indeed, we look upon them as if from a distance, as if we have a God's-eye view of them in some way.

ii) *Participatory-involved writing*: While in dialogical-prospective-relational writing, as a part of us being involved with those others, we cannot not be accountable to them; we have a sense of our responsibility toward them. And if asked by them as to why we make the claims we do about them, we feel we must respond to their request; we must justify ourselves to them in ways that they can accept (or can give good reasons for rejecting).

iii) *Responsibility to colleagues*: Thus, in the former style, our first (ethical) responsibilities are to you as a professional reader and to our shared discipline, and we must write in a way justifiably connected with our supposedly shared theoretical interests (as sociologists, anthropologists, psychologists, historians, etc.).

iv) *Answerable to those others or an 'otherness'*: While in the latter style, one of our major responsibilities is toward those others, or othernesses, *of whom* or *of which* we speak and write. Thus in this dialogical-prospective-relational writing, we cannot write simply in relation to a fixed and constant theoretical interest; we must write in a way that *respects* our currently shared but changing conversational or dialogical relations to them, or to 'it', that respects 'who' they 'are' or 'what' it 'is'.

Moving on from where we actually are — relinquishing utopian dreams

To turn now to what all this means for how we can conduct our inquiries into the nature of our own human affairs within our academic disciplines, and especially in the communication discipline: It means, I think, instead of working in terms of what people *argue* are the *ideally* are 'the best' ways, ideas, theorizations, or practices – and seeking to discover in our inquiries what we take to be these pre-existing, ideal things.... we must accept that we ourselves continually bring such 'things', the subject matter of our studies, into existence.

This, however, is an unusual orientation. As intellectually active adults, our focus is more usually on knowledge as conceptualized, on propositional knowledge – as Argyris (2003) has noted, "actionable knowledge requires propositions that make explicit the causal processes required to produce action" (p.444). But as young infants, we lack such well-defined forms of knowledge; if we are later to gain this kind of 'knowledge' of the 'things' around us, we must first be able to recognize them and move around in relation to them in our everyday practices as the 'things' they 'are', that is, as the 'things' they are taken to be by the others around us – and such practical recognitions cannot be taught us at this stage by trying to teach us propositions or by offering us facts linguistically.

So, although we may continually talk of our understandings as coming into existence as a result of our *prior* "thoughts," "ideas," "knowledge," or "deliberate plans or decisions" – and that, as a result, it seems perfectly reasonable to seek the namable causal processes responsible – the fact is, such processes can *only* be seen as *having been at work* in people's performances, *after* they have been completed[21].

And this, it seems to me, is the case with many more of our named topics of study in the behavioural sciences and communication disciplines: what are in fact *outcomes* of a person's actions, *after* those actions have been performed, are taken as components of the overall process within which they are *produced*, and as a result, the *theories*, *models*, etc, that we produce are, to put it academically, are *after the fact*, and *beside the point* – they set us 'looking backwards', and 'repeating the past' as if the indeterminate future we now face was already determined. Indeed, as 'nameable things' they are often, in fact, *foreshadowed* in the very *ways* in which, prior to our investigations, we commit ourselves to a particular way or ways of looking into the phenomena before us. Thus, as I see it, 'something else' altogether guides us in the performance of our actions than the nameable things whose nature we seek to discover in our inquiries. So how can we proceed?

Someone who has been very clear about the need to adopt such a method – a method that *he* in fact calls a method of comparisons, in which we articulate what an experienced phenomenon *is like* – is Amatya Sen (2009) in his book, *The Idea of Justice*. He begins it by quoting Charles Dickens's who, in *Great Expectations*, put these words into the mouth of the grown up *Pip*: "In the little world in which children have their existence, there is nothing so finely perceived and finely felt, as injustice" (p.vii) – where the grown up *Pip* is recollecting a humiliating encounter with his sister, *Estella*. In other words, he wants to begin his inquiries, not by asking what a perfectly just society would look like, but from our *felt sensing of a something being* unjust, from our *disquiets*, form our feelings of *things being not quite right*.

Why? Because: "What moves us, reasonably enough," he remarks, "is not the realization that the world falls short of being completely just – which few of us expect – but that there are clearly remediable injustices around us which we want to eliminate" (p.vii). Thus, as I suggested above, by situating ourselves within a particular practical situation within which we can gain a *shared sense* – along with all the others around us – of a particular *injustice* at work; there is a real chance of us all, working together, of arriving at a way of remedying it. For we can all find in such a situation both, a guiding motivation, and, as we mentally move about within it, *ways to bring to light* the resources we need to move on from that injustice – where the *ways* we need will involve our *theories*.... to be used, not as explanatory devices, but as *objects of comparison* to help us in coming to a *felt sense* of what the particular injustice in question *is like*.

So here – if we want to focus on in justices and the ethics at work in our *relations* to each other – we end with a new *orientation* towards our inquiries in the communication discipline, compared with it as to do with the transmission of messages within the context of social interaction: a practice-based rather than a theory-based approach. An approach that does not exclude attention to 'relational things' like its theory-based cousin. And as such, it will give rise to a whole new set of expectations, a new horizon of future goals and endeavours. However, unlike its more instrumental, theory-based cousin, we will not be able to expect any *final* answers to our *general* questions – we will never know *what* actually communication *is* – for our way of proceeding will *not* be to do with 'seeing patterns' out in the world, but with 'sensing similarities' within our lives together.

This will not mean, however, that we can do away with *theory*; we will still need it; but instead of our arguing with others over which is a *best ideal*, all our theories will find a *use* – a metaphorical and/or poetic use – in bringing to light similarities (and differences) within our task of clarifying what a particular sensed injustice *is like*.

In setting out the possibility of this new *orientation* for our studies in communication in this fashion, I am reminded of how Thomas Kuhn (1970) ended his account of *The Structure of Scientific Revolutions*; he said: "We are all deeply accustomed to seeing science as the one enterprise that draws constantly nearer to some goal set by nature in advance. But need there be any such goal? If we can learn to substitute evolution-from-what-we-do-know for evolution-toward-what-we-wish-to-know, a number of vexing problems may vanish in the process" (p.171).

And this, of course, is what I am proposing here: that we relinquish the still unfulfilled – and, as I see it, *forever unfulfillable* – dream of gaining the very general results we desire in our inquiries, and to be content with the limited, partial, and situated results we *can in fact obtain* – which, in the end, will, I believe, perhaps surprisingly, turn out to be of far greater practical use and value to us. Indeed, as each new result is obtained and each small change in our surroundings effected, if Bateson (1979) is correct about the nature of co-emergence, then we can expect human cultural development to exhibit similar, unpredictable, co-emergent, innovative outcomes to those that occur on a smaller scale everyday amongst us in our dialogically-structured practices. And in our practices, we will alter (develop) new environment(s) within which the others around us (and our children) will develop their mentalities. Hoping, in the past, always for jam tomorrow, we have ignored too much of what is readily available to us, all of us, today... and today... and today (Shotter, 2013).

Notes

1   In physics, the behaviour of a wave or particle, in the social and behavioural sciences, a person's meaning, attitude, personality, or abnormality of some kind.

2   As is well known, friction, air resistance, and other contextual details are usually ignored in physical theories, just as Chomsky (1965) talked only of "an ideal speaker-listener" (p.3), and again, ignored in his theories of linguistic competence how we shape our utterances to the circumstances of their utterance.

3   I say 'can' here, as I begin to suspect that in today's somewhat chaotic environments, basic turn-taking skills may sometimes not be being well learnt.

4   See comments in Vygotsky (1978) on the genesis of children's pointing gestures in mothers' reactions to their reaching movements: "from an object-oriented movement it becomes a movement aimed at another person, a means of establishing relations. The grasping movement changes to the act of pointing " (p.56).

5   As Wittgenstein (1953) notes, "if language is to be a means of communication there must be agreement not only in definitions but also (queer as this may sound) in judgments" (no.242), i.e., in the values people sense in what is happening around them.

6   See Kuhn (1970, pp.4-5) for an account of the questions to which a scientific community has to have answers to before effective scientific research as such can begin.

7   See note 4: Implicit in a good enough mother's facial expressions, tones of voice, and other more informal aspects of her expressions, are, of course, her valuations, her judgments as to what is in fact taking place.

8   Here, of course, I am straightaway, seemingly, giving a name to a range of as yet un-well-known phenomena; however, I am using a noun phrase contrastively, as an indicative name, to highlight a distinction within a context.

9   I have taken the term 'performative' from John Austin (1962, 1970), who pointed out that all our utterances 'do things' out in our social world, even

those that merely seem to be stating facts.

10 "The language-games are rather set up as objects of comparison which are meant to throw light on the facts of our language by way not only of similarities, but also of dissimilarities" (no.130).

11 "Conscious experience is a widespread phenomenon... But fundamentally an organism has conscious mental states if and only if there is something that it is to be that organism – something it is like for the organism" (Nagel, 1974, p.436).

12 Our "tryings" are of a different logical type (see Bateson, 1979) from our "achievements," in that they are invisible, non-locatable, relational things rather than objective things that can be pointed at and located in a place at a point in time.

13 For we must remember that metaphors can conceal as well as reveal (Lakoff & Johnson, 1980).

14 Wittgenstein (1953): "Something that we know when no one asks us, but no longer know when we are supposed to give an account of it, is something that we need to remind ourselves of. (And it is obviously something of which for some reason it is difficult to remind oneself.)" (no.89).

15 Elsewhere (Shotter, 2005), I have called these signs of direction in thought, "action guiding anticipations."

16 Winnicott (1988) with respect to mothering, called it a "facilitating environment" (p.24).

17 "We come into the world moving. We're precisely not stillborn. Indeed, movement forms the 'I' that moves before the 'I' that moves forms movement" (Maxine Sheets-Johnstone).

18 "The origin and primitive form of the language game is a reaction; only from this can more complicated forms develop. Language – I want to say – is a refinement, 'in the beginning was the deed'[Goethe]" (1980, p.31)... "But what is the word 'primitive' meant to say here? Presumably that this sort of behavior is pre-linguistic: that a language-game is based on it, that it is the prototype of a way of thinking not the result of thought" (1981, no.541).

19 As Geertz (1973) notes: "The ethnographer 'inscribes' social discourse; he writes it down. In so doing, he turns it from a passing event, which exists only to its own moment of occurrence, into an account, which exists in its inscriptions and can be reconsulted" (p.19). Inscription devices are thus a set of practices that work to provide visible traces of the sequences of events that go to making up the otherwise invisible unfolding of dynamical events. Indeed, a major part of our task in our inquiries into our everyday affairs consists in devising situations within which such traces can become available to us.

20 What Barad (2007) has in mind here is Niels Bohr's resolution of the wave-particle duality paradox by noting that "wave" and "particle," as classical concepts, i.e., metaphorical terms referring to entities 'out there' in the external world, are only given determinate meanings in relation to different, indeed mutually exclusive, apparatuses, and that as such they refer to different, mutually exclusive phenomena, not in fact to independently existing physical objects. Bohr thus leaves it open as what the 'real' nature of physical reality actually is! This, of course, is in line with Wittgenstein's (1953) claim that

all our 'name' words only have determinate meanings within the confines of specific language-games.
21 James' (1890) "Psychologist's Fallacy" (p.196) again.

References

Argyris, Chris (2003). Actionable knowledge. In H.Tsoukas and K. Christian (Eds.) *The Oxford Handbook of Organization Theory*. New York: Oxford University Press. pp.423-452.
Austin, John (1962). *How to do Things with Words*. London: Oxford.
Austin, John (1970). *Philosophical Papers*. London: Oxford University Press.
Bakhtin, Mikhail M. (1986). *Speech Genres and Other Late Essays*. Trans. by Vern W. McGee. Austin, Tx: University of Texas Press.
Bakhtin, Mikhail M. (1993). *Toward a Philosophy of the Act*, with translation and notes by Vadim Lianpov, edited by M. Holquist. Austin, TX: University of Texas Press.
Barad, Karen (2007). *Meeting the Universe Halfway: Quantum Physics and the Entanglement of Matter and Meaning*. Durham & London: Duke University Press.
Bateson, Gregory (1979). *Mind in Nature: a Necessary Unity*. London: Fontana/Collins.
Bergson, Henri (1922). *Creative Evolution*. London: Macmillan.
Bergson, Henri (1974). *The Creative Mind: an Introduction to Metaphysics*. New York; Citadel Press.
Bernstein, Richard J. (1983). *Beyond Objectivism and Relativism: Science, Hermeneutics, and Praxis*. Philadelphia: U of Pennsylvania Press.
Billig, Michael (1999). *Freudian Repression: Conversation Creating the Unconscious*. Cambridge: Cambridge University Press.
Chomsky, Noam (1965). *Aspects of the Theory of Syntax*. Cambridge, Mass.: M.I.T. Press.
Descartes, René (1968). *Discourse on Method and Other Writings*. Trans. with introduction by F.E. Sutcliffe. Harmondsworth: Penguin Books.
Dewey, John (1910). "What is thought?" Chapter 1 in *How we think*. Lexington, Mass: D.C. Heath, pp.1-13.
Foucault, Michel (1972) *The Archaeology of Knowledge*. trans. A.M. Sheridan, London: Tavistock.
Garfinkel, Harold (1967) *Studies in Ethnomethodology*. Englewood Cliffs: Prentice-Hall.
Geertz, Clifford. (1973). *The Interpretation of Cultures*. New York: Basic Books.
Gergen, Kenneth J. (2009). *Relational Being: Beyond Self and Community*. Oxford & New York: Oxford University Press.
Gibson, James (1979). *The Ecological Approach to Visual Perception*. Boston, MA: Houghton Mifflin.
James, William (1890). *Principles of Psychology*, vols. 1 & 2. London: Macmillan.
James, William (1912) A World of Pure Experience, Chapter 2 in *Essays in Radical Empiricism*. New York: Longman Green and Co, pp.39-91.
Kuhn, Thomas S. (1970). *The Structure of Scientific Revolutions, 2nd Edition, Enlarged*. Chicago, Il: University of Chicago Press.

Lakoff, George and Johnson, Mark (1980). *Metaphors We Live By*. Chicago: University of Chicago Press.

Lao Tzu (1967). *Tao te Ching*, trans. by D.C. Lau. Harmondsworth: Penguin Books.

Law, John & Mol, Annemarie (1994). Regions, networks and fluids: anaemia and social topology. *Social Studies of Science*, 24: 641-671.

Mills, Charles Wright (1940). Situated Actions and Vocabularies of Motive. *American Sociological Review*, 5, pp.904-913.

Nagel, Thomas (1974). What is it like to be a bat?. *Philosophical Review, 83*. pp.435-451

Nussbaum, Martha C. (2001). *Upheavals of Thought: the Intelligence of Emotions*. Cambridge, UK & New York, USA: Cambridge University Press.

Heidegger, Martin (1969). *What is a Thing?* Chicago: Regnery Press.

Heidegger, M. (1976). *What is Called Thinking?* New York: Harper-Perennial.

Ryle, Gilbert (1949). *The Concept of Mind*. London: Methuen.

Scott, Marvin B. and Lyman, Stanford M. (1968). Accounts. Reprinted in D. Brissett and C. Edgeley (Eds.) *Life as Theater: a Dramaturgical Sourcebook*. New York: Aldine. 1990, pp.219-241.

Shotter, John (1984). *Social Accountability and Selfhood*. Oxford: Blackwell.

Shotter, John (2005). Inside processes: transitory understandings, action guiding anticipations, and withness-thinking. *International Journal of Action Research*, 1(1), pp.157-189.

Shotter, John (2006). Understanding process from within: an argument for 'withness'-thinking. *Organization Studies, 27(4)*, pp.585-604.

Shotter, John (2010a). Bateson, double description, calibration, abduction, and embodiment: preparing ourselves for the happening of change. *Human Systems*, 21(1), pp.68-92.

Shotter, John (2010b). Situated dialogic action research: disclosing "beginnings" for innovative change in organizations. *Organizational Research Methods,* 13(2), pp.268-285.

Shotter, John (2013). Agentive spaces, the "background", and other not well articulated influences in shaping our lives. *Journal for the Theory of Social Behaviour*, XX(X), pp.xx-xx.

Vygotsky, Lev S. (1978). *Mind in Society: the Development of Higher Psychological Processes*. Edited by M. Cole, V. John-Steiner, S. Scribner, and E. Souberman (Eds.) Cambridge, MA: Harvard University Press.

Winch, Peter (1958). *The Idea of a Social Science and its Relations to Philosphy*. London: Routledge and Kegan Paul.

Wittgenstein, Ludwig (1953). *Philosophical Investigations*, translated by G.E.M. Anscombe. Oxford: Blackwell.

Wittgenstein, Ludwig (1980). *Culture and Value,* introduction by G. Von Wright, and translated by P. Winch. Oxford: Blackwell.

Winnicott, Donald (1988). *Babies and their Mothers*. London: Free Association Books.

Innovations in
Systemic Inquiry

II

A Solidarity Approach: The Rhizome & Messy Inquiry

6

Vikki Reynolds

Introduction

A Solidarity Approach aims to hold all of the inquiry process to the ethics and practices of activist solidarity and in line with an ethic of justice-doing (Reynolds 2010a, 2011a). This writing illuminates this inquiry process which was created for my PhD dissertation. The approach calls on Deleuze and Guattari's concept of the rhizome (2008) to describe the networked communities (Lacey 2005a) in which my activism and paid work occur. This writing begins with describing my work supervising and training community workers and therapists who work within contexts of social injustice alongside people who are marginalized and oppressed. Next, a description of the interconnectedness of these communities and the usefulness of the concept of the rhizome in activism, community work and a Solidarity Approach to inquiry is offered. A hopeful scepticism around inquiry and writing is made public, and I will show how these concerns were addressed. Some of the work from Clarke (2005), Lather (1993, 2010), and Law (2004) that supports this engagement with a messy inquiry, an ethic of justice-doing and a Solidarity Approach will be discussed. Some strategies for the Solidarity Approach are outlined and I illuminate an Expansive Inquiry in which my work and ethical stance are placed at the centre of the inquiry in order to resist replicating appropriation or exploitation of oppressed people and workers. This work is then re-situated back into the rhizome, where there are possibilities of expansiveness and de-centering my work which, while useful, is only a connected filament that is profoundly co-created, inter-dependent and may be the stuff that foments other useful work.

The context: Supervising community workers struggling in the margins

The context of this inquiry is centered in my work as a clinical supervisor and consultant with community workers and therapists working in the margins of society with oppressed people, many of whom are exploited, racialized[1] and colonized. We are responding to human suffering, which is loosely talked about in medicalized ways as trauma or addiction. The context of our work is the realm of human suffering, which exists because people's human rights are not respected and because we have constructed an unjust society. I have supervised a center for survivors of torture (Reynolds 2010b) and supervise a rape crisis center, addictions teams and housing and shelter workers in Vancouver's Downtown Eastside, which is the poorest off reserve area in Canada. This work occurred alongside queer, Two Spirit, gender variant and transgender workers[2], and direct action activists addressing a multiplicity of oppressions. All of these workers, activists and clients have profoundly contributed to this work.

A Supervision of Solidarity (2010c), which is how I describe my work, encompasses an ethical stance for *justice-doing* which is a response to the suffering, indignity, and violations of social justice that is the context of much of this community work.

Dire need compelled me to create practices that can be of use to the workers I supervise. Teachings from activist cultures have informed me on this path alongside community workers and clients, and my engagement with these ideas has proven useful on the ground. At times I have felt an affinity with Irish playwright Samuel Beckett's character who states, "I can't go on: I'll go on"(1958, p.178). The absurdities faced by workers and clients within contexts of poverty and dislocation amidst great affluence and political apathy are often reminiscent of Beckett's austere and surreal landscapes. Despite not knowing what I was going on to, I found that something I dare to call a faith in solidarity helped me to go on.

Being of use has required immediate responses. This could not wait for better training, the arrival of the right teacher, or finding the right book. Taking what I have learned from activist cultures, from progressive therapeutics trainings (Waldegrave & Tamasese 1993; Anderson 1997; Sanders 1997; Bird 2000; White 2007; Madigan 2011) and from my family and culture, I responded to need with action. A teaching from American anarchist theorist Noam Chomsky informs this work:

> "Social action cannot await a firmly established theory of man [sic] and society, nor can the validity of the latter be determined by our hopes and moral judgments. The two − speculation and action − must progress as best they can, looking forward to the day when theoretical inquiry will provide a firm guide to the unending, often grim, but never hopeless struggle for freedom and social justice" (2005, p.116).

Counsellors, shelter workers, and other community workers who had participated in a Supervision of Solidarity (Reynolds 2010b, 2011b) let me know that they found the solidarity practices useful and in line with fostering sustainability and addressing the spiritual pain they experience when they are forced to work in ways that are not in line with their ethics (Reynolds 2009).

A hopeful scepticism

Norwegian qualitative researcher Steinar Kvale's "hermeneutics of suspicion"[3] has proven a useful practice for me in articulating and making public my ethical concerns with research, inquiry and publishing. Hermeneutics is the art of interpretation which resists authoritative truths, and engages with multiple meanings from different voices. This hopeful scepticism requires that theorists' claims are held in abeyance until the practice can be shown to reveal the theory. With this phrase Kvale invites us to take a critical distance from the claims we make, and invites a hopeful yet sceptical position, open to the possibility that our practices may reveal something other than our intentions.

Histories of appropriation have made me sceptical about researching or writing anything informed by activism. I do not want to exploit clients or workers by writing exotic tales of torture and dramatic pain. I am also cautious about claiming knowledge that has been created by unnamed collectives of activists and putting my name to it. Work with survivors of torture and political violence taught me that engaging in research and publishing is not a neutral activity. Research on therapeutic work with survivors of torture has been studied at places such as the School of the Americas, where torturers are trained (School of the Americas Watch, 2009). [4] I have been careful in selecting what will be revealed and what might be risky in all of my writing, trainings and teachings. I remain aware I am not the one at risk.

Maori researcher, Linda Tuhiwai Smith, offers this caution on the legacy of research for colonized people:

> " 'research' is probably one of the dirtiest words in the indigenous world's vocabulary...It stirs up silence, it conjures up bad memories, it raises a smile that is knowing and distrustful...The ways in which scientific research is implicated in the worst excesses of colonialism remains a powerful remembered history for many of the world's colonized peoples. It is a history that still offends the deepest sense of our humanity" (1999, p.1).

American Black critical pedagogy educator bell hooks writes about the risk of activists' work and knowledge being appropriated and subsumed by people working from academic frameworks, particularly in relation to early writings from feminist communities (2000). Publishing was a useful tactic to get feminist perspectives legitimized specifically in academic discourses. However, this knowledge became the property of academics and was distanced from the activist communities which developed it. According to hooks, feminist activists became less relevant and were not seen as qualified to speak of feminism when these feminist discourses were finally legitimized by academic institutions.

When I began my PhD I recognized and was attuned to these risks. At the same time, I was encouraged by many practitioner and trainer colleagues to make public the ethical positioning I had relied on as I developed some useful practices. As an activist I am always striving to change the social context in *just* directions. Making an offering to knowledge in an academic context is part of a diversity of tactics that aims to promote *just* social changes. I felt compelled and in some small and humble way collectively accountable to bring this work to a wider audience.

bell hooks evokes a spirited solidarity when she writes:

"I came to theory because I was hurting— the pain within me was so intense that I could not go on living. I came to theory desperate, wanting to comprehend — to grasp what was happening around and within me. Most importantly, I wanted to make the hurt go away. I saw in theory then, a location for healing" (1994, p.59).

Imelda McCarthy (2001) from Ireland's Fifth Province team writes of the necessity to make public the privatized pain of clients that individualized practices, such as individual therapy, can contribute to. McCarthy describes how "public problems become private and privatized issues" in therapeutic practice:

"It is crucial that the private issues of clients need to be entered into the public arena if social change is to occur. This publication does not refer to the specific details of confidential material but of the themes and trends... The private and the public cannot be separated when one works with the poor; otherwise we are in danger of creating yet another arena for their silencing and further oppression" (2001, pp.271-272).

hooks and McCarthy's invitation to make public the privatization of suffering has accompanied me and encouraged me to engage with making my work more public, with an aim to contribute in some way to the social change McCarthy envisions.

Bridging the worlds of activism and academia is at the heart of my work. Theorizing is not a neutral practice. I believe that theorizing holds the promise of *justice-doing* and that liberatory theorizing can engender liberatory practices. I have approached theory with an intention of excavating histories of both acts of resistance, and of acts of justice. Theorizing has been useful in my activist work by drawing links across differences, and making public acts of power that are often obscured in the mystification of media, and what passes for normal: the way things are. Theorizing informed by liberatory intentions can open up possibility: the way things might be. In this work I borrow on the hope of bell hooks, who believes in the possibility that theory can be liberatory in social justice work (1984).

The rhizome

Activists' understandings of the rhizome are informed by the work of Deleuze and Guattari (1987). They use the rhizome to describe horizontally linked, non-hierarchical forms of social organization, thought, and communication. In botany, a rhizome is a horizontal plant stem, which exists underground, and from which the shoots and roots of new plants can be produced. Growing horizontally underground, rhizomes are able to survive extreme weather. The rhizome has been picked up in activists' cultures for its usefulness in dismantling hierarchy and power structures, while inviting a form that is more organic, responsive, co-creative and alive (Smith 2010, 2011). New Zealand/ Aotearoa narrative therapist John Winslade has investigated the usefulness of Deleuze's work in narrative therapy and conflict resolution (2009). Activist/scholar Anita Lacey illuminates the work of networked communities (2005a) and offers rich accounts of the multiple ways that the rhizome has informed activist networks and movements, including the riot girrrl network and the Anarchist Teapot Collective in London. The spirit of the rhizome is illustrated beautifully by Canadian anarchist and liberatory educator Scott Uzelman:

> *"Running bamboo often gives rise to unwitting bamboo gardeners. A single innocent shoot can stand alone for several years and then suddenly an entire field of bamboo begins to sprout. This leaves the unsuspecting gardener with a new bamboo garden that stubbornly resists attempts to get rid of it. While on the surface each shoot*

appears to be an individual, related but separate from its neighbors, underground all are connected through a complex network of root-like stems and filaments called a rhizome. During the years the gardener watched a single bamboo shoot grow tall, underground the bamboo rhizome grew horizontally, spreading throughout the yard, storing nutrients in anticipation of a coming spring. Like the bamboo garden, social movements are often rhizomic organisms growing horizontally into new terrains, establishing connections just below the surface of every day life, eventually bursting forth in unpredictable ways" (Uzelman 2005, p. 17).

A Solidarity Approach

As an activist working and living in the rhizome of interconnected communities striving towards social justice I wanted to approach inquiry in line with my ethics of solidarity and justice-doing. Solidarity speaks to our hopes and practices that move us towards our collective liberation, and the belief that our paths towards something *just,* are woven together.

The ethics of solidarity require that I do not replicate exploitation or abuses of power in my work or the inquiry of it. Solidarity requires that I begin all of my work from a decolonizing place, trying to hold myself accountable to my settler privilege on the unceded indigenous territories in which I live and work. I hold a decolonizing and anti-oppression frame for all of my activism and my paid and unpaid work (Dua & Lawerence 2005; Reynolds 2010a; Walia 2012). This requires an intersectional analysis (Crenshaw 1995) that takes on oppression on all fronts attending to lines of power and disadvantage. My relationship to solidarity is imperfect, and I embrace an imperfect solidarity as an anti-perfection project (Reynolds 2010d, 2011c). And this makes it possible for me to go on without needing to be perfect, but knowing I can respond to oppression with action and engage accountability to repair imperfect actions.

Metis Response-Based therapist Cathy Richardson created a Metis Methodology for her PhD dissertation (2004), which held her entire process accountable to the cultural practices, traditions and ethics of her Metis culture. After consulting about my fears and concerns, Cathy inspired me when she suggested that what I needed was to create a Solidarity Approach that would help me hold all of my PhD process accountable to the ethics and practices of solidarity from my activist culture.

The engagement with solidarity is recursive, messy, and non-linear in this work. In fact, the same ethics that were the subject of this inquiry informed the inquiry process, the practice and the writing recursively. A Solidarity Approach became my response to the question of how I could hold all of my inquiry accountable to understandings and practices of solidarity that are at the heart of my work and activism.

An Expansive Inquiry

Alongside other academic/activists I believe that "Social researchers should always be the most vulnerable — not those being studied or 'left' behind once the research is complete" (Fine, 2006, p. 88). Writing myself into the work, and examining my own theory and practice invited enough-accountability for me to engage in line with this ethic. I put the development of my own practice, and my ethical stance for my work forward as the subject of this inquiry. I was encouraged in this direction by my dissertation instructors, Sally St. George and Dan Wulff who speak of research as daily practice, where they encourage practitioners to "examine data from our own clinical work to more richly understand our practices and societal discourses" (2012).

This Solidarity Approach led to an engagement with inquiry rather than research. This is important as inquiry allows for the messy, fluid, emergent dialogues that I thought would be more generative and useful than categories, evidence or truth. Ken Gergen, an American Social Constructionist, describes collaborative inquiry as a process in which the interests of participants inform the direction of the inquiry (2005).

For this project I could have researched the work of other practitioners and evaluated and categorized the results to judge if they were in fact engaging ethics. Instead of researching the work of others and distilling it down to results (or truth), I invited people into my practice. I was not looking to deliver a perfect model of practice, or any manualized tools. What I was interested in articulating was my ethical stance from which generative practices emerged. I did not want to reify any of my practices, such as the Solidarity Group — I used it mainly to invite other workers to explore and co-investigate my ethical stance. My hope was that practitioners would respond by creating their own practices in line with some of our collective ethics for *doing justice*, expanding possibilities outwards from this experience. In consultation, my dissertation advisor Ken Gergen described my process as an Expansive Inquiry, and sketched a picture:

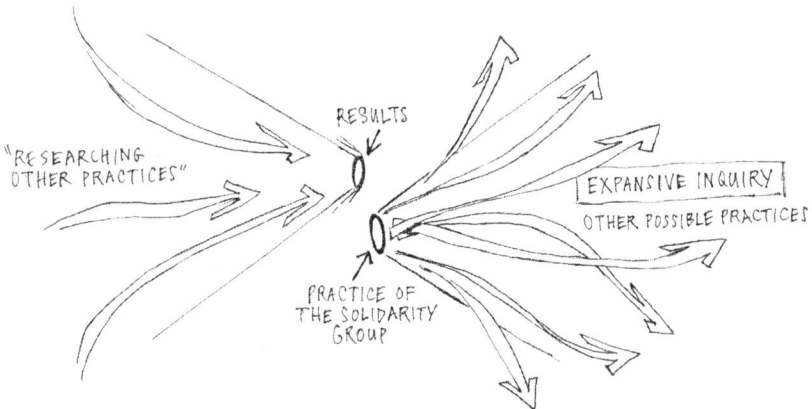

Solidarity Practices describe the practices I have developed as they all follow from a commitment to an ethical stance for justice-doing. The rhizome drawings illustrate that the Solidarity Practices emerge organically from the ethical stance, which is comprised of the Guiding Intentions:

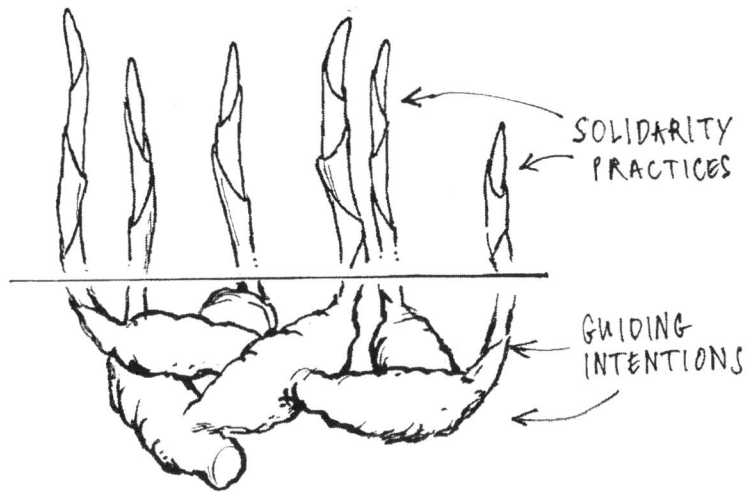

The Solidarity Practices that arise from the Guiding Intentions include Solidarity Groups [5], Solidarity Teams, the Witnessing Supervision Interview, and *people-ing the room*, among others (Reynolds, 2011b). The Solidarity Group practice was chosen for use in this inquiry because of the energy, interest and usefulness which the group inspired in the community workers who participated in it.

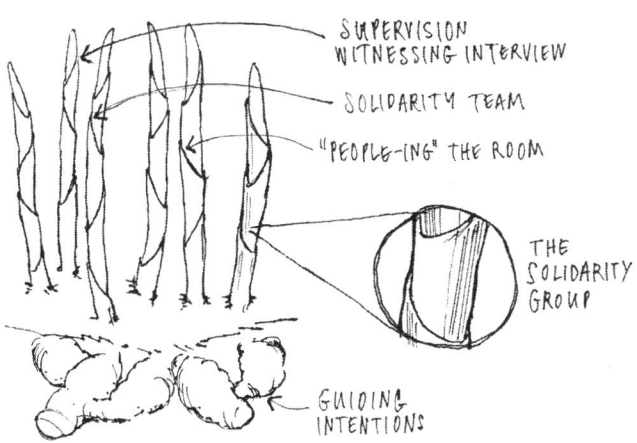

The reflections and critiques offered by workers participating in Solidarity Groups became the stuff that contributed to articulating and describing the particular Guiding Intentions from which the practices grow.

Messy and fluid inquiry

The pragmatic approach to inquiry of Patti Lather, an American feminist poststructuralist social science researcher prioritizes action/ activism. Lather speaks of catalytic validity, and asserts that the value of research should be based on how it can be used, not how it can be measured (1993). As anarchists say, 'talk-action=zero'. My work and activism is informed by anti-colonial struggle, feminist and queer theory and anarchist theory. The threads of this collective and possibly inconsistent theorizing (Newbury 2011) name power, address structural abuses of power and contest the construction of normal. It also requires a complex understanding of power, and acknowledges people's acts of both resistance and solidarity as acts of power (Reynolds 2010b; Wade 1997). I aim to respond to oppression and resistance to make social change in line with a decolonizing and anti-oppressive stance and direct action. I wanted my inquiry to attempt to do the same.

Queer theory has been inspiring for me in this process as it invites fluidity, which is movement from the fixed and certain to the confused and unstable, a privileging of flow and mutability, a refusal to be stable or static, and an ability to morph (Butler 1990; Jagose 1996). Engaging with fluidity helps us to resist constructing dialogues that are sedimented, reified, static, and immutable (McNamee 2008). Fluidity also offers a resistance to definition or explanation.

Working to discern the differences between description, under-standing and explanation has been liberatory. Austrian philosopher Ludwig Wittgenstein writes that, "We must do away with all explanation, and description alone must take its place" (in Shotter 2008, p.13). Explanation is a finite process that claims to state what something truly means. Description, on the other hand, brings people closer to the experience and creates a space for the reader's own perspective. Norwegian therapist, Tom Andersen, critiqued his earlier claims to explanation in an epilogue saying, "If I had written the book today the words explain and explanation would have been replaced by understand and understanding" (Shotter & Katz 1998, p.81; Andersen 1991, p.158). I was not after a rigid stable explanation of my work, but a fluid and useful engagement with it.

Janice DeFehr, a Canadian social construction informed therapist, introduced me to compelling practices of dialogical approaches to inquiry that invite a messy and generative process to emerge (DeFehr 2008, 2007; Lather 2010; Law 2004). This excited me as I wanted to find a way to attend to outliers in my inquiry, reflections that were in the margins not the centre, as that is where activists are, as well as many people I know as workers and clients. Imelda McCarthy captured my interest speaking of her Irish informed understanding that "the illumination is in the margins" (personal communication, 1996). McCarthy credits her culture-informed reading of *the Book of Kells* with this teaching (Kearney *et al.* 1989). *The Book of Kells* is a precious copy of the gospels in which the text is surrounded by beautifully painted borders containing elaborate celtic knots. I wanted to amplify teachings from the margins that were evoked in my inquiry.

Outliers can be silenced in research, and I engaged a spirit of solidarity to resist producing normalizing, heteronormative research. I didn't want to 'prove' anything. As Leonard Peltier, a political prisoner and American Indian Movement leader says, "We're not supposed to be perfect, we're supposed to be useful" (1999, p.10). I wanted to engage queer and anarchist space, "spaces of justice" (Lacey 2005b), and deliberately forged "spaces of inclusion" (Lacey 2010a). This required resisting the disappearances that result from using mutually exclusive categories. African-American critical race theorist Kimberly Crenshaw's work on intersectionality problematizes categories as a taken for granted useful way to make meanings of information. Crenshaw contests the creation of separate identity categories such as race and gender, "The categories we consider natural or merely representational are actually socially constructed in a linguistic economy of difference" (1995, p.375). Categories are always influenced by power and always exclude. They can obscure more than they reveal as they silence outliers and dissenting voices, which I was finely attuned to as an activist in the current political climate of the criminalization of dissent.

In response to these concerns and intentions for the inquiry process I engaged with Adele Clark's postmodern response to Grounded Theory, which she calls Situational Analysis (2005). Clark resists analysis that delivers the truth of situations, and employs messy mapping to make space for outliers, complexity and divergent voices. Messy Mapping invites the person doing the inquiry to show up, not disappear, in the decision making process of deciding what will be attended to, what resonates and what is of use. From this lovely mess of responses a more ordered or understandable story of the experience can be told.

Messy inquiry allows for attending to what is of interest and what resonates. Over eighty practitioners who participated with me offered reflections and critiques of their experience from within the practice of Solidarity Groups. These groups were not homogeneous, and varied in the number of workers involved and the context of the work. Some occurred as part of paid supervision work, others were hosted at conferences, trainings and team days. Questions were offered to evoke responses, but these questions changed in the process as better questions were offered to me, and as some workers responded by writing emails, or phoning, or catching up afterwards for dialogue in person. As well my interest and focus was transported by some of the experiences of the group, and I inquired about different aspects of the work. Engaging with a messy process allowed for continually redirecting the inquiry based on what participants found interesting and what they were paying attention to. I also attended to my own interests, reading, resonating thoughts, and emergent practices. These generative responses informed both the doing of the Solidarity Group and the attempts to describe the Guiding Intentions that grounded it.

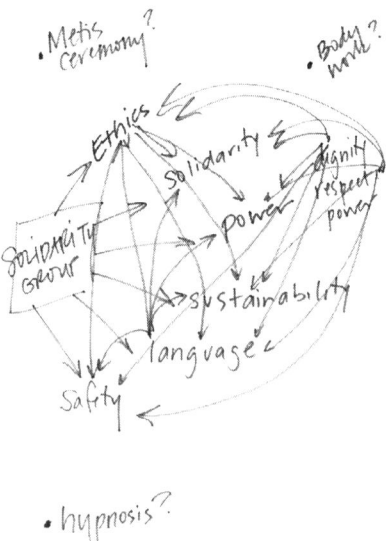

The diagram above is a skeletal retelling of the messy map created from practitioners' responses to what they thought were the ethical underpinnings of my practice and our collective experiences in the Solidarity Groups. Using this messy map, I discerned six Guiding Intentions. Committing these Guiding Intentions to writing required that I order them in some way. Despite using letters instead of numbers I couldn't get outside of rank ordering in the writing. To destabilize the notion that these Guiding Intentions exist in a hierarchy I used Deleuze and Guattari's rhizome to illustrate them, allowing for more fluidity and mess.

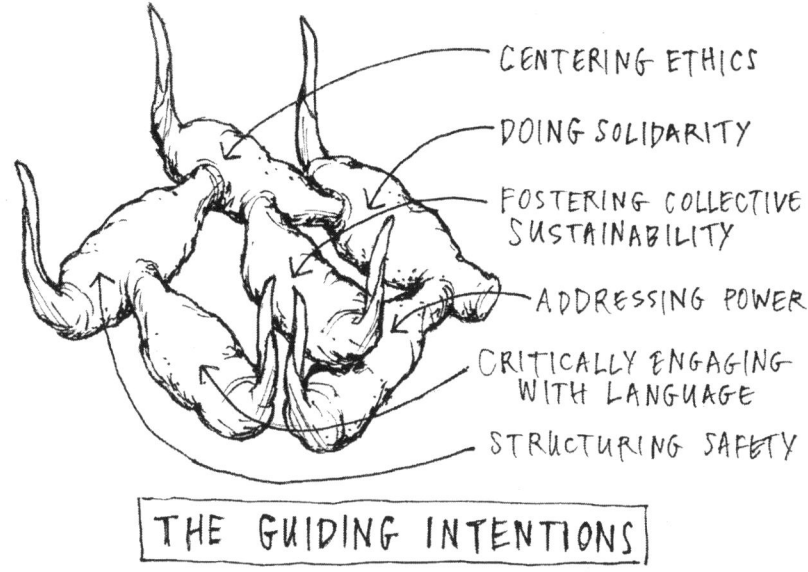

CENTERING ETHICS

DOING SOLIDARITY

FOSTERING COLLECTIVE SUSTAINABILITY

ADDRESSING POWER

CRITICALLY ENGAGING WITH LANGUAGE

STRUCTURING SAFETY

THE GUIDING INTENTIONS

Like a rhizome, the Guiding Intentions were rough around the edges, disorderly, not of equal size, and resisted mathematical precision. They defied mutually exclusive categories, and grew into and out of each other, The Guiding Intentions that emerged in the inquiry were: centering ethics, doing solidarity, fostering collective sustainability, addressing power, critically engaging with language, and structuring safety. (See Appendix 1 for a description of the Guiding Intentions. For a rich description there is a chapter on each Guiding Intention in the dissertation [Reynolds 2010a] *Doing justice as a path to sustainability in community work*).

Guiding Intentions coexist in relationship with each other, much as the filaments of a rhizome. They are linked, overlapping, living, and fluid. For example, all of the Guiding Intentions are inextricably linked with Structuring Safety, and yet Structuring Safety is itself considered a Guiding Intention. Taking one Guiding Intention out of the rhizome for investigation is required, but artificial, as they exist relationally, and need to be re-connected in the rhizome, with the other Guiding Intentions in order to be useful, much as an ethical stance requires intersectionality, solidarity, and is immensely inter-dependent.

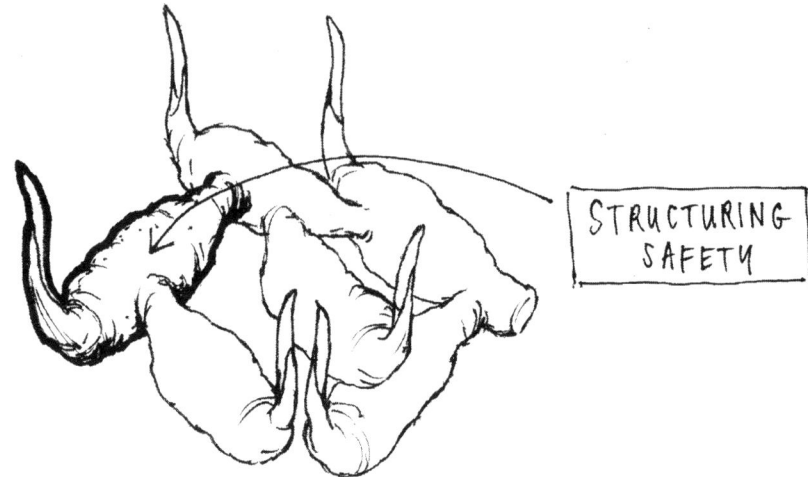

The writing of this ethical stance and the six chapters which offered rich descriptions of the Guiding Intentions which comprised it can be read in any order. They could have been organized in different ways, as the rhizome can be entered onto at any point and defies a static order. The Guiding Intentions are differentiated under six headings to provide clearer understandings, but there could have been ten headings, or four. These six Guiding Intentions identify the main threads of my ethical stance, and they also flow well into the themes that I follow in practice. For the purposes of clarifying the Guiding Intentions I differentiated them from each other. In practice and in action, however, it is not possible, nor required, to completely separate one Guiding Intention from another.

These Guiding Intentions differed from principles in that they had fluid boundaries and were not mutually exclusive. Guiding Intentions were more slippery to operationalize than a set of principles. Practice is messy, and people do not actually engage with linear principles. The Guiding Intentions were offered as an heuristic, which is a possible way of moving towards a goal (Moustakas 1990). This differs from principles which may comprise an algorithm which is a set of specific steps that will lead to a predetermined and known end.

This ethical stance is not finite or fixed, but always in flux, expanding in width and depth with changes in texture and tone as experience, community workers, and clients inform and transform me, and as we counter influence each other, our communities and our environment. This reflexive process of examining and re-creating my ethical stance follows critical educator Paulo Freire's teachings of praxis (1970). Action is followed by reflection, which informs actions which are more *just*, which rolls into further reflection, and so it continues. Popular Education teaches that acting without theorizing can be unsafe and ineffective (Fanon 1961; Freire 1970). Without this understanding of theorizing as a reflexive exercise I could replicate oppressive practices, or more simply, use power in unethical ways.

In consultation John Winslade offered this insightful critique of my use of the term 'theory' in the Solidarity Approach, particularly as it denotes a "level of abstraction" when my inquiry is alive and practice-based. He suggests Deleuze's understandings of 'concepts' as a more useful description:

> "Deleuze talks in one place about the task of the philosopher as being to generate 'concepts' that people can use (the rhizome is an example) and it seemed to me that this is in part what you are doing. Working to identify from the discourse at the local level expressions that can be treated as useful for doing meaning-making around and doing justice with" (personal communication, 2012).

Strategies for a Solidarity Approach

Many strategies were engaged to promote the spirit of solidarity throughout this inquiry. Some of the most useful ones are outlined here. (They are not rank ordered.)

1. Not researching people who are exploited
The centre of this inquiry was my work, which I invited workers I supervised to critique and reflect upon as an accountability practice.

2. Resist contributing to dead knowledge
It was important that this work matter, that it could possibly make a contribution to social change and that I did not engage with inquiry primarily to earn a higher degree. As Lather says, this work tries to do something, not say something.

3. Frontline worker consultant and reader
An intention of the work was to welcome all workers, including those unfamiliar with social justice language and therapeutic language into the work. To serve this purpose a new community worker, Jaime Wittmack, served as an outside reader and a cultural consultant (Waldegrave &

Tamasese 1993). Jaime read all of the drafts and offered a critique to encourage clear-enough writing, accessibility, and promote the purpose of the writing, which was to engage and invite, not marginalize. This consultation was generative in multiple ways. For example, Jaime encouraged the use of footnotes not merely as references, but to expand the text while keeping it uncluttered. She reflected that extensive references inside the writing distracted her from the ideas, and left her feeling 'stupid'. Jaime suggested that the people being referenced be introduced, and I took the opportunity to identify their profession and culture to give newer readers some context and possible connection to the knowledge. Jaime taught me to write in ways that honoured and welcomed the workers I was most trying to be of use to.

4. Networked communities of cultural consultants
Cultural consultants from anarchist and activist communities, queer and transgendered communities, as well as refugees and survivors of political violence and torture played an important role in this inquiry. These cultural consultants offered critiques of this writing and my work and analysis with an aim towards more accountability and resisting the appropriation of ideas. The qualification for these consultants was not their academic certification but rather their life experiences and positionings. These generative critiques freed me from being paralyzed by guilt, and helped me resist a false humility that could have silenced what I do know and have done. This inspiring and committed collection of folks served as my Solidarity Team (Reynolds 2011b) for this inquiry.

5. Referencing widely
References are a gift to the reader and, to invite more accountability, I identified my references in terms of their multiple cultural locations. Referencing widely, and attributing cultural knowledges to more than published works, helped historicize the knowledges of communities that could otherwise be disappeared. The history of the ideas and practices is as important to hold in collective memory as the more accessible published accounts of the ideas. This use of extensive referencing invited more history-making from the communities which have informed this work.

6. Resisting appropriation
While my ethical stance was fully my own and I held myself accountable to its claims, I acknowledge that it was co-created in important and meaningful ways. The teachings of the people I worked alongside who are refugees, activists, and survivors of torture and political violence are

central to this stance. It is important to acknowledge the differential price extracted from people from the global south and racialized and minoritized people from the global north. I recognized the generosity which has enabled them to teach me and for me to benefit from their lived experiences. Part of this writing was a testament and witnessing of these ideas, offering an invitation into the rich histories of these ideas and practices in activist cultures and social movements. This stance of accountability, which is a teaching from activism, embodied my resistance to appropriation, which is always a risk for persons and groups holding non-academic and alternative knowledges.

7. Co-writing

This inquiry, like all of my work, was profoundly collaborative, so I worked to make the collaboration public by referencing widely, inviting reflections and co-authors, and weaving my relationships with real people into the scholarship, honourings and acknowledgments. Co-writing some of these stories helped bring the ideas from the academic realm into practice. Negotiating permission for this storytelling required slowing down the process and extensive back-and-forth dialogue. As part of this co-writing I engaged with real-time storytelling in hopes of offering a retelling that was close to the experience. This also allowed a person's own voice to carry their wisdom, as opposed to me interpreting and possibly appropriating their knowledge. I was invited into real-time storytelling by Arden Henley (1994, 1992), who credited the idea to the work of David Epston (1989) and most particularly David's inspiring story of *Dory the Cat*.

8. Public domain and free access

Because this inquiry was so profoundly collaborative the book is available for free download. Other writers have registered their work as Copyleft. Anyone can use it, morph it, and copy it, as long as they don't capitalize on it — sell it. In this sense it, like much activist collective wisdom, becomes part of the commons we hold collectively.

9. Engaging inconsistently with anonymity

In order to fully credit and name people's contributions and not subsume their ideas into my voice I resisted ideas of total confidentiality. The mixed approach to confidentiality was not smooth, and I reluctantly participated in the marginalizing of some communities by perpetrating the use of pseudonyms. The aim in doing this was to avoid putting workers at risk for sharing their knowledges. For example, in relating the story of Tina, who identified herself as an Aboriginal transgendered woman, I had the choice to steal her voice, silence it, or participate in making her knowledge sharing *safe-enough* by using a pseudonym. I have not resolved my ethical struggle and discomfort in relation to Tina, and my response to this is to work towards justice alongside other allies so that in a possible future she may use her own name and experience that as a *safe-enough* thing to do. A consistent use of confidentiality would smooth over this discomfort, but would also mask important differences in access to power that were made public by this messy and inconsistent use of pseudonyms and names.

10. Liberatory language practices
An important solidarity strategy was to commit to using language in ways that resisted the social construction of pathologizing and marginalizing identities. The possibilities created by language practices that assist people in being seen in ways they experience as liberatory inspired me. With this in mind I invited people participating in this inquiry to self-identify their gender, culture and orientations.

American queer theorist Judith Butler problematizes the binary of gender, man/woman, especially as it denies queer identities and alternative possible spaces (1990). I used androgynous language constructions such as 'them', 'they', 'our', and 'this person'. My purpose was for people to self-identify, or choose not to identify their gender. Some participants who self-identify as differently gendered people struggle to live and be seen outside of the binary of man/woman. The point is not to use inclusive and space-making language only when speaking of people who exist outside of the gender binary, but to use it everywhere to expand possibility for everyone's preferred and liberatory identities.[6]

11. Making discomfort and fear public
The ethical tensions experienced in the inquiry process were not smoothed over, but made public. This was of course flawed because my awareness and analysis is imperfect. Part of the aim was to invite more critique and generative engagement with the ethical struggles the inquiry engendered.

Emerging transformations: Holding onto a fish that is morphing into an octopus.

The reflexivity of this inquiry process has greatly informed my approach to the work and changed the practice itself. The participants engaged in the Solidarity Group served as witnesses for my work and for the Guiding Intentions that inform my practice. Several practitioners have caught me up on the value of participating in the process, an ethic that Tuhiwai Smith speaks of in Decolonizing Methodologies (1999).

Engaging in this process has contributed to the emergent creation of new practices in my work with community workers. This inquiry has invited generative conversations with colleagues which are unlikely to have occurred without this project. The critiques made by the cultural consultants, and the dialogues these consultations fostered, have been expansive and illuminating. I experience all of these unexpected developments as nourishing support for my own sustainability. My experiences in this inquiry have transformed me in terms of holding a more enriched and useful critical analysis. The experiences of activism and community work recursively transform and counter-inform each other as we bring learnings across domains of practice.

The collective dialogue from inside the practice is breathing new life into the doing of the Solidarity Group. In response to this still-continuing collaborative transformation, I experience writing up this work as akin to holding onto a fish that is morphing into an octopus.

Unsettled fears and discomforts

Inquiry does not exist without risk despite our *just* intentions. In a Solidarity Approach, like all anti-oppression activism, we strategize to hold our work accountable to our collective ethics. As American activist/ musician Ani DiFranco says, "Any tool is a weapon if you hold it right" (1993). I believe that the Solidarity Group can be used in harmful ways if it is picked up in a mechanistic or formulaic way divorced from the ethics for justice-doing on which it is rooted. If the ethical stance is read or presented as finished, fixed, correct and righteous it can also be used oppressively.

A lesser fear is that the work could be de-contextualized and de-politicized. Activists have seen this happen to many of our tactics and practices. For example, *Adbusters* magazine was initially a fresh voice of deconstructing capitalism's hegemonic advertising system (Adbusters: Journal of the Mental Environment). Over time, however, anti-ads became trendy and *Adbusters* finally became an unofficial textbook for advertisers, ultimately becoming a tool of selling (Heath & Potter 2004*)*. The potential for liberatory tactics to be de-politicized or co-opted (Hayden 2008) is not paralyzing for me. As activists we know that our tactics of resistance are anticipated and their effectiveness over time will be purposefully minimized. In a spirit of solidarity we respond to this with creative ways of being that bring forth our ever emergent resistance and the next liberatory tactic.

In contrast, the fear of my participation in the appropriation of activist culture is paralyzing. To this end, I have referenced widely, invited, pursued and sought out critique from diverse people who have the moral courage to confront me as a practice of solidarity. This is not based on righteousness, but on my experiences of being the person who has transgressed, and who others have needed allies against (Reynolds 2010d).

This inquiry has occurred at the cost of my engagement with more direct forms of activism in terms of time and resources. I will probably not be able to smooth over my discomfort regarding the elevation of my status and the undeniable privilege that comes with academic qualification. This discomfort is not the same as guilt, as Chomsky invites us to not posture with false modesty, but acknowledge that in a diversity of tactics there are roles some of us accomplish easier and more usefully, and that we are less suited to other pieces of the work. Like many social justice oriented activist/academics I plan to be accountable for this academic privilege.

Re-situating the work back into the rhizome

Part of a Solidarity Approach requires that the work that is held up for consideration be re-situated within the rhizome, returning to the networked communities who fostered it. From here it might decompose and possibly nourish other work, or it could be morphed, changed, or reused.

Here the work settles as a re-connected piece of something far greater, something Lacey describes as contributing to spaces of justice (2005b). It becomes part of, another node of social justice activism and liberatory theorizing: No more and no less.

The value of the ethical stance described in the Guiding Intentions and of the practice of the Solidarity Group lie in how they are used. In bridging decolonizing anti-oppression activism and inquiry my hope is that practitioners will take up this invitation to join in a collaborative inquiry, and contribute multiple and generative responses to the Guiding Intentions and develop new practices. It has been increasingly sustaining for me to hear back from community workers who have taken up this invitation and furthered the diversity of possible practices that share a spirit of solidarity. Like "rhizomic organisms growing horizontally into new terrains, establishing connections just below the surface of every day life, eventually bursting forth in unpredictable ways" (Uzelman 2005, p.17).

Dedication

For Arden Henley, Cathy Richardson and Allan Wade, who encouraged me back to the academy, and continue to feed my hungry hope for liberatory pedagogy that does more than make room for direct action activists, but meets us in the rhizome.

This writing took place on Indigenous land which has never been surrendered.

Acknowledgments

This work is profoundly collaborative, and co-created by diverse fellowships of activists, workers, clients, teachers, colleagues and family who have inspired, critiqued and taught me across time. Thanks to Gail Simon for finding value in my solidarity inquiry, affinity in the rhizome with her 'underground writing', and fostering our lovely and imperfect solidarity. My advisors at the TAOS Institute, Ken Gergen and Sallyann Roth allowed room for a Solidarity Approach, without which I could not have completed my academic writing. Other faculty, Sheila McNamee, Sally St. George, Dan Wulff and Imelda McCarthy, were generous with their expertise, time and critique. Fellow students, Christine Dennstedt, Aileen Tierney, Ottar Ness, Janet Newbury and Janice De Fehr continue to shoulder me up in the work, offering excellent and generative critique. Jeff Smith, John Winslade, Sheila McNamee, Mr. Peaslee, and Ken Gergen served as my Solidarity Team for this project. Their solidarity has been more important to me than they can know. Thanks to Marie Hoskins, who invited me to lecture her graduate students at the University of Victoria. The expansive critique which followed contributed to this writing. Finally, my appreciation for the creativity and talent of Kent Peaslee for the diagrams, and Yvonne Hii for layout.

Appendix1. An ethical stance for justice-doing

My ethical stance for *justice-doing* is comprised of six Guiding Intentions:

A. Centering Ethics

The centre of my supervision is our relational ethics and ethical positioning as we respond to clients' varying needs from within contexts of power. When practitioners cannot act in accord with our ethics we experience spiritual pain. Spiritual pain speaks to the discrepancy between what feels respectful, humane, and generative, and contexts which call on us as community workers to violate the very beliefs that brought us to this field. I centre my inquiry on the ethical stance of the practitioner, our collective ethics, and how these ethics are revealed in practice.

B. Doing Solidarity

My understandings of solidarity are derived from time honoured activist traditions of looking for points of connection and weaving people together. I attend to both practices of resisting oppression and promoting social justice. This spirit of doing solidarity acknowledges that our struggles to promote social justice are interconnected.

C. Addressing Power

Addressing Power speaks to witnessing both resistance and acts of justice-doing. It also invites cultural and collective accountability. Accountability requires a complex analysis, in which the multiplicity of sites of both power and oppression are acknowledged and addressed.

D. Fostering Collective Sustainability

Sustainability refers to aliveness, a spirited presence, and a genuine connectedness with others. It requires more than resisting burnout, more than keeping a desperate hold on hope; and yet it encompasses both of these capacities. We are sustained in the work when we are able to be fully and relationally engaged, stay connected with hope, and experience ourselves as being of use to clients across time. Sustainability is inextricably linked with an alive engagement with a spirit of social justice, and openness to our transformations as practitioners across time.

E. Critically Engaging with Language

Language can be used to serve or resist abuses of power. I hold an overt intention of utilizing language in liberatory ways. Critically engaging with language also acknowledges the dialogue that exists outside of words, and invites languaging the body.

F. Structuring Safety

Co-creating relationships of *enough-safety* outside of the binary of safe and unsafe helps to structure safety (Bird 2000). All conversations across difference are risky, and are of greater risk to some than to others. The possibility of doing harm by replicating some kind of oppression is one potential risk. I am also aware of the limitations of accountability. Social justice is better served by creating contexts in which the transgression is less likely to occur. This requires Structuring Safety (Reynolds 2010c).

Notes

1 The terms *minoritized* and *racialized* are used for the purpose of naming the power and intention required in the racist and colonial project of re-constructing the majority of the world's people as a collection of minorities.
2 "Queer" has been adopted by groups of people I work with, both workers and clients, who do not identify as strictly heterosexual. Using queer as an

umbrella term to include folks who self-identify as lesbian, gay, bisexual, Two Spirit, questioning and queer, is problematic for many reasons (Fassinger & Arsenau, 2007). Primarily people who self identify as lesbian, for example, may not resonate with queer theory or politics at all, and be subsumed by that term. As well, some folks who do identify as queer mean specific things by it, such as resonating with queer theory in ways that do not align them with gay or lesbian identities, and find using the term queer as an umbrella term mystifies and erases the queer politics and ethics that are at the heart of their preferred ways of identifying (Aaron Munro, personal communication, 2012). People I work alongside who identify as queer may be in any of these groups, but primarily identify outside of heterosexual normativity, which refers to discourses which promote heterosexuality as normal. People who I work alongside who self-identify as Two Spirit refer to their cultural location as Indigenous people who do not identify as heterosexual: Two Spirit refers to rich cultural knowings as well. People who I work alongside who identify as transgender or trans do not identify strictly with the gender they were assigned to at birth, and may transition culturally, socially and/ or physically to a gender in which they feel more congruent, which could be something other than male or female (Nataf 1996; Devon McFarlane, personal communication, 2011). Many people do not identify their gender in any way, and others identify as gender variant, gender non-conforming or gender queer, meaning something different than trans and outside of the normative gender binary (Janelle Kelly, personal communication, 2011). All of these terms are problematic, contested and evolving. I am using these terms for clarity and because groups of folks I work alongside have settled on this imperfect phrasing for now (Reynolds 2010b).

3 Kvale (1996 p.203) borrows the term "hermeneutics of suspicion" from the work of French philosopher Paul Ricoeur (1970). "His hermeneutic is always informed by both a suspicion which makes him wary of any easy assimilation to past meanings and as hope that believes in complete appropriation of meanings while warning 'not here', 'not yet'. Via suspicion and hope, Ricoeur plots a hermeneutic course that avoids both credulity and skepticism" (White 1991, p.12).

4 "The School of the Americas... is a controversial U.S. military training facility for Latin American security personnel located at Fort Benning, Georgia, made headlines in 1996 when the Pentagon released training manuals used at the school that advocated torture, extortion and execution." Consult the School of the Americas Watch website for a critique of this military project (School of the Americas Watch, 2009).

5 The Solidarity Group is described extensively in my dissertation (2010a) and in an article entitled A Supervision of Solidarity (2010c). The Solidarity Group emphasizes our collective sustainability with a specific aim to build solidarity and an orientation for justice-doing. At the center of the conversation are themes connected to centering ethics, doing solidarity, addressing power, fostering collective sustainability, critically engaging with language, and structuring safety. This is different than organizing therapeutic supervision around specific problems and individual workers. The Solidarity Group is only one component of the necessary supervision of therapists,

with an emphasis on collective sustainability of the therapeutic community and their relational ethics. In the Solidarity Group the supervisor is not the primary resource, this role is played by a community of workers. Although one person is interviewed, the centre is the whole group. In Solidarity Groups the therapeutic community is being supervised collectively. In many ways, it does not matter who is speaking as the entire group is at the center. As the supervisor I look for themes that resonate with the principles of a Supervision of Solidarity. I attend to emergent experiences which hold meaning for the therapeutic community, not necessarily the individual being interviewed. These experiences may be acts of justice, ethical struggles, startling successes, painful losses, or other occurrences which hold meaning collectively. As the supervisor it is my task to ensure that all participants are witnessed in the conversation, and that people are woven together.

6   An excellent example of binary busting language is the adoption of the term *pomosexuality* by some members of some queer communities. "Pomosexuality lives in the space in which all other non-binary forms of sexual and gender identity reside – a boundary-free zone in which fences are crossed for the fun of it, or simply because some of us can't be fenced in. It challenges either/or categorizations in favour of largely un-mapped possibility and the intense charge that comes from transgression. It acknowledges the pleasure of that transgression, as well as *the need to transgress limits that do not make room for all of us*." (my emphasis) Queen & Schimel (1997), p.23.

References

Adbusters: Journal of the Mental Environment. Vancouver, British Columbia: Adbusters Media Foundation.

Andersen, Tom (1991). *The reflecting team: Dialogues and dialogues about the dialogues*. New York: Norton.

Anderson, Harlene (1997). *Conversation, language, and possibilities: A postmodern approach to therapy*. New York: Basic Books.

Beckett, Samuel (1958). *The Unnamable*. New York: Grove Press.

Bird, Johnella (2000). *The heart's narrative: Therapy and navigating life's contradictions*. Auckland, New Zealand: Edge Press.

Butler, Judith (1990). *Gender trouble: Feminism and the subversion of identity*. New York: Routledge.

Chomsky, Noam (2005). *Chomsky on anarchism*. B. Pateman (Ed.). Edinburgh: AK Press.

Clarke, Adele E. (2005). *Situational Analysis: Grounded theory after the Postmodern Turn*. London: Sage Publications.

Crenshaw, Kimberle (1995). Mapping the margins: Intersectionality, identity politics, and violence against women of colour. In K. Crenshaw, G. Gotanda, G. Peller, & K. Thomas (Eds.), *Critical race theory: The key writings that formed the movement* (pp.357-383). New York: The New Press.

DeFehr, Janice (2008). *Transforming Encounters and Interactions: A Dialogical Inquiry Into the Influence of Collaborative Therapy In the Lives of Its Practitioner*. Retrieved from http://www.taosinstitute.net/

DeFehr, Janice (2007). *Dialogical methods of social inquiry*. Unpublished paper.

Deleuze, Giles & Guattari, Félix. (1987). *A thousand plateaus: Capitalism and schizophrenia*. London: Athlone Press.

DiFranco, Ani (1993). My IQ. On *Puddle dive* [CD]. Righteous Babe Records.

Epston, David (1989). *Collected Papers*. Adelaide, Australia: Dulwich Centre Publications.

Fanon, Frantz (1961). *The wretched of the earth*. New York: Grove Weidenfeld Publishers.

Fassinger, Ruth & Arsenau, Julie (2007). "I'd rather get wet than be under the umbrella": Differentiating the experiences and identities of lesbian, gay, bisexual, and transgendered people. In K. Bieschke, R. Perez, & K. Debord (Eds.), *Handbook of counselling and psychology with lesbian, gay, bisexual and transgendered clients* (2nd ed., pp.19-50). Washington, DC: American Psychological Association.

Fine, Michelle (2006). Bearing witness: Methods for researching oppression and resistance-A textbook for critical research. *Social Justice Review,* 19(1), 83-108.

Freire, Paolo (1970). *Pedagogy of the oppressed*. New York: Continuum.

Gergen, Kenneth (2005). *An invitation to social construction*. Thousand Oaks, CA: Sage Publications.

Hayden, Tom (2008). *Writings for a democratic society: The Tom Hayden reader*. San Francisco, CA: City Lights Books.

Heath, Joseph & Potter, Andrew (2004*). The rebel sell: Why the culture can't be jammed*. Toronto, Ontario, Canada: Harper Collins.

Henley, Arden (1992). Dory the cat runs away. *Australia and New Zealand Journal of Family Therapy,* 13(4).

Henley, Arden (1994). Stories that have heart: Narrative practices with children and their families. *Journal of Child and Youth Care,* 9(2).

hooks, bell (1984). *Feminist theory: From margin to center*. Cambridge: South End Press

hooks, bell (1994). *Teaching to transgress: Education as the practice of freedom*. New York: Routledge.

hooks, bell (2000). *Feminism is for everybody: Passionate politics*. Cambridge, England: South End Press.

Jagose, A. (1996). *Queer theory: An introduction*. Melbourne, Australia: Melbourne University Press.

Kearney, Phil; Byrne, Nollaig O'Reilly & McCarthy, Imelda Colgan (1989). Just metaphors: Marginal illuminations in a colonial retreat. *Family Therapy Case Studies,* 4(1), 17-31.

Kvale, Steinar. (1996). *Inter-views: An introduction to qualitative research interviewing*. London: Sage Publications.

Lacey, Anita (2005a). Networked communities: Social centres and activist spaces in contemporary Britain. *Space and Culture: The Journal.* 8(3), 286-299.

Lacey, Anita (2005b). Spaces of justice: The social divine of global anti-capital activists' sites of resistance. *CRSA/RCSA,* 42(4), 407.

Lather, Patti (1993). Fertile obsession: Validity after poststructuralism. *The Sociological Quarterly,* 34(4), 673-693.

Lather, Patti (2010) Engaging *Science Policy: From the Side of the Messy*. New York: Peter Lang.

Law, John (2004). *After method: Mess in social science research*. London: Routledge.

Lawrence, Bonita & Dua, Enakshi (2005). Decolonizing Anti-Racism. *Social Justice: A journal of crime, conflict and world order*. Vol. 32, No. 4. 120-143.

Madigan, Stephen (2011). *Narrative Therapy*. Washington: American Psychological Association.

McCarthy, Imelda (2001). Fifth province re-versings: The social construction of women lone Parents' inequality and poverty. *Journal of Family Therapy*, 23, 253-277.

McLaren, Peter & Leonard, Peter (1993). *Paulo Freire: A critical encounter*. London: Routledge.

McNamee, Sheila (2008). The Lindberg Lecture. *Transforming dialogue: Coordinating conflicting moralities*. Retrieved from http://pubpages.unh.edu/~smcnamee/dialogue_and_transformation/LindbergPub2008.pdf

Moustakas, Clark. (1990). *Heuristic research*. Newbury Park, CA: SAGE Publications.

Nataf, Zachary (1996). *Lesbians talk Transgender*. London: Scarlet Press.

Newbury, Janet (2011). A Place for Theoretical *In*consistency. *International Journal of Qualitative Methods*. 10 (4): 335-347.

Peltier, Leonard (1999). *Prison writings: My life is my Sundance*. New York: St. Martins Griffin.

Queen, Carol & Schimel, Lawrence (1997). *Pomosexuals: Challenging assumptions about gender and sexuality*. San Francisco, CA: Cleis Press.

Reynolds, Vikki (2009). Collective ethics as a path to resisting burnout. *Insights: The Clinical Counsellor's Magazine & News., December 2009, 6-7.*

Reynolds, Vikki (2010a). *Doing justice as a path to sustainability in community work*. PhD thesis. Taos Institute. Retrieved from http://www.taosinstitute.net/vikki-reynolds1

Reynolds, Vikki (2010b). Doing justice: A witnessing stance in therapeutic work alongside survivors of torture and political violence. In J. Raskin, S. Bridges, & R. Neimeyer (Eds.), *Studies in meaning 4: Constructivist perspectives on theory, practice, and social justice*. New York: Pace University Press.

Reynolds, Vikki (2010c). A Supervision of Solidarity. *Canadian Journal of Counselling*, 44(3), 246-257.

Reynolds, Vikki (2010d). Fluid and Imperfect Ally Positioning: Some Gifts of Queer Theory. *Context*. October 2010. Association for Family and Systemic Therapy, UK, 13-17.

Reynolds, Vikki (2011a). Resisting burnout with justice-doing. *The International Journal of Narrative Therapy and Community Work*. (4) 27-45.

Reynolds, Vikki (2011b). Supervision of solidarity practices: Solidarity teams and people-ing-the-room. *Context*. August 2011. Association for Family and Systemic Therapy, UK, 4-7.

Reynolds, Vikki (2011c). The role of allies in anti-violence work. *Ending Violence Association of BC Newsletter*. (2) 1-4

Richardson, Cathy (2004). *Becoming Métis: The relationship between the sense of Métis self and cultural stories*. Unpublished doctoral dissertation. University of Victoria School of Child and Youth Care.

Ricoeur, Paul (1970). *Freud and philosophy: An essay on interpretation*. New Haven, CT: Yale University Press.

Sanders, Colin (1997). Re-authoring problem identities: Small victories with young persons captured by substance misuse. In C. Smith, & D. Nylund (Eds.), *Narrative therapies with children and adolescents* (pp.400-422). New York: Guilford.

School of the Americas Watch (January 26, 2009). Human Rights Advocates Face Six Months in Federal Prison for Nonviolent Direct Action Opposing the School of the Americas (SOA/ WHINSEC). Retrieved January 28, 2009 from http://www.soaw.org/pressrelease.php?id=143

Shotter, J. (2008). *Conversational realities revisited: Life, language, body and world*. Chagrin Falls, OH: Taos Institute Publications.

Shotter, John & Katz, Arlene (1998). 'Living Moments" in dialogic exchanges. *Human Systems: The Journal of Systemic Consultation & Management*. Vol.9 No. 2.pp.81-93.

Smith, Jeff (2010). Entering the Rhizome: A description of a music therapy street outreach program. *The Drumbeat*, 11(2), 10-12.

Smith. Jeff (2011). *Just orientations: Analysis of membership categorization during Response-Based conversations about violence and resistance*. Unpublished doctoral dissertation. University of Victoria School of Child and Youth Care.

St. George, Sally & Wulff, Dan (2012, 2, 12). *Research as Daily Practice*. SOWK 655, Edmonton, Alberta.

Tuhiwai Smith, Linda (1999). *Decolonizing methodologies: Research and indigenous peoples*. London: Zed Books Ltd.

Uzelman, Scott (2005). Hard at work in the bamboo garden: Media activists and social movements. In A. Langlois, & F. Dubois (Eds.), *Autonomous media: Activating resistance and dissent* (pp.17-27). Montreal, Quebec, Canada: Cumulus Press.

Wade, Allan (1997). Small acts of living: Everyday resistance to violence and other forms of oppression. *Journal of Contemporary Family Therapy*, 19(l), 23-40.

Waldegrave, Charles & Tamasese, Kiwi (1993). Some central ideas in the 'Just Therapy' approach. Australian and New Zealand Journal of Family Therapy, 14, 1-8.

Walia, Harsha (2012). Decolonizing together: Moving beyond a politics of solidarity toward a practice of decolonization. Retrieved from http:// briarpatchmagazine.com/articles/view/decolonizing-together

White, Erin (1991). Between suspicion and hope: Paul Ricoeur's vital hermeneutic. *Journal of Literature and Theology*, 5, 311-321.

White, Michael (2007). *Maps of narrative practice*. New York: Norton.

Winslade, John (2009). Tracing Lines of Flight: Implications of the Work of Giles Deleuze for Narrative Practice. *Family Process*, Vol. 48, No. 3, pp 332-346.

Performative Practices, Performative Relationships: in and as Emergent Research

7

Saliha Bava

Introduction

I have been in love with research since I accompanied my mother on her doctoral data collection trip when I was nine years old. My first formal attempt at research was eight years later in the last year of my high school or grammar school. Subsequently, I went on to do research projects in my Bachelors, Masters, Post-Graduate and Doctoral programs. From 1998, I formally started supervising research projects. My research encounters made me curious about the process of research itself.

By the time I was in my Doctoral program, I was determined to make the focus my research the methodological constructions themselves and not solely apply methodological formulas to a substantive issues (or area of inquiry). Often the first time a graduate student is immersing herself[1] in research is during her doctoral dissertation where there will be an emphasis on learning about research process. The traditional idea is to learn the methodology as per the research questions that are preferred within the discipline or by one's research advisor. Experimenting with methodology may not be considered good scientific research (Bernstein 2000).

Scientific research has been reduced to empirical methodologies that are often located within the positivist paradigm. Often, such popular methodologies are considered the true and tested pathways we use for knowledge construction. However, methodological canons are not always reflective of the researcher's philosophical orientation but they shape what we see which is the substantive area (subject matter/ area of inquiry or research focus) of study. What we see is shaped by how we see it (Pearce 2007). The result is a philosophical disconnect between the methodology and the researcher's framework which guides the substantive. This disconnect occurs because the area of inquiry is expected to change and evolve overtime; as it is the subject that is under

---

[1] I will use the male and female gender interchangeably throughout the chapter, to cultivate the image of researchers as contextual beings (gendered in this case).

knowledge construction, while popular methodologies which are the pathways we use for this knowledge construction are not expected to change (Bernstein 2000). This distinction is inherently reflective of a modernist view point where the constructed knowledge is independent of the knower or ways of knowing. Further it fuels the false notion that methodologies do not shape knowledge, thus creating the notion of objectivity. This myth of objectivity is double layered: free of researcher bias and methodological bias.

The process of inquiry is shaped by a community of researchers, people like you and me, who deem certain methodologies as established and thus credible. Researchers and methodologies are embodiments of values and assumptions. Both as researchers and in our ways of knowing we habituate and cultivate certain practices. These practices are value and community-based. Thus, not only is the knower shaping that which we know but the pathway to knowing also shapes that which we know.

The path to knowing is discursive, that is, a responsive dialogic process. Dialogue or conversation is performative, i.e. it is constitutive. By constitutive, I mean that through the discursive process the inter-locutors bring into being that which they name. We are doing/acting when we are speaking or communicating with each other (Gergen 2009; Pearce 2007). In the process of coordinating (Gergen 2009) the activity of dialogue with each other we create the meaning of that which we are speaking. We are creating meaning together that constitutes itself and shapes what emerges next. Such joint action could be experienced as understanding, next steps and/or action items.

Thus, the activity of dialogue, inherent to the research process and our participation within communities of research practices shapes the emergence of methodologies. Any development of new method-ologies or ways of knowing are often referred to as emergent methods (Hesse-Biber & Leavy 2006). However, Hesse-Biber and Leavy claim "Emergent methods are often driven by new epistemologies on knowledge production, which in turn creates new research questions (methodologies) that often require an innovation in methods" (p.xxx). I agree that new methodologies emerge as a response to changing issues such as, "to unearth previously subjugated knowledge" or "new research questions" (p.xxx). Additionally, in the process of doing any research project new methodological practices are potentially being created and recreated. In this chapter I will illustrate how research is a "made-up" activity and thus emergent. I will introduce the notion of research as a community of practice and a construction followed by research as performance and performative. Further, drawing on examples from supervision of research I will introduce an alternate notion of *emergent research.*

Research as community of practice and research as performance and performative form the basis for what I identify as emergent research. I am claiming that all research is *made up* and inherently emergent thus we need to approach research not only as a planned or designed process but also as a messy, chaotic process with surprises that requires one to improvise during the process. And as research supervisors we need to be able to be responsive, playful and flexible with our students or advisees in the process. Let's read on to explore why and how.

Research as Communities of Practice

Community of practice is a term coined by Jean Lave and Etienne Wenger in 1991 which Wenger expands on in his book *Communities of Practice* (1998). According to Wenger "Communities of Practice" are groups of people who share a concern or a passion for something they do and how to do it better as they interact regularly. He emphasizes that it has three elements –domain, community and practice – that sets apart a community of practice from a group of people who share an interest or are in a geographical or online community. It is a group of members who are *practitioners* with *shared domain of interest* who *interact and learn together* and *share resources* (tools, stories, experiences and ways of addressing a problem) (Wenger 1998).

Each research project is not only a product of a community of practice but the concept of research itself is a community of practice. Based on Wenger's notion of Communities of Practice, research methodologies are domains that have groups of practitioners who share stories of tools and approaches when they interact (through conferences, journals, books, online discussions etc). They learn from each other about their shared area of interest (experimental design, observation, interviewing, content analysis, autoethnography, etc). So, not only do we have methodologists grouped by types of methodologies but we also have an umbrella group, to which we all belong by our shared interest in research. The act by which this book was produced and is in your hand is a statement of such a community of practice. This book is a resource for furthering our community of practice about research methodologies by systemic practitioners. This is one of the ways we create traditions and rituals of practice.

McNamee (2004) states, that we create traditions and rituals by coordinating our situated activities. And research is one such tradition that has been created to constitute how knowledge is produced. Research practices that emerge as rituals become standards of practice and grow as the community of practice grows. Over time, these standards of practice get calcified as credible and legitimate practices and determine which processes can be labeled as "research." In the scientific and academic communities, we value the knowledge that is produced in the course of research. Media often privileges such knowledge and promotes it as legitimate knowledge (Figure 1) while distorting it or reconstituting it (depending on your perspective).

We have created traditions, as illustrated in the comic (Figure 1) titled *The Science News Cycle,* where we value the exclusivity of research based knowledges[2] over lived and practitioner knowledges even as it filters through our everyday news sources. In the West, the status of knowledge produced via research is valued higher than the knowledge produced via practice or everyday lived experiences. In fact, we have set up practices where one needs to validate the practitioner's knowledge via research for it to achieve legitimacy; i.e. the distinction of scientific credibility. (How else would you term this distinction?) Practice is seen as more an everyday activity while academic and scientific research is viewed as a more rarified set of communities and practices. We create a dichotomy between research and practice, failing to see research as a form of practice.

People tend to be immersed in "practice" by the very act of living and working in their everyday contexts. Research on the other hand, is crafted within rarified spaces as bounded practices that must embody certain traditions such as research questions, hypothesis, design, validity, reliability, trustworthiness, for example, to be counted as research. And in some disciplines, to be deemed as scientific, the gold standard is the adoption of the experimental research design, specifically the randomized controlled trials, especially in USA (Christ 2014; Denzin 2008). Thus, research spaces become not only rarified spaces but can also become calcified. Whatever innovation occurs has to be within these bounded walls of research to be deemed scientific. Further, we have created methodological practices which are stratified; a form of classism in the guise of classification or categorizing of methodologies. By classism I mean practices by which we create privilege for one set of practices, ways of being and/or people over another. One broad classification continues to hold quantitative as a premier research method

---

[2]   I am using the notion of knowledge here to connote it as a product or commodity to be marketed, sold and acquired.

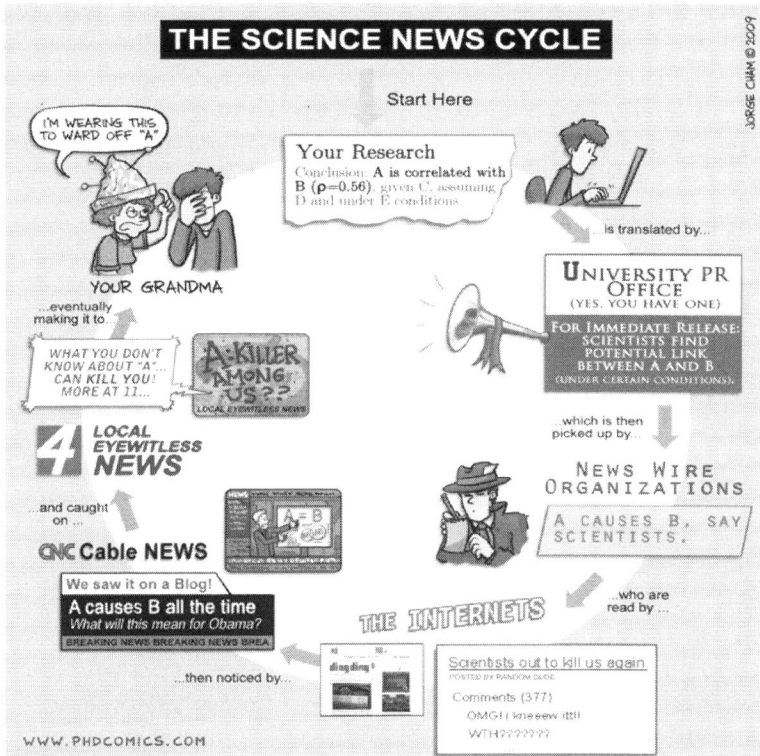

Figure 1. How research results get reconstituted through the news cycle

Source: "Piled Higher and Deeper" by Jorge Cham www.phdcomics.com http://www.phdcomics.com/comics/

compared to qualitative which Denzin (2008) refers to as the "paradigm disputes of the 1980s" and "the paradigm dialogue." This represents the continued legacy of positivist, dualistic thinking. However, there is a move towards mixed methods and increased appreciation of qualitative methods identified as the "third methodological moment" (Teddlie and Tashakkori 2003, p.9).

In a knowledge-based economy (Druker 1969; Smith 2002) where we are seeking equality and equity, the question is whose knowledge counts? And who decides whose knowledge counts? Research is a base for knowledge production and researcher's assumptions of knowledge production need to be critically reflected on. We need to ask the question who does it serve to have a class-based approach towards research methodology? One answer, for example, might be that it serves the people who have access to conduct "gold standards" of research in order to undermine practice-based forms of knowledge, privileging instead practices that are identified as "scientific" forms of knowledge production.

Thus, I invite us to view the performance of "what is research" and how we research (the methodologies) as forms of practice that is grown in coordination with each other as members of the research community. And as we grow, we collectively define what acceptable performances are, and thus we grow our communities of practice. Let us now explore what is research as performance.

Research as Performance

I view performance as a social constructionist turn, so there is no one way to define it. "All performances or actions that are culturally categorized as 'performance' are socially constructed due to the collective consensus of that socio-cultural group within a particular time-space (historical period)" (Bava 2005, p.173). An interdisciplinary notion, performance has multiple definitions depending on the context of its use. Denzin (2003) states "Performance is an act of intervention, a method of resistance, a form of criticism, a way of revealing agency... performance is a form of agency, a way of bringing culture and the person into play" (p. 9). I prefer to draw on Kaye's (1994) notion that performance "may be thought of as a *primary postmodern mode*" (emphasis added, cited in Carlson 1996, p.123). For me performance is "related to the blurring of the boundaries between art and science, literary and scientific, real and virtual, and nature and nurture" (Bava 2005, p.172).

I see currently four ways in which the notion of performance is being used in research discourses. Firstly, as an activity, that is the production of "a thing" that we present as a research project (Bava 2005). From this view point, all research projects are performances. Secondly, it refers to researches that are art-based. The whole production of research is through the medium of art or the purpose is to produce art or inquiry of art and design through the practice of it (Barrett & Bolt 2007). Such work is sometimes also referred to as "practice-led research[3]" (Barrett & Bolt 2007; Hasseman 2006) though it applies to disciplines beyond art and design. Thirdly, as identified by Denzin (2003) performance is a movement of resistance, intervention and a political change-maker. This includes both the way research is produced and the "results" being presented as poetry, prose, art, theater and movies etc. And lastly, the

---

[3] See special issue "Practice-led Research" of Media Information Australia, February 2006.

notion of performance is being increasingly drawn on as a means of evocatively expressing one's research results using art-based methods, such as poetry, stories, theatre, movies etc (Gergen & Gergen 2012; Piercy & Benson 2005). The last two notions of research as performance, are not mutually exclusive rather they depend on the researcher's intentions and how the researcher positions research as a political activity.

Research as performance can be seen in at least two ways: as a form of theatre and/or as a textual performance. Theatres have the potential to give voice. Brecht, German playwright and theater director, states that in the form of popular theatre, called bourgeois theatre, one hangs up their brain along with their hat (Boal, n.d.). Theatre of the Oppressed (Boal 1997) grew in resistance to the bourgeois theatre as an art form for social transformation to unpack the power constructions by engaging in discursive practices via theatre. Thus, rather than viewing research as a form of bourgeois theatre but as a form of activism, we move away from it being as a representational act to a dynamic space for social discourse (Denzin 2003; Madison 2008). In the latter view, research performances are not only giving voice to the subject of inquiry but more so to the research participants, who are not simply objects or subjects of the study, but are co-creators of what is at the heart of the research focus. In the process of giving voice to the heart of the subject matter, there is also the researcher, who has a voice and a supervisor. For instance, as a research supervisor, it is critical for me to create space, conditions for researchers to be directors of their play, for them to have their voice such that I am creating an alternate form of theatre rather than one where the advisees suspend their thinking when adopting research methodologies. I want them to actively question and shape their methodologies in dialogue with their participants as an act of responsiveness. How do we do that? One way is to reflect on research (processes, relationships and outcomes) as a form of theatre and another is to view it as a textual performance.

Research is a text; a performance text of a particular community. Each knowledge community will prescribe and perform what are their dos and don'ts of research practices. A knowledge community can be defined along discipline lines (e.g. management studies, psychology, sociology, economics, marketing, etc) and/or methodology lines (e.g. experimental, ethnography, phenomenology, autoethnography, narrative etc). A distinctive example of this is the research report that is developed at the end of a project which is formatted and styled according to the established communities of practice such as American Psychological Association (APA) or Modern Language Association of

America (MLA) or Harvard style. In the Taos Institute-Tilburg Doctoral programme, where I am an advisor, our students are not told which style to follow but are required to stick to a consistent format. This guideline gives the student space to develop a style that fits with the material and intent that they are crafting within the scope of their inquiry. I think this is critically important. Research reports, though viewed as part of the research process, are seen within a modernist scientific framework as a reporting tool: a story about the research, rather than seeing the reports as part of the tool that is shaping the narrative of research focus. Once again, the idea of objectivity is subversively present within the performance of what is labeled as the "Research Report." Our research reports are political playgrounds (whose voice, who speaks for whom, whose voice is heavier, who decides and how is it decided) (Madison, 2008) which are located within our communities of practices and the context of research. Our experience of the research narrative is shaped not only by its presentation but also in how it engages the reader. Richardson talks about the written performance in academic writing in her book *Fields of Play* (1997). Not only does she introduce the notion of writing as research but also the notion that the written style is not neutral. She states how the academic writing is performed to keep the researcher within the folds of the academia while it fails to engage the reader. To understand the purpose of such a textual performance, let us explore the notion of text in performance.

Research: A Performance Text

W. B. Worthen, a performance theorist, draws on Roland Barthes' uses of the word *text* in performance studies, to state that there are "three interlaced ways we think of a "text": (1) as a canonical vehicle of authorial intention; (2) as an intertext, a field of textuality; (3) as a material object, the text in hand" (1995, p. 14). Drawing on Worthen's interpretation of Barthes, I will unpack research as a textual performance.

Research as a vehicle for authorial intention (power and traditions): In most disciplines, research is used as the authoritative voice to proclaim or sanction practices. It carries the status of being legitimate and credible. Thus, as consumers of knowledge we value statements that are based in research. In fact, we have created the myth that if something is researched, it is fact. We don't see how research is a production and so are "facts" that are produced by research processes. Research which was constructed as a tool now becomes the vehicle for authorial power and a self- perpetuating process to keep alive the traditions by which it was created (Bateson 1972).

***Research as intertext, a space for 'play, activity, production and practice'*:** Research is not just an activity it is also a practice of the communities we belong to and their production. An intertextual (Lemke 1995) production that we hope gives us entry into a particular community and/or is making of that community. In the process of making of communities there is often play and textual politics. We play with textuality and conventions as witnessed in a number of recent works (Barrett & Bolt 2007; Denzin & Giardina 2008; Gergen & Gergen 2012). Elizabeth Bell, performance theorist, states,

> *Textuality [Research] plays with the notion of writing itself-its conventions, its histories, and its interplay with other works in the canon-challenging anyone's claim to authority and enforcement. In this use, texts [research] are open fields, a place of 'play, activity, production, and practices.' (2008, p. 77 parenthetical insertions are mine)*

Research a material object: This is the most common or familiar view of research as performance. In performing research we create a thing called a report or dissertation which is a material object. We often point to the report as if it is the research. Rather it is one of the objects that is crafted in the process of doing an activity that we call research. The production of the research and the report are both performances. One can view both as objects, though the latter is the one that carries the materiality in its form. And we fail to see the materiality of the process or for that matter the process as product.

Research Supervision: An Example of a Situated Performance

Supervision, as the name suggests is inherently hierarchical. As a collaborative practitioner my focuses shifts from the role to the relationship with the question of 'how to re-script the conventional performance of supervision?' I attempt to create a practice of reflection and dialogue about our relationship and process in my supervision to cultivate an openness for us to explore what is being produced in our advising relationship. I use the terms supervision and advising interchangeably to refer to the process of guiding or mentoring a researcher. I stay curious by asking questions such as "how are we working to create this relationship?" or "what do you want me to listen to/for?" I make this a public performance and invite the advisee to reflect with me on how our relationship is fostering and shaping his/her research. Our research is an embedded practice. And one of the spaces that the research is embedded is within our relationship (in addition to the context of the discipline and study, with the participants, committees and universities). So it is important for me to seek reflection on our relationship in relation to the project itself and the researcher's expectations and goals. Such a conversation foregrounds both our relationship and its relationship to the project. These conversations are also spontaneous. It is an invitation to be in a relational and responsive space that is constitutive of the process rather than be in a role. Thus, I attempt to foreground supervision as a space of spontaneous play, activity, production, practice and a product of dialogue, reflection, and responsiveness that is constitutive of our relationship.

In this section I have described how, from a performance theory perspective, research can be understood as forms of practice that can be viewed as theatre, as a vehicle, as a place of play, as an activity, as a production, and as an object – all at the same moment. Furthermore, not only can research be performance but it can also be understood to be performative. In the following section, I describe how research is performative.

Performative: Making of (Research) Practices

Research is Performative
Performative is that which we make in the process of naming and enacting it to be as such. In comparing research to text (as above), I invoke Worthen's (1995) notion that "Barthes' sense of *text* is self-consciously performative" (p. 15). *Research is performative.* I identify the following three processes/movements by which to understand the making of research or its construction as performative:

1. Speech acts: According to speech act theorist J. L. Austin (1975), certain utterances are declarative and constitutive of creating particular realities, though later Austin "purported that *every speech is an act*" (Pandey 2008, p.151). Drawing on Austin's view, utterances such as "As a researcher I state" or "Research results reveal" or "Based on scientific research" are declarative and constitutive of what gets created as being real or factual since they are uttered as being research driven.

2. Language movements or moments/Communicative action: The activity of pointing and naming something, is a way of making it into an entity or reality. This activity of pointing and naming happens in language which Harlene Anderson and Harry Goolishian refer to it as "communicative action" (1988, p.378). For instances, researcher often 'explain' their results. These explanations are "made-up" as they are plausible ways of understanding results. They become tentative statements awaiting verification. Or one could say potential hypotheses for another research. Explanations are sense-making practices which are constitutive. We declare or birth a possible reality in the course of giving explanations. It also can function like the game we called Chinese whisper game[4] that I played as a child in India. In this game a phrase or a sentence gets transformed some times as it is whispered by one person to the next. In Figure 1 (above), we observe a similar process where, in language, research explanations moves through the news cycle. The explanation or its understanding gets reconstituted by the media channels to be responsive to its audience or to make news. In language movements, new realities are produced. Language movements are possibilities of coordinated action (Gergen 2009) outlined in the third point here.

On shifting our gaze from invoking structure to invoking communicative action we are stepping from performance into the performative space. Rather than performing functions of set roles, we are engaged in a creative activity of mutual engagement and inquiry. This mutual engagement and inquiry is not limited to the dissertation topic rather it starts out by inquiry into the advisory/supervisory relationship that we are seeking to create. I often start out by asking my advisee or student, "what is important for you in this topic and how would you like me to listen and attend to it within our relationship?" It is within this mutual engagement that we script our performances as advisors/supervisors and advisees/supervisees. Thus, we are improvising our relational dance just like we are improvising the research process. The relationship is emergent like the inquiry. And they shape each other.

---

[4]   Chinese whisper game is where people get in a circle and one person starts by whispering a sentence or word in her neighbor's ear. Then the receiver whispers it to the next person and thus it travels through the circle until it gets back to the first person, who says it out aloud and states the original phrase or word. In the course of it going around the circle, the phrase or word change based on what one hears.

3. Coordinated actions: "Only in coordinated action does meaning spring to life" (Gergen 2009, p.31). According to Gergen, all human action lies within co-action. It is within the relational space that we bring to life the world as we know it. Coordinated action is a process of communicative action of making meaning. What I say here are words on a page, but in our back and forth, within our relational space, we bring these ideas to life. This process is no different than when I am positioned as a research supervisor.

Our way of being, what we say and do, is shaped and understood within the relationships that host those actions. Similarly, the whole process of research is a coordinated activity among the various people (researchers, participants, advisors, reviewers, publishers etc). The meaning created in the relational responsiveness between the researcher and participants or among the committee members with the researchers is a communicative action. It is through this coordinated action that the conducted activity is deemed to be research *and* real.

In these ways, the process of enacting design and methods and naming it to be as such, we make the thing called *research*. The supervisory process is one such research process we make in enacting it to be as such.

Supervision: An Example of a Performative Relationship

As stated earlier supervision is a situated practice that is traditionally structured to be a hierarchical relationship which tends to emphasize the static performance of the roles rather than the dynamic nature of the relationships. Being a supervisor or a research student is a relationship not just a role. Though we use a noun to identify our position, our gaze needs to be on the performative, the practice of what we are constructing and not on the noun which constitutes a dormant or static performance.

How to be, that which we are being *and becoming*, is shaped in the conversations and the relationships we share with our advisee and the various people within that context. Drawing on Bakhtin's (1986) notion of text and context, our conversations and relationships are the texts which become the contexts for the emerging (becoming) relationships. Research advising as a learning context is a conversation about the processes, relationship and the community (McNamee 2007) and not limited to the content or focus area of the research. Thus, an advisor who positions himself/herself as a learner within the research process creates space for an emergent process.

My expertise, as a supervisor, lies in the attention to the practices and the values of my advisee and my own rather than mechanistically applying a series of skills to the process of advising. It is at the intersection of these values and practices that we constitute our supervisory relationship.

Central to the process of advising for emergence is the notion of *coordinating performative practice*. As an advisor, I position myself as a person who is cultivating and coordinating practices with my advisee to help us develop a performative gaze. I believe by developing our performative or constitutive gaze, we can value the messiness of our research process and stay open to emergence.

For instance, with one of my advisees, Greg[5], I had a sense that our relationship was bounded in some kind of a formal relationship of what it means to be advisor and advisees. Greg was an established practitioner and had facilitated many student activities and teaching as part of his career. We often socially chatted about his life outside his dissertation sphere. Yet I felt I didn't have a sense of Greg outside of his dissertation world, though he had located his topic as having a personal note. During one of our meetings, I brought up my sense of how something was amiss for me. We explored together how we understood our conversations. How we decided where we had bounded the dissertational space. During that meeting, I ventured to learn more about Greg's passion and hobbies and what he did in his free time. I discovered that he was a photographer and a creative; a part of himself that he kept out of his dissertation. We then explored how we go about making choices about what is in and what is out when we construct research spaces and what counts as skills and what doesn't. Later during a workshop which I was facilitating, we were exploring creative methodologies and how to think outside the box and we made a new connection about his process. We realized that the understanding that we created was not how to step outside his box, but rather how to bring Greg's creative presence into the box he had demarcated as research. Since, then Greg has been exploring his approach not only in writing but also via photographs and pictures. Thus, by coordinating our views of research, we reconstituted the notion of research.

Emergent Research

Drawing on the notions of research as performance and performative, I will introduce the notion that all research is emergent. By emergence

---

[5] Name changed to protect confidentiality.

I mean what is created, in the communicative action, among people. Thus, with every interaction, research and research designs are reborn as illustrated in the example with Greg. Emergence is not just the "order arising out of chaos" (Holman 2010, p.18). Rather it is inclusive of the messy process of chaos and meaning making; the back and forth of messiness *and* making order. The two cannot be unlinked. Chaos is the sense of disorder and disequilibrium that *seems* unclear and unknown to us. It is the liminal space where there are many options and nothing is yet clear. In chaos, there are numerous possibilities and one has to actively engage in sense making (order). The process of sense making is a creative social/relational process which occurs in dialogue, collaboration and coordination (Anderson 1997; Gergen 2009; McNamee 2004, 2007). This communicative action, is what John Shotter (2004) identifies as 'withness'-talk which is a "spontaneous, expressive, living, bodily, and responsiveness" activity (p. 205). Such a dialogic activity is a process of understanding and sense making which occurs in language communities we habituate, utilizing the traditions we have created along with anticipation of "what-next might happen" (Shotter 2004, p.205). This process can include what Holman identifies as differentiation and coherence (2010). She defines differentiation as *becoming* distinct or unique and coherence as "a stable system of interaction" (Holman 2010, Kindle Locations 533-534).

Holman has adopted the notion of emergence as a way of life. She states "My own story has become more open-ended and nonlinear as my quest for *uncovering* the deeper patterns of these methods" (2010, Kindle Locations 171-172, emphasis added). In this statement, lies the difference of her view from mine with regard to emergence. Holman's view of emergence is reflective of the field of complexity and chaos theory where one of the goals is to discover (uncover) "deeper patterns." Mining for such patterns and discovering them becomes the way we start to see the world around us and makes the existence of these patterns independent of the person(s) who discovered the pattern. However, from a constructionist and performative view it is in our language communities that we *make* these patterns – they are 'made' or come into being through the co-creative practices and processes in our research. And we recognize, through our spontaneous, reflective responsive practices, our construction of reality. Our claim that reality is made of patterns is a temporal myth or a cultural construct. Pattern making is created from the sorting and dividing parts of an interconnected whole. These patterns cannot be separated from the knower (maker) (Bateson 1972) or the community of knowers. Further, as Bateson (1972) points out in his Introduction to *The Steps to Ecology of Mind,* pattern making cannot be separated from the substance which it is classifying. What are the implications of the performative emergent view for research?

From Holman's view, one could conclude that emergent research is one that breaks apart from the status quo to create a uniqueness that differentiates itself and creates a coherent system. This view fits closely with Hesse-Biber and Leavy's view as espoused in their book *Emergent Methods in Social Research.* I am referring to what Hesse-Biber and Leavy (2006) identify as the new methods which are crafted in response to the "complex questions that arise from a range of newly emerging theoretical perspectives" (p.xxx).

However, my view of emergent research also recognizes the chaotic messy space of any research. It is where, in communicative action, the creative responsive process of making methods of inquiry arises out of the vocabulary of the discipline, substantive/focus area of inquiry, context and in collaboration with people (supervisors, participants, committee of readers, institutional review boards, colleagues, friends, and family etc) invested in the research. The resulting methodology might be traditional or it can be innovative and possibly disruptive of the traditional. The key emphasis is on the process of communicative action and the evolving process of making the direction and purpose of an inquiry, the research question(s) and the crafting of the method, which all go hand in hand, thereby being responsive to the local context and in synch with our epistemic position. Such a process *recognizes that the performance of research is performative,* that is, it creates the thing that we call research by the activities (traditions or new rituals) that are commonly referred to as designs and methods.

Another important implication of the emergent perspective applies to the notion of research outcome. Research has typically tended towards sort and divide (a way to analysis) discover and name patterns (Bateson 1972). "Analysis was seen as the best means to make sense of our world" (Holman 2010, p.19). Analysis typically means breaking down the whole into parts to make meaning. Holman's view is that because of limited capacities we were unable to study complex systems but the study of emergence is back in favor due to increase in nonlinear mathematical models that allow us to study whole systems. Further, the analysis focuses on outcomes, however from an emergent perspective not only outcome but also "our relationships, how we interact with each other, and how we relate to our environment" (Holman 2010, p.101) become central to the inquiry. The latter has been one of the central foci for systemic practitioners. Thus, approaching research as emergent relocates that focus on activity in research relationships, interactions and what is being created as well as on outcome (what is created). However, as Bateson (1972) who draws on Alfred Korzybski, Polish-American philosopher cautions us *"the map is not the territory"* (p.455) that is, the named interactions and relationships (our analysis identified as patterns or forms = outcomes) are not the "material" or "substance" rather they are forms (Bateson 1972, p.xxxii). Thus, emergent research reminds us that the research outcome is a temporal activity and it is one way of understanding and not *the* way of understanding.

Thirdly, emergent research highlights that methodology and the area/focus of the inquiry are interlinked and intertextual activities shaping each other (Hesse-Biber & Leavy 2006). These linked, mutually shaping processes can be viewed as performance and performative. The process of designing methodology and implementing it could be viewed as a textual performance as described above. However, in the process of applying methodologies, we adapt practices to our own process and create what we call methodology. This process of making, labeling and declaring it to be so is the performative element that the members of a research community coordinate with each other via papers in journals and conferences. Such coordination is what further builds our communities of practice while we make new methodological practices; thus, recognizing that all of research is made-up and is continuously re-making itself.

Conclusion

Coming back full circle, I love the process of making. I believe all researchers are designers and makers of methodology - not simply consumers of methodology. In this chapter I aim to encourage readers to be curious not only about the products that arise out of the research process but also about the communicative actions and discourses that produce the narratives of research and their methodological practices; and about the processes that link the methodology to the research focus (substantive). I illustrate the performative practices and relationships which are the making of emergent research by drawing on the processes of research supervision. I suggest that research is a developed activity in the communities of practice that we inhabit. While research is an activity of the communities of practice that we inhabit simultaneously it is being reborn and redesigned leading to its emergence and reconstitution. Thus, inspiring a playful quality towards conventions and traditions as an expressive responsive activity created with its stakeholders and from within the context of the inquiry.

In closing, drawing on Bakhtin (1986), research - the construct, the processes, the relationships and outcomes and what we mean by each of these terms- is constantly being reborn. He states,

> *there can be neither a first nor a last meaning; it [anything that can be understood] always exists among other meanings as a link in the chain of meaning, which in its totality is the only thing that can be real. In historical life this chain continues infinitely, and therefore each individual link in it is renewed again and again, as though it were being reborn. (1986, p.146. Parenthetical insertions are mine)*

References

Anderson, Harlene (1997). *Conversation, Language and Possibility*. New York: Basic.

Anderson, Harlene & Goolishian, Harold (1988). Human systems as linguistic systems: Preliminary and evolving ideas about the implications for clinical theory. *Family Process, 27*, 157-163.

Austin, John Langshaw (1975). *How to do Things with Words: The William James Lectures delivered at Harvard University in 1955*, 1962. Eds. J. O. Urmson and Marina Sbisà. Oxford: Clarendon Press.

Bakhtin, Mikhail (1986). [2010 reprint] Speech Genres and Other Late Essays. Trans. V.W. McGee, Eds. Caryl Emerson & Michael Holquist. Austin, Texas: University of Texas Press.

Barrett, Estelle & Bolt, Barbara (2007). *Practice as Research: Approaches to Creative Arts Inquiry*. New York: I. B. Tauris.

Bateson, Gregory (1972). *Steps to an Ecology of Mind*. London: Paladin.

Bava, Saliha (2005). Performance Methodology: Constructing Discourses and Discursive Practices in Family Therapy Research. In D. Sprenkle & F. Piercy (Eds.), *Research Methods in Family Therapy* ((2nd ed.; pp. 170-190). NY: Guilford Press.

Bell, Elizabeth (2008). *Theories of Performance*. Thousand Oaks, CA: Sage Publications.

Bernstein, Charles (2000). *Frame Lock*. Retrieved: http://epc.buffalo.edu/authors/bernstein/essays/frame-lock.html

Boal, Augusto (1997). *Theatre of the Oppressed*. Trans. Charles A. & M. L. McBride. New York: Theatre Communications Group.

Boal, Augusto (n.d.). Retrieved: http://brechtforum.org/civicrm/event/info?id=12647&reset=1

Carlson, Marvin (1996). *Performance: A critical introduction*. New York: Routledge.

Christ, Thomas. W. (2014). Scientific-based research and randomized controlled trials, the "gold" standard? Alternative paradigms and mixed methodologies. *Qualitative Inquiry, 20*, 72-80. doi: 10.1177/1077800413508523

Denzin, Norman (2008). The new paradigm dialogs and qualitative inquiry. *International Journal of Qualitative Studies in Education, 21*, 315-325.

doi:10.1080/09518390802136995

Denzin, Norman (2003). *Performance Ethnography: Critical Pedagogy and the Politics of Culture*. Thousand Oaks, CA: Sage Publications.

Drucker, Peter (1969). *The Age of Discontinuity; Guidelines to Our Changing Society*. New York: Harper and Row.

Gergen, Kenneth. (2009). *Relational Being: Beyond Self and Community*. New York: Oxford University Press.

Gergen, Kenneth & Gergen, Mary (2012). *Playing with Purpose: Adventures in Performative Social Science*. Walnut Creek, CA: Left Coast Press.

Hasseman, Bradley (2006). A manifesto for performative research. *Media Information Australia, 118*, 96-106

Hesse-Biber, Sharlene & Leavy, Patricia (2006). *Emergent Methods in Social Research*. New York: Sage Publications.

Holman, Peggy (2010). *Engaging Emergence: Turning Upheaval into Opportunity*. Berrett-Koehler Publishers. Kindle Edition.

Lemke, Jay L. (1995). *Textual Politics: Discourse and Social Dynamics*. Bristol, PA: Taylor & Francis Inc.

Pearce, W. Barnett (2007). *Making Social Worlds: A Communication Perspective*. NY: Wiley-Blackwell

Piercy, Fred & Benson, Kristin (2005). Aesthetic forms of data presentation in qualitative family therapy research. *Journal of Marital and Family Therapy, 31*, 107-119.

Madison, D. Soyini (2008). Narrative poetics and performative interventions. In Norman K. Denzin & Michael D. Giardina (eds.). *Qualitative Inquiry and the Politics of Evidence*. Walnut Creek, CA: Left Coast Press.

McNamee, Sheila (2007). Relational practices in education: Teaching as conversation. In Harlene Anderson & Diane Gehart, (eds.) *Collaborative Therapy: Relationships and Conversations that make A Difference*. London: Routledge.

McNamee, Sheila (2004). Relational Bridges Between Constructionism and Constructivism. In J.D. Raskin and S.K. Bridges (Eds.), *Studies in Meaning 2: Bridging the Personal and the Social in Constructivist Psychology* (pp.37-50). New York: Pace University Press.

Pandey, Rishikant (2008). *Speech Act and Linguistic Communication*. New Delhi: Concept Publishing Company.

Richardson, Laurel. (1997). *Fields of Play: Constructing an academic life*. New Brunswick, New Jersey: Rutgers University Press.

Shotter, John (2004). Expressing and legitimating 'actionable knowledge' from within 'the moment of acting'. *Concepts and transformation, 9*, 205-229.

Smith, Keith (2002). "What is the 'Knowledge Economy'? Knowledge Intensity and Distributed Knowledge Bases". Discussion Papers from United Nations University, Institute for New Technologies, No. 6. Retrieved: http://www.intech.unu.edu/publications/discussion-papers/2002-6.pdf

Teddlie, Charles &Tashakkori, Abbas (2003). Preface. In A. Tashakkori and C. Teddlie (eds.). *Handbook of mixed-methods in social and behavioral research*, (pp. 9–15). Thousand Oaks, CA: Sage.

Wenger, Etienne (1998). *Communities of Practice: Learning, Meaning and Identity*. UK: Cambridge University Press.

Worthen, William B (1995). Disciplines of text/sites of performance. *The Drama Review, 39*, 13-28.

8 Reporting from inside the Emerging Process of Becoming Research Consultants

Jacob Storch and Karina Solsø

When studying different qualitative research practices, one can easily recognise that many of the skills central to such practices are similar to those applied by systemic practitioners. We make use of questioning and conversational skills. We participate in social interplay with clients or participants. We reflect on the reality that our presence is neither neutral nor objective, and instead we pay particular attention to how our actions form and shape the context we all participate in and subsequently what kind of social reality we are creating.

Despite the apparent similarities we experience, there are important differences that need to be reflexively addressed in order not to miss out on important nuances or differences. This chapter adopts an insider perspective of a consultancy community in the process of developing a research unit and practice. This process results in many reflections on what it means to carry out a systemic inquiry in the practical activities of consultancy and research. It is from within our own experiences of this development in both practice and identity that we wish to explore some of the themes that have arisen in our conversations on what we find ourselves doing as practitioners who are simultaneously consultants and researchers.

We commence our reflections with a conversation that illustrates some of the many issues we are facing that we need to reflect upon in order for us to continually immerse ourselves in the process of forming our identity and practice as systemic inquirers.

Karina: Jacob, there is something I would like to talk to you about concerning my research. I could really use an external view on a dilemma that I am facing.

Jacob: OK.

Karina: As part of a piece of consultancy I have been doing, I have had an experience with a group of executives which has generated some interesting material for me in relation to some of the ideas that I am working with right now in my research. I had the idea that it might be interesting for this group to read the

	text I am going to write and I am reflecting upon how I can do this.
Jacob:	So what's the dilemma?
Karina:	The dilemma arises as I can feel that there is something ethical at stake here. I actually feel like giving this group feedback on some of the patterns that I notice may be influencing their way of working. However, I do not have a meeting with them where there is an obvious opportunity to do that. This places me in the difficult situation of having to find another occasion to do this. It was in the middle of thinking about this that I got the idea that I could 'take advantage of' my position as a researcher to invite them into a more reflexive position of curiosity. You know there is a strong interest in research these days, and who would not want to listen to research reflections about themselves? So I am thinking about telling them that in my research I am interested in the type of things that happened at that very meeting, and that I would like to use that experience as data. I thought I could tell them that I would be happy to share it with them if they would be interested.
Jacob:	And you are thinking about the ethics of doing this?
Karina:	Yeah, because I am concerned as to whether I am taking advantage of the authoritative discourse of 'research' in order to increase my chances of getting to talk to them. And what I intend to tell them might not necessarily be what they want to hear.
Jacob:	So it is a kind of a feedback that you want to give them? Show them what you see?
Karina:	Yes. I feel there is some potential for me as a consultant to *integrate* some of the practices that arise in my research into my consultancy work. I mean, in my research work I have time to immerse myself in my practice and to achieve a more reflexive understanding of my experiences. I have been thinking that this might be a way of doing consultancy. I have often felt constrained as a consultant as a result of contracts with clients that specify the purpose and the methods of the consultancy. However, I can experience some interesting things in relation to my clients that are not part of the formal contract. It is sometimes difficult to find opportunities to share these experiences and reflections, especially if they concern patterns or themes that for various reasons can be

difficult to talk about. I think that the research tradition and practice has something interesting to offer a consultancy practice. The potential is to offer a description or a mirroring of my experience of a different kind than that of normal consulting. Now I find myself in this particular situation in which this dilemma arises, and I am trying to find out how I can go on in a way that I don't feel that I am violating an ethical obligation.

Jacob: OK. I can relate to your dilemma. I think it is important to be cautious when we offer that kind of feedback. I have twice experienced trouble in consultations because I have shared with them what I was experiencing from my research position. It is one thing for the researcher to make a shift in identity. It is another thing to be conscious of the kind of identity that you create for the other since we risk positioning our client as an audience to our findings rather than as participants in a conversation. In this case I had inadvertently turned them into contributors to and subjects of a research project rather than simply the client or the buyer of consultancy that they had thought they were. Inevitably, this discordance affects their opportunities to respond accordingly and thus their story of themselves. The risk is to say something in one context that we implicitly anticipate that they can transgress into their workday conversation and way of being together, which they obviously fail to do.

Karina: Yes. There are indeed a lot of things to consider for doing this. I also think about the risk of being fired from the job. I think that we risk being fired from the assignment by transparently sharing some of my thoughts and ideas. I have just come to the conclusion that I think it is sometimes better for a consultant to find complementary occasions to offer these observations to clients rather than 'just' meeting the objectives of the contract. We experience lots of interesting things when we are working with our clients that we want to address. Often we just do it whenever there is an opportunity during a conversation. However, sometimes I experience that what I want to address is 'bigger' or more central than what is expressed in the responses in-the-moment. I think that timing is important to do this. And this is the kind of situation I find myself in now.

Jacob: I think that it might be important for you to reflect upon the position from which you are articulating these things. Are you reflecting from your position as a researcher or as a consultant? Who is speaking? And do the people you speak with know how you want them to respond?

Karina: My immediate idea was to reflect upon the theme from my position as a researcher since this is the position in which I have come to think about all this.

Jacob: It's worth considering that research and consultancy are different forms of practice which pursue different ideals. As a consultant you pursue an ideal of trying to help the client, which may or may not be an issue in research.

Karina: No, I can see that. In my research I do not have to be aware of the fact that I might get fired from the job. In my research, my writing is more unfiltered with regard to emotions and feelings that might be associated with reading it. I think this is something I should think some more about. I need to be aware of the different ideals and reflect upon my own position in order for me to go on here.

The above conversation is important to us because it expresses the conversational practices that we find ourselves in as we try to make sense of the distinction between being a systemic consultant and being a systemic research practitioner.

The chapter is divided into three parts. First, we reflect in more detail on how we understand ourselves as systemic practitioners. Second, we introduce two personal reflections of how we have worked with systemic inquiry in our practice as researchers. Third, we discuss some of the methodological themes that we find as central to our development of practices.

Developing an Integrated Systemic Research Practice

When I discover something that works with a family, I will try it on a different family to see if fits here as well. If it works here too, I will act deliberately never to do it again! (Cecchin[1])

The conversation we have shown here illustrates some of the many difficulties that we face as systemic consultants in developing a research practice. Both of us work in a systemic consultancy helping clients with the challenge of enabling change in their organisational life. In our

---

[1]   Quote from conversation in supervision, 2002

organisation over the past few years, we have created an internal research community in order to further expand our community's capacity to learn and grow. The community consists of consultants with doctorate degrees and a number of doctorate students. Through research, we want to move as a knowledge community away from only presenting the research-based work of others to developing and presenting our own research and, in so doing, offer accounts with their own internal validity of how we work and succeed as consultants.

Being Systemic - Self and Organisation

[T]he thing actually at stake in any serious deliberation is not a difference in quantity, but what kind of person one is to become, what sort of self is in the making, what kind of a world is in the making. (Dewey 1922/30, p.216-217)

For us, being systemic is an attitude. It is the commitment to curiosity over inference and the desire to question metaphors and what they conceal as opposed to staying loyal to one speech practice.

This attitude led the pioneering Milan Group to challenge established practices in therapy by replacing the notion of therapy with that of consultation in order to denote the conversational nature of that practice as opposed to the more diagnostic traditions. They expanded the position of neutrality into one of curiosity and hypothesising (Selvini Palazzoli, M. Boscolo, L. Cecchin, & G. Prata, 1980, Cecchin 1987), and later introduced the notion of *irreverence* (Cecchin, Lane, & Ray, 1992). In our view, this attitude – the concern with open endings and with imagination over certainty – is one of the most important characteristics of the systemic practitioners and theorists.

Further, being systemic denotes an ontological presence, a certain way of being in the world. Being systemic is a recursive iterative processes of actions in which identity evolves. So one's way of being becomes a performative act, a social construction in motion, where the very words and actions both form the social world in which we live and simultaneously shape the speaker in an ongoing recursive process. The view held by systemic theory practitioners is that of emerging identifications of selves in the making. A key characteristic of this literal community is its ability to reflexively shift positions or change attitudes towards novel ways of relating, to create new and enriched languages rather than sticking to old language habits.

Following this line of thinking, we immediately recognise that to study organisations, we must direct a great deal of attention to the processes of becoming, since we engage ourselves in the living dynamics of organising the fluctuating nature of the living. That is, we take the process of self-creation seriously.

Studying the process of becoming is fundamentally different from a traditional scientific position in which the subject of inquiry is stable rather than emergent. This calls for some reflection in relation to the attitude of the researcher. Whereas the traditional scientific attitude identifies with the ability to generalise across cases, to abstract, and to finalise, the systemic attitude has to do with 'being on the edge', continually paying attention to the micro details of what is unfolding rather than remaining in certain fixed and closed patterns of interpretation. While the traditional approach produces methods and action-guiding ideas, the systemic tradition suggests that the inquirer must be reflexively aware of the way one is oriented in the moment-to-moment relational responsive process. Conducting systemic inquiries calls for excellence in orientational skills rather than pure reasoning (Shotter 2006).

As systemic inquirers we thus take an irreverent stance towards overly detailed descriptions, plans, procedures and scripts in order for us to carry out our exploration. Too much 'planning' puts us in danger of not being able to 'be on the edge' – that is, to be actively engaged and present in a way that enables us to pay close attention to what is happening in the micro processes of the living. However, we do need to have some action-guiding anticipations in order for us to go on. We have a need for 'orientation', which is a need to feel 'at home' in our surroundings – that is, to become increasingly relationally responsive to the many different ways of relating to our surroundings (Shotter 2007).

'Being on the edge' rejects the traditional scientific question, 'Am I describing things as they really are?' and replaces it with the question introduced by Rorty who says that the pragmatists '... substitute for this traditional question the practical question, "Are our ways of describing things, of relating them to other things so as to make them fulfil our needs more adequately, as good as possible? Or can we do better? Can our future be made better than our present?"' (Rorty 1999, p.72). By saying this, Rorty is adopting the same fundamental attitude that is found in the systemic tradition of irreverence (Cecchin et al. 1992; Lang, Little & Cronen 1990).

Where irreverence is associated with professional practices within therapy and consultation, we find with Rorty a much broader significance attributed to this ambition. Rorty doesn't limit irreverence to a professional practice but to the very challenge of self-creation originally articulated by Nietzsche. In Rorty's view, this must be one of the primal tasks of living in an anti-representational world view, a view which is shared by the systemic community by large. Throughout his writings one will easily recognise this challenge as the urge to invent new vocabularies as a primary task of philosophy, literature and science. Rorty advocates for a redescriptive practitioner – that is, one who '... aims to keep reinvigorating the conversation by finding new descriptions capable of making the world seem fresh all over again; they want to elicit a "sense of wonder that there is something new under the sun"' (Rorty 1980, p.370). As such, what we have come to see as one of the basic qualities of being systemic is the ability not to arrive at a singular description but to continually explore the processes of becoming by being on the edge, paying close attention to what is happening moment by moment as an emerging way of making sense of experience, resisting the temptation to create finalised conclusions and instead creating new vocabularies.

Jacob's story: staying in the mess - and learning language

A central lesson that I have learned from experience is to acknowledge 'the mess' that arises during research processes. To stay in the mess means suspending any Cartesian anxiety, the tendency to bring things to conclusion and order, and instead remaining in the processes of exploration. What we learn from staying in the open is the many inter-pretational openings that emerge from experiencing data from within the process of its making. During a research project into our own organisation and practice during the years following the financial crisis, it was only very late into the project (two years) that the research narrative came together and produced the necessary operative distinctions needed in order to bring it to conclusion. The event that brought it to cohesion was a comment made by a consultant in the organisation one afternoon. He said that it was funny to think about it, but it was as if the whole process over the past year had made us more systemic than we were before. I asked him if he could explain in more detail what he meant by this, and he replied (Storch 2011):

> *There must be coherence between our 'inner dialogue' and the way*
> *we practise systemic consultation. I will name this the emergence of*
> *a collective moral obligation regarding the individual responsibility*
> *to help oneself and the organisation to sustain and develop the*
> *capacity to coordinate meaning into coordinated action.*
>
> *   This approach has in my view been strengthened in a period*
> *of recession where we had to be 'exemplary' in the sense that we*

as an organisation faced serious challenges. It has meant that we as employees can address and raise issues on equal terms with the management. This is possible because of the shared sense of moral obligation described above. An essential part of this is that the management recognises the importance of mutual trust in the leader-employee relation in the sense that every member of the organisation is responsible for helping coordinate meaning in the organisational multiverse.

This entire response from the employee made it possible to articulate a beginning and an end to the narrative of the research, yet it also pointed towards whom we had become, leading us forward into new possible stories. Thus, staying in the open and continually keeping an open agenda as to what counts as data in the research allow for certain moments to emerge, moments which have a particular unique quality, a felt experience of things coming together to form a transformational wholeness. Dewey (1925) refers to these moments as *consummatory* dimensions of experience, meaning, in Cronen's words, 'the creation of moments that have the feeling of finality, or a moment of elegant "fit" embracing form and feeling in a unifying moment' (Cronen 2000, p.6). Not only do these moments change the qualitative experience of the episode, they also produce within us, in our way of being able to relate to the otherness around us, a different orientational knowing, a different sensibility that enables us to anticipate the 'moves' of others in the social interplay. To put it in Wittgenstein's (1953) terms, we learn how to draw on different 'grammatical abilities', denoting our knowing how to go on in particular contexts and, in this case, into the 'not yet actualised'. In order to engage in the not yet actualised, we need a new literal horizon (Storch & Ziethen, 2012) in order to put that newness into language, since our current language practices only allow us to arrive at known inferences and consequently, when we do research, we risk assimilating our inquiries into known categories, which would compromise our systemic attitude of being on the edge. Let us elaborate this point a bit further.

Both Rorty (1991) and Shotter (2006) argue that all contexts can be divided into two kinds, one of which sees inquiry as developing a new set of attitudes towards something already known in one's repertoire. For Shotter, this is associated with *assimilating* something into an already existing and known category. He warns that doing this often makes us ignore the unique characteristics of a situation and *important deviations* that may advance new practice and knowledge.

The other kinds of contexts, Rorty argues, are the ones where one develops a new set of practices 'toward which one had previously no *attitudes*' (Rorty 1991, p.94). Doing so becomes a process of imagination and language-learning as opposed to inference. These attitudes are not developed 'at an intellectual level, as something one can talk about to others' (Shotter 2006, p.2) rather, they are aspects of an orientational difficulty in which 'knowing how to go on' becomes a felt dimension of the dynamic process of living relationships and a matter of 'being responsive to the unique details of a situation by one's actions within it' (Shotter 2006, p.2). Rorty further argues that 'to create one's mind is to create one's own language, rather than to let the length of one's mind be set by the language other human beings have left behind' (Rorty 1989, p.27). If one sees knowledge as something that can be captured or brought to a conclusion, one is inclined to assimilate into pre-existing ideas. Hence, to re-create is to expand, and it is in the process of acting that knowledge is lived as a series of practical judgments that create not only who we are but also re-iterate our knowledge about who we can become and what kind of world this becoming is taking place in. Innovation is not only about developing things; it is about developing who we are in the world we create as we try to figure out who we are becoming. Knowledge is an ongoing activity and trying to capture it, drawing conclusions about it, or locate it as something within people's minds will eventually fail in practice. Instead, one needs to step into the process of the unfolding in order to make sense of the world as it expresses who we are and what kind of world we choose to live in.

In my own research practice I (Jacob) have experienced a great advantage in adopting in new vocabularies or metaphors, the use of which challenged my way of seeing, talking and making sense of the episodes I was inquiring into. These new words enabled me to notice my preferred ways of talking about or relating to the kind of episodes I was in and in so doing produced differences that made it possible to express for the first time the purpose of my research as I invented the language by which it was possible to articulate. In my case, that was to take up a neopragmatic philosophy and merge it into a systemic language. Doing so caused a creative shift from working within one set of ideas to seeing the same situations in different ways, creating tensions, differences and bridges between ideas, thereby elaborating a novel expressive research language.

Karina's story: reflexivity

In researching one's own experience, findings arise from the researcher's reflections on his experiences. Entering situations with the attitude of not knowing, suspending the tendency to conclude, potentially leads the researcher to create novel understandings of what is unfolding. However, one of the basic systemic ideas relates to the role of the researcher in the activity of arriving at conclusions. This leads to important questions: What is my own role in the interpretational process of collecting and reflecting on my material? How do I relate to my own habitual thinking, second by second, as I conduct my inquiries?

When I (Karina) started my doctorate at the Complexity Research Group at the University of Hertfordshire, my first project (for the first six months) focused on the development of my own thinking during my life. In that project I gave a narrative account of the influences and experiences that inform my current thinking as a consultant and as a researcher. Based on narratives and reflections from different phases of my life, I deconstructed my own thinking in order to be able to detect the patterns and ways of thinking that inevitably form my ways of making sense when I am carrying out my inquiries.

The importance of doing the first project in this particular way is justified in relation to the idea that we are paradoxically forming and being formed at the same time (Stacey & Griffin 2005). I am forming the patterns in my life while at the same time being formed by them. More specifically, when I participate in social processes both as a consultant and as a researcher, I am forming the situation I find myself in while at the same time being formed by it. The following section is a small piece of my first project:

Reflecting upon the way I moved into the Christian community and into Attractor[2], I recognise a pattern of 'belonging'. It is very natural to me to take part in a community, connecting with people, finding things we have in common, and so on. Reflecting on it now makes me think that there are things to be aware of. I think it is mostly a good thing (also as a consultant) to be able to engage in and create strong relationships with other people. On the other hand, I critically ask myself if this kind of immersion in the social groups I find myself in is also a way of retreating from the struggle to reflect upon what I think and feel about the values and norms of the group. This theme is especially interesting at this very time, since I have just entered into a new group of people at the management doctorate with a strong common attachment to specific theoretical ideas.

---

[2]   Attractor is the consultancy company in which I work.

In order for me to be able to take the position of not knowing, I need to be able to critically reflect upon the patterns of my thinking, the patterns of my interpretations. Being on the edge in how I pay attention to what is going on in a research process involves paying attention to my own role in the sense-making process.

In 'Experience and Nature' John Dewey explores the basis of our experience. He emphasises that all experiencing arises from our *habitual* beliefs and expectations. When I enter a situation as a researcher or a consultant, my experience is influenced by my past experiences and my anticipations of the future. Dewey states:

The things of primary experience are so arresting and engrossing that we tend to accept them just as they are – the flat earth, the march of the sun from east to west and its sinking under the earth. Current beliefs in morals, religion and politics similarly reflect the social conditions which present themselves. Only analysis shows that the ways *in which we believe and expect have a tremendous affect upon* what *we believe and expect.* (Dewey 1958 p. 14)

When we carry out our inquiries and explorations, we are arrested and engrossed by the things of our primary experiences. The way in which the world appears to us is highly influenced by our habits; we interpret the situations we find ourselves in based on our own life history with all the layers of meaning that are embedded within it.

Reflecting on the quote above, one of the things that I have come to think more critically about is the need to belong. How does my need to feel at home with people enable and constrain my ways of reflecting upon what is going on in a social process? How do the patterns of my own thinking influence my sense-making?

When we are in the midst of a consultancy or research inquiry, our way of making sense of what we are experiencing is, first and foremost, informative about the patterns that characterise our own way of making sense.

Where the natural sciences aim for an objective position from which the world can be expounded, a systemic position takes the subjective experience and the interpretation of it as its starting point. As systemic researchers we acknowledge the fact that we cannot escape or exceed our own life experiences, our contingencies.

[Life experience] is already overlaid and saturated with the products of the reflection of past generations and by-gone ages. It is filled with interpretations and classifications, due to sophisticated thought, which have become incorporated into what seems to be fresh, naïve

empirical material. It would take more wisdom than is possessed by the wisest historical scholar to track all of these absorbed borrowings to their original sources. If we may for the moment call these materials prejudices (even if they are true, as long as their source and authority is unknown), then philosophy is a critique of prejudices. These incorporated results of past reflection, welded into the genuine materials of first-hand experience, may become organs of enrichment if they are detected and reflected upon. If they are not detected, they often obfuscate and distort. Clarification and emancipation follow when they are detected and cast out; and one great object of philosophy is to accomplish this task. (Dewey 1958, p.37)

This statement points to important reflections: first, if I do not detect the results of past reflection – that is, if I do not try to discern the way in which my own patterning process influences my way of making sense of what I am experiencing – I will probably obfuscate and distort what I am exploring. The conclusions that I will be able to articulate will reveal more about my own interpretations and classifications than about the phenomenon that I am exploring. However, the results of past reflection also have the potential to become organs of enrichment if I am able to continually detect and reflect upon them.

In relation to the small section from my first project cited above, I have while writing identified a 'need to belong' as a pattern in my way of relating. Even though this 'need' is one that I obviously share with a lot of people, I find it important to pay attention to the way in which it influences my way of acting as a researcher and a consultant. This pattern (as well as every other pattern) can obfuscate and distort my ability to make sense of what is happening. However, paying attention to this pattern can potentially help me to use this pattern constructively in my way of interpreting what is going on.

This is an invitation to self-reflexivity, which calls into question how I know what I know and how I have come to know it. It is an invitation to explore my own *role* in making sense of what I am trying to make sense of in my consultancy and research inquiries (Mowles, forthcoming). Management researchers Alvesson and Skjöldberg (2009) point to the ability of interpreting our own interpretations as a key ingredient in our endeavour to become more skilful in our ways of acting. Our interpretations of how we are interpreting make it possible to deconstruct what we are doing and how we are doing it. It is a way of calling into question the things of our habitual experience that we take for granted. It is this way of continually reflecting upon our own ways of making sense that entails the potential for clarification and emancipation. Engaging with this kind of self-reflexive process compels us to relate critically to the habits and patterns of our thoughts and to free ourselves from their potential tyranny.

There is an interesting paradox going on here, I think. I argue that we cannot escape our contingencies, but at the same time we should put a lot of effort into detecting them. How does that make sense?

I will inquire into this question in relation to the experience that led to the conversation described in the beginning of the chapter.

As a part of an overall change process I facilitated as a consultant, a conversation in a group of executives occurred in which something interesting happened. In the immediate experience of the situation, I was quite struck by some of the things that happened. Some of the directors were articulating dissatisfaction with the way in which the managers at the organisational level below them were acting in the change process. They thought the managers were navel-gazing too much in that process, and that as executives they should 'raise the bar', creating a more ambitious context for the process so that the managers would understand that it was not time to look inward – it was time to act. I had myself witnessed the process of 'looking inward' that had referred to and I found it understandable and natural that a change calls for reflection about one's own identity as a manager. In this particular conversation in the group, there was some disagreement as to how they should try to 'raise the bar'. The meeting ended with the directors clearly feeling dissatisfied with the way the managers were responding to the need to change. When I came home and took time to reflect upon the situation, I became more and more occupied with what to me seemed like a very typical but destructive pattern: that each level of the organisation was months ahead of the level below, and the higher level would get impatient and dissatisfied with what to them seemed to be the slow pace in the lower level in responding to the need for change.

Thinking back on that situation now, I can still feel the annoyance and the frustration in relation to that impatience. However, by inviting myself to take a self-reflexive stance, which means thinking about my own thinking about this, I realise that my annoyance and frustration had to do with some of my own moral ideals and values. In my (personal) view, the power to define that is associated with climbing higher and higher in the organisational hierarchy calls for a continuous ability to be reflexive. This is, to me, the moral claim of being a leader.

Thus, through the reflexive process of coming to realise that I am triggered by something that has to do with my own interpretation process, I think I am able to respond to the situation in a more reflexive and skilful way. I cannot put aside my emotional responses in relation to my experiences, but I can subject them to reflexive thinking, thereby recognising the themes in my experience, and continually pay attention to how my way of experiencing influences my very experiences. This helps me to not get 'caught up' in my own interpreting process but to instead be able to meet the situations I find myself in with openness to perceive what is happening. I am not totally free from my contingencies, but I am reflexive about the way they inform my way of making sense.

This relates to the way Rorty understands the importance of realising one's contingencies. The ability to track one's contingencies is related to the ability to realise the opportunity for imagining a new and better future, since 'an ironist cannot get along without the contrast between the final vocabulary she inherited and the one she is trying to create for herself' (Rorty 1989, p.88). As a consultant and a researcher I need to reflect on the habits or the vocabulary that I have inherited through my ways of making sense of my experiences.

Methodological considerations

In this chapter we have been arguing for an emergent and exploratory approach to research that is based on a specific understanding of what it means to 'be systemic'. We have been advocating for an orientational approach to systemic inquiry in which the ability of the researcher to suspend judgment and conclusion is central.

This methodology is linked to the notion of Feyerabend, who says that a 'theory of science that devises standards and structural elements for all scientific activities and authorises them by reference to "Reason" or "Rationality" may impress outsiders – but it is too crude an instrument for the people on the spot, that is, for scientists facing some concrete research problem' (Feyerabend 1975, p.1). Here, research scientists need to inquire into 'possibilities not yet actualized' (Shotter, 2007 p. 64) and this task is best explored using much more dialogically situated practices than classical sciences allow. For, as Shotter (2007) continues, 'research sciences must be rooted in the same kind of accountable human communication that grounds all our practical dealings with each other in our daily lives' (p. 67) so that, to put the issue in technical language, we do not 'lose the phenomena' (Garfinkel 2002). This emphasises the importance of not losing those 'guiding' and 'connecting' feelings that actors make use of in acting in ways 'responsive' to the situation they are in.

As systemic inquirers we are therefore necessarily practitioners exploring concrete phenomena in relation to concrete situations. Our phenomena are related to our practice and we cannot distance ourselves from our own participation in our research process.

This leads to a research position in which it is the embodied experience of the researcher that is the starting point of the research rather than pure rationality in the collection and interpretation of material.

This way of conducting our inquiry leads to an exploratory and emergent methodology. Our research questions and claims emerge both from our immediate experience of participation and as we retrospectively make sense of our experiences. We are using the term research here not as a linear process of making hypotheses and finding results but instead an emergent and iterative process of making sense of our experiences in order for us to find out how to 'go on'.

The ongoing changes in our interpretation about what we are creating in our research are inherent in inquiry and there is no external or privileged position from where justifications can be made (Rorty, 1980). Hence, justification is a matter of creating agreement among a group of people so that the descriptions available serve the purposes they intend to achieve, so that the question of whether we are representing correctly gets set aside and replaced with the practical question that we also have introduced earlier on: '*Are our ways of describing things, of relating them to other things so as to make them fulfil our needs more adequately, as good as possible? Or can we do better? Can our future be made better than our present?*' (Rorty 1994, p.72).

This notion provokes further reflection as we are carrying out our inquiries: how does my way of participating contribute to the findings that I am creating? And this immediately raises the question about validity: How can we justify that this methodology contributes to the knowledge and the continual development of practice?

These questions are practical questions, and they have to do with how we, as inquirers, relate to the people we deal with. Thinking back on the conversation in the beginning of this chapter, one of the important difficulties is precisely about Karina's ideas about how to participate in the inquiry, her ethical and practical dilemmas about her position as being either researcher *or* consultant.

The understanding that emerged during the earlier conversation was related to the different identities or different positions of being either a consultant or a researcher. As experienced consultants we train ourselves to become increasingly aware of the meaning that our participation has with regard to what gets created, and furthermore, our ability to be able to give an account of our practical judgments as we respond to the emergent reality of consulting is continuously elaborated.

Our relationships to our clients are always contractual. The client's wishes and definitions are the context for our ways of inquiring. Of course, we interpret these invitations differently since we bear different contingencies. However, the overall idea of inquiry in the context of consultation is related to the contractual relationship with the client.

The experience of being in contractual relationships with our clients has provided an interesting lesson over time that we find important in relation to research. In the consultant-client relationship, we have clear formulations about where to end. In this context, the consequences of our ways of acting become very obvious. When we utter a sentence, we immediately produce a context for a response that helps us in our ongoing orientation. We thus have to be very aware of the constitutive power of language and be ready to reflect upon that in relation to the meaning that emerges during an inquiry.

This is one of the things that become apparent in the earlier conversation between the two of us. We are committed to different purposes as consultants and as researchers. As consultants our ways of acting are justified in relation to a contractual relationship which does not apply in the context of research.

There is something methodologically important to pay attention to here. As consultants we are constantly justifying our actions in relation to a contract, which enables us to conduct our inquiries in the way that we do, being aware of the consequences of the constitutive power of language.

As researchers we have no formal contract that specifies the purposes of our explorations. However, our inquiries do have an effect on the ongoing evolution of the science that we are taking part in. This is an invitation to pay attention to our own idiosyncratic ideas about the purposes of our research.

Rorty makes an important contribution here:

Pragmatists – both classical and 'neo' – do not believe that there is a way things really are. So they want to replace the appearance-reality distinction by that between descriptions of the world and of ourselves which are less useful and those which are more useful. When the question 'useful for what?' is pressed, they have nothing to say except 'useful to create a better future'. When they are asked

'Better by what criterion?', they have no detailed answer, any more than the first mammals could specify in what respect they were better than the dying dinosaurs. (Rorty 1999, p.27)

Rorty's point is important to us because he highlights that change is inherent in inquiry and that there is no external or privileged position from where justifications can be made. Rather, justification is a matter of creating agreement among a group of people so that the descriptions available serve the purposes they intend to achieve.

From a practical perspective this points to the nature of the community in which conversations about research take place. This can be grasped in a broad sense: How is the conversational discourse (in general) in the sphere of research, and how do we contribute to that conversation? At the same time it can be grasped in a more local sense: How can we create local research communities in which the conversations contribute to the evolution of practice? At Attractor we are still in the formation phase of our research community, and one of the things that we are methodologically obligated to pay attention to is how our ways of reflecting upon and critiquing each other's work contribute to the findings that we are creating.

Conclusion

in this chapter we have addressed some of the practical considerations that have arisen in our movement in practice and identity towards becoming researchers. We have explored what we think is crucial in taking a systemic attitude in systemic inquiries, namely the ability to take a not-knowing position in which we try to continuously suspend the tendency to abstract and conclude. This involves being on the edge of one's own need to understand and determine what is going on, remaining open towards multiple continuations of the conversation. This relies not on a desire to control the inquiring process towards predetermined hypothesis or goals. Rather, carrying out inquiries from this position relies on what Shotter calls 'a sense of sureness', which is a confidence in one's actions that something interesting will occur sooner or later. Methodologically this leads to an emergent research position in which the researcher constantly aims towards openness to the many potential conclusions that might arise in the joint activity of inquiry.

We have explored this form of inquiry through two practical experiences which point towards two different and yet connected activities that are related to this research position.

The first is the ability to stay in the mess and in language learning. To stay in the mess is to suspend the desire to bring things to order and instead remain in the process of inquiry. This attitude allows for the opening of many interpretations that arise from the patience of experiencing the material from within the process of its making. Inspired by the ideas of Rorty, the central activity then becomes the activity of language learning. Rorty points to the important process of creation in which we potentially find ourselves in our experimentations with metaphors and new concepts. It allows for the experience of something that was not there before, something new.

The second is the practical experience of coming to pay attention to our own role our interpretational processes. To carry out systemic inquiries involves the constant questioning of our own thinking about our experiencing. It involves detecting the patterns of our experiences and ways of making sense as a prerequisite for our ability to remain open in the experience of what is going on. This process of reflexivity is something in which we as researchers continually must find ourselves. As we move on step by step in the iterations of inquiry and sense making, we must pay attention to the way in which our way of going on is formed by our own history with all its layers.

As such, both examples illustrate aspects of what it takes to see a research process as a social construction in motion. It requires us to pay attention to 1) our tendency to reach conclusions based on already known metaphors and concepts rather than staying in the mess and being open to new understandings, and 2) our tendency to reproduce our own life history if we do not critically pay attention to our interpretational process.

We are aware of the fact that these descriptions might sound intangible and fluffy. For sure, these are not descriptions that produce rules and procedures for how to go on in complex situations. However, our view is that the everyday life that we try to explore is not a manuscript. Everyday life has its own emerging, fluctuating indeterminacy. Carrying out systemic research is first and foremost about finding a way of relating to the mess of everyday life that allows for multiple and potentially novel descriptions of reality.

References

Alvesson, Mats, & Sköldberg, Kaj (2009). *Reflexive methodology: new vistas for qualitative research*. London: Sage.

Cecchin, Gianfranco (1987). Hypothesising, Neutrality and Circularity Revisited. *Family Process*, <u>26, 4,</u> pp.405–413.

Cecchin, Gianfranco; Lane, Gerry & Ray, Wendel A. (1992). *Irreverence: A strategy for Therapists' Survival*. London: Karnac Books.

Cronen, Vernon E. (2000). Practical Theory, Practical Art, and the Naturalistic Account of Inquiry. Prepared for the conference: *"Practical Theory, Participation, & Community"*. Baylor University, January, 2000 [http://www3.baylor.edu/communication_conference/cronen.htm].

Dewey, John (1922/1930). *Human Nature and Conduct An Introduction to Social Psychology*. The Modern Library. Reprint by Kessinger Publishing.

Dewey, John (1925). *Experience and Nature*. New York: W.W. Norton & Company.

Dewey, John (1958). *Experience and Nature*. London: George Allen & Unwin, Ltd.

Feyerabend, Paul (1975). *Against Method*. London: Verso.

Garfinkel, Harold (2002). *Ethnomethodology's Program: Working out Durkheim's Aphorism*. Boulder: Rowman & Littlefield Publishers.

Lang, Peter; Little, Martin & Cronen, Vernon (1990). The Systemic Professional – Domains of Action and the Question of Neutrality. *Human Systems: The Journal of Systemic Consultation & Management*. 1, pp.39-55.

Mowles, Chris (forthcoming). *Managing in uncertainty: complexity and the paradoxes of everyday organisational life*. London: Routledge.

Rorty, Richard (1980). *Philosophy and the Mirror of Nature*. Princeton University Press.

Rorty, Richard (1989). *Contingency, irony, and solidarity*. Cambridge University Press.

Rorty, Richard (1991a). *Objectivity, Relativism and Truth. Philosophical Papers Vol. 1*. Cambridge University Press.

Rorty, Richard (1991b). *Essays on Heidegger and Others, Philosophical Papers Vol. 2*. Cambridge University Press.

Rorty, Richard (1999). Ethics Without Principles. In *Philosophy and Social Hope*. London: Penguin Books.

Selvini Palazzoli, Mara; Boscolo, Luigi; Cecchin, Gianfranco & Prata, Guilliana (1980). Hypothesising-circularity-neutrality. *Family Process, 19,* pp73-85.

Shotter John (2006). Organizing multi-voiced organizations: action guiding anticipations and the continuous creation of novelty. Draft Paper httt://pubpages.unh.edu/~jds/Essex.htm

Shotter John (2007). With What Kind of Science Should Action Research Be Contrasted?, In *International Journal of Action Research*, 3, 1-2, 2007.

Storch Jacob (2011). *Systemic Thinking, Lived Redescription, and Ironic Leadership: Creating and Sustaining a Company of Innovative Organisational Consulting Practices*. Professional Doctorate Thesis, University of Bedfordshire.

Storch, Jacob & Ziethen, Morten (2012). Recurrence vs. re-description - the relationship between instrumental and artistic practices. *The Danish Journal of Coaching Psychology*.

Wittgenstein, Ludwig (1953). *Philosophical Investigation* (G.E.M. Anscombe, trans.). Oxford: Basil Blackwell.

Writing Essays as Dialogical Inquiry   9

Lisen Kebbe

Introduction

When KCC in London, 2006, started the first cohort of the systemic practice-based doctoral program, there were no given ways of how "to do" research. There was though the wish to make some kind of non-traditional, cutting edge, mind-blowing qualitative action research. The first years of study were revolutionary for me as to what research is and can be. It was hard to grasp the task of finding or creating research methodologies that would fit practice and honor our practice relationships. In the same vein, I grappled with how to reflexively intertwine theory and philosophy.

During these years there were several frustrating stand-stills, but the research process in itself had ways of creating organic growth. This paper is a reflection on how the writing of essays became my main ally in exploring my practice. Since essay writing does not call for a fixed or finalized analysis so much as opening up a multitude of aspects, it has been a liberating paradigm for me and in the end it also became my way of presenting and constructing my research. I draw on Bakhtin, Cunliffe, Richardson, Shotter and Vygotsky amongst others.

Beginning the doctoral studies

In the late warm summer of 2006, a group of nine doctoral candidates met with Peter Lang, Martin Little and John Shotter in the shabby-chic quarters that used to house KCC at 210 Wyvil Road, in Vauxhall London. I was one of them and had worked with Peter Lang in Sweden for about ten years but never visited the physical location of KCC before. It was with great expectation that all twelve of us started the first doctoral program that was going to be the jewel of the KCC crown. I remember entering the library on the first floor, balancing a cup of coffee and wildly scribbling in my notebook while mainly John talked about dialogue and responsiveness. The whole situation was bewildering. Nevertheless, the course, as well as my fellow candidates, filled me with excitement and curiosity. This paper is an attempt to tell how my frustrated way-finding process turned into the craft of systemic dialogical professional research through writing.

My research project concerned family meetings with business families who were approaching succession, a practice I had developed within my consultancy firm together with Jenny Helin. This field of work is performed on the border connecting management consultancy and family therapy. The research focus was to help families during their succession process to deepen family relations as well as to develop their business. To help deepen family relations *as well as* developing the business at the same time contrasted with the paradigms of mainstream family business research and consultancy. Family and business are commonly seen as two very separate systems where the first is emotional/relational and the second rational/ economical. Usually families are seen as the unprofessional element when mixing the two systems. This can be thought to harm the business as well as being seen as the cause of severe conflict in families. The aim of my studies was to turn these beliefs upside down. I firmly believed it was possible to facilitate conversations and appreciate the interconnections between family and business and, in that way, help families find their own ways "to go on".

At first I felt very self-assured in relation to my research project. In my systemic consultancy practice, I had been working with facilitation of conversations; the task was going be to "prove my point" of how efficient it would be to manage successions in family businesses in that way. But even though I had had a systemic practice for more than ten years, I lacked the awareness of the need to integrate the philosophy of research with practice. So when it came to ideas around research, my conventional training as a psychologist from another time and place, made "traditional" science methods seem "natural" and obligatory for "real research". And there were the ideas that it had to be done from an "outside objective stance with the aim to find the truth". Envisioning the future, I saw myself presenting a thesis with advice on "how to manage family meetings" - probably a manual that easily could be used by consultants involved in these kinds of tasks. My work was going to be to report on the conversation with six different families that we had planned to have as a base for showing "how to do it". This was roughly my pre-understanding of how to manage the professional systemic doctoral process when the studies started.

Getting immersed into the process

As time went by the succession project rolled on. The conversations were audio-taped and transcribed. There were seminars in London with

Shotter and others, fellow doctoral students became friends and we had lengthy conversations amongst ourselves. Apart from the seminars and the conversations, my days were filled with extensive reading. Shotter, Vygotsky, Anderson, Richardson, Andresen, Ellis, Bateson, Seikkula, Wittgenstein, Bakhtin, Cunliffe, Gadamer, Gergen and many more filling my every day between working hours. This was a time up-rooting old knowledge, widening my mind, experiencing frustration mixed with bliss! Loads and loads of disparate ideas were swirling around making my head spin.....

After a couple of years, all conversations with the six family businesses had been audiotaped. I had met each family three times and each conversation had taken three hours; a staggering amount of transcriptions were done. In the first paper I used Shotter's (1993, 2008) notion of "joint action" and was pinpointing the very sequences where it seemed that something new was emerging and transforming in the dialogue. The study concerned moments in the transcript and focused on passages where I thought "*it*", a joint action, had happened. The writing was great learning, but still it was writing by looking at the process from an outside position and in a technical way.

But how to write a thesis?

The writing process had started, but still I was struggling with how to make it a *systemic* thesis. I was sweating with all the *"big"* research questions. How could I find a form for my research that would address my research topic in a sensitive way? What methodology could I use that would make sense of all my transcribed conversations, field notes and all the theory and philosophy I was taking in? What could be counted as "data"? What would make up a meaningful wholeness? I wanted make it possible to view family business succession in a new light.

While working with the families I became aware of that family conversations that were "safe enough" created responsiveness among the family members and this in turn made new connections possible for them and for me, which in turn made the succession process unfold.

Slowly I began to realize that it was how these interconnections came about that had to be the focus of my studies. I found myself wondering how I could make an account of these subtle processes and how I could find a way of doing research that could create an understanding for what it takes and what happens? I needed to find a philosophical base from where the systemic research methodology could be built. Hence my study explored my own practice: a first person qualitative action research with the aims of i) developing my practice; ii) changing the way we perceive successions in family businesses; iii) communicating these ideas and practices with family business families, the systemic community and with the family business research field. My colleague, Gail Simon calls this concurrency of practice and research, "Praction Research": a form of action research used for: "critical, relational reflexivity to sustain respectful and irreverent movement across and between ideology, theory and practice" (Simon 2012).

This sounded revolutionary and challenging and fitted my need to be able to use all the different material I had already gathered and still wanted to find out more from. I had to find a way that supported reflexive movements between practice, philosophy and maybe also sociology. I found myself becoming greatly interested in placing family business succession in a historical, gendered and cultural perspective.

Central to all systemic practice and research is language, dialogue and communication. This applies to all kinds of language usage; spoken and silent, as well as 'live' and written language. The systemic philosophy builds to a large extent on the developments in the 'linguistic turn' (Anderson & Goolishian 1988, 1989; Alvesson & Sköldberg 2008). The linguistic turn rose out of social constructionism and postmodern thinking and viewed language as the central element that creates our social lives. The traditional research perspective is to view language as the means by which we describe realities of others from an outside, expert stance. This contrasts with systemic social constructionism which views language as a relational language system by which we constitute our reality and create meaning. This was my main guide in my systemic research practice. And, as Ann Cunliffe so beautifully puts it, "meaning is created as language plays through us, as words, sounds, rhythms, and gestures evoke verbal and emotional responses" (2002, p.129). So, if language is viewed as the ontology through which our social world is built, then research is one powerful way to construct this social reality.

How can knowledge be created when language is the ontology?

I was preoccupied by two questions. What kind of research methodologies and what kind of epistemology would fit my aims? How can anything be known and how does it come to be known (Whitehead & McNiff 2006)?

Central to the systemic approach is the postmodern and social constructionist view that there is no grand narrative, no objective truth to be found, that social knowledge is situated and local and it is impossible to 'discover any objective truth' about our social lives (Lyotard, 1984). Instead we are constantly in the process of co-constructing our realities (Hedges, 2005). We generate meaning through our conversations and these, in turn, co-construct our reality. Central to my take on the systemic is also the Bakhtinian view on dialogue as embedded in people through language (Shotter 2008; Cunliffe 2003; Anderson 1997; Helin 2011; Vedeler 2011). My experience is that when people meet in a dialogical moment something unique is always created. What is spoken is as much a product of the listener's anticipation as of the speaker's utterances. The meaning making happens in a joint process between persons (Shotter 2008). The meaning of words and the meaning of utterances are always infinite; there are always openings for new meaning-making.

My dissertation aimed to create knowledge that could develop new ways of *seeing* successions as well as to develop new ways of facilitating succession processes. Lyotard inspired and awoke my curiosity when he asks us to "invent allusions to the conceivable which cannot be represented" (1984, p.84). What could that look like? It might set the context for a way of doing research that would rather portray important moments grasped "in the stream of life" (Wittgenstein 2001) than report and analyze from an outside so called objective stance. It would allow reflexive interplay between practice, writing, reading and reflecting on the total research project in line with Simon's Praction Research (2012).

Could essay writing be the answer?

I had for a long time heard about essay writing and many researchers only write in essay form. Asplund, the Swedish grand old social psychologist does so, for example, in "Marvelling Over Society" (1970, not translated into English), and so did Lyotard in the ground-breaking "The Postmodern Condition" (1984). Freud is another well-known example of a writer that always used the essay form when writing about his cases where he interfolds his own feelings and surprise over his findings that make the case studies come alive. So could my thesis be organized as several fairly independent essays, like beads on a string? This could be a way to connect with the ideas of Lyotard (1984, p.81) when he asks us to "invent allusions to the conceivable which cannot be represented"?

The French author, Montaigne, was the first to put a name to this form of writing and he published his first essays in 1580. Montaigne lived in Bordeaux, in the midst of religious wars where fundamentalist Catholics and Protestants killed each other. At eleven, he witnessed the beheading of Protestants in the town square. He later worked as a judge at the court of the Parliament but before turning forty, he sold his official position and returned to his little castle and started writing. Montaigne declared that he wanted to withdraw and live in the company of the Muses; he wished to be free and personal in his writings. He was the first to use the term *essaie* by which he meant an attempt, a trying out, a first draft or a test. His essays are reflections on philosophy, poetry and on his own very personal views and wisdom. Montaigne continued to elaborate on the essays his whole life. He rewrote and published them several times, they were never finalized (Stolpe 1986).

Zaidie Smith refers to Virginia Wolf when she writes in the *Guardian* (2009):

> *an essay is an act of imagination, even if it is a piece of memoir. It is, or should be, "a form of thinking, consciousness, wisdom-seeking", but it still takes as much art as fiction.*

The Swedish writer and critic Horrace Engdahl writes about essays:

> *The essay is a survivor from the world of the 'lantjunkare' (noble soldier during the 17th century), the last remains of an old conversational culture that got the kiss of death when time managers became a necessity for every man and woman. In the era of data bases and two minutes tableaus, essays are as strange as carriages pulled by horses. Texts that won't be summarized! It is the last refuge for ancient, time consuming, personalized structures of meaning that are hard to reproduce, they carry the disregarded name; knowledge. (Gustavsson 2010, in my own translation)*

In Engdahl's words, essay writing is rather a way of writing that has its source in the deeply felt wish to express something that is not easy to reproduce, this undoubtedly reverberates with Lyotard's request. I wanted to set up a way of writing that would do justice to the very complex and multi-voiced experiences I was collecting. So I started to experiment to allow connected and disparate material to dialogically "speak to one another" in the text. In the process of connecting transcribed material, philosophy, history, my own experiences, my emotions and reflections and so on in the writing, my inner voice (Vygotsky 1986) was activated. Through the act of writing, new ideas were emerging and in the re-writing and re-writing and re-writing new ways of perceiving the world were released and surfaced.

Essay writing does not ask for finalized analysis, but is open to a multitude of aspects. This was a liberating paradigm and it fitted my needs. If there is no single grand narrative to be told and if truth is local, I could not act as if the world I was working in was stable and just waiting to be discovered. It was only a matter of finding a form of writing that was open to the multifaceted and dynamic world that is so hard to reproduce; a way of writing that would allow for many furrows and not force all my thinking into *one* track.

The writing

As the writing evolved it became an important tool for 'analyzing' and sensitizing me to the 'organic life' of the conversations and enabling me to 'see' and become aware of what was happening in my Praction Research. The writing made it possible to be more responsive to the relational understanding that gave me a "practical grasp of the changing, moment-by-moment links and relations" (Shotter & Katz 1996, p.16). But at the same time when working with research into my own practice it was important to also create a distance to the practice to be able to "see" it and reflect over it both when it came to the involvement with family members and the way of working. Essay writing became the royal road to the kind of distance that at the same time allowed for withness (Shotter 2008). The writing made it possible to move between different perspectives and let them fertilize each other.

I will here give an example of one of the first times it happened that the writing process in itself opened up for totally new insights. Bateson (1972, 1979, 1988) had been my companion for some length of time and I was hooked on the importance of context and realized that it is really true that without context there is no meaning. Words, actions and everything always exist with a background, in a situation; words, in themselves, do not have any meaning.

Then one afternoon when taking a walk, I met my old teacher and remembered a quarrel we had had in class about forty years ago regarding a poem by Strindberg. When seeing him and remembering our argument, I realized that the different contexts we had been in had resulted in conflicting interpretations of the poem. He was talking about Strindberg's view of a "rotten" Swedish society a hundred years earlier which the poet metaphorically attacked in his poem through his words "tearing down houses to let in air and light". My context was of another kind: as students we were in the midst of rioting against the tearing down of a beautiful ancient house on our school grounds and we wanted to keep it for our after school social time. It was impossible for me to imagine ripping away houses as a liberating metaphor. When meeting the teacher on the boardwalk that day, I realized that our realities and contexts at that time had been completely antagonistic which naturally elicited opposite interpretations of the poem. When understanding this, the notion of context leaped out of the book and hit me full on!

After this insight from the meeting with the teacher, my writing took off. Now I had found a well I could draw on. The continuous writing with overlapping layers of reflexivity between context, theory, dialogue and do on helped me to understand the importance of context more deeply and over a wider spectrum. Emerging out of this came an understanding of the current situation in the family I was working with in addition to important professional aspects of the facilitation process. The writing process facilitated my ability to move around in my research material in many directions which felt extremely meaningful. At the same time I started to feel like a storyteller and opened up an inner dialogue with a future reader which created a kind of distance necessary for reflexive connections.

At the time I was working with a farming family that were going to hand over the farm from third to fourth generation. The mother in the family, Elsa, and her daughter in law, Anna, had earlier been distant with each other and each alluded to very different ways of life when talking about the future of the farm. However, I had noticed that they recently had found some common ground but I did not understand what had happened. Then the realization came that they had started to talk about horses, a subject first taken up by Anna's husband almost a year earlier when he reflected in our conversation over what future possibilities a farming life could carry. Although Anna seemed not to connect to this idea at that time, I now understood that she had asked Elsa about giving a horse as a birthday present to Disa, her three year old daughter. Both women had earlier in their lives been "horse-groomers", but in spite of the ten years Anna had been a part of the family it was not until now they were able to share this interest. The horse story had been inaccessible to me our more traditional succession talks. But when I was searching through my transcripts and field notes of talks with Elsa and Anna, I found that the "horse story" had started a couple months earlier. Later they were talking about restoring a stable on the farm that not had been used for ages, not since Elsa had kept her own horses there. This new project now involved all family members, including Anna's family of origin. Yet at that time, the succession process concerning the family business seemed to have stalled. Nevertheless, the succession process was kept alive through the horse related activity across the three generations of women in the family. This background apparently unrelated activity created energy, goodwill and a sense of progress which enabled the whole of the succession to roll on. Through the writing process, I understood that our conversations had created some common contexts for the women that made it possible for them to start to talk and cooperate in new and creative ways. I called the essay I wrote, "A Shared Context can Create Wings for the Succession" (Kebbe 2012, p.138).

In the writing process my embodied experience and reflections of the material I was working with could now move in flux from focusing on experiences with the family, both caught in the transcipts and in my memories of being with them, together with private memories that were evoked and the theory I was working with at the time. What differentiated the writing process from the mere thinking around these matters, besides the stabilizing effect, was the dialogue with the written text and with future readers. This created an inner forum for movement between different perspectives. A forum that made it possible to switch focus on what was written - if it made sense, if it took the dialogue with the reader a step further and so on. At the same time the writing process opened up for a dialogue between my own consiousness and my inner speech (Vygotsky 1986). I was as hooked on Vygotsky and felt I had a glimpse of what his views meant on the social construction of language and language usage. I was thrilled by his writings about our social multi-layered and fluid inner speech and of the possibility of words having infinite variations of meanings. In Vygotsky's own words: "A word relates to consiousness as a living cell relates to a whole organism, as an atom relates to the universe" (1986, p.256). It is astonishing to reflect over what multitudes of meaning and possible connections a single word in a context can open up for and what possibilities that can create.

This process was facilitated, validated and to a large extend also inspired by reading Richardson who is one of my guiding stars. She writes "I write because I want to find something out. I write in order to learn something that I didn't know before I wrote it" (1994, p.517). She considers writing a method of inquiry and encourages researchers to write and re-write and to reflect over their own process while doing it. To strengthen the individual voice and to be more fully present in our work, more honest and more engaged she says is to take on the postmodernist possibilities for qualitative writing. The important thing is that the writing is a part of the whole of the research process. It is not a reporting of what has been going on; it is in the writing that everything happens. As Richardson says we have to use writing as the method of analyzing. Essay writing makes it possible to make connections and associations in the writing where literature, transcriptions and the reflections of the writer are used reflexively. The essay has an aim, but the writer is flexible and open for the connections that are awakened in the writing process. This makes for "Aha!" experiences in the writing process that, in turn, makes for new connections.

My essays

From the beginning the essays I wrote were solitary pieces. But as the process went along I noticed that if they were ordered according to a time line it became a way of telling a story about the succession process in the Bjärges family, the sole family I came to choose for my research project. However, it is not THE story, since there are many more ways to narrate what happened during the five years I followed them. But by the added time perspective connections were created between the parts and made it easier to follow the work we had been doing. Furthermore, the sequencing of the "story" made me at the end of the study write a couple of essays that I felt were 'missing' to give a "clear enough picture" of what this research process had involved and to be able to view the succession process in a new light.

The essays became my way of reflexively bring together new learning that the listening to the audiotapes and reading of the transcriptions made visible; it has been amazing how every new contact with the conversations created new ways of understanding and connecting to what had happened. I agree with Etherington (2004, p.62) when she challenges the writer to "let go of structure and embark on a journey into the unknown; to reflect on self and others and to move beyond cognitive processes"

The free form with different parts yet without a given structure makes it possible to write and re-write over and over again without disturbing the whole of a thesis. The basic assumption in the essay is to find a way where it is possible to "sketch". It is not meant to give a full picture of a research process but rather to give a perspective on a special phenomenon. Compared with traditional storytelling which has a plot and the telling is a finalized story, the ideas in an essay are dwelled upon without the need to finalize "a story".

Until now I have only reflected over writing the single essays and that was my perspective for a long time. I wrote eight essays concerning the family conversations dealing with different insights I got and with different stages in the succession process. But the more essays I had gathered, the more it showed that they did not only have to do with family conversations. The essays situated my work with the families in a philosophical, historical, gendered world which made it important to write essays also from other perspectives than from within the family conversations. I also had an immense need to situate the systemic approach within the philosophy of science and put effort into that. One essay was built on some interviews with lawyers and accountants. I wanted to find out if what I called "mainstream consulting" was really happening out there in "real life". And I can assure you – it does. I also had to get acquainted with the field of family business research. But maybe the most interesting thing was to explore how the philosophy underpinning the view on family businesses, and the consulting in the field, have their roots in feudal society which is a strictly gendered culture. There have been laws to protect the rights of the oldest son to inherit the estate in order to keep the riches assembled. Today this way of acting is not protected by law but these values are still thought of as "natural". All the different essays I wrote can be read independently but together as a whole they "sing a new tune".

Each of the essays in my thesis can be seen as a different attempt to make sense in the study. They have their own inner logic that are not mirrored through the whole of the thesis. At the same time they do "speak with each other" and give a kaleidoscopic picture of the whole, a process that could have been presented in an infinite number of different ways. The writing process has been very meaningful to me. It has been my tool to understand what I was doing and the world I was moving in and co-creating. My hope is that it will interest the reader. I think that essays offer engaging texts because they are open to many perspectives and it is hopefully easy for the reader to fill in the gaps and connect to the text in a personal way. In this way essay writing supports the dialogue with the reader.

At the end I want to say

It is important to embark on the writing process from the beginning of undertaking research or an inquiry and to stay in it, because I now see the possibility to use writing as the main methodology to shape the research. It does not mean that you should start writing to learn how to write –more, it is a form of ongoing reflections that reflexively integrate your practice, your reading, your conversations, your earlier life, and your hopes for the future etc. Usually we believe that we should start by collecting data and then commence the writing. From the beginning I was also stuck in that way of thinking and ended up with an enormous pile of transcripts before I started my writing. But with the essay format, there is no problem to start the writing at once - this freeing process develops into a reflexive process.

Writing in the research process is often taken for granted. In the beginning of the research process we often think of the writing as a way of reporting. Nevertheless, it is good to think that different genres of writing create different contributions and different ways of working. To read many different kinds of research, to test writing in different genres is a way to explore and find what suits you and your kind of research best. What kind of writing gives you the most energy and creates most ideas that will take you further in your research and what way of writing gives you the feeling that it is possible to find what you want to say.

Something to beware of though, is that the essay form gives you little help to structure your work and you may find yourself opening up for too many tracks that doesn't guarantee clarification or greater understanding of your practice. As you may understand from my presentation above, I was balancing on that border. If you run the risk of drowning, a good supervisor is needed, or the essay way of writing might not help you create the kind of research you are dreaming of.

I also invite you to reflect over the fact that a text can never be innocent. As I wrote earlier research is one way of constructing reality, both for the writer and the reader. Writing is never only a question of aesthetics it is also an utterance with ethical considerations. You always write from a certain perspective, it is always an answer to one or many utterances (Bakhtin, 1984). You make it possible for some voices to be heard while others are silenced. This makes what you write an ethical matter and it has to be valued as such. What realities are you creating for those that have collaborated with you when making the study for your readers and for yourself? And which dialogues and narratives do you want to open up and why?

Writing *this* essay has given me the opportunity to reflect over my own writing process while being immersed in some systemic practice research which has been interesting for me to look back on. There are no truths about how my writing process really evolved. I have used vague memories of what it was like in the beginning of the doctoral program but have applied all the experience the long studying process has given me while telling you about my struggles and my victories.

References

Anderson, Harlene (1997). *Conversation, Language, and Possibilities*. New York: Basic oBoks.

Asplund, Johan (1970). *Om Undran Inför Samhället*. Lund: Argos.

Bateson, Gregory (1972, reprinted 2000). *Steps to an Ecology of Mind*. Chicago: University of Chicago Press.

Bateson, Gregory (1979). *Mind and Nature: A necessary Unity*. New York: Bantam.

Bateson, Gregory & Bateson, Mary Catherine (1988). *Där änglar är rädda att gå*. Stockholm: Symposium.

Bakhtin, Mikhail (1986, reprinted 2002). *Speech Genres & Other Late Essays*. Texas: University of Texas Press.

Gustavsson, Bjørn. (2010). Horace Engdahl: Ärret efter drömmen. Available at: *http://ovanmyramissionshus.blogspot.co.uk/2010/01/horace-engdahl-arret-efter-drommen.html*.

Cunliffe, Ann (2002). Social Poetics as Management Inquiry A Dialogical Approach. *Journal of Management Inquiry*, Vol.11, No.2, 128-146.

Cunliffe, Ann (2003). Reflexive Inquiry in Organizational Research: Questions and Possibilities. *Human Relations*, 56(8), 983-1003.

Hedges, Fran (2005). *An Introduction to Systemetic Therapy with Induviduals*. New York: Palgrave.

Helin, Jenny (2011). *Living moments in family meetings*. Jönköping: Jönköping International Business School.

Kebbe, Lisen (2012) *Keep the Conversation going. A Study of Conversational Spaces during Family Business Succession*. Doctoral thesis. University of Bedfordshire. Available at: http://uobrep.openrepository.com/uobrep/handle/ 10547/234472

Lyotard, Jean-François (1984). *The Postmodern Condition: A Report on Knowledge*. Minneapolis: University of Minesota Press.

Montaigne, Michel de (1580, reprinted 1986). *Essayer, book 1*. Stockholm: Atlatis.

Richardson, Laurel (1994). *A method of Inquiry*. London: Sage.

Shotter, John (2008). *Conversational Realities Reloaded*. Chagrin Falls, Ohio: Taos Institute Publications.

Shotter, John (1994). Conversational realities: From within persons to within relationships. *The discursive construction of Knowledge conference*. University of Adelaide.

Simon, Gail (2012). Praction Research: A Model of Systemic Inquiry. *Human Systems Journal of Systemic Consultation and Management*. Vol. 23:1 pp. 103-124. Available at: https://docs.google.com/file/d/0B5TWuGoJVPe_UDNYdGJ5NXl1dGs/edit?pli=1

Smith, Zadie (2009). An essay is an act of imagination. It still takles quite as much art as fiction. *Guardian News and Media Limited*.

Vedeler, Anne Hedvig (2011). *Dialogical Practices Diving into the Poetic Movement*. Doctoral thesis. University of Bedfordshire. Available at: http://uobrep.openrepository.com/uobrep/handle/10547/223011

Whitehead, Jack & McNiff, Jean (2006). *Action Research Living Theory*. London: Sage.

Wittgenstein, Ludwig (2001). *Philosophical Investigations*. London: Blackwell.

Vygotsky, Lev (1986). *Thought and Language*. Massachusetts: MIT Press.

10 Conversational Reflexivity and Researching Practice

J. Kevin Barge, Carsten Hornstrup and Rebecca Gill

The three of us share a passion for qualitative research methods and the practice of reflexivity in research. Kevin and Carsten have worked together over the last decade with a MSc program in systemic leadership and have developed a number of training techniques and tools for organizational practitioners for working with reflexivity as they conduct qualitative research. Rebecca has been developing reflexive research methods in the context of shadowing as a tool for qualitative research (Gill 2011; Gill, Barbour, & Dean 2014). In this essay, we want to take our recent work on issues regarding reflexivity and qualitative research methods and focus our attention on a concept that we have been developing that we call *conversational reflexivity*. To ground this concept in concrete practice, we draw on the experiences that Kevin and Carsten have had through their involvement with the MSc programme in systemic leadership.

Kevin and Carsten have been involved over the last 10 years with a MSc program for practitioners that is informed by systemic constructionism, appreciative practice, and dialogue. At the heart of this programme are a set of activities that involve a research component, both smaller writing projects as well as a MSc dissertation, that move practitioners to inquire into some aspect of their professional practice. The MSc is designed around the premise that managers, leaders, and consultants need to be able to take a research position toward their professional practice and to develop an ability to generate actionable knowledge that invigorates and transforms not only their individual practice, but the practice of people they work with. The MSc has generated a number of dissertations in a variety of organizations including educational (Henriksen 2009), social services (Christiansen 2011), medical (Breddham 2008), and financial (Peterson 2011) over a range of practices such as strategy (Biering,2010), inspection processes (Chard 2005), assessment (Pouslen 2006), leadership development (Hornstrup 2006), and knowledge management (Falkensfleth 2009).

When teaching and supervising research projects within the MSc program, a primary assumption that informs our practice is that managers, leaders, and consultants need to adopt a reflexive position toward the conduct of inquiry. The importance of working reflexively within one's research practice is an idea that is embedded in most, if not all social and human science paradigms as well as humanities-based research. For post-positivist or normative researchers, reflexivity tends to be treated as methodological reflexivity which emphasizes the researcher taking into account how the choice of particular research methods, including research design and analytical tools, influence the type of knowledge claims that can be drawn and their validity (Johnson & Duberly 2003). For critical and interpretive researchers, reflexivity has been equated with self-reflexivity, being aware of how one's own biases and presumptions as well as the beliefs and assumptions of the research community they participate in shapes the production of knowledge (Alvesson & Skoldberg 2000).

Given that a systemic constructionist approach to practice is imbued with a distinct flavor given its unique set of epistemological, ontological, and ethical commitments (see Barge 2004a, 2004b, 2007; 2012; Barge & Fairhurst 2008), an important question to address is, "How is reflexivity practiced and performed if one adopts a systemic constructionist approach to research practice?" To answer this question, we begin by articulating what we mean by practice-based systemic constructionist research. We then offer a concept, conversational reflexivity, that provides a way of accounting for the way practitioners work with reflexivity as they conduct practice-based systemic constructionist research. At the heart of this concept is the notion that reflexivity involves managing conversations between and among people and texts over time in ways that are relationally-responsive, use difference as a resource for meaning making and action, and resonate with the people we work with and who read our work.

Practice-Based Systemic Constructionist Research

As our understanding of research has evolved whilst working with the MSc programme, we have used a variety of terms to describe the kind of approach we use when we teach and train people in qualitative research methodology, including systemic constructionist research (Barge 2006) and practice-based evidence (Barge, Hornstrup & Henriksen 2010). For the purposes of this paper, we want to integrate three central concepts that animate our approach—practice, systemic, and social constructionism—and focus on what we call practice-based systemic constructionist research (PSCR). Practice-based systemic constructionist research focuses on the ways that individuals and groups work affirmatively and use differences to notice, name, and transform unfolding relational practices within patterns of communication over time. There are several key ideas in this definition that pick up on our earlier thinking regarding research methods (e.g. Barge 2006; 2009).

First, PSCR focuses on *practice* and centers on articulating the evolution of patterns of communicative acts over time and the kinds of social worlds these evolving patterns construct in the forms of episodes, identities, relationships, and cultures. Building on Craig's (2006) definition, a practice may be defined as patterns of communicative acts that occur within a particular site, are linked to a particular professional, personal, or relational identity, or are linked to the performance of a particular activity. We can therefore explore the practice of an organization (site), the practices associated with being a manager, a leader, or a consultant (identity), as well as the practices associated with specific duties, responsibilities, or projects such as strategic planning, staff development, and assessment (activity). What is important to PSCR is that it centers on the patterning of communicative messages over time between individuals, groups, and organizations and gives specific attention to the kinds of episodes, identities, relationships, and cultures these patterns invite and discourage as people attempt to coordinate their behavior. For example, Falkensfleth (2009) was interested in exploring the practice of knowledge sharing within her hospital and centered her dissertation around the kinds of communication interventions and meetings that would facilitate knowledge sharing among units in her hospital and create partnership and develop her practice. Her dissertation is a good example of what most of our MSc students do when they conduct their research projects; they examine a specific practice in their home organization (site) that is related to their position within the organization (identity), which is related to some professional responsibility they must perform as part of their organizational position (activity).

Second, PSCR employs *systemic explanations* to account for patterns of meaning making and action versus individualistic explanations. Drawing on Bateson (1972), Barge (2006) highlights that there has been a tendency for researchers in the social sciences to highlight more linear variable-analytic accounts of why a particular pattern of communication exists and what consequences they create. For example, there has been recent interest in issues related to the occurrence of workplace bullying or mobbing (Tracy, Lutgen-Sandvik & Alberts 2006). If one were to create a linear variable-analytic account of this phenomenon, one might seek psychological explanations that would use individual-based variables such as personality traits to account for the occurrence of workplace bullying which might generate claims like, managers who are narcissistic and have a high need for power are more likely to engage in workplace bullying. On the other hand, one might create more structural-based explanations relying on more macro-level explanations to offer an account for the occurrence of workplace bullying such as, upper-level management has created a climate that makes workplace bullying permissible. While both of these explanations appear different as one employs more micro-level variables to explain the occurrence of workplace bullying and the other macro-level variables, they share a similar explanatory logic in that they reduce the situation's complexity by developing an account for the occurrence of workplace bullying using linear explanation that relies on cause-effect logic where one entity (read independent variable) leads to another (read dependent variable).

PSCR moves from linear, singular explanations to systemic explanations that emphasize how various stories, metaphors, narratives etc. connect to one another to provide an account of the integrated complexity of a particular practice at this particular moment in time in a specific place. Rather than assume simple linear causality, drawing on Bateson (1972), the focus becomes on identifying the various feedback loops that connect elements in a system and exploring how the configuration of connections invites or discourages certain patterns of behavior and engenders particular consequences. The burning question is, "How does it make sense for the people involved in a current practice to co-ordinate their meaning and action in this fashion?" For example, let's say in the process of investigating workplace bullying within a specific organization, we generate the following data and interpretations:

- The onset of reported incidents of workplace bullying occurred when the new CEO was appointed and implemented a new set of performance objectives.

- The CEO believes that organizational performance is enhanced when employees feel invested in the organization's purpose and mission.

- Employees in the organization suggest that the typical conversations they have with their supervisors tend to be one-way with supervisors telling employees what to do. Collaborative participative decision-making is discouraged.

- There are a set of stories floating about in the organization that employees who dissent from company norms and directives are either reassigned to less desirable jobs or have their contracts terminated.

- The organization is in a financial crisis and unless it is turned around quickly, there is a question of how long it can survive.

- The founder of the organization had a personal motto, "Only the strong survive."

Rather than try to reduce the explanation of why the practice of workplace bullying persists in this organization to a single factor or variable, we become more interested in looking at how these different facets combine into an integrated story that captures the complexity of the situation. In this instance, we might generate an explanation that is grounded in a story of "heightened pressure":

> *The organization has a history of emphasizing "getting it right" the first time as its founder emphasized strength and toughness. The managers feel pressure to get it right, so they take personal responsibility and adopt an autocratic style where they tell their employees what to do. This tendency has only been heightened given the perilous economic conditions of the company, and managers feel even more pressure to get it right if the company is going to survive. Employees have learned a pattern that if they resist what the manager says, they will likely be transferred or fired. The new CEO may have unintentionally triggered bullying as another pressure is given the edict to supervisors, "Hit your new performance objectives!"*

What this "heightened pressure" explanation does is take several distinct elements—the founder's story, the story of the new CEO, the economic story of the organizations, and the supervisor-employee stories—and weaves them together into a coherent narrative. It is the way that these various elements connect, reinforce, and contradict each other that provide a systemic explanation for the increase in bullying behavior. While certain elements may carry more weight than the others, they join together in a single narrative that respects the various elements or what Barge (2004a) has called a systemic story. This process of creating systemic explanations is analogous to the process of abduction where an explanation that provides an integrated account of the particulars regarding why people are doing what they are doing makes sense to them (Shepherd & Sutcliffe 2011).

Third, PSCR emphasizes *affirmative practice*. Drawing on inspiration from Appreciative Inquiry (Cooperrider & Whitney 1999) and the concept of positive connotation from Milan Systemic Family Therapy (Boscolo, Cecchin, Hoffman & Penn 1985), PSCR focuses on what gives life and energy to a human system. Many approaches to Appreciative Inquiry conflate affirmation with a strong focus on the "positive," but our perspective is that affirmative practice needs to be conceived more broadly, focusing on what generates life and energy within a system, which sometimes means needing to work with and transform strong negative emotion, fragility, and vulnerability (Barge & Oliver 2003; Barge & Fairhurst 2008). In terms of taking a research position that emphasizes affirmative practice, this can take at least two different forms when conducting inquiry. On one hand, affirmative practice can be used to actively intervene and participate in a human system, which emphasizes managers, leaders, and consultants designing and conducting inquiry in ways that direct the attention of the participants to what generates life and energy in a human system. For example, this may involve conducting individual or group interviews regarding best practices, what works well in an organization, core values, and dreams. Many of these questions are standard practices associated with appreciative interviewing. On the other hand, affirmative practice can be used to cultivate an observing position toward a human system that emphasizes researchers cultivating an appreciative ear and eye when analyzing the material they have generated. When cultivating an observing position, researchers give particular attention to what is working well in the organization, remembering that even if the participants offer negative stories about the organization, these negative stories have a shadow side where a problem is simply a "frustrated dream." In the present example, a manager who is working affirmatively with workplace bullying might frame and design inquiry regarding "how do we get our relationships right so they are respectful and humane?" This kind of framing and subsequent design is appreciative in nature in that it picks up on a core value within the organization regarding "getting it right" but also connects it to a future dream, having constructive workplace relationships, which is the "frustrated dream" within workplace bullying. When reflecting on the material that has been created, when reading examples where organizational members have felt abused, the researcher may listen for the hopes and aspirations of what a healthy relationship might look like, one where they are not abused but valued.

Fourth, PSCR focuses on generating *productive differences* throughout the research process to create more complex nuanced descriptions, interpretations, and interventions. Within the research methods literature, particularly the literature involving mixed methods, there is an emphasis on using member checks and multiple sources of data to engage in triangulation (Lindlof & Taylor 2010). Triangulation involves using a variety of data sources to create an account that emphasizes what is common across them and is typically viewed as providing a method for making stronger claims particularly when multiple sources lead to the same conclusion. Rather than engage in logics of inquiry that emphasize confirmation and commonality, PSCR employs a logic of inquiry that emphasizes divergence and difference. PSCR purposefully employs the notion of difference when generating and analyzing data. For example, if we begin with the notion that any person's view of a system is inherently partial, it becomes important to interview different members of a human system in order to generate a more complex story regarding the system. If we also recognize that our view and interpretation of the data is inherently partial, then it is imperative to introduce difference into our analyses so they become challenged and disturbed. In the present example, this might mean interviewing people at different levels within the organization from different departments in order to capture the diversity of perceptions regarding the organization. It might also mean that we use multiple analytical tools, such as narrative, grounded theory, and discourse analysis, to create different interpretations of the data. This is similar to what Ellingson (2008) refers to as crystallization. It is possible that different data sources, analysis tools, and interpretations may lead us to similar conclusions, but our starting point is to engage in a process aimed at fostering divergent interpretations, and then exploring their connections, which may or may not lead to convergence.

Fifth, PSCR is *generative*. Drawing on action research, collaborative forms of inquiry, and participatory action research (Coghlan & Brannick 2005), we believe that research needs to enable new patterns of meaning making and action. Practice-based systemic research is aimed at developing an awareness of our and other's practice in a way that generates actionable knowledge to deepen, extend, and transform self and other's practice reflexively. Pearce (1994) highlights that human beings can take at least two different positions toward their experience and the experience of others. A first-person perspective creates research and knowledge that answers the question, "What do I or we do next?" This kind of question is future-oriented as an individual, group, or organization has to make sense of a situation and develop a line of action. A third-person perspective creates research and knowledge that answers the question, "What are they doing?" This kind of question is more retrospective in nature as it attempts to demonstrate knowledge about a human system by identifying what language games they are engaging and what these games produce.

From our perspective, PSCR's highest-level context is the first-person perspective. As a manager, leader, or consultant, we are always wrestling with choices of what we should do next and how we enable the groups we work with to make wise choices about what they are going to do next and the kinds of effects they wish to invite. This does not diminish the importance of conducting research that takes more of a third-person perspective, which emphasizes retrospective sense making and observer-generated descriptions of the unfolding patterns of communication. But the knowledge generated by third-person perspectives needs to be put in the service of a first-person perspective. The descriptions should help create springboards for future meaning making and action; they need to generate actionable knowledge. For example, in the MSc dissertations we have been involved with, it is not uncommon for our students to generate data from their teams and analyze it, creating a third-person description of relevant themes and patterns. However, the research does not stop at that point. The analysis is often then used to create a reflecting session where the group engages with the analysis, challenges it, deepens it, and oftentimes generates a set of actionable next steps that may be taken. When people engage in such reflecting sessions, they begin to co-create the future as they generate new insights that lead to new patterns of meaning making and action.

Practice-based systemic research can focus on either one's individual practice as a manager, leader, or consultant, the practice of a team or organization, or the functioning of a wider system. The question that animates PSCR is, "What can I or we do next?" This future-oriented question moves researchers to generate actionable knowledge that can generate new forms of meaning making or action. Such actionable knowledge is more likely to be useful when it focuses on affirmative practice and purposefully incorporates difference. The tacit metaphor that informs PSCR is that of the improvised conversation. To improvise means you have to be in the moment and make wise choices from within the flow of the research process. These choices may range from very micro-choices such as what question to ask during an interview or what you (pre) consciously notice in the research scene or more macro-choices regarding the various pieces (e.g., interview, analysis, document collection) that need to be in place and how they are sequenced. Such choices involve situated reflexivity in the moment as to how one manages the communication flows and relationships among and between people and texts.

Practice-Based Systemic Constructionist Research and Conversational Reflexivity

Reflexivity has been an important term in the social and human sciences. Though many different definitions and perspectives toward reflexivity exist, there are two common approaches to reflexivity that have been articulated in the literature: (1) textual reflexivity (Alvesson, Hardy, & Harley 2008), and (2) relational reflexivity (Hosking & Plutt 2010). Alvesson et al (2008) suggest that textual reflexivity centers on the ways that researchers write up their research with a focus on how "textual practices are used to evoke and present various forms of reflexive analysis" (p. 481). Cunliffe (2003) observes that a metaphor of otherness tends to characterize postmodern, poststructural, and deconstructionist approaches to qualitative research, approaches that are closely aligned with textual reflexivity. The metaphor of otherness operates from the assumption that meaning is created through the interplay of differences among texts, particularly the interplay of presence and absence and the oppositional logics among multiple texts. Researchers surface multiple, and often contradictory, sets of meanings by closely pulling apart the different voices, social languages, discourses, language games, and genres within a single text or by juxtaposing various texts against each other.

Relational reflexivity draws attention to the way that reflexive practices are embodied in the unfolding research conversations among researchers and research participants as well as members of other linguistic communities such as academic peers, institutional review boards, and journal editors. The emphasis on social construction imbues research with an interventive flavor as the utterances performed in conversation, by either the researcher or a member of another linguistic community, shape the meaning making process, inviting certain forms of meaning making and discouraging others. For example, ethnomethodological studies of research interviews highlight that the knowledge produced in interviews is a collaborative accomplishment emerging from the joint action between interviewers and research participants (Talmy 2011). Cunliffe (2003) suggests that this form of reflexive practice involves, "acknowledging the constitutive nature of our research conversations; constructing 'emerging practical theories' rather than objective truths; exposing the situated nature of accounts through narrative circularity; [and] focusing on life and research as a process of becoming rather than already established truth" (p.991).

Rather than treat reflexivity as a textual or relational process, we prefer to treat reflexivity as a conversational process that involves the coordination of multiple conversations including various human and nonhuman actors including research participants, the literature, field notes, members of a research team, editorial board members and the like (Pearce & Pearce 2006). Like many forms of qualitative research, PSCR involves the generation of texts such as interview transcripts, notes and flipcharts from meetings, memos, emails, and personal journals through ongoing conversations with organizational members, external organizational constituencies, and professional colleagues outside the workplace. PSCR also involves coordinating conversations among people in the form of group interviews as well as collective data analysis sessions with participants. It is not uncommon for individual or group interviews to be used initially to generate texts which the researcher then uses to generate an analysis, and then to subsequently engage individuals and groups in conversation as co-researchers to analyze the texts. The line between reflexivity between and among texts and reflexivity between and among people is often blurred as people actively engage in conversation with one another about the texts to generate new insights and activity. We suggest that the notion of conversational reflexivity as a useful concept for exploring the way that practitioners can work with reflexivity during inquiry and the way the coordinate between and among texts and people.

Conversational reflexivity may be articulated as a focus on the ways conversations between and among texts and people disrupt the meaning making process and introduce alternative forms of meaning making that influence the construction of the research process and knowledge claims. These conversations may occur internally, where researchers engage in self-reflection on their research practice and knowledge claims or externally where individuals engage in collective reflections with their co-researchers. We find conversational reflexivity to be a useful concept for several reasons.

First, conversational reflexivity integrates textual and relational reflexivity within a single framework. Organization and management theorists acknowledge that both types of reflexivity are useful (Alvesson et al 2008; Cunliffe 2003); however, they serve different purposes. Conversational reflexivity provides a framework that values the contribution of each and allows us to examine three different kinds of research conversations: (a) conversations between and among texts, (b) conversations between and among people, and (c) conversations between and among texts and people.

Second, conversational reflexivity acknowledges that different modes of reflexive practice exist, unfolding and intertwining over time. Hibbert et al. (2010) observe that temporal aspects of reflexivity are often overlooked, which neglects the way that researchers move between different modes of reflexivity. For example, field notes are commonly employed in ethnographic work. In terms of textual reflexivity, researchers need to pay attention to how they keep reflexivity alive in the notes they use to construct their analysis, how they give attention to multiple voices, discourses, and perspectives, and how they account for the way their positionality influences their knowledge claims. The way field notes are constructed influences one's subsequent relational reflexivity when engaging with others in the field. Conversational reflexivity facilitates examining how our writing and dialoguing practices become intertwined and mutually implicated over time.

Third, conversational reflexivity recognizes that modes of reflexive practice are layered. Operating within the framework of textual reflexivity, Alvesson and Skoldberg's (2000) model of reflexive interpretation highlights four levels of interpretation (empirical material, interpretation, critical interpretation, and self-critical and linguistic reflection) and the interaction between levels. In a similar vein, Ellingson's (2008) notion of crystallization emphasizes using multi-level analysis, employing different analytic genres, in order to develop detailed rich descriptions. Working from a relationally-reflexive position, Barge and Oliver (2003) highlight several different conversational tools for inviting and coordinating people's interpretations. Brannick and Coghlan (2005) suggest that action research cycles be coupled with individual experiential learning cycles that emphasize experiencing, reflecting, interpreting, and taking action in order to be fully reflexive. Action research cycles embody a more relationally focused form of reflexivity, whereas individual experiential learning cycles emphasizes epistemic reflexivity. These different examples highlight how various modes of reflexive practice can be layered onto each other. The notion of layering in conversational reflexivity draws attention to issues regarding which modes of reflexive practice serve as higher-order contexts for working with and interpreting lower-order levels of reflexive practice as well as the shape and form of the conversations between levels.

Fourth, conversational reflexivity emphasizes situated judgment. A key issue in qualitative research is what kind of reflexivity or reflexive practice is needed at a particular moment in time. This requires researchers to make situated judgments about when to engage particular modes of reflexivity and these judgments are informed by the way that researchers formulate the problem at hand. A wide variety of literatures ranging from management and leadership studies (Grint 2005; Schon 1984) to family therapy (Boscolo, Cecchin, Hoffman & Penn 1985) observe that the way a problem is formulated or set defines how elements in a system connect with each other and the kinds of communication that are needed or legitimated by that particular problem formulation. When researchers articulate a problem in a particular way, then certain modes of reflexivity become more relevant than others. For example, if a researcher frames the problem as the need to elicit more reflexive accounts of their participant's research experience, then a mode of what Walsh (2003) calls interpersonal reflexivity may be warranted in order to invite a conversation that does this. Of course, the conundrum is that problem setting is itself a reflexive activity and as such, the researcher has had a hand in constructing the articulation of the very problem that informs their choices regarding reflexive practice.

Viewing reflexivity as an improvised activity that occurs within conversation focuses attention on the way that practitioners orchestrate the interactions among texts and people. What makes working with research conversations in a reflexive manner challenging is that they are situated and dynamic. They are situated in the sense that they are unique and novel given the particular time, space, and participants, and they are dynamic as the collective action of the researcher and participants introduce new elements into the research process that must subsequently be addressed. Therefore, it is critical for researchers to give attention to the ongoing quality of the conversation and what they wish to create by having certain conversations and not others.

Managing Conversations and Practice-Based Systemic Constructionist Research

When we think about research as a conversation interesting questions emerge, "What are the qualities of good conversations?" and "How do we foster good conversations between and among texts and people?" While several possibilities exist for articulating what qualities characterize "good" research conversations, we suggest that there are three qualities that can be used to inform and assess our research conversations: (1) research conversations should be relationally-responsive, (2) research conversations should involve difference work, and (3) research conversations and their portrayals should be resonant and provocative.

Research conversations should be relationally-responsive

When we inquire into our own or others' practice we must coordinate multiple conversations with pre-existing organizational texts such as reports, mission statements, and strategic plans and the texts we create in the form of interview transcripts, field notes, or visual or audio recordings, as well as people and groups that help us co-create and analyze data. Practitioner-researchers must orchestrate conversations within and among texts and people or what might be termed a network of nonhuman and human actors (Ashcraft, Kuhn & Cooren 2009). This means that practitioner-researchers should be mindful of what conversations they need to have, what human or nonhuman actors they need to have them with, and how they will connect in a meaningful way to the other actor in the conversation. As practitioner-researchers begin to think about what conversations they want to invite texts and people into or how texts and people invite practitioner-researchers into conversation, they need to work through the following kinds of questions:

- What kind of conversations do you want to have?

- How do you want to have this conversation?

- With what or whom do you want to have this conversation?

- When do you want to have this conversation?

- Where do you want to have this conversation?

- What supports need to be in place in order for you to have the conversation you desire?

Conversational reflexivity foregrounds the importance of research conversations being relationally-responsive to the contingent details of the moment and the flow of unfolding conversation. Relationally-responsive conversations emphasize the importance of being present within a conversation and paying attention to the unique particulars of a situation so one can connect with others in ways that honor the uniqueness and complexity of the situation as opposed to imposing an *a priori* research plan and design onto the situation and others (Scharmer 2009). Shotter (2010) talks about the importance of engaging in "withness thinking" with others, which means that we need to respond to one another from within the emerging flow of conversation and pick upon the contribution that each is making. How can we do this in terms of different kinds of research conversations?

Text-to-person conversations. Text-to-person conversations are the conversations that practitioner-researchers or their co-researchers have with written, audio, or visual texts. For example, after one has conducted fieldwork, a number of texts may have been created that a practitioner-researcher might engage with including field notes, interview transcripts, video-recordings, and the like. How does a practitioner-researcher generate relationally-responsive conversations with texts or encourage such conversations between their co-researchers and texts? Similar to jazz, such conversations tend to be improvisational as the researcher has a toolkit that s/he works from. It is not uncommon for researchers when they propose a research study to have a preliminary analysis plan in place. However, to be relationally-responsive, a researcher has to make choices in the moment of how to engage the empirical material in light of what the material provides, the expectations of others in the research community, the purpose of the study, and the expectations of the client. For example, in our experience most practitioner-researchers have a general sense of what they might like to do in the analysis; however, this becomes refined as they work with the material. They notice certain things such as key words that keep being mentioned, the heavy use of metaphoric language, or the frequency of stories, which attracts their attention and moves them to rethink what analysis they might use. If they become intrigued with language use, they might employ discourse analysis. Texts have an "uptake" to them, which means there are certain kinds of linguistic or nonlinguistic triggers that a practitioner-researcher might pick upon that become a focus for inquiry. Texts speak to us as the "uptake" invites us into certain kinds of conversations. As a result, practitioner-researchers may read the text in different ways that leads them to different kinds of analysis, many of which were unanticipated.

How can practitioner-researchers broaden their ability to read texts differently? One way is offered by Weick's (2007) notion regarding the generative property of richness. Weick (2007) argues that researchers need to read widely so that they can employ a wide variety of frameworks, ideas, and concepts to engage with texts. When we have rich interpretive repertoires to draw on as researchers, the possibility that we can generate fresh insights to the material and pick up on elements from the text that others may not give attention to is enhanced. Another way that practitioner-researchers can broaden their ability to read texts differently is to purposefully juxtapose different texts with one another and see how elements of one text may or may not connect with another. This is the notion of intertextuality, which means placing one text in conversation with another (Kristeva 1984). For example, one might use key ideas from organizational documents like mission statements, memos, and strategic plans and explore their connections to the texts generated from individual or group interviews. What appear to be text-to-text conversations are in actuality text-to-person-to-text conversations as text-to-text conversations are always mediated by a person, either practitioner-researchers, co-researchers, or practitioner-researchers collectively working with their co-researchers.

Person-to-person conversations. Conversations between and among people within research projects also need to be reflexive. The primary challenge here is how to work with people to co-create conversations in ways that are relationally-responsive and generative. The kinds of conversations that one can have vary by stakeholder as well as purpose. Person-to-person conversations can involve several different conversational partners, including members of one's team or unit as well as organizational members and units that are external to the team or unit in focus, and individuals or groups that are external to the organization such as clients or other external partners or collaborators.

The kinds of person-to-person conversations associated with research can fulfill different purposes. Dempsey and Barge (in press) propose several different kinds of conversation that are involved with collaborative research:

1. Co-missioning: Coordinating people's stakes in the research process, the purpose for the research project, and the end-in-view for the inquiry.

2. Co-design: Developing a structure for the way empirical material will be generated, analyzed, and used in subsequent meaning making and action.

3. Co-reflection: Collaborative work that analyzes and interprets the empirical material that has been generated.

4. Co-action: Action-oriented conversations that focus on possible future action and activity that might be undertaken in light of the interpretations and information generated from engaging in the inquiry.

For example, Henriksen (2009) offers an excellent example of these kinds of conversations in play. Henrikson (2009) was a headmaster at a school and was interested in working collaboratively with members of his staff to develop their strategic competence. He actively involved his staff when completing the ethics board proposal, which allowed members of his staff to have a voice in determining the purpose and flow of the research (co-missioning and co-design conversations). He and his staff subsequently met on a regular basis to work through the material that had been generated, interpret it, and use it to determine subsequent lines of action (co-reflection and co-action conversations). A point we wish to make is that person-to-person conversations can be used throughout a research project; the question becomes what kinds of conversations are most useful to generate new forms of sense making and action when, and with whom.

Reflexivity within person-to-person conversations turns on one's ability to manage the flow of conversation in a way that responds to earlier moves in the conversation and gestures toward new possibilities for meaning making and action that others can follow. As Pearce (1994) observes, understanding the flow of any conversation means working with the conversation triplet. Pearce (1994) suggests that the meaning of any act is determined by the utterance that precedes it and what follows it. Reflexive practice involves sequencing one's conversational moves in ways that pick up on elements of earlier moves, affirm them, and then making a gesture that extends these lines of conversation. This process may occur preconsciously or intuitively in a type of reflex action or may be more conscious and reflective (Cunliffe, 2004). Working reflexively necessitates managing the flow of emergent conversation in a way that preserves coherence, movement, and evolution.

Let us provide two examples of how this reflexive process might work in conversation both at a micro-level as well as a macro-level. At a micro-level, we are referring to the ways that practitioner-reseachers manage conversation uttcrance-by-utterance. For example, MSc students frequently use systemic or circular questioning to conduct interviews (see Hornstrup, Loehr-Petersen, & Madsen, 2012, for a description of systemic or circular questioning). Systemic or circular questioning is reflexive in nature as it builds off previous responses and tries to connect various utterances. Practitioner-researchers pay attention to some element in the utterance by another, ask a question that picks up on that element, and depending on how the other responds to their question, adjusts their next conversational move.

Working at a more macro-level means focusing on the connections among episodes within the flow of the research project versus individual utterances. Pearce and Pearce (2000) and Spano (2001) refer to thinking about the flow of episodes within a research projects as event design. How should different events of conversational episodes be sequenced in ways that build off each other and are coherent? A conversational episode is a communicative sequence that has a distinct beginning, middle, and end and a through-line that connects the distinct utterances into a coherent pattern. For example, we can talk about individual or group interviews, data analysis sessions, and feedback sessions as conversational episodes. When we take a more macro-level view toward person-to-person conversations, we treat the episodes as if they were a single utterance and become interested in how the sequence of episodes build on each other and cohere with one another. Reflexivity at this level becomes concerned with emergent design work. Typically a research project has some kind of pre-planned design associated with it, however, this design is subject to change as things unfold. For example, Kevin was recently involved with a research project that had a very clear co-missioning conversation where the understanding was that he and a group of researchers would work with a health organization to design an event that would bring members of the organization in dialogue with groups of a faith-based community. However, leadership within the health organization did not feel the organization needed members of the research team and the role of the research team was redefined from designers of the event to advisors, which led to a different kind of meeting than was originally anticipated. It became important to design a different kind of meeting because the situation changed (leadership now wanted the research team to be advisors versus designers) and the research team's hope was that this meeting would build on this change and open up a new role for the research team.

Research conversations should involve difference work

A second quality of generative research conversations is that they need to treat the conversation as difference work and attempt to foster multiple points of view and perspectives. Difference work involves creating and introducing differences into the conversation to bring additional perspectives, frameworks, and viewpoints into play. Difference becomes an important resource for meaning making and action as difference enlarges the experiential base for creating interpretations, rending judgments, and taking action. Practice-based systemic constructionist research is grounded in the belief that we need to foster divergent reads and interpretations of situations from various vantage points and then connect them with one another into some kind of coherent whole that moves meaning making and action forward. Difference work is like the process of refraction. When light is passed through a prism the process of refraction allows us to see light in a different way as being comprised of myriad colors. In linguistic terms, this is analogous to Bakhtin's (1981) observation that what appears to be singular language, story or discourse is actually multiple. For example, what we might take to be a single language, story, or discourse is actually a distillation of multiple discursive elements from the past. Moreover, people may narrate events in different ways. Therefore, it becomes important to focus on issues of difference and use difference as a meaningful resource to tease out dissimilarities and divergences in the empirical material that may otherwise go unnoticed.

Conversational reflexivity involves offering multiple readings of the phenomena, which emphasizes crystallization and kaleidoscopic approaches that emphasize difference and divergence, as opposed to triangulation, which privileges consensus and similarity (Ellingsen, 2008). In the MSc dissertations we have been involved in, differences in the way practitioners can work with and introduce difference into their data generation and analysis can take many different forms:

1. *Playing with time*: Oftentimes researchers will use future-oriented questions to dislodge participants from present ways of thinking and inspire fresh perspectives. This is then followed up with "backcasting" questions that work with the participants from the present to the future.

2. *Playing with position*: Different reflecting positions are created that emphasize different takes on the material. For example, domains theory offers three different positions that can be used to reflect on a communicative pattern—the domains of explanation, aesthetics, and production (Lang, Little, & Cronen 1990). Other frameworks that students have often employed to foster diverse perspectives toward the material include CMM (Pearce 2007), the LUUTT model (Pearce & Pearce 1998), student analysis groups etc.

3. *Playing with layers*: Often students will not use a single analyzing tool but incorporate multiple analyzing tools used in sequence. For example, a student may begin with a metaphor analysis of then draw on elements of narrative analysis to tease out stories relating to different metaphors.

4. *Playing with communication media and modes*: We have been impressed with the various tools the students use to create differences. For example, students often listen to their own interview record-

ings and transcribe them, which brings a different experience to the analysis. Or, they relive the interview by simultaneously listening to the recording and reading the interview transcript, which moves to recreate the bodily sensations they may have felt during the interview. Christiansen (2011) used an interesting projective technique using Visual Explorer, which uses photographs to encourage narrative story telling.

5. *Playing with insider-outsider positions.* Students often use student groups to help analyze their data as well as groups from within the organization they work with.

Research conversations and their portrayals should be resonant and provocative

As we conduct our inquiry, we want to make sure that our conversations with our research participants and the stories we develop about our research conversations with texts and people, become distilled into our analyses and are resonant and provocative to participants and readers of our work. Our participants become our co-researchers, which means that the interviews we conduct with them, the reflecting sessions that we have them, and/or other types of meeting are meaningful and inspiring. For those who read our research stories in the form of essays, articles, book chapters, and the like, they too need to resonate with the experience of the reader and provide inspiration. Whether these stories are about the research process itself, how it was co-missioned and conducted, or about people's experience, they need to simultaneously connect with people's experience and gesture toward future patterns of meaning making and action. Resonance is achieved when our conversations and stories have a sense of narrative fidelity, coherence, and engagement.

Fisher (1989) suggests that there are two dimensions that can be used to assess narratives. The first, narrative fidelity, refers to people's sense of whether a narrative has "a ring of truth." Does the constructed narrative "ring true" given people's experience? The second, narrative coherence, refers to whether the plausibility of the narrative to what degree does the narrative hang together and present a coherent sensible interpretation of events. When people experience narratives as having a sense of fidelity and coherence to them, they become more persuasive and can enable action.

We would add a third concept, narrative movement, to Fisher's notions of narrative fidelity and coherence. We choose the term movement purposefully as it directs our attention to narratives and stories that move us, which have some emotional connection. The notion of movement not only highlights the notion of forward movement, it foregrounds the creation of new future possibilities. The notion of movement as something we find interesting and provocative is hinted at in Davis' (1971) work, which explores what it is that makes a theory interesting. Operating within a phenomenological framework, Davis (1971) argues that a theory becomes "interesting" when it challenges the taken-for-granted phenomenological ground of a particular community. For example, one way to account for the rise of asset-based, strength-based, and appreciative approaches to management is that they challenged the dominant ground of management theories that were rooted in a problem-solving deficit-based logic. We would suggest that for a narrative to become moving, it has to provide a fresh insight into the situation or issue. It also needs to provide a different take on the situation, something that challenges our assumptions and surprises and delights us or perhaps even saddens us, and provokes us into action.

For research conversations, this means working in a relationally-responsive way that not only foregrounds difference when we meet with our co-researchers, but also challenges their thinking and introduces new ways of making sense of their social worlds. Negative strong emotion still resonates and is generative, but may need to be transformed. For our research stories, we need to find ways to portray our work in engaging ways that capture the complexity of the work we are doing and convey its emotional and inspirational impact.

Making Judgments and Conversational Reflexivity

The purpose of this essay has been to articulate the concept of conversational reflexivity as a way for practitioner-researchers to work reflexively when conducting inquiry. Conversational reflexivity is associated with a number of core animating values including playfulness, generativity, experimental attitude, curiosity, co-creation, and increasing the possibility space for alternative forms of meaning making and action. At this point, we want to invite you into a conversation with us about where we can take our thinking next. In that spirit, we pose three questions that have captured our interest and ask you to also think through the possible responses.

The first question is, "What is that allows practitioner-researchers to improvise and work with emergence?" Conversational reflexivity privileges emergence and improvisation. What kinds of experience, preparatory activities, skills, and abilities allow us to improvise and make changes to our process in a way that honors our research aims and purposes and makes sense to the people we are working with? If PSCR is co-created with others and requires us to be present in the moment, it will be important to identify the kinds of abilities, resources, and practices that enable us to work with emergent complex situations.

The second question is, "What tensions must be managed when working with conversational reflexivity?" As we have co-created this chapter, a number of trade-offs and tensions emerged regarding the way we work with co-missioning, co-design, co-reflection, and co-action conversation. For example, some of the tensions we might face when working with conversational reflexivity include:

1. Consciousness—How do we manage our conscious and preconscious resources to respond to an emerging situation? When does (pre)consciousness become an enabling resource or obstacle to our inquiry?

2. Preparation—How do we manage the tension between the process needing to be planned/structured and emergent/unstructured from within the flow of inquiry?

3. Curiosity—How open do we keep the process to encourage divergence and when do we need to focus on convergence and narrow our thinking?

4. Reflection: How do we manage the tension between the need to be reflective and take action? How do we develop a sense of timing regarding when to engage in reflection and when to take action?

5. Playfulness: How do we keep the space open to play with different ideas and interpretations and maintain a focus on getting things done, in the domain of production?

6. Positionality: How do we manage the tensions between being a practitioner but also needing to take a research position toward our practice?

This brief listing represents a small sample of the possible tensions one may engage when working with conversational reflexivity. What other tensions do we need to give attention to and how can they be managed?

The third question is, "How can we deepen and broaden our practices for conversations that take place within and among texts and people?" We have identified some different ways that people have worked with conversational reflexivity in the form of examples from MSc students. What other practices can we develop? Our essay has focused on how we might cultivate difference but has not explored issues of timing, pacing, and sequencing. What role does time and timing play in the practice of conversational reflexivity?

As Bakhtin (1981) has said, the dialogue is never-ending and it is unfinalizable. We look forward to continuing the conversation regarding the ways that conversational reflexivity can be used to develop practice-based systemic constructionist research.

References

Alvesson, Mats, & Skoldberg, Kaj (2000). *Reflexive methodology: New vistas for qualitative research*. London: Sage.

Alvesson, Mats, Hardy, C., & Harley, B. (2008). Reflecting on reflexivity: Reflexive textual practices in organization and management theory. *Journal of Management Studies, 45,* 480-501.

Ashcraft, Karen L., Kuhn, Thomas R. & Cooren, François (2009). Constitutional amendments: "Materializing" organizational communication. *Academy of Management Annals, 3,* 1-64.

Bakhtin, Mikhail M. (1981). *The dialogic imagination*. Austin, TX: University of Texas Press.

Barge, J. Kevin (2004a). Antenarrative and managerial practice. *Communication Studies, 55,* 106-127.

Barge, J. Kevin (2004b). Reflexivity and managerial practice. *Communication Monographs. 71,* 70-96.

Barge, J. Kevin (2006). Living systemic constructionist management research. *Human Systems, 17,* 257-280.

Barge, J. Kevin (2007). The practice of systemic leadership: Lessons from the Kensington Consultation Centre Foundation. *OD Practitioner, 39,* 10-14.

Barge, J. Kevin (2009). Basics of social constructionist research. In W. L. Hurwitz & G. Galanes (eds.), *Socially constructing communication: Catching ourselves in the act*. Cresskill, NJ: Hampton Press.

Barge, J. Kevin (2012). Systemic constructionist leadership and working from within the present moment. In S. Ospina & M. Uhl-Bien (eds.), *Advancing relational leadership theory: A conversation among perspectives* (pp.107-142). Charlotte, NC: Information Age Publishing.

Barge, J. Kevin & Dempsey, Sarah (2014). Engaged scholarship as democratic conversation. In L. L. Putnam & D. Mumby (eds.), *The handbook of organizational communication*. pp.665-688. Thousand Oaks: Sage.

Barge, J. Kevin, & Fairhurst, Gail T. (2008). Living leadership: A systemic constructionist approach. *Leadership, 4,* 227-251.

Barge, J. Kevin; Hornstrup, Cartsen & Henriksen, Jan (2010, April). *Practice-based evidence and action research*. Paper presented at Qualitative Research in Management and Organizational Conference, Albuquerque.

Barge, J. Kevin & Oliver, Christine (2003). Working with appreciation in managerial practice. *Academy of Management Review, 28,* 124-142.

Bateson, Gregory (1972). *Steps to an ecology of mind*. Chicago: University of Chicago Press.

Biering, Christian (2010). *Systemic strategic management in the Royal Danish*

Air Force. Unpublished MSc dissertation, University of Bedfordshire, Bedfordshire, UK.

Boscolo, Luigi; Cecchin, Gianfranco; Hoffman, Lynn & Penn, Peggy (1985). *Milan systemic family therapy*. New York: Basic Books.

Breddham, Christina. (2008). Collaborative knowledge sharing and development. Unpublished MSc dissertation, University of Bedfordshire, Bedfordshire, UK.

Chard, Alex (2005). *Youth offending teams and inspection: Understanding the impact on the management of service*. Unpublished MSc dissertation, University of Bedfordshire, Bedfordshire, UK.

Christensen, Thomas. N. (2011). Co-creating dialogical processes at meetings. Unpublished MSc dissertation, University of Bedfordshire, Bedfordshire, UK.

Coghlan, David & Brannick, Teresa (2005). *Doing action research in your own organization* (2nd ed.). London: Sage.

Cooperrider, David L., & Whitney, Diana (1999). *Appreciative inquiry*. San Francisco: Berrett-Koehler.

Craig, Robert T. (2006). A practice. In G. J. Shepherd, J. St. John, & T. Striphas (Eds.), *Communication as…Perspectives on theory* (pp.38-48).Thousand Oaks, CA: Sage.

Cunliffe, Ann L. (2003). Reflexive inquiry in organizational research: Questions and possibilities. *Human Relations, 56,* 983-1003.

Cunliffe, A. L. (2004). On becoming a critically reflexive practitioner. *Journal of Management Education, 28,* 407-426.

Davis, Murray S. (1971). That's interesting! Toward a phenomenology of sociology and a sociology and phenomenology. *Philosophy of the Social Sciences, 1,* 309-344.

Ellingson, Laura L. (2008). *Engaging crystallization in qualitative research*. Thousand Oaks, CA: Sage.

Falkensfleth, Merete. (2009). Sharing knowledge within a hospital. Unpublished MSc dissertation, University of Bedfordshire, Bedfordshire, UK.

Fisher, Walter R. (1989). *Human communication as narration*. Columbia: University of South Carolina Press.

Gill, Rebecca (2011). The shadow in organizational ethnography: Moving beyond shadowing to spect-acting. *Qualitative Research in Organizations and Management, 6,* 115-133.

Gill, Rebecca; Barbour, Joshua B., & Dean, Marleah (2014). Shadowing in/as work: Ten recommendations for shadowing fieldwork practice. *Qualitative Research in Organizations and Management*, 9, 69-89.

Grint, Keith (2005). Problems, problems, problems: The social construction of "leadership". *Human Relations, 58*, 1467-1494.

Henriksen, Jan (2009). Leading through language: The creation of reflexive relationships. Unpublished MSc dissertation, University of Bedfordshire, Bedfordshire, UK.

Hibbert, Paul, Coupland Christine and MacIntosh, R. (2010) Reflexivity: Recursion and Relationality in Organizational Research Processes. *Qualitative Research in Organizations and Management*, 5:1 47-62.

Hornstrup, Carsten (2006). *Stories of systemic leadership*. Unpublished MSc dissertation, University of Bedfordshire, Bedfordshire, UK.

Hornstrup, C., Loehr-Petersen, Jesper & Madsen, Jørgen. G. (2012). *Developing relational leadership*. Chagrin Fall, OH: Taos Institute Publications.

Hosking, Dian Marie & Pluut, Bettine (2010). (Re)constructing reflexivity: A relational constructionist approach. *The Qualitative Report, 15,* 59-75.

Johnson, Phil, & Duberly, Joanne (2003). Reflexivity in management research. *Journal of Management Studies, 40,* 1279-1303.

Kristeva, Julia. (1984). *Revolution in poetic language*. New York: Columbia Press.

Lang, Peter; Little, Martin, & Cronen, Vernon (1990). The systemic professional: Domains of action and the question of neutrality. *Human Systems, 1,* 39-56.

Lindlof, Tom R., & Taylor, B. Copeland (2010). *Qualitative communication research methods* (3rd ed.). Thousand Oaks, CA: Sage.

Pearce, W. Barnett. (1994). *Interpersonal communication: Making social worlds*. New York: HarperCollins.

Pearce, W. Barnett. (2007). *Making social worlds: A communication perspective*. Malden, MA: Blackwell Publishing.

Pearce, W. Barnett, & Pearce, Kimberly A. (1998). Transcendent storytelling: Abilities for systemic practitioners and their clients. *Human Systems, 9,* 167-184.

Pearce, W. Barnett, & Pearce, Kimberly A. (2000). Extending the theory of the coordinated management of meaning (CMM) through a community dialogue process. *Communication Theory, 10,* 405-424.

Petersen, Jesper. K. (2011). How can we at AAMS co-create a sustainable organizational agility? Unpublished MSc dissertation, University of Bedfordshire, Bedfordshire.

Poulsen, Mia. (2006). *Appreciative inquiry and future visioning as an approach to training needs analysis*. Unpublished MSc dissertation, University of Bedfordshire, Bedfordshire, UK.

Scharmer, C. Otto (2009). *Theory U: Leading from the future as it emerges*. San Francisco: Berrett-Koehler.

Schön, Donald A. (1984). *The reflective practitioner: How professionals think in action*. New York: Basic Books.

Shepherd, Dean A., & Sutcliffe, Kathleen M. (2011). Inductive top-down theorizing: A source of new theories of organization. *Academy of Management Review, 35,* 361-380.

Shotter, John (2010). *Social construction on the edge: "Withness"-thinking and embodiment*. Chagrin Falls, OH: Taos Institute Publications.

Spano, Shawn (2001). *Public dialogue and participatory democracy: The Cupertino community project*. Cresskill, NJ: Hampton Press.

Talmy, Steven (2011). The interview as collaborative achievement: Interaction, identity, and ideology in a speech event. *Applied Linguistics, 32,* 25-42.

Tracy, Sarah J.; Lutgen-Sandvik, Pamela & Alberts, Jess K. (2006). Nightmares, demons, and slaves: Exploring the painful metaphors of workplace bullying. *Management Communication Quarterly, 20,* 148–185.

Walsh, Russell (2003). The methods of reflexivity. *The Humanistic Psychologist, 31,* 51-66.

Weick, Karl. E. (2007). The generative properties of richness. *Academy of Management Journal, 50,* 14-1.

11 The Impact of Dialogical Participatory Action Research (DPAR)
Riding in the peloton of dialogical collboration

Ann-Margreth E. Olsson

The use of dialogical collaboration both in the emerging coaching and participatory action research (PAR) reflexively expanding and diffusing effects as well as intensifying the progress and the processes in the social workers' practice as well as the researcher's. Not only became the research characterised of being participatory but also dialogical (DPAR). The processes of the conducted action research became metaphorically talked about as going on a cycling tour riding in a peloton of dialogical collaboration. In the dynamic flow of dialogical interplay the participants found the directions how to go on exploring and learning using 'living tools' as 'delta reflecting teams' using 'listening ears' and 'listening questions'

This is about a study where it became important that the used research supported and strengthened the empowering and mobilizing movements in the rest of the practice. It started with an ambition to create systemic collaboration inviting clients into partnership in social work practice and emerged into a dialogical reflecting inquires. The interest here will be focused on the practice of the emerging research processes – mutual processes of joint actions (Shotter 1980), creating expanding and diffusing effects as well as intensifying the progress and the processes in the study. These processes became talked about as a dialogical travel, a tour of interaction likened to the interplay in a peloton in a cycling tour – a polyphony of actions and voices and other things in joint actions of dialogue. The conducted participatory action research (PAR) (Whyte, Greenwood & Lazes 1991a) emerged into a style characterised by the dialogical interplay named Dialogical Participatory Action research (DPAR) (Olsson 2010).

A professional and theoretical practice

My research tends to be conducted from within my work as a dialogical coach and trainer to social workers working with children and families. This work is inspired by systemic ways of talking and creating knowledge. By researching my practice, I have been well-placed to advise on training and policy making in the county of Scania (Skåne) in the south of Sweden (Olsson 2005, 2008). Using systemic practice such as curiosity, inquiring and exploring what works and how, learning by doing (Dewey 2007) and reflecting in and on (Schön 2002) new efforts and alternatives, exploring, dreaming, designing and delivering, again and again in an ongoing circular process and flow, we co-create new orientation in how to go on. We *become* in relation to one another (and others and otherness) and our social world is created in our communication, the lived practice generates new learning. These ideas emanate both from ideas of action research (McNiff, Lomax & Whitehead, 1996; Reason & Bradbury 2006b) and systemic practice (Anderson 1999; Bateson 1987, 2000; Watzlawick, Beavin, Bavelas & Jackson 1967) as well as from the area of leadership and organisation, Appreciative Inquiry (AI) (Cooperrider & Whitney 2005) adapted to many other areas (cf. (Trajkovski, Schmied, Vickers & Jackson 2013). In this language plays a crucial part working with a view of social constructionism (Burr 1995) (Gergen & Gergen 2003; Gergen 2009).

In the dialogical approach I am foremost influenced by John Shotter and his view on dialogical processes as living interaction; spontaneous, chiasmatical, mutual, expressive, embodied responsiveness (Shotter, 2002, 2004a, 2004d). Shotter uses the term chiasmic (Shotter 2004c, 2005b) following Maurice Merleau–Ponty (2004), in the sense of intertwining in one another (Shotter & Gustavsen, 1999). Dialogical interplay is about moving in a mutual living and expressive responsiveness, responding to and addressing one another, other and otherness in *joint actions* (Shotter 1980, 2003b). The simultaneously ongoing interplay and mutual responsiveness in joint actions heighten the quality (Shotter 1993). Something (a third) is born in between the two and neither you nor I are "to blame" (Shotter 2004b). Shotter used to call this relational dynamic *joint action* (Shotter 1984, 1993, 2000). The dialogical reality constructed between them seems to "just happen" without an author, like if "a third agency is at work in all dialogical realities" (Shotter 2004b p.3). The joint actions are impossible to divide and recognise from each other (Shotter 1987) so the outcome of any exchange cannot be traced back to the intentions of any of the individuals involved (Shotter 2004b).

Metaphorically it could be seen as if we were in a 'mishmash' of relationships, of communication and interactions interweaved and entangled from within (with and in) our interplay. Based on this view, it is inevitable then that the research participants and I become travellers on a tour of joint actions in a practice, not just in terms of theory *or* practice but in a combination which I liken to the interplay in cycling in a peloton in a cycling tour – a polyphony of voices and actions and other things in a joint action of dialogical interplay.

The research process as a tour

The processes in this kind of study cannot be described as going from an initial design to the final presentations of results. This study is more a tour on a winding road – an ongoing flow of living practice of research, social work and coaching, creating a mixture of phases of exploring, reflecting and analysing, spreading and diffusing results and new ideas, testing, outlining and re-orientations in how to go on. There is much movement in the roles people take on during this process.

Example
55 social workers and their managers in seven municipalities invited me in to become the social workers' coach. I took part of their practice focusing on how to improve their listening to the voices of children and other clients as well as inviting and involving clients into collaborative social work. From the beginning I introduced a dialogical approach and Appreciative Inquiry (AI) in the coaching. I had the idea that development of a combination of an appreciative approach and systemic inquiry with curiosity and exploration together with dialogical interplay with involving dialogue, would bring about new opportunities in the desired direction, new orientation in how to go on, both in the research processes and in the processes of the systemic project. I suggested that the conducted research and the action project should have the same *style*. In my mind was that what was expected from the social workers to involve and invite the clients into partnership and collaboration should also be expected from the researcher (me) and vice versa co-creating sustainable reflexively learning capacity and infusing an approach for everyday use and life. At the same time this was a direction of the diffusion. The original idea from the County Administrative Board of Scania (the local state government) was to create many small events with diffuse boundaries, hoping that the ideas that unfolded will become widely spread through creating 'ripples on the water', or as Björn Gustavsen calls it: 'ripples in the water' effects (Gustavsen 2008).

My background and identity as a social worker and many years of experience as a manager in social organisations probably made a difference to how well the participants joined in with the research. For example, it was easy for me to join their grammar (Wittgenstein 2001) and the geography of their different places, sectors and activities, living space and hierarchies in the social workers' arenas and other professional networks. Using Michel Foucault ideas of discursive practice (Foucault 1972), this could be expressed as me moving, acting and talking from within the discourse and the relations of power. New understandings can be created through discourse between people engaged in the inquiry process (Greenwood & Levin 1998). For this to occur, a mutually understandable discourse is required, and this is achieved through living together over time, sharing experiences, and taking actions together (Greenwood & Levin 1998). I use my experience and familiarity to communicate in different contexts and from different positions.

Not just any tour – a cycling tour. The peloton at work.

As a way of describing and understanding the unfolding researching movements and emerging impacts on coaching and research projects, the metaphor of going on a tour – and more specifically to me as a cyclist, a cycling tour and riding in the peloton has been very helpful. It is a tour where we have some ideas about the end-in-view beforehand (Dewey 2007) and have sketched out some possible routes but mainly trust that new orientations on how to go on will emerge in the dialogical interplay between the participants as the tour goes on.

In the voyage tour I see how the participating social workers and I travelled, guided by the (re-) narrating of examples using (verbal) systemic signposts and directions in the action research – for example, the ideas of curiosity (Cecchin 1987), co-construction and co-creation (Lang 1991), dialogue as mutual spontaneously living communication in responsiveness (Shotter 2002) and learning in action, in reflecting on and in action (Schön 2002). The research participants were, through and in the context of the action projects and the coaching, speaking more and more about dialogical and more democratic meetings where more voices could be heard. We were riding in an ocean of systemic ideas stopping at some of the possible halts of narratives, getting a sense of how much more there was to explore and highlight, catching a glimpse of how many other different directions there were to choose, but also finding inspiration and fresh support on how to go on. Using this metaphor of a cycling tour, I think of the research process metaphorically as the joint action of cycling together in a peloton.

Joint action in the peloton
In the peloton, I am cycling amongst all the other participants or some of them, and we are going fast. A lot is happening. Sheltered from the

wind (by the protection of the others around us) everything seems to go easy and smooth. Those in front are taking the brunt of the nasty wind, sucking and pulling us up to their speed. They have got the direction, how to go on, I am following the flow.

At the same time, I have to be very careful, paying a lot of attention to every movement implanted, flowing and streaming in the group. Every little movement of the other participants, especially from those in front of us, is transplanted and transformed in relation to everybody else in the peloton. I am sensitive to what is happening around me; the speed, fragrances, sounds and movements. I am paying attention and responding in relation to my surroundings, the condition of the roads, my body's signals as well as from the bike. I am riding relaxed, not too tense in muscles and nerves; I let the bike go with me. I am enjoying the ride, the company, the flowers on the verges, the birds in the sky, the church towers in the horizon and the bike. We become like a united body – the movements and the anticipations are in us as an embodied whole of the peloton. I do not have to wait for my companions' next moves and they don't have to complete their moves before I can understand their message/response sufficiently for me to respond to it in practice and guiding me to know, or give an orientation of, how to go on, to understand where they might possibly move next (Shotter, 2008). In this background of relational dynamics, a ceaseless flow of expressive-responsive, living, embodied activity spontaneously continuously, which occurs between us and the others and the othernesses around us in our meetings with them, as me on the bike in the peloton, we all carry out our daily lives (Shotter 2004b). The joint actions are so closely interwoven and intertwined with each other and everything else and everybody else in the moment, so nobody can notice the differences or the parts or how they are being connected, influencing and mutually responding in the chiasmatic interaction. This is what happens in a dialogically involving communication. It is an imperceptible flow or movement you can sense – sense it in your body. Shotter calls it embodiment (Shotter 2003a). Anne Hedvig Vedeler, Norwegian systemic family therapist, calls it *resonance* (Vedeler 2008) – a resonance heard and felt from within the field of the peloton, in the interplay between the riders, guiding and giving orientation on how to go on, respond and ride further.

Noticings

What I do during this journey of dialogical and systemic action research is to track and together with participants, choose examples, ideas and narratives given in the context of the action projects and research which we experienced as *striking* or unique examples (Shotter 2000, 2008), useful for bringing the emerging ideas in the projects and the systemic ideas into further learning and developments, disseminating them as ripples on the water (Gustavsen 2008) into new contexts. We focus both on what is working and successful and, unlike solution-focused coaching, explore difficulties and (what was told about as) failings. The use of the expression *striking examples* comes from Shotter (2000, 2008) connecting to Ludwig Wittgenstein (2001).

In a Swedish context the expression "being struck" is a common metaphoric expression which I often use in questions within the context of coaching, noticing that this seems to increase the responsiveness in the dialogue. The joint search for striking moments seems to help the participants to 'Stop – Look – Listen' in their memories within the contexts of the coaching process (Arendt 1978; Dewey 2007; Shotter 2005c). I am asking them for details in the moment, often in chronological order and in small steps. The purpose is also to bring the participants *into* the situation, remembering *from within* (Shotter 2000), to seek participatory understanding, avoiding an approach from the outside as observers (Shotter 2004a)

The striking examples emerged in different contexts: in dialogical conferences (Shotter & Gustavsen 1999), meetings with reflecting teams and delta-reflecting, in meetings with clients and from within the dialogues in the coaching. It was examples that emerged for the social workers and/or for me as important and significant for the progress and impact of the projects and the study. The narratives of these examples, emerging in the coaching and in other meetings, became important for me to study more closely and hear other people's understanding – that is the participants' understanding and interpretations (Whyte 1991b). Involving the participants in the on-going analysing (in action research analysing is constantly recurring (Elliot 2001) in the study; inviting to reflect and delta-reflect, to read excerpts of transcriptions or drafts of my manuscripts, to watch selected parts (I selected) of the video-recordings or other exercises aiming at making me hear other voices in understanding the progress and results of the study, became a further linking of the inquiry to the actions.

Contributions from the participants have not only been of great value for the development of the coaching and the conduct of the research, they were indispensable, absolutely necessary, for the outcome of this study. However, when you/I involve participants, you/I also have to be ready to pay attention to what they produce, highlight and ask for, as well as take into serious considerations what they want you/me to do or not do. So involving participants you as researcher also have to be prepared to cut, change and re-write chapters. I sent the participants drafts of and information about my further use of what they had contributed. I sent them both drafts and completed manuscripts giving them opportunities to respond and ask me to leave out or change parts. This way of opening up opportunities to change at the very last moment put me several times in great trouble. Once I had to re-write almost a whole manuscript just before I was going to leave it for publishing. At the same time, all these steps and considerations ensured that the participants really gave their approval and consented to what I was doing, not only in the beginning when we set the context for the collaboration and made a contract with the participating clients (these were also documented in written and signed documents) but throughout the entire journey.

The emerging and ongoing DPAR

I tried to attain a "good enough" quality as coach using different sources and ways of improving my approach. The ongoing research facilitated and increased my opportunities to hear the voices of the social workers, which was my most important source of improvement. The ongoing research seemed to authorize me to inquire more about the coaching as well as arrange special events where I invited the participants to reflect on and co-create narratives, delta-reflecting, about the emerging systemic dialogical practice. Everything became documented by video recording. This gave me the opportunity to both alone and together with co-researchers listen to and reflect on what was heard in the delta-reflections and explore further whenever I wanted to.

Delta Reflecting Teams
By using systemic ideas with *reflecting teams* (Andersen 1987, 1992, 2003), new ways of using these ideas and forms emerged. Keen to hear more, new and different voices in the research, I invite participants to connect to their own experiences and to bring forth narratives of their own into the reflecting teams. They both reflect on what they hear in the session and on their own narrating seeing this narrating and reflecting as co-creating new *veins of narratives as in a delta* (here: of different storylines). This expanded form of reflecting team I have come to call *delta-reflecting teams*. In Swedish, the word *"delta"* is used both in the meaning of "participate" or "share" as well as the dividing of the mouth of a river into several river channels.

In Delta Reflecting Teams, participants are encouraged to reflect on what they hear and see, expand the reflections with new narrating, and contribute with experiences of their own and whatever they want to bring into the dialogue. The rules for the ordinary reflecting team, according to Andersen (1987), is that there should be no reference to things not pertaining to the conversation seen or heard. However, the teamwork and the interaction sometimes also grow and flow over into what we can call several *outflows* and *inflows* of narrating <u>not</u> seen or heard earlier in the conversation. In connection to the subject(s) this facilitated the polyphony. More became told and heard with new nuances.

Listening ears and listening questions

At one of events when all the participants came together, two messages really struck me in relation to myself as coach. It was when one of the participants emphasized how I was using what she called *listening ears* and *listening questions*. I found these expressions very nice, catching the response and interplay I was hoping to contribute within the dialogical coaching very well and strengthening me to continue in the way I now approached the participants in the coaching. Something had made the difference in our conversations which had made it possible for me as coach to ask a lot of questions and still make it possible for us participants to experience the conversations as dialogical and mutually involving. I had asked myself how it could be possible to have a living dialogue in the coaching when new questions often became my way of responding. Why did our meetings not turn into monological coaching instead of a joint inquiry into dialogical interaction? I think the social worker, in inventing the expressions *listening ears* and *listening questions*, captured what she perceived in my participation as a participation in a resonance. In *resonance* you not only listen but also try to be responsive on an emotional level and take in the whole context of the other person's utterance being responsive to intonation, words, breathing, pauses, and bodily movements (Vedeler 2008). It is about placing yourself completely at the other participants' disposal, to live and act from within the responsiveness in relation to the others and otherness completely accessible in the moment, absolute presence.

Living tools

During these years of ongoing practice including writing about the study and what unfolded, I have noticed how my awareness of how I use social constructionist and systemic ideas has increased as well as my knowing and abilities to use these ideas in practice. I have continued coaching and supervising social workers, getting new commissions and learning more and more about social work, coaching and action research. As I see it, the systemic and dialogical methods and techniques become *living* in use, changed and changing, reflexively influencing and being adapted from within the relational dynamic of joint actions in use. Connected to this I more and more have found myself talking about using *living tools* in my practice.

My interest became more and more focused on the dialogical practice of the emerging research processes – mutual processes of joint actions. These joints actions are creating expanding and diffusing effects as well as intensifying the progress and the processes in the study. Connected to my interest in cycling and each summer focusing on the Tour of France, the project and my research became talked about as a dialogical travel, a tour of interaction likened to the interplay in a peloton in a cycling tour – a polyphony of actions and voices and other things in joint actions of dialogue. The conducted participatory action research (PAR) (Whyte et al. 1991a) emerged into a style characterised by the dialogical interplay I named it Dialogical Participatory Action research (DPAR).

A model of DPAR

Below, I have sketched out some punctuations in an attempt to further reveal how and to what DPAR emerged to in this unique study and in these local conditions and circumstances – the meaning used and reflexively emerging in this study and context. These punctuations have guided me in my actions in relation to the participating social workers and others in the study.

1. A participatory, emancipatory and democratic process, concerned with developing practical knowing from within actions, aiming to improve practice – informed, committed, intentional actions with a worthwhile purpose. "Action research is wedded to the idea that change is good" (Denscombe 2009, p.124).

2. To make explicit and transparent the processes through which the knowing and the impact are emerging – systematic inquiry made public – the processes and the results as open and accessible as possible.

3. To bring together action and reflection, theory and practice – create new forms of understandings "since action without reflection and understanding is blind, just as theory without action is meaningless" (Reason & Bradbury 2006a, p.2).

4. To research "... *with, for* and *by* the involved persons and commu-

nities, ideally involving all stakeholders both in the questioning and sensemaking that informs the research, *and* in the actions that is its focus" (Reason & Bradbury 2006a, p.2).

5. "... it is necessarily insider research, in the sense of practitioners researching their own professional actions" (McNiff et al. 1996, p.14).

6. Cyclic processes where actions, reflections and inquiries are interwoven in dialogical conversations and interplay, creating new responsive understandings of ways of going on, giving new orientations pointing towards *another kind* of future (Shotter 2004b) – open-ending outcome (Hart & Bond 1999).

Below, I have tried to outline a figure of the cyclic processes in the *ongoing flow of living in the research peloton*. The figure is <u>not</u> doing justice to how intertwined the different phases become in each other <u>nor</u> does it show the endless amount of variations emerging in the interplay. It could both be read as an illustration of the conducted DPAR and the conducted coaching.

Figure 1. Dialogical Participatory Action Research (DPAR) — the ongoing living flow of the research peloton

⇓⇑

⇔ actions in practice ⇔ reflections in actions ⇔

⇓⇑

⇔ "stop look listen" ⇔ reflections on actions ⇔ appreciative inquiry ⇔

⇓⇑

⇔ responsive understanding from within⇔ partnership ⇔

⇓⇑

⇔ learning by doing ⇔ new orientation ⇔

⇓⇑

The research was conducted from within the practice and vice versa – the practice was conducted from within the research. It was not applied research with a separation between thoughts and actions (Greenwood & Levin 1998) or theory and practice (Shotter 2005a). Valid knowing was derived from practical reasoning engaged from within the actions

(Greenwood & Levin 1998). The unfoldings in the practice were integrated with the research and vice versa – in joint actions (see above about the dialogical flow in the peloton) – and the participants, including myself as coach, were researching practitioners.

Reflections and more

The idea emerging that the conducted research and coaching should have the same *style* as was expected from the social workers to involve and invite the clients into partnership and collaboration, seems to have made 'a difference that make a difference' (Bateson 2000). All this became both about to create sustainable reflexively learning capacity and to infuse an approach of dialogue for everyday use and life. At the same time this was a direction of the diffusion.

The narrative about cycling in a peloton is metaphorically illustrating the dialogical interplay in the emerging DPAR in the study. This entangled and intertwined relational dynamic of actions, joints actions, became the characteristic style of the research in relation to the conducted coaching as well as my development. We were all learning by doing (Dewey 2007) and inquiring (Dewey 1938) and by reflections in and on our actions (Schön 2002), testing and exploring (Dewey 1991), developing and improving both the social work and the coaching as well as the research actions and processes.

I read Timothy Gallwey's books on coaching, relating both to my earlier experiences as coach and how I was developing my actions here and now. From Gallwey I picked up ideas about learning, using an approach of fascination in relation to whatever you were doing and using. This will increase your feeling for rhythm, timing, listening and the present. Gallwey continues (Gallwey 1997): There are also so many choices to pay attention to in the present, to start with observation without judgment and choose (only) one detail to change (the rest will also be changed in relation to the changing of the chosen detail). Prepare yourself by imagining the change and let yourself go – let it happen – "just" let it go. Again, explore the results and the differences without judging, and so on. All this I found extremely helpful; the non-judging exploration, the preparation followed by actions with readiness for evaluation afterwards, again without judgement, and with focus on being in the moment – being in the present.

The above connects to the prerequisite of living dialogues where I became more and more aware of the importance of being in the present to make it possible to be responsive in relation to other participants, myself and otherness in the moment. The use of dialogue made the meetings between the social workers and myself easier, inspiring confidence and trust in the relationship between us. This probably also had something to do with my earlier experiences, my age, my identity as a social worker and accustomedness to move in social organisations, talking the language in the dominating discourse – joining the grammar.

References

Andersen, Tom (1987). The Reflecting team: Dialogue and Meta-Dialogue in Clinical Work. *Family process, 26*, 415-428.

Andersen, Tom (1992). Relationship, Language and Pre-understanding in the reflecting Processes. *A.N.Z.J. Fam.Ther., 13*(2), 87-91.

Andersen, Tom (2003). *Reflekterande processer. Samtal och samtal om samtalen.* Stockholm: Mareld.

Anderson, Harlene (1999). *Samtal, språk och möjligheter. Psykoterapi och konsultation ur postmodern synvinkel* (C. Brodin & K. Hopstadius, Trans.). Stockholm: Mareld.

Arendt, Hannah (1978). *The life of the mind. One/Thinking Two/Willing.* London: Secker & Warburg.

Bateson, Gregory (1987). *Ande och Natur. En nödvändig enhet* (C. G. Liungman, Trans.). Stockholm/Lund: Symposion Bokförlag & Tryckeri.

Bateson, Gregory (2000). *Steps to an ecology of mind.* Chicago and London: the University of Chicago Press.

Burr, Vivien (1995). *An Introduction to Social Constructionism.* London and New York: Routledge.

Cecchin, Gianfranco (1987). Hypothesizing, Circularity, and Neutrality Revisited: An Invitation to Curiosity. *Family process, 26*(4), 405 - 413.

Cooperrider, David L. & Whitney, Diana (2005). *Appreciative Inquiry. A Positive Revolution in Change.* San Francisco: Berett-Koehler Publishers.

Denscombe, Matryn (2009). *Forskningshandboken – för småskaliga forskningsprojekt inom samhällsvetenskaperna* (P. Larson, Trans.). Lund: Studentlitteratur.

Dewey, John (1938). *Logic – The Theory Of Inquiry.* New York: Henry Holt and Company.

Dewey, John (1991). *How we think.* New York: Prometheus Books.

Dewey, John (2007). *Democracy and Education.* Teddington,Middlesex: Echo Library.

Elliot, John (2001). *Action Research for Educational Change.* Philadelphia: Open University Press.

Foucault, Michel (1972). *Vetandets Arkeologi* (C. G. Bjurström, Trans.). Staffanstorp: Bo Cavefors Bokförlag.

Gallwey, W. Timothy (1997). *The Inner Game of Tennis* (Revised edition ed.). New York: Random house.

Gergen, Kenneth J. (2009). *Relational being. Beyond Self and Community.* Oxford: Oxford University Press.

Gergen, Kenneth J. & Gergen, Mary (Eds.). (2003). *Social Construction. A reader*. London. Thousand Oaks. New Delhi: SAGE Publications.

Greenwood, Davydd J., & Levin, Morten (1998). *Introduction to Action Research. Social Research for Social Change*. London: SAGE Publications.

Gustavsen, Bjørn (2008). Action research, practical challenges and the formation of theory. *Action Research, 6*, 421-437.

Hart, Elizabeth & Bond, Meg (1999). *Action research for health and social care. A guide to practice*. Buckingham and Philadelphia: Open University Press.

Lang, Peter (1991). Organisations: Conundrums, Chaos and Communication. In M. M., P.-S. M. & W. E. (Eds.), *Effective Management*: British Association of Social Workers.

McNiff, Jean; Lomax, Pamela, & Whitehead, Jack (1996). *You and your action research project*. London: Routledge.

Merleau-Ponty, Maurice (2004). *Lovtal till filosofin. Essäer i urval*. Stockholm: Brutus Östlings Bokförlag.

Olsson, Ann-Margreth (2005). *Barnets socialsekreterare. Coaching i dialogiska utredningar* (Vol. 4). Malmö: Länsstyrelsen i Skåne län.

Olsson, Ann-Margreth (2008). *Hörs barnet? Studie om hur socialsekreterare gör barns röst hörda i utredningarna* (Vol. 2008:3). Malmö: Länsstyrelsen i Skåne län.

Olsson, Ann-Margreth (2010). *Listening to the Voice of Children. Systemic Dialogue Coaching: Inviting Participation and Partnership in Social Work*. Unpublished PhD, University of Bedfordshire, Luton.

Penn, Peggy (1985). Feed forward: Future questions. Future maps. *Family Process, 24*, 299 - 311.

Reason, Peter & Bradbury, Hilary (2006a). Introduction: Inquiry and Participation in Search of World Worthy of Human Aspiration. In P. Reason & H. Bradbury (Eds.), *Handbook of Action Research* (pp. 1- 14). London: SAGE Publications.

Reason, Peter & Bradbury, Hilary (Eds.). (2006b). *Handbook of Action Research*. London: SAGE Publications.

Schön, Donald A. (2002). *The Reflective Practitioner. How professionals think in action*. Aldershot: Ashgate Arena.

Shotter, John (1980). Men the magicians: the duality of social being and the structure of moral worlds. In C. A.J. & J. D.M. (Eds.), *Models of Man* (pp. 25-28). Leicester: British Psychological Society.

Shotter, John (1984). *Social Accountability and Selfhood*. Oxford: Blackwell.

Shotter, John (1987). The Social Construction of an "Us": Problems of Accountability and Narratology. In R. Burnett, P. McGhee & D. Clarke (Eds.), *Accounting for Personal Relationships: Social Representations of Interpersonal Links* (pp. 225-247). London: Methuen.

Shotter, John (1993). *Cultural Politics of Everyday life: Social Constructionism, Rhetoric, and Knowing of Third Kind*: Open University Press, University of Toronto Press.

Shotter, John (2000). *Conversational Realities - Constructing Life through Language*. London: SAGE Publications Ltd.

Shotter, John (2002). Spontaneous responsiveness, chiasmic relations, and consciousness inside the realm of living expression. Retrieved 2002-10-23, 2002.f

Shotter, John (2003a). Being 'moved' by the embodied, responsive-expressive 'voice' of an 'other'. Retrieved 2004-10-13, 2004, from http://pubpages. unh.edu/~jds/Tornio.htm

Shotter, John (2003b, October 3lth - 4th, 2003). *Inside the moment of speaking: In our meetings with others, we cannot simply be ourselves.* Paper presented at the Psychologies and Identities Conference, University of Bergamo, Italy.

Shotter, John (2004a). Dialogue, depth, and life inside responsive orders: from external observation to participatory understanding. Retrieved 19 oktober, 2004, from http://pubpages.unh.edu/~jds/PerformingKnowledge.htm

Shotter, John (2004b, 2004-12-09). The embodied practitioner: Toward dialogic-descriptive accounts of social practices. *The Role of the Social Sciences Today* Retrieved 20 January, 2005, from http://pubpages.unh. edu/~jds/page8.html

Shotter, John (2004c). *On the edge of Social Constructionism: 'Withness'-thinking versus 'Aboutness'-thinking.* London: KCC Foundation.

Shotter, John (2005a). *Inside Organizations: Action research, management and 'withness'-thinking.* London: KCC Foundation.

Shotter, John (2005b). The Role of 'withness'-thinking in 'going on' inside chiasmically-structured process, Organization Summer School Workshop

Shotter, John (2005c). *Wittgenstein, Bakhtin, and Vygotsky: Introducing dialogically-structed reflective practice into our everyday practices.* Paper presented at the Relations and resources - in the field of special education, Copenhagen.

Shotter, John (2008). *Conversational Realities Revisited: Life, Language, Body and World.* London: Taos Institute Publications.

Shotter, John (Ed.). (2004d). *Dialogical dynamics: Inside the moment of speaking.* Amsterdam and New York: Benjamins, John.

Shotter, John & Gustavsen, Bjørn (1999). *The role of "dialogue conferences" in the development of "learning regions": doing "from within" our lives together what we cannot do apart.* Stockholm: Stockholm School of Economics.

Trajkovski, Suza; Schmied, Virginia; Vickers, Margaret & Jackson, Debra (2013). Implementing the 4D cycle of appreciative inquiry in health care: a methodological review. *Journal of Advanced Nursing, 69*(6), 1224-1234.

Vedclcr, Anne IIedvig (2008). *Resonance.* Unpublished manuscript, Oslo.

Watzlawick, Paul; Beavin Bavelas, Janet & Jackson, Don D. (1967). *Pragmatics of human communication. A study of international patterns, pathologies, and paradoxes.* New York and London: W.W. Norton & Company.

Whyte, William Foote; Greenwood, Davydd J. & Lazes, Peter (1991a). Participatory Action Research. Through Practice to Science in Social Research. In W. F. Whyte (Ed.), *Partcipatory Action Research.* London: SAGE Publications.

Whyte, William Foote (1991b). Comparing PAR and Action Science. In William Foote Whyte (Ed.), *Participatory Action Research* (pp. 97-98). London: SAGE Publications.

Wittgenstein, Ludwig (2001). *Philosophical Investigations* (G. E. M. Anscombe, Trans.). Oxford: Blackwell Publishers.

12 Pragmatic Inquiry
A research method for knowledge creation in organisations

Andreas Granhof Juhl

Pragmatic inquiry is presented in this chapter as a stringent and coherent philosophical approach to research in organisations and organisational development based on the work of Lyotard (1984), William James (James 2000), John Dewey (Dewey 1916, 1938; Brinkmann 2006), John Austin (Austin 1997), Ludwig Wittgenstein (Wittgenstein 1989, 1994) and Gregory Bateson (Bateson 1972, 1984).

Pragmatic inquiry is presented as a research approach that changes an organisational relationship to knowledge from that of traditionalist and knowledge consumer to that of knowledge producer, so that the organisation creates new knowledge based on practice. Knowledge that is useful for and validated in practice.

What is pragmatic inquiry and when is pragmatic inquiry a useful approach to knowledge creation in organisations?

In "The postmodern condition" Lyotard argues, that "the grand narrative has lost its credibility" (Lyotard 1984, p.37) sending institutions into a crises of legitimation, since no a priori narrative can legitimate the existence of the institution. This postmodern condition creates a situation where the organisation can only create legitimation through performativity. As a consequence of this postmodern condition most organisations use extensive resources to document its effectiveness. Although this is necessary, it is not sufficient since it implies no concept of knowledge. To create a postmodern and pragmatic understanding of knowledge, Lyotard argues for a connection between knowledge, language and efficiency using Wittgenstein's notion of language games and John Austin's notion of performativity (Ibid.). Knowledge, regarded in classical scientific terms as a passive and accurate description of reality, does not show how knowledge from a pragmatic philosophical perspective creates the organisational outcome. Dewey called his work instrumentalism to show how knowledge must be evaluated from its ability to "perform" certain desired end-states (Dewey 1916).

Following Lyotard's ideas in an organisational context, organisations need to reflect on their own view of knowledge and efficiency and the relation between the two. To illustrate how this relationship can be constructed in different ways, let me introduce a simple distinction between the "traditionalist", the "knowledge consumer" and the "knowledge producer".

In an organisation that takes the position of the "traditionalist", knowledge is habitual and reproducible. Different learning theorists, for example, Dreyfus and Dreyfus (1999) and Lave and Wenger (Lave, 1999), implicitly support this understanding of knowledge. Dreyfus and Dreyfus argue that experts in a field use tacit knowledge to make subtle discriminations in practice. *"[The experts] need to almost exclusively trust their intuition and make almost no comparative analysis of alternatives"* (Dreyfus & Dreyfus 1999, p.61). Implicit in this understanding of expertise lies an understanding of knowledge as stable and reproducible. Taking a similar approach to knowledge, Lave and Wenger are known to criticize abstract teaching and suggest that learning happens in communities of practice (Lave 1999). To organisations, this means that learning too a high degree is a matter of socialization to existing organisational practices within strong communities of practice (Ibid.). The position of the "traditionalist" seems the obvious choice in organisations where knowledge has a largely stable character. But this position is challenged in organisations where constant change in knowledge is the norm. In such organisations, reproduction of habit is no longer possible. This gives the organisation the challenge of finding a new position in relation to knowledge and efficiency.

The position of "knowledge consumer" offers the organisation a relationship to knowledge where the needed knowledge is found, bought and implemented in the organisation to overcome the strategic challenge.

Example

It has been politically decided in Denmark that schools are to increase their ability to ensure inclusion of pupils that would previously have been excluded and sent to special schools. Besides changing the economic structure for schools to increase a school's motivation to ensure inclusion, this also involves the discussion raised above: what new knowledge does the school need in order to create the desired end-state? In one municipality the schools were offered to choose either the LP-model, an analytical model, or positive psychology developed by Seligman among others. In either case this means that the school takes the position of the knowledge consumer buying and implementing the needed knowledge.

The example shows the obvious strengths and weaknesses with the position of knowledge consumer. On the positive side, the organisation can secure its legitimacy by using standardized knowledge. Further knowledge development is cost efficient for the organisation that can either buy it or acquire the knowledge for free. But the knowledge consuming position also has weaknesses. The relationship between knowledge and desired end state is blurred leading both teachers and leaders to ask the obvious question: Does LP and positive psychology *really* enable the schools to create an increased level of inclusion? The trouble for the knowledge consuming organisation is that this question must always be answered by "Yes, we expect it to do so". The organisation cannot know what results will follow using the knowledge since they have no experience using the knowledge. In short: *the knowledge consuming organisation cannot, at the time of acquiring the new knowledge, have any real experience about the performativity of the knowledge.*

To challenge the position of both "the traditionalist" and "the knowledge consuming" position, the position of "knowledge producing" organisation is suggested as useful for organisations, where new knowledge is needed to reach new objectives. The new situation is meet by the organisation through a series of knowledge creating processes based on practice and creating new knowledge that is both useful for practice and validated in practice. I call this pragmatic creation and validation of knowledge *pragmatic inquiry* and describe this below. From a pragmatic perspective this is a normal relationship to knowledge and inquiry processes. As Dewey writes:

> "Systematic advance in invention and discovery began when man recognized that they could utilize doubt for purposes of inquiry by forming conjectures to guide action in tentative explorations, whose development would confirm, refute or modify the guiding conjectures" (Dewey 1916, p.121).

Such an approach to inquiry processes challenges both "the traditionalist" and "the knowledge consuming" position and many other classical approaches to research by putting the practitioner and the creation of new practices and knowledge in the foreground. As John Shotter writes:

> "Thus, the major difference between practitioner initiated and oriented inquiry and academically initiated and oriented research, i.e. coolly rational research, is that such research aims at reliable, repeatable, publically criticisable results, results that can be

generalized to apply in many different contexts, while practitioners are concerned in their inquiries with gaining an orientation, a sense of "where" they are placed in relation to their immediate surroundings, and the surrounding field of real possibilities open to them for their next step". (Shotter 2009, p.6)

Pragmatic inquiry overcomes this dualism. The knowledge producing organisation needs to base its knowledge production on practice and to be useful in practice. I use the term "pragmatic inquiry" for such knowledge producing processes where the nature of knowledge is practitioner sensitive and conducted with two purposes:

- that the inquiry is grounded in the practice of the practitioners
- that the inquiry is to be useful for both the practitioners engaged in the inquiry and for a wider range of practitioners

I will argue that these two criteria are both necessary and sufficient to secure the pragmatic validity of the inquiry. Doing this the organisation becomes legitimate by being able to create the results needed to be efficient and by creating a clear relation between the knowledge and the results created by the organization.

Pragmatic inquiry and a new relationship between knowledge and knower

From a pragmatic point of view it is important to recognize and appreciate the intimate relationship between knowledge and knower. Vernon Cronen draws attention to this relationship:

"The scientist, seeking episteme or truths about the natural world, does not change the objects of study by his or her inquiry. However, as the Greeks well knew, the study of rhetoric led to the development of new practices in oratory. If today new forms of intervention change practices in families and organizations, the objects of our own inquiry are changed by the act of inquiry. Thus, in the arts of praxis the relationship of the knower to the known is never an objective one. The knower is always a participant". (Cronen 2000, p.3).

As Vernon Cronen formulates, an inquiry approach has the implication of changing both the field being observed and the observer. That the researcher influences the field being researched is well documented and shown experimentally by Robert Rosenthal (Rosenthal 1968; Juhl

& Madsen 2011). In his original studies Rosenthal showed that by manipulating psychology students' expectations to the performance of the rats they were to use in experiments, Rosenthal influenced the actual performance of the rats. Similarly he proved in the famous subsequent study, "Oak School experiment", that the manipulation of students' test scores induced an increase in positive expectation amongst the teachers of 20% of their pupils' performance (Rosenthal 1968). As it turned out these 20% subsequently had a statistically better result in their exam one year later. Rosenthal experimentally shows that the psychology student and the teacher influence the field being studied by having certain expectations.

In some research traditions, this can be regarded as a mistake. In pragmatic inquiry generating knowledge about this relationship is the purpose of doing the inquiry. Going into the substance of Dewey's work on inquiry, Dewey defines inquiries as

"The intentional endeavour to discover specific connections between something, which we do, and the consequences, which result, so that the two become continuous. Their isolation, and consequently their arbitrary going together, is cancelled: a unified developing situation takes its place. The occurrence is now understood" (Dewey 1916, p.119).

Furthermore, Dewey goes on to remark,

"Experience as trying involves change, but change is meaningless transition unless it is consciously connected with the return wave of consequences, which flow from it" (Ibid. p.113).

Dewey's notion of inquiry challenges the Dreyfus brothers' and Lave & Wenger's understanding of knowledge. In producing new knowledge, the practitioner cannot have a purely intuitive approach to knowledge, as Dreyfus and Dreyfus have argued (1999). And knowledge does not exist as something finished that new organisational members can be socialised into. Instead the practitioner becomes what Schön calls a reflective practitioner by increasing the practitioner's ability to both reflect-in-action where *"we may reflect in the midst of action without interrupting it... our thinking serves to reshape what we are doing while we are doing it"* (Schön 1987, p.26) creating on the spot experiments as well as being able to *"reflect* on *our reflection-in-action"* (ibid. p.31) as a kind of meta-reflexive ability. The expert is no longer seen as being intuitive in his judgements but rather being an expert by the ongoing reflection on the doing and being of the practice. By doing this, the practitioner frees himself from the risk of reproducing old habits. Following Schön's argument, *"a skilled performer can integrate reflection-in-action into the smooth performance of an ongoing task"* (Ibid. p. 29) enabling the practitioner to *"know how to go on"* (Wittgenstein, 1989, 1994). This is important since the inquiry is concerned with practice, and practitioner difficulties *"[are] orientational or relational difficulties, to do with how we spontaneously respond to features in our surroundings"* (Shotter 2009, p.6).

What is pragmatic inquiry and how does pragmatic inquiry structure knowledge-creating processes based on and useful for practice?

The recognised Danish expert on Dewey, Professor Svend Brinkmann, describes Dewey's approach to inquiry like this:

> *(1) All experimentation involves action, to arrange change in our surroundings or in our relationship to it.*
>
> *(2) Further, experiments are not arbitrary, but build in hypothesis, ideas and the like, that appear relevant to the specific focus of inquiry.*
>
> *(3) Finally, the results of the experiments are the creation of a new situation, in which the objects are in a renewed relationship with each other, and where we can claim to have knowledge because we have experienced relationships between our active doing in the world and the consequences of that doing. All scientific knowledge is therefore knowledge about relationships (and not knowledge about isolated substances or elements) (Brinkmann 2006, p.79)*

I will make two reflections about Dewey's notion of inquiry.

Firstly, it helps practitioners turn practice into hypothesis worth testing in order to improve the situation in the organisation. By consciously connecting the return wave of consequences, which flow from the process, each of these situations creates a process of inquiry for the practitioner that helps answer the question for the inquiry.

Secondly, it is important that both the question for the inquiry and the way the inquiry is made is based on practical judgements about "what will work in this situation?" As Coolican (1999) and Kvale (2002) point out, the researcher should address three questions to construct a research approach. I will address the first two questions and then move on to the third:

1. *What is to be researched?* In the knowledge producing organisation the answer to this question has to show a connection between the expected knowledge created and the ability of the organisation to create results in relation to the strategies of the organisation.

2. *Why is the research made?* As described with Lyotard, this question can always be answered in two ways. The knowledge created is necessary for the organisation to be efficient. And by creating a clear connection between efficiency and knowledge, the organisation secures its legitimacy in a wider political and societal context.

Example

Pragmatic inquiry was initially developed during my professional doctorate program in systemic practice with the focus: *How can I, on the basis of my own work as a consultant, create an account of how to succeed as a consultant?* As a result of this work, a model called "the consultancy room" was developed and tested and validated in 3 different organisations.

Example

In a municipality in Denmark the work with people with dementia was located in one organisation. The organisation was given two objectives. Firstly, to create nursing and caring activities for people with dementia. Secondly, to create useful knowledge for everybody working with dementia in the municipality. To reach the second objective the organisation, with much debate, created a "university of practice" giving internal consultants the task of producing knowledge about successful work with people with dementia.

Example

In a municipality in Denmark, schools struggled to find the useful knowledge base to ensure inclusion for children in the schools. An organisation, the Centre for Inclusion, was created with the purpose of supporting the schools ensure inclusion. The employees in the centre were typically psychologists and speech-hearing therapists. A group of 14 people designed a process of pragmatic inquiry inquiring into the question: How can we create the knowledge needed to secure inclusion in the schools? Knowledge that the schools can use and knowledge we can use to support the schools?

Even though the three examples above are different, they share some important elements. In all the examples, the organisation needs new knowledge to meet new objectives, so the position of traditionalist is no longer possible. As an answer to this the organisation takes the position of knowledge production to secure its efficiency and thereby its legitimacy in a wider political and societal context. But the examples also different and indicate the importance of the third question that Coolican and Kvale point to:

3. *How* to do the research? I will answer this question more fully using my own research in organisational consultancy as illustration. My intention in doing this is to make the theoretical ideas in pragmatic inquiry as a research approach clear to the reader.

Pragmatic inquiry as a method for knowledge creation

Based on Dewey's notion of inquiry *"to discover specific connections between something, which we do, and the consequences, which result, so that the two become continuous"* (Dewey 1916, p.119), every pragmatic method must be concerned with the connection between action and consequence. The inspiration from Dewey helped me create a simple 4-step method illustrated in this model:

Figure 2. 4-step inquiry method

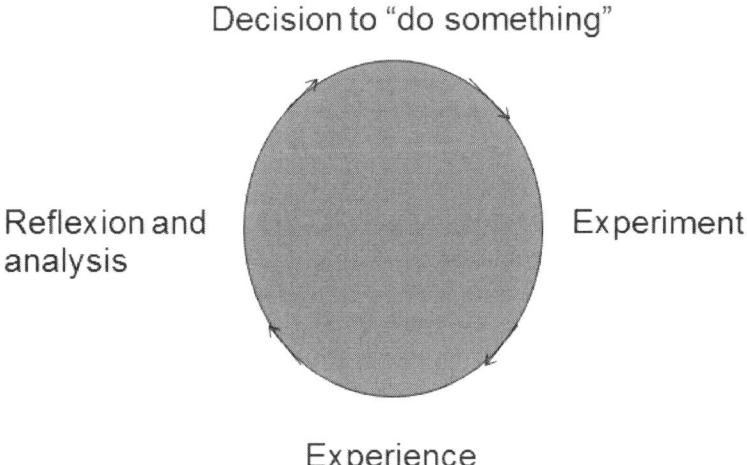

Step 1: Decision to "do something"
Experiments are not arbitrary but are built on hypotheses and ideas that appear relevant to the specific focus of inquiry. Step 1 is about making it

possible for the researcher to meet the world with what Dewey referred to as an "experimental attitude" (Cronen 2000), looking for unseen connections. Part of this process involves deciding what question is to guide the inquiry. In my research into organisational consultancy one hypothesis was that different approaches to organisational change could help the consultant design successful change processes together with the organisation.

Step 2: Experiment
With Brinkman's words *all experimentation involves action, to arrange change in our surroundings or in our relationship to it*. So having decided on a question for inquiry in Step 1, Step 2 is experimenting and doing.

Step 3: Experience
With Dewey's words *"the intentional endeavour to discover specific connections between something, which we do, and the consequences, which result, so that the two become continuous"* (Dewey 1916 p.119). Experience is seeing connections between "doing" and "consequence of doing". In relation to my research question this was important because if using different approaches (the systemic, the appreciative, the strategic, for example) does not lead to different consequences then, by William James' definition of the "pragmatic method" (James 2000), they are not different.

Step 4: Reflection and analysis
Step 4 is analysing the experience and reflecting on the new connections created by the experiment. Below I will describe a 2-step method to make such an analysis. It is important that Step 4 will create a new situation with new questions that can be utilised for inquiry purposes. So step 4 is also about creating the foundation for formulating new questions for inquiry.

Step 5: (back to Step 1): Decision to "do something" - again
This step is included to show that this method does not end but continues and thereby create a position of i) reflexive practitioner for the employee and ii) knowledge production for the organisation. Based on previous experiments, the inquiry in step 5 will be different from that in step 1 with new questions and new actions.

Three questions of importance construct pragmatic inquiry as a coherent and clear research method to create new knowledge in organisations:

- What kind of research is being conducted: quantitative or qualitative?

- What counts as data?

- How is data used?

What kind of research is being made: quantitative or qualitative?

A pragmatic approach to inquiry means that the research approach is chosen because the approach helps to achieve the "what" and the "why" defined in the research. This is what Silverman calls a pragmatic argument (Silverman 2005). A pragmatic approach to choice of method is opposed to choices based on personal favourites, expectation from a research supervisor, or because it is a dominating approach at the University. Burck supports this saying *"we can think of quantitative and qualitative research methodologies as best suited to different kinds of research questions posed at different levels, for different audiences, but crucially interlinked"* (Burck 2005, p.238). So a first choice has to be made about a quantitative or a qualitative approach.

In my own research I used Karpatchof (2000), Silverman (2005) and Burck (2005) to make this choice. According to Karpatchof, the quantitative approach is preferable, when the researcher is aiming at de-contextualised and de-personalized knowledge in order to create more objective and general knowledge. Therefore the researcher should use a larger population to secure generability. Burck supports this arguing that quantitative research is useful when conducting "outcome studies" (Burck 2005) looking at measurable data.

Karpatchof argues that a qualitative method is preferable, when the field to be studied is context-specific going into the detail of what is being researched (Karpatchof 2000). Silverman argues in similar ways stressing that the two approaches should not be seen as dichotomies, but in research processes with sufficient time and money to go hand in hand so that the qualitative method is used to look at detail and the quantitative method is used to look at variance (Silverman 2005). Burck supports this saying

> *"The types of research questions which qualitative research method-ologies address are often open-ended and exploratory, aiming to generate hypotheses rather than to test them. Systemic clinicians often pose questions of this kind, asking how therapeutic change comes about, and exploring subjective experience, meanings and processes" (Burck 2005, p.238)*

Using Karpatchof, Silverman and Burck looking at my research in organisational consultancy, the quantitative method could be useful if I wanted to measure success, find out how often I used different theories or if I wanted to look at a wider "population" of consultants. But the purpose of my research was *aiming to generate hypotheses rather than to test them* about how the consultant can increase his practical abilities: how do I know and decide about what to do next in order to create success? And do this by looking at similarities and differences at a practical level since *"depth rather than breath is what characterizes a good research proposal"* (Silverman 2005, p.80). With this purpose and using the arguments from Silverman (2005), Burck (2005) and Karpatchof (2000), I was best served using qualitative methods.

This raises the question of which qualitative methods to use? Going into the details of constructing a research approach I will address the two pending questions described above: What counts as data? How is data used? I will approach these questions with the inspiration from the pragmatic literature and the work of Dewey, James, Wittgenstein, Rorty, Cronen and Bateson.

What counts as data in pragmatic inquiry?

Taking a practical and pragmatic approach to research leaves the researcher with the fundamental question: How do I collect data about practice without disturbing the practice being researched?

Firstly, if the practitioner doing the pragmatic inquiry puts a tape recorder, video camera or extra researcher in the room, this will change the situation and the conversation. In short, the practitioner will not get the everyday kind of data he or she is looking for. In my own research I use Rosenthal's work to argue that the examples presented in my thesis would not have taken place like they did, had they been called "part of an experiment" or had there been a camera in the room recording the interaction.

Secondly, researching into practice the trouble for any practitioner is in advance how to choose what situations to accept as data and which not to. In pragmatic inquiry this is "solved" taking a practical approach to data meaning "everything is potentially data" with a re-writing of Schein's originally statement that "everything is data" (Schein 1999). This pragmatic approach to data has the obvious and practical advantage that the researcher can use field notes, memories, mail correspondences, etc. to create stories from practice and for use in practice. In my research, I use the term "example" as the basic unit of data for analysis.

In the following, I will first present four arguments for this definition of data followed by a critical reflection on this choice, reflecting on what I included and excluded in my research.

Firstly, Silverman's rule number 1 is that the researcher should "*Begin in familiar territory*" (Silverman 2005, p. 39). My own practice was familiar even though developing due to the research. A critical perspective could be that I did not take other consultants' work into account. But as Wolcott argues, the researcher should "Do less more thoroughly" (Wolcott, cited in Silverman 2005, p.85). In my research, I use this argument to support my choice about using my own practice and not that of other or more consultants.

Secondly, deciding that "everything is potentially data", every episode is of importance. This has the implication that deviant examples become part of the research and that the researcher steps into the position of the reflexive practitioner (Schön 1987) as I argued above. In my own research, this would not have been the case, were I to choose particular situations or insist on documenting these examples with video or tape recorder.

Thirdly, that everything potentially is data raises the question if pragmatic inquiry is a case study. Punch defines a case study as:

"The basic idea is that one case (or perhaps a small number of cases) will be studied in detail, using whatever method seems appropriate. While there may be a variety of specific purposes and research questions, the general objective is to develop as full an understanding of the case as possible" (Punch, cited in Silverman 2005, p.126)

If one chooses to see the researcher or organisation as "a case", this definition of case study is valid for the research. In my research I choose to see each of the examples as a case in the sense that I used *whatever method seems appropriate* from emails to memories to field notes. But each case was not treated as a case study *to develop as full an understanding of the case as possible*. Rather, differences and similarities between the examples were the focus, as I will describe below using Bateson's method of double description (Bateson 1972, 1984).

Fourthly, Pawson et al argue in favour of a wide range of sources of knowledge and additionally not to create a hierarchy in this classification of knowledge:

Our chosen classification is based on the different sources of social care knowledge, identified as: Organisational knowledge, Practitioner knowledge, User knowledge, Research knowledge,

Policy community knowledge. Several decisions informed this choice of classification system. Three key intentions, however, were that (...) the classification should send out the message that:

• all these sources have a vital role to play in building up the social care evidence base, there being no hierarchy implied in the above list

• it is important not to neglect sources of knowledge that are tacit, that currently lack prestige and seem less compelling

• information needs are variable, and there is flexibility and diversity within the recommended schema in order to help users find appropriate evidence for their particular requirements (Pawson et al 2003)

Pawson strengthens the argument in pragmatic inquiry that "everything is potentially data".

Finally, a critical perspective on this definition of data is necessary. When everything potentially is data, how does the researcher make distinctions between what to include and what to exclude from the research? Since obviously not every example can be used, where does the researcher draw the line? And how is this choice made? The researcher can use three questions to make such choices:

- *What can be learnt from the example about my research question?* In my research this was connected to how to create success and to behave professionally as consultant.

- What are the similarities and differences between the examples?

- What examples are deviant and how can they be used in the research?

Taking a pragmatic approach to data that "everything is potentially data" has the consequence that examples regarded "the same", not being "different" or "deviant" in some way could be excluded from the research.

How is data used in pragmatic inquiry?

In this section I will present a two-step method based on pragmatic ideas and methods to turn examples and data into richer and useful narratives. In Step 1, data and examples are turned into narratives about results of the research using Bateson's method of double description looking at similarities and differences. Step 2 is validating and enriching the narratives by putting them into use in various contexts. In my research these 'various contexts' included texts addressing examiners of my doctoral thesis, books I wrote on the subject of consultancy translated to two languages, discussions of research material with customers and colleagues, and reflections on the use of these practices in my own work. This is the part of the research building on pragmatic ideas from John Dewey (Dewey 1916, 1938; Brinkmann 2006), Vernon Cronen (Cronen 2000), William James (James 2000), Richard Rorty (Rorty 1997), Ludwig Wittgenstein (Wittgenstein, 1989, 1994) and Gregory Bateson (Bateson 1972, 1984). In the following I will show how they influenced pragmatic inquiry as a research approach, and I will describe steps 1 and 2 in detail.

Step 1:

Bateson's idea of double description is that new knowledge is created when *"two or more information sources come together to give information of a sort different from what was in either source separately"* (Bateson 1984, p.21) His often used example is seeing where depth emerges in the combination of two eyes. *"The two-eyed way of seeing is itself an act of comparison"* (Ibid. p.87). Comparison means taking account of both the similarities and the differences of the examples.

In order to make such a double, or in my case multiple, description, three questions can guide researchers when collecting examples and turning them into results. Each question has its own purpose. I will describe one question at a time and look at what came out of asking them when conducting my research.

Question 1: What can be learned from the example about the research question?
In my case this meant looking at what can be learned about how to create success and to behave professionally as consultant? The purpose of this question is twofold.

First of all, it supports a research position as reflexive practitioner both reflecting *in* the situation and *looking back* on the situation. This action learning based approach to my own work accelerated learning and could have become a thesis in its own right.

Secondly, the question supports the creation of two types of knowledge. One connected directly to Dewey's idea of inquiry, where knowledge is created *"because we have experienced relationships between our active doing in the world and the consequences of that doing"* (Brinkmann 2006, p.79). But also knowledge of a more imaginary kind thinking of "what might have happened, if I had done...?"

In my research, the results that came from working with question 1 supported the hypothesis, making clear how different approaches to organisational change were brought into the situation and what other approaches could have been used.

Question 2: What are the similarities and differences between the examples?
Question 2 follows directly from Bateson's notion of double description and has the main purpose of generating new knowledge. In my research, I noticed two results came from working with this question. Firstly, the focus on similarities showed that in my practice, I had a tendency to choose between a "set" of well-known positions. Even though I at a theoretical level would say that "every situation is unique" drawing on Heraclitus' idea that you are never stepping into *the same* river twice (Næss, 1965), this was not reflected in my own practice. For example, the idea of working with best practices from appreciative inquiry showed itself in many examples. These results became part of the research results and what I finally called "the consultancy room", a three dimensional figure of distinctions that the consultant can use to orient him- or herself in practice. One of these dimensions consists of "distinctions of position" and does so because looking at similarities between examples showed that I continually used six distinct consultancy positions.

Secondly, the focus on differences made me see something more clearly that I hadn't seen before. What I ended up calling "distinctions of system" and "distinctions of time", the two other dimensions of what I ended calling "the consultancy room", had not been clear to me before in my consultancy work.

Question 3: What examples are deviant and how can they be used in the research?
The purpose of this question in pragmatic inquiry is to secure that everything can indeed become data and thereby secure a rigour in the research method. In my research this question did not, however, add anything new that was not already looked at in the question about differences in question 2.

To summarize Step 1, a Batesonian analysis is one way to make a pragmatic inquiry, because it turns examples into results by looking at differences and similarities in the examples. But to fully meet the pragmatic ideas of usefulness, a Step 2 is needed.

Step 2:

To make a full pragmatic inquiry, the results in Step 1 need to be put into use with the possibility to create new and deviant examples. Further the results from step 1 need to be tested in conversations with others. In my research these conversations were with colleagues and customers about the work being done. This part of the pragmatic inquiry builds on two pragmatic ideas.

The first idea is that *"theories become instruments"* (James 2000, p.19[1]). An idea James shares with Dewey, who called his own position one of *instrumentalism* (Egeblad & Høgh Laursen 2000). What Dewey and James share is an understanding that theories in any domain should be evaluated by their usefulness to create something: solve a problem, achieve a goal etc. James calls this the "pragmatic method" (James 2000). If the theory does not have practical consequences, the theory hasn't "said" anything. The theory is never to be seen as a final truth about the world. If the researcher sees theories as instruments, the researcher must put the theories into use as part of the research in order to validate the theories. I will return to this below addressing the validity of pragmatic inquiry. In my own research Step 2 showed that taking different positions did lead to different ways of consulting in practice.

The second pragmatic idea in step 2 is Rorty's notion that *"truth is a word that we use about those convictions that we can agree upon"* (Rorty, cited in Haack 2000, p.54[2]). This is a very practical notion of truth, because it implies that the researcher needs to "test" his results through conversations with others asking: Does this theory help us create what we hope to create? The term agreement is not to be understood simply as consensus but that the theory has the intended consequence. In order to meet this criteria and to make this move with the results from the research, I initiated three different types of conversations as part of Step 2 in using the data.

One context of conversations was conversations to do with research. These conversations took place with research supervisors, examiners and colleagues at the professional doctorate programme at University of Bedfordshire. The intention and consequences of these conversations was to create pragmatic inquiry as a research approach that was both useful and had a clarity and rigour to it.

Another type of conversation was conversation to do with practice and the usefulness of the results. To get into conversations with colleagues and customers about both critical and supporting perspectives on

---

[1]   My translation from Danish.
[2]   My translation from Danish.

the results, I began writing and publishing about working and using the consultancy room. This was done initially with the article *"The professional process consultant"*[3] and then by publishing the book by the same name[4].

The publications had the intended consequence and initiated conversation with both customers and professional colleagues. Some of the comments were positive and supported the model. Others were critical raising important questions to reflect about. Some questions were already answered but were to implicit in my presentation of the results and other questions developed the research even further.

A final type of conversation took place in training courses and had a theoretical perspective. As a consequence of the research and the results from it, I initiated two types of education. One was a course at the University in Aarhus. One was an open course at diploma level for leaders and consultants from both public and private organisations about "the professional process consultant" based on the book.

I give these conversations some space because an important element in pragmatic inquiry is that working with and validating data is not done in the study chamber reading and re-reading data. Validation is done by looking at how the theories are useful in creating a desired outcome in collaboration with others. This leads to the last section of the research description: a critical perspective on pragmatic inquiry as a research method to create new knowledge in organisations.

A critical perspective: Validity and how it is accounted for in pragmatic inquiry

In this chapter I have so far presented pragmatic inquiry as a research method to generate new knowledge in organisations. I have been doing this by working with three questions: What is to be researched? Why is this to be researched? And lastly, how is the research being done going into themes of data and how data is used. But to present a strong and coherent research approach, I additionally need to take a critical perspective on pragmatic inquiry as a research model. To do this I will address what Coolican (1999) points out to be the most important questions: the questions of validity and how this is accounted for in pragmatic inquiry.

Validity is viewed differently from a quantitative and a qualitative tradition. In a quantitative tradition of measuring, the theme of

---

[3]   My translation from Danish.
[4]   Published in Danish in 2009, published in Swedish in 2013 and in ongoing negotiations to be translated into English.

validation is asking if the researcher is measuring and addressing what they are intending to measure? (Ibid.).

Working with qualitative methods *"validation becomes a question of choosing between competing and falsifiable interpretations"* (Kvale, 2002 p.235[5]). Kvale points to three different perspectives on validity in qualitative research and can be used to show how validity is accounted for in pragmatic inquiry.

Validity defined as "quality in the research process"

Kvale's first perspective on validity in qualitative research is to secure *quality in the research process*. In this section I will show how I secured quality in the research process in four different ways.

Following Kvale, the first way to secure quality in the research is by the researcher taking a self-reflexive and self-critical position in order for the researcher not to believe too much in just one interpretation of the data. This self-critical position is built into pragmatic inquiry. This section is one example. Above I described how putting results into use and discussing them with research supervisors, colleagues, students and customers tested the results. This was done in order to secure a quality in the research process by creating a continued critical position in relation to the research being done.

The second way Kvale addresses quality in the research process is by securing an "internal coherence".

> *"Rather than being concerned, for example, with the representativeness of the sample used in the qualitative research project, you should concentrate on whether it was internally consistent and coherent. Does it present a coherent argument? For instance does it deal with loose ends and possible contradictions in the data?"* (Smith 1996, p.192)

Smith's idea is closely connected to *Question 3: What examples are deviant and how can they be used in the research?* As mentioned above in step 1, the consequence of this question is that *loose ends and possible contradictions in the data* are built into the data collection and analysis – not left behind.

The third way to create quality in the research process is continually looking at if the *what, why and how* of the research are connected in a meaningful way.

---

[5]   My translation from Danish.

The fourth way Kvale defines quality in research is by looking at the ways theoretical reflections are drawn upon to strengthen the argument. In my research this happened in all chapters where several theorists were drawn upon to build a strong argument about the theoretical foundation for the results.

Communicative validity

Kvale's second perspective on validity in qualitative research is to secure a communicative validity (Kvale, 2002). In my research communicative validity was addressed in two ways:

Firstly, as the ongoing conversation with research supervisors, colleagues, students, and customers mentioned already.

Secondly, I worked with communicative validity by writing the examples in the thesis in such a way that the reader was able to follow what went on and see what theoretical ideas inspire me to do, what I did. Further I made extensive comments and reflexions about the examples in the thesis to let the reader see what theoretical and practical reflections come out of the situations.

Pragmatic validity

As a third perspective, Kvale points to pragmatic validity. In short: qualitative research is only valid, if it is useful. The important point in pragmatic validity is that research is not "just" *grounded in* practice but the research must also be *useful for* practice. Meaning, that the research is leading to new actions for either the person being researched (in my research this was myself), the person researching (in my research this was myself) or people reading about the research. In this section I will return to pragmatic authors, present their arguments for this approach to validity and show how it is used in my research.

Pragmatic literature and pragmatic authors take on validity show a clear focus on practice as the basis for any pragmatic inquiry. Rorty using the inspiration of William James says:

> "*Let us see truth as, in James's phrase, "what it is better for us to believe", rather than as "the accurate representation of reality" ... "accurate representation" is simply an automatic and empty compliment which we pay to those beliefs which are successful in helping us to do what we want to do*" *(Rorty 1979, p.10).*

As with the earlier quote from Rorty, that "*truth is a word that we use about those convictions, that we can agree upon"* (Rorty, cited in Haack 2000 p. 54[6]), one could misinterpret Rorty to say that truth is only a matter of seeking consensus. But Rorty builds on Dewey's work, so this is not the case. Theories are neither true nor not true but are instruments that people do things with, as I showed earlier with Dewey's position as *instrumentalism* (Egeblad & Høgh Laursen 2000). Where the term "truth" might give us an idea of something stable and independent of human action, Dewey preferred the term "warranted assertability". "Warranted" indicates that a theoretical claim has to be grounded in practice and experience, and "assertability" indicates that the same claim has implications for our further thinking and doing (Brinkmann 2006). In the end a theoretical idea should help us know *how to go on*, as Wittgenstein frames it (Wittgenstein 1989, 1994). In pragmatic inquiry ethics therefore becomes a matter of showing how the knowledge can be used for something good and useful. In connection to "the knowledge producing" position this means creating a clear connection between the knowledge created and the purposes and strategies of the organisation.

In my research pragmatic validity was been dealt with in two ways.

Firstly, the data, the examples was actual cases from my practice. By using successful examples about work as consultant, the presentation of cases are both accounts of what happened and indicators for future practices. By doing this, the examples strengthened the pragmatic validity of my thesis.

Secondly, the model created, the consultancy room, was again both rooted in practice and gives the practitioner both ideas to "what to do" as well of giving a way to reflect in and on practice.

Summary

In this text I have presented *Pragmatic Inquiry* as a research method for knowledge creation in organisations. I have used the work of pragmatic philosophers such as Lyotard (1984), William James (James 2000), John Dewey (Dewey 1916, 1938; Brinkmann 2006), John Austin (Austin 1997), Ludwig Wittgenstein (Wittgenstein 1989, 1994) and Gregory Bateson (Bateson 1972, 1984) to argue, that organisations in a postmodern reality need to take a knowledge producing position, where knowledge about performing is created. I have argued that this challenges and changes typical organisational views of knowledge that are most often based on a "traditionalist" or "knowledge consuming" position.

---

[6]   My translation from Danish.

Further, I have used my own research in organisational consultancy as a case to show how pragmatic inquiry gives a coherent research method for practitioners. A four-step method has been presented to help practitioners take an experimental attitude and become researchers in their own practice. Bateson's method of double description has been presented as one way of turning everyday practice into research narratives with *usefulness* as the prime criteria for validity.

References

Austin, John (1997). *Ord der virker*. Reproset. København.
Bateson, Gregory (1972). *Steps to an ecology of Mind – Collected essays in anthropology, psychiatry, evolution and epistgemology.* London: Intertext Books.
Bateson, Gregory (1984). *Ånd og natur – En nødvendig enhed.* Rosinante. Charlottenlund.
Brinkmann, Svend (2006). *John Dewey, en introduction.* Hans Reitzels forlag. Danmark.
Burck, Charlotte (2005). Comparing qualitative research methodologies for systemic research: the
use of grounded theory, discourse analysis and narrative analysis. *Journal of Family Therapy*, 27: 237–262.
Cameron, Kim (2008). *Positive Leadership: Strategies for Extraordinary Performance.* Berrett-Koehler. USA.
Coolican, Hugh (1999). *Research methods and statistics in psychology.* London: Hodder & Stoughton.
Cronen, Vernon (2000). *Practical theory and a naturalistic account of inquiry.* Conference paper.
Dewey, John (1916). *Democracy and Education.* The Macmillan Company. 288 pages. Dewey, J. (1938) *Logic: The Theory of Inquiry.* New York: Henry Holt & Co.
Dewey, John (1938). *Logic: The Theory of Inquiry.* New York: Henry Holt & Co.
Dreyfus, Hubert & Dreyfus, Stuart (1999). Mesterlære og eksperters læring.. In: Nielsen, K. & Kvale, S. *Mesterlære – læring som social praksis.* Pp 54 – 75Hans Rietzels forlag.
Egeblad, Anders & Høgh Laursen, Henning (2000). PHILOSOPHIA – Tidsskrift for filosofi. Årg. 26, 5 – 14.
Haack, Susan (2000). *PHILOSOPHIA – Tidsskrift for filosofi.* Årg. 26.
James, William (2000). *Hvad pragmatisme betyder.* PHILOSOPHIA – Tidsskrift for filosofi. Årg. 26, 15 – 30.
Juhl, Andreas Granhof & Madsen, Anne Krogh (2011). Pygmalion-effekten: Når forventninger skaber virkeligheden In *20 psykologiske eksperimenter - der ændrede vores syn på mennesket.* Pp127 - 142. Plurafutura publishing.
Karpatschof, Benny (2000). *Forelæsning om Kvalitativ og kvantitativ metode.* Københavns Universitet (Lecture at University of Copenhagen)
Kvale, Steinar (2002). *Interview.* Hans Reitzels Forlag. København.
Lave, Jean (1999). Læring, meterlære, social praksis. In: Nielsen, K. & Kvale, S.

Mesterlære – læring som social praksis. Pp 35 – 53. Hans Rietzels forlag.

Lyotard, Jean François. (1984). *The Postmodern Condition.* Manchester: Manchester University Press.

Næss, Arne. (1965). *Moderne Filosoffer.* Vintens Forlag. København.

Pawson, Ray; Barnes, Colin; Boaz, Annette; Grayson, Lesley & Long, Andrew. (2003). *Types and quality of social care knowledge Stage one: a classification of types of social care knowledge.* ESRC UK Centre for Evidence Based Policy and Practice. (working paper without pagenumbers)

Rorty, Richard (1989). *Contingency, irony, and solidarity.* Cambridge University Press.

Rorty, Richard (1997). *Philosophy and the mirror of nature.* Princeton university press.

Rosenthal, Robert (1968:1992). *Pygmalion in the Classroom. Teachers Expectations and Pu- pils' Intellectual Development.* Irvington Publishers.

Shotter, John (2009). *Some relations between practitioner initiated and oriented inquiry and 'coolly rational' forms of 'research': 'Systemic thinking' and 'thinking about systems'.* Notes from the Professional Doctorate Course at Bedforshire University.

Schön, Donald A. (1987). *The reflective practitioner. How professionals think in action.* New York: Basic Books.

Silverman, David (2005). *Interpreting Qualitative Data: Methods for Analysing Talk, Text and Interaction.* London: Sage.

Smith, Jonathan (1996). Evolving issues for qualitative psychology. In Richardsson, J. T: E. (red.) *Handbook of qualitative research methods for psychology and social sciences.* 189 - 202 BRP Books.

Wittgenstein, Ludwig (1989). *Om Vished.* Forlaget Philosophia. Århus.

Wittgenstein, Ludwig (1994). *Filosofiske undersøgelser.* Gyldendal Bogklubben.

13 Using CMM to Define Systemic Reflexivity as a Research Position

Christine Oliver

One of the things that continually confronts me is the challenge and opportunity of managing meanings about the context in which we perceive and into which we act. (Pearce, 2011, personal communication)

Bushe & Marshak (2009) suggest ... 'there appears to be a rather large gulf between academics who study change from narrative and interpretive premises and ... practitioners who use dialogical methods' (p. 362). Systemic research practice could be said to exemplify dialogical method in the way that it does not treat data gathering, meaning making and intervention as discrete, sequential entities, but rather, it assumes that they are simultaneously integrated in ongoing interaction processes (Oliver & Fitzgerald 2012). In this chapter, I will offer one way of narrowing the gulf between academic and practitioner, developing a language for defining the *system* in focus through articulating and elaborating relevant aspects of Coordinated Management of Meaning (CMM) Theory (Barge 2004; Oliver 1992, 1996, 2005, 2013; Pearce & Cronen 1980; Pearce 1989, 1997) for the research context. This process will enable reflexive exploration of the meaning and impact of cyclical patterns in our co-construction of communicative contexts.

In dialogical research processes, meaning making is treated as contested, temporary, partial and contingent. For instance, if a research participant were to say 'women are emotional', the researcher with a dialogical sensibility might inquire into this as a temporary and partial narrative with possibilities for narrative development, and might take the position that this is one of many narratives that this participant could tell, each narrative contextualised by historical and current communicative, relational and power dynamics. Depending on the perceived relevance of the particular utterance to the goals of research, specific interaction experiences with different women might be explored to facilitate a more contextualised and nuanced narrative, and those experiences, linked to cultural, family and relational narratives or scripts, identifying grounded links between the person's experience of women and emotion.

The goal in a dialogical research process is to identify narratives and patterns of communication collaboratively, with relevant *system* members, for the benefit of *system* development (Marshak & Bushe 2012; Oliver & Fitzgerald 2012). This commitment fits with the aims of the critical research tradition as expressed by the work of Alvesson & Deetz (2000), who define the research task as a complex interplay between the development of *insight* (interpretation of the local), *critique* (investigating the local through connecting micro practices and macro discourses), and *transformation* (connecting insight to social action). I suggest that in the systemic research context, however, the development of insight and critique are usually goals at a higher contextual level than the goal of transformation. While it is acknowledged that research conversations have consequences for the research participants, and that the researcher is accountable for their contribution to those implicative effects, the development of narratives and patterns of communication is not usually the primary task of the researcher, but is more a secondary commitment, whereas transformation is more usually the higher order context shaping sense making for other systemic practitioners such as therapists and consultants.

The focus in any qualitative research context is, of course, to explore the meaning of social phenomena, not to count instances or make claims about frequencies (Silverman 2000). Alvesson (2003, p.30) points out, however, that, "there are not many efforts to develop a theoretical frame to understand context issues". He also suggests that it would be innovative to provide studies that combine critical and non-critical perspectives. It is proposed here that a position of *systemic reflexivity*, employing and developing CMM as a framework for systemic inquiry and analysis, can offer a structure for interpreting a complexity of contexts, perspectives and interests, and combine critical and 'non critical' approaches to research, critical in so far as different levels of discourse and context are linked, but 'non critical' in the appreciative stance that is taken in exploring how those contexts are made.

For Alvesson & Deetz (2000, p.113), reflexivity in research shows itself as "an interpretive, open, language sensitive, identity conscious, historical, political, local, non authoritative and textually aware understanding of the subject matter". This seems a useful working definition but it also seems necessary to locate reflexive practice in research in the context of a vocabulary for describing the *system* in focus. If the vocabulary framework for *system* is not defined, we become unclear about what we might select out for attention and give voice to, and how to relate reflexively to what we make relevant. CMM facilitates this task of structuring our systemic vocabulary, enriching inquiry into our practices.

The chapter will unfold in the following way:

I will begin with an introduction to the concept of *systemic reflexivity* and go on to identify how CMM can facilitate description, hypothesis and interpretation of the *system*. A more concrete vocabulary will then be offered for CMM as a research tool with a case example for illustration.

Introducing systemic reflexivity

Although many writers have discussed reflexivity (for instance, Burnham 2005; Cunliffe 2002; Dallos & Draper 2005; Van der Haar & Hosking 2004), *systemic reflexivity* has not previously been offered as a concept in the systemic field. However, one definition of it has emerged in some work on decision making in career development (Tams & Marshall 2011). Tams & Marshall (2011) define *systemic reflexivity* as a subjective meaning making process facilitated by the observation of contradiction and incoherence in social systems and the consideration of personal impact on those social systems. This description fits well with a critical approach, seeking out the problematic, but within the systemic tradition we might be more interested in the relationship between coherence *and* incoherence or connection *and* disconnection or contradiction. I will be drawing attention later in the chapter to the usefulness in a contextual analysis of a focus on these relationships and, in particular, to the quality of *(in)commensurability* in systemic narratives and patterns of communication.

My use of the term *systemic reflexivity* is inclusive of such systemic observation, taking seriously the idea that the ways that we think, feel, talk, listen, act, and construct narratives about those interactions, have consequences for self and others in the *systems* of meaning and action within which we participate. However, it not only invites consideration and inquiry of those *systems* of meaning and action but assumes a (partial) moral responsibility for their outcomes and for facilitating *systemic reflexivity* for and with other participants of the *system*. Further, if advocating systemic observation, evaluation and recalibration, the notion of *system* itself needs specification, a task not undertaken by Tams & Marshall (2011).

Van der Haar and Hosking (2004) helpfully connect the notion of reflexivity to two different theoretical traditions. A constructivist approach focuses on the curious inquiry of the individual in relation to their own narratives, a meta-cognitive activity. A constructionist approach has a socio-relational focus, where the individual treats their actions as constitutive of social and political realities. The concept of *systemic reflexivity* incorporates both approaches to reflexivity, emphasising the ability to act consciously, with purpose, towards the systemic provenances and effects of one's actions in and on the *system*. This approach fits with and extends that of Frosh and Barraitser (2008) who define reflexivity as "an interactively critical practice that is constantly reflected back on itself and is always suspicious of the productions of its own knowledge" (p.350). *Systemic reflexivity* is less concerned with 'suspicion' but more, aspires to participate consciously in the construction of the system with commitment to accountability for one's part in that construction.

This conceptualisation of *systemic reflexivity* articulates a complex, CMM influenced view of *system* building on previous usage (von Bertalanffy 1968; Boscolo et al 1987; Campbell et al 1989; Campbell & Huffington 2008; Dallos & Draper 2005; Watzlawick et al 2011). Specifically it provides unique detailing of a framework for thinking about what counts as a *system*, comprising hypothesised interactive patterns of *emotion, meaning* and *action* shaping and shaped by narratives and part narratives of culture, relationship and identity (Oliver et al 2003; Oliver 2005, 2008, 2010). This view of *system* will be elaborated in detail later in the chapter, illustrated by a case example, but first I will trace something of the development of the conceptualisation of *system* in the systemic literature.

What is a system?

The notion of *system* has taken many forms in the literature (Pearce 1997). Early systems theory, based on first order cybernetics, assumed the objectivity of the 'outside' observer, treating the *system* in modernist, mechanistic terms but did have some application for human interaction, expressing some principles that are helpful for considering reflexivity (von Bertalanffy 1968). For instance, the notion that any action within a *system* stimulates a response which becomes feedback *to* the *system*, implies the possibility of reflexive learning, containing the idea that *system* participants can reflect on their behaviours and the consequences of those behaviours for future action. Bateson (1972) highlights the significance of feedback in conceptualising a *system* as a unit structured on feedback with its interacting parts exerting mutual influence and connected to each other in observable and coherent patterns. The characteristics and patterns of a *system* are seen as evolving and not possible to predict or control (unlike earlier mechanistic notions of *system* which were based on the possibility of control). Actions, in these terms, are always responses to what has gone before and responses are actions, in circular relationship.

The innovative work of Watzlawick et al (2011 reprint) in the 1960s, building on Bateson's contribution, places communication at the heart of the systemic enterprise and links it to context and interaction. They identify the vicious circles that emerge when discrepant punctuations of communication become repeated patterns, and highlight the role of meta-communication in resolving such difficulties. They make the point that 'the ability to meta-communicate appropriately is not only the *conditio sine qua non* of successful communication but is intimately linked with the enormous problem of awareness of self and others' (p.34), implying the significance of reflexivity. They define the concept of pattern in communication as shown by 'repetition or redundancy of events' (p.99).

While this chapter develops the concept of pattern in relation to awareness of self and others, hypothesising connections between behaviour, thought, emotional responses and their narratives of influence and consequence, the focus for Watzlawick et al (2011) is only patterns of observable behaviour, as symbolic meaning is said to be 'objectively undecidable' (p.26). The claim in this chapter is not for 'objectivity' but for a heuristic framework that facilitates research orientation, hypothesis and interpretation.

Dallos & Draper (2005) make the point that what counts as a *system* is always a hypothesis of the observer. They suggest that communication feedback can either lead to change or stability of existing patterns depending on how open or closed to information (and learning) the *system* is. Communicative *systems* need both patterns for healthy survival and development. In the 1970s and 1980s, the Milan group, less overtly behaviourist than earlier *systems* approaches, building on Bateson's work (1972) and others, highlight the significance of the co-creation of shared meaning in relationships through communication processes, in their efforts to treat families suffering complex mental health problems (Palazzoli Selvini et al 1978 1980; Cecchin, 1987; Boscolo et al 1987). Their work draws attention to how pathological patterns of identity and relationship are constructed interpersonally and have interpersonal effects. Their work shifts attention towards a second order cybernetic view of *system* where the systemic practitioner is invited into a position of reflexivity, less an expert stance, more one of collaboration in conversation. The Milan approach encourages curiosity and challenge towards meanings and their links with action, for self and others, not assuming that this stance will inevitably lead to productive outcomes but stimulating conditions for greater choice in decision making and action (Cecchin 1987).

Campbell et al (1989), applying Milan thinking to the organisational consultancy context, suggest that patterns of meaning/belief and behaviour develop in relation to organisational tasks which in turn affect communication and relationships. For instance, if in a community mental health team meeting the social workers usually experience their contribution as not valued, this will likely affect their narratives about relationships with service users and with management, which will in turn shape their behavioural responses. Consultants using a systemic approach stimulate conversations that facilitate development of these beliefs and behaviours, with a central aim of increased systemic awareness. Campbell et al (1989) speak of consultants facilitating a self-reflective position in relation to beliefs and behaviour of organisational participants. It is notable that there is no vocabulary for emotion in this approach to thinking about *systems*; the emphasis is on beliefs and behaviours, yet emotion is usually co-existent with cognition as we might hypothesise in relation to the example above. The notion of *systemic reflexivity* developed in this chapter offers a vocabulary for linking emotional responses of *system* participants to meaning and action and the narratives shaping those responses (Oliver 2004b, 2005, 2013; Oliver et al 2003).

The notion of *system* will build through the chapter as CMM is incorporated into the narrative. However, it is useful to highlight at this stage that the circular linkage between meaning and behaviour has been a core focus for the systemic enterprise for some years. What will be useful will be to put more flesh on the bones of meaning and behaviour, incorporating emotion into the vocabulary, so an accessible vocabulary is provided for practical research use.

System through the lens of CMM

The task of the researcher
I have suggested that the task of the systemic researcher might be to facilitate insight and critique as primary commitments and trans-formation as a secondary commitment (Alvesson & Deetz 2000). For Pearce (1989, 1997, 2011), whose work with Cronen originally developed CMM conceptualisation (Pearce & Cronen 1980; Cronen & Pearce 1985), the process and form of communication should be the object of inquiry, insight and critique for the researcher and, in particular, the useful questions to ask are: *how was this social world made; what social*

worlds are we making; and what social worlds do we want to make?

In these terms, the task is to facilitate insight and transformation of the *interpersonal logics* expressed by *system* participants' narratives and patterns of communication, through inviting reflection on and critique of *system* participants' acts of communication, interpretation and coordination. In doing so, the researcher contextualises and re-contextualises emotional expression, meaning making and behaviour. This approach invites researchers to draw attention to and inevitably intervene in conscious and unconscious dimensions of communication. The *unconscious*, in this vocabulary, refers to those aspects of experience not yet given narrative form. Cronen & Pearce (1985) argue that "no social system can operate with near total consciousness of its own structure from a third person position at all times" (p. 83). To be human is to be not always conscious of the narratives shaping and limiting communication. The researcher's own logic of meaning and action thus encourages narratives of purpose, potentially positioning research participants with conscious agency in their *coordinations* of *interpersonal logics* (Cronen & Pearce 1985). It is important to add that narratives of the unconscious have historically taken an expert position where 'relationality was bracketed for many decades' (Mitchell, 2000) but the development of intersubjectivity theory has asserted the significance of relational and communication contexts for making sense of individual behaviour and it is in this spirit that I am using the word unconscious (Benjamin 2004; Mitchell 2000).

Interpersonal logics

A *system* within this vocabulary can be represented by the quality of *(in)commensurability* in *interpersonal logics* of *emotion, meaning* and *action* shown in the coherence and connections of coordinated narratives and patterns of communicative interaction. *Interpersonal logics* are a good location for examination of the *system*. They arise from our experience and shape and limit our interpretation of behaviour and meaning, our emotional responses, our sense of appropriate action and our vocabulary of purpose. To illustrate, a father might interpret (*make meaning of*) his son's expression of independent thought as a criticism of him, might feel belittled (*feel emotion*), and in that context might feel obliged to act defensively and criticise his son (*undertake action*). His logics for making meaning and guiding action might be predicated on an experience in his family of origin of belittlement, having felt, for example, emotions such as rage and shame, linked to his own parents' misuse of power, shaping his logic for *emotion, meaning* and *action* and stimulated within the present communication episode. In this chapter, I develop the notion of *interpersonal logics* further, through giving attention to the emotional and unconscious dimensions of *emotion, meaning* and *action*. The CMM account has not historically identified the role of emotion in communication exchanges, subsuming it in the category of *meaning*.

Logical force

The CMM notion of *logical force* is useful in highlighting variability of consciousness of purpose and emotion and their role in the communication and *coordination* of our *interpersonal logics* of meaning and action. Prefigurative (no conscious narrative of purpose) and practical force (conscious narrative of purpose) represent a horizontal continuum of this variability and contextual and implicative force, a vertical continuum where contextual force refers to the strength of the *interpersonal logics* that contextualise a communication episode and implicative force refers to the strength of the implication of the current communication episode for developing or challenging meanings of higher contextual levels such as narratives of *culture, relationship* and *identity*.

To continue with hypothesising from the example above of the father:

Prefigurative force: 'if my authority is questioned I have to defend myself'. No *practical force* is evident. The father does not have a (reflexive) narrative of how his actions may affect his relationship with his son or their experiences of identity and relationship.

Contextual force:

family narrative – 'control is the only way to handle difference/disagreement'

relational narrative – 'only one party can be right'

identity narrative – 'self esteem is contingent on being right'

Implicative force: low (see Figure 1)

Coordination

Coordination has been defined as an activity where we attempt to realise our goals – for instance, *cultural, relational, identity* goals... the communication enactments we engage in to construct our "visions of the good, desirable and expedient" and to constrain "the bad, ugly and

Figure 1. logical force

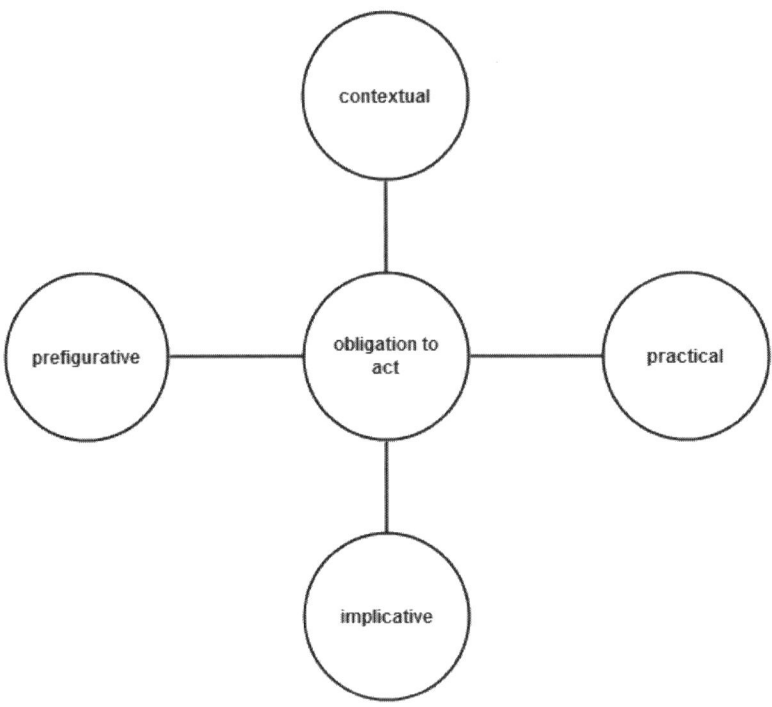

obstructive" (Pearce 1989, p.20). Pearce points out that "coordination is inherently difficult in human communication because the meaning of messages is determined by their enmeshment in various moral orders (or logics) whose content cannot be assumed to be either constant or commensurate with each other" (p.59). He suggests that well formed *coordinations* are "collaborative artistic accomplishments" and that *incommensurate interpersonal logics* will result in failures of *coordination* (p.38). However, here I want to emphasise how *unwanted* repetitive patterns might also be thought of as examples of well-formed *coordination*. When people engage in consciously unwanted patterns, they very often offer a narrative of felt compulsion or obligation to act in the way that they do, experiencing an absence of choice and a strong emotional pull, implying a strong unconscious influence in communication construction. In CMM language these are instances where prefigurative and contextual forces are strong. I propose that even when the social worlds we create may be consciously unwanted and may at first glance seem poorly coordinated, they may well be opaquely unconsciously well coordinated. Further, I show the usefulness for the researcher in highlighting, where relevant and purposeful, the unconscious *commensurability* of apparently *incommensurate interpersonal logics* and the place and role of emotion in constructing (un)conscious *(in)commensurate interpersonal logics*.

Figure 2. incommensurability in the context of commensurability

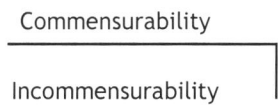

Thinking about coordination in this way invites us to explore and consider narratives about purposes that may be outside consciousness and require conscious incorporation for communication participants to meet their conscious goals. The following section will offer a theoretically grounded practical language.

CMM as a practical research tool

Contextualised by the thinking above, the systemic focus for the researcher becomes communication acts, comprising conscious and unconscious responses and linkages of *emotion, meaning* and *action,* taking place within communication *episodes,* often taking the form of patterns that repeat over time becoming embedded in the *system* as conscious narratives and unconscious part narratives of *culture, relationship and identity* shaping future linkages and patterns of *emotion, meaning* and *action* within communication exchanges. In those exchanges we draw consciously and unconsciously on *interpersonal logics* for our *emotional, meaning* and *action* responses and the communication patterns that develop over time may be consciously wanted or unwanted by *system* participants (Pearce 2007; Oliver 2005).

To make sense making meaningfully manageable for the researcher in the face of systemic complexity, I propose a framework of three forms of pattern, *reactive, paradoxical* and *reflexive,* for describing conscious and unconscious *coordination* of communication and contributing to a contextual analysis of *interpersonal logics* of *emotion, meaning* and *action* and the narratives that shape them (Oliver 2005). This framework provides the possibility of holding sufficient structure and complexity to enable the researcher to make sense of the system so as to promote insight, critique and transformation within a collaborative, reflexive process with research participants.

Reactive patterns are represented by linkages between *emotion, meaning,* and *action* characterised by an emotional experience stimulating a desire for fight or flight, linked to poor reflective capacity and a predominance of contextual and prefigurative force. Such a communication *culture* sets a context for poor meta-communication, shaping rigid symmetrical or complementary *relationships* where the position of the other is delegitimised, which further sets a context for *identity* narratives of exclusive legitimation. Communication *coordination* is characterised by apparent fragmentation and polarisation both within and between narratives, between narratives and episodic *emotional, meaning* making and *action* responses, with a prefigured and contextual difficulty in taking action to transform the communication experience. Unconscious *well-formed coordination* occurs when there is *commensurability* between the protective/defensive purposes of relevant *system* participants, though the conversational effects may appear to be *incommensurate* with conscious goals.

Figure 3. reactive pattern

▲ *Culture*: predominance of contextual and prefigurative force; poor meta-communication

Relationship: rigid symmetry or complementarity with the position of the other delegitimised

Identity: poor agency and exclusive legitimacy

___

Episodic pattern of communication

Emotion: fear

Meaning: threat

Action: protect through control

Paradoxical patterns, developed from the concept of strange loops in the CMM literature, (Cronen, Johnson & Lannamann 1982; Oliver et al 2003) are in the form of a figure of eight, where linkages of *emotion, meaning* and *action* stimulate the opposite meaning at each contextual level. These patterns also show strong prefigurative and contextual force and are contextualised by processes of unconscious splitting, fragmenting the pattern lived from the story or narrative told, so that when an individual or group are conscious of one experience of *emotion, meaning* and *action*, they become unconscious of its opposite. *Cultural, relational* and *identity interpersonal logics* in symmetrical or complementary form, tend to be contradictory, ambivalent or polarised and when experiencing the pattern, participants show a tendency to lack reflective capacity and meta-communicative abilities. Coordination is oscillatory and unstable; the felt experience may include a sinking awareness of being in an impossible pattern. Unconscious *well-formed coordination* will occur here also where there is a fit of protective purposes for *system* participants, leading to complementary *commensurability*.

Figure 4. paradoxical pattern

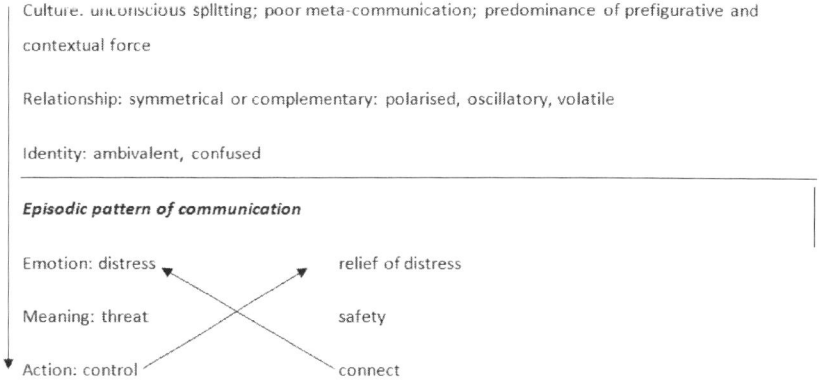

Culture. unconscious splitting; poor meta-communication; predominance of prefigurative and contextual force

Relationship: symmetrical or complementary: polarised, oscillatory, volatile

Identity: ambivalent, confused

Episodic pattern of communication

Emotion: distress   relief of distress

Meaning: threat   safety

Action: control   connect

Reflexive patterns are those characterised by the conscious desire to act purposively to make sense of and coordinate rich social worlds, and by reflexive abilities whereby individuals and groups show preparedness to reflect on and evaluate the ways their own *narratives, part narratives* and *emotion, meaning and action patterns*, are contributing to the social realities of the system. A *culture* of respect (but not necessarily agreement) for the position and perspective of the other, and preparedness for reflective learning sets a context for *relationships* of self/other legitimation, linked to *identity* narratives of partial legitimation, i.e. the individual takes a position of reflexive humility in relation to their own views and experiences and is curious about those of the other; practical and implicative forces predominate.

Figure 5. reflexive pattern

Culture: predominance of implicative and practical force; good meta-communication; desire for
learning

Relationship: respect for position and perspective of the other

Identity: strong agency and partial legitimacy

Episodic pattern of communication

Emotion: curiosity

Meaning: emotion and difference are not to be feared

Action: explore experience

Coordinated Management of Meaning as analysis of interpersonal logics: a story from practice

The following story comes from a psychotherapy setting within adult mental health services in the NHS where I work as a systemic psychotherapist. It illustrates how CMM can bring understanding and develop action within relationships, be it personal or professional. This account is about work with a couple I am calling here, Kath and Mike. In session 1, they present their concern as relational conflict, shown through distressing arguments which they find impossible to control or transcend. *Coordination* appears to be poor and *interpersonal logics* of *emotion, meaning* and *action,* appear *incommensurate* with neither person able to achieve their goals as individuals or for the relationship, nor are they able to meta-communicate about their *coordination* without exacerbating the conflict.

Mike's explanation for the arguments is that his wife is mentally ill. He believes that her experience of sexual abuse as a child plays a large part in her mental instability. Kath's explanation for the arguments is that Mike has anger management problems and treats her like a mentally ill person. Both describe problems with intimacy; initially Mike blames the sexual abuse, implying the fault is with Kath, but when this is explored, it emerges that he is unable to be intimate with Kath because he feels like he is abusing her. Kath feels furious and helpless in the face of this perception and expresses anger with Mike for believing that her childhood experience is 'to blame', without his owning the part his own childhood experience might play in their difficulties.

Both Kath and Mike feel compelled to act antagonistically and competitively with each other, showing prefigurative and contextual force with weak implicative and practical force. Both complain about the behaviour of the other, describing the other in complementary, simplified and diminishing terms. *Incommensurable interpersonal logics* appear to be at play suggesting the usefulness of exploring the possibility of *unconscious commensurability* as a contextualisation of the *incommensurability*. This is facilitated by inquiring into the *emotion, meaning and action interpersonal logics* and patterns within argument episodes and relevant historical episodes where logics were formed and reinforced, with the purpose of exploring and appreciating how this couple *system* was made and, potentially achieving greater implicative force in the system whereby conscious and unconscious *coordination* can integrate.

Some important themes come out in Session 2. Firstly, Kath reports that both her parents denied that sexual abuse by her father had occurred. In fact her mother threatened to cut off contact with her, initially emotionally, and later physically if Kath continued to speak of the abuse. This experience of not being believed, combined with the injunction to suppress memories and emotions linked to the experience of abuse, influence Kath's contribution to her current relational predicament, constraining her freedom of emotional expression while provoking profound feelings of rage and distress.

Then, Mike tells how both his parents behaved aggressively towards him with the emotional effects of fear, helplessness, diminishment and shame. He felt disrespected and unimportant. Mike's mother had a mental health diagnosis of depression, her communication often characterised by aggression. He describes how there was no room for his vulnerability in the family dynamic, that if he showed 'weakness' he was bullied. Kath reports a similar 'bullying' experience in their current arguments, feeling her own opinions and needs are discounted and that she is 'forced' to comply with his opinions and needs. Kath claims that her fear of his aggression constrains her ability to raise and discuss difficult subjects that he may feel to be provocative.

There are more developments in session 3. Kath begins to cry and Mike responds: "this is no time for tears". This utterance provoked the following exchange:

K: you don't like me to have emotions; you think I'm crazy like your mother.
M: I don't like it in my house.
K: you are the one that brings it into the house with your aggression; the

irony is that you lose control much more than I do. I'm not mentally ill; I am distressed about our situation.

M: you are mentally ill because you were abused by your father.

T: if you did not think of Kath as mentally ill, how might you relate to her differently?

M: I would approach intimacy differently. I can't trust her because I am not sure she is not mentally ill.

T: she has been crying. Do you see that as a sign of mental illness?

M: it shows a lack of control.

K: don't patronise me. I'm crying because my husband thinks I am mentally ill.

M: I do see that I am partly responsible for making things worse.

The following is a CMM analysis of the above episodic *coordination* and its interpersonal logics.

K: (tearful)

M: this is no time for tears

Communication act	Narratives
Emotion: vulnerability in the context of tears	Family culture: vulnerability prohibited
Meaning: distress is prohibited/weak	Relationship: aggressor/ victim
Action: control of emotional expression	Identity: aggression permitted

K: you don't like me to have emotions; you think I'm crazy like your mother.

Communication act	Narratives
Emotion: anger at emotional prohibition	Family culture: disowned and disbelieved abuse
Meaning: anger is prohibited	Relationship: aggressor/ victim
Action: show distress about the prohibition	Identity: mentally ill

M: I don't like it in my house.

Communication act	Narratives
Emotion: fear of distress	Family culture: vulnerability prohibited
Meaning: distress is prohibited/weak	Relationship: aggressor/victim
Action: control of emotional expression	Identity: aggression permitted

K: you are the one that brings it into the house with your aggression; the irony is that you lose control much more than I do. I'm not mentally ill; I am distressed about our situation.

Communication act	Narratives
Emotion: distress at emotional positioning	Family culture: disowned emotions
Meaning: positioning is invalid	Relationship: aggressor/victim
Action: reject positioning	Identity: protest is not legitimate

M: you are mentally ill because you were abused by your father.

Communication act	Narratives
Emotion: fear	Family culture: vulnerability prohibited
Meaning: emotional stance is challenged creating vulnerability	Relationship: aggressor/victim
Action: position Kath as vulnerable facilitating disowning of his own vulnerability	Identity: no vulnerability permitted

T: if you did not think of Kath as mentally ill, how might you relate to her differently?

Communication act	Narratives
Emotion: reflexive feeling of stuckness and rigidity Meaning: hypothesis that the feeling is communicated unconsciously from the couple and evaluate that context shift is needed Action: ask hypothetical future question	Therapy culture: usefulness of recognising and inquiring into therapist's own emotional experience and its associated narratives Relationship: therapist/client Identity: facilitator of linkage between emotion, meaning, action and narratives shaping them

M: I would approach intimacy differently. I can't trust her because I am not sure she is not mentally ill.

Communication act	Narratives
Emotion: fear Meaning: mental illness means danger Action: acknowledge fear of mental illness while positioning Kath as mentally ill and responsible for intimacy problem	Family culture: no trust in family members' emotional responses Relationship: aggressor/victim Identity: difficulty trusting validity and safety of own and partner's emotions

T: she has been crying. Do you see that as a sign of mental illness?

Communication act	Narratives
Emotion: reflexive feeling of incongruity Meaning: stifling rather than expression of crying might be more likely to lead to mental illness Action: attempt to challenge the linkage between crying and mental illness	Therapy culture: usefulness of recognising and inquiring into therapist's own emotional experience and its associated narratives Relationship: therapist/client Identity: facilitator of linkage between emotion, meaning, action and narratives shaping them

M: it shows a lack of control.

Communication act	Narratives
Emotion: fear of distress Meaning: distress is prohibited/weak Action: control of emotional expression	Family culture: vulnerability prohibited Relationship: aggressor/victim Identity: no vulnerability permitted

K: don't patronise me. I'm crying because my husband thinks I am mentally ill.

Communication act	Narratives
Emotion: despair Meaning: it is impossible to get my voice heard Action: tears	Family culture: disowned abuse; distress prohibited Relationship: aggressor/victim Identity: mentally ill

M: I do see that I am partly responsible for making things worse.

Communication act	Narratives
Emotion: empathy	Family culture: vulnerability prohibited
Meaning: acknowledgement	
	Relationship: aggressor/victim
Action: reposition self as contributing to pattern	
	Identity: developing awareness of contribution to relational pattern

In response to this exchange, the therapist highlights how both seem to have different perceptions of whether expressions of vulnerability demonstrate a capacity or incapacity in communication. Mike, fearful of vulnerability and weakness, prohibits Kath's expression of emotion which in turn stimulates her frustrated protest as she becomes more distressed because her freedom of expression is constrained; linking to her past abusive experience and her mother's response to hearing about it.

Discussion of interpersonal logics

Mike
Hypothesising from a researcher position, in Mike's family experience, vulnerability was feared and prohibited and translated into aggression. His *emotional* logic in the face of his own vulnerability is: '*emotional* expression creates fear of breakdown'; the *meaning* logic in this context is 'emotional vulnerability means weakness'; the *action* logic is: 'when feeling vulnerable, protect yourself by aggressive action and control'.

Kath
For Kath, *emotional* suppression in the context of abuse and rejection creates an *emotional* logic of fear of breakdown; the *meaning* logic is: 'vulnerability means lack of protection and outrage'; the action logic is: 'show distress about the wrongs done to you'.

Complementary interpersonal logics
Their complementary interpersonal logics of *emotion, meaning* and *action* about the expression of emotion, seem to be *incommensurate*, Mike fearing emotional expression and Kath fearing emotional suppression. Mike's action logic is: when faced with my own emotional

vulnerability, disown it and position Kath as vulnerable instead. Kath has grown up with an abuse dynamic whereby the physical (and psychological) boundary between herself and others is disturbed, inviting her to coordinate with this abusive positioning, leaving her with deep feelings of rage. However, the direct expression of rage and protest has been disallowed in her family culture, so she disowns rage and instead positions Mike as the raging aggressor. Her action logic is: when faced with my own rage, disown it and position Mike as aggressive. She begins to challenge her action logic in the therapy episode, in protesting about how she is positioned, in denying that mental illness is a totalising narrative. Mike too, attempts to express other feelings than rage when he expresses vulnerability in talking about his fears and begins to own his contribution to their relational patterns. In fact in session 4, he redefines the therapeutic contract and in so doing, recontextualises their relative responsibilities, by acknowledging that he and Kath make equal contributions to their difficulties and that he is in therapy for himself as well as for her, enabling a more equal positioning of vulnerability.

In considering the *interpersonal logics* of this couple, neither person had a negotiating voice in their families of origin. They both experienced abuse, Mike physical and emotional, and Kath, sexual and emotional. Their struggle with expression of emotion and its associated fear of breakdown, took a complementary form and appeared at first glance to be *incommensurate*. Through placing *commensurability* at a higher level of context in the analysis of *interpersonal logics,* it became possible to appreciate that the couple's reactive patterns, when conjoined, took on a paradoxical quality which made it almost impossible to escape without meta-communication abilities.

However, the explicit meta-communicated *coordination* offered by the therapeutic process enabled the beginnings of an implicative force and the possibilities of practical force whereby a vocabulary of intention and purpose becomes more possible and coordinated goals potentially consciously negotiated. The *coordination* of communication begins to show more ability to speak about emotion rather than it being enacted in reactive or paradoxical patterns governed by contextual and prefigurative force. See below for a diagram of the paradoxical pattern that emerged out of the analysis of narratives and communication acts above.

Figure 6. paradoxical interpersonal logics

Family culture	Disowning of abuse and emotion. Poor reflexive and reflective abilities. Poor meta-communication abilities. Contextual and prefigurative forces strong.
Relationship	Conflicted complementary relationship. A belief in the justice and 'rightness' of one's own position; belief in the illegitimacy of the position of the other. For Kath: the other positioned as abusive and controlling. For Mike: the other positioned as vulnerable and disturbed.
Identity	Individual narrative about rage and distress but exclusive legitimacy.
Communication episode	Aggressive argument.
Emotion	Kath: fear of breakdown Mike: fear of breakdown
Meaning	Kath: vulnerability is threatening Mike: vulnerability is threatening
Action	Kath: "you are abusing me" Mike: "you are mentally ill"

Systemic reflexivity from the researcher's position

Reflecting on my position as a participant researcher in the therapeutic process, and at a different research stage, thinking and writing about the process, I will structure my observations using Van de Haar and Hosking's distinction about reflexivity as both a meta-cognitive activity and an activity constitutive of social realities (2004).

From a meta-cognitive perspective, I am conscious that I value observation and inquiry into my own narratives. Through this research process, there is strong contextual and practical force from my professional narrative that I am obliged to invite purposeful and coordinated agency for all participants, in the context of therapy, where the goal of transformation is primary, and as a secondary commitment in the context of research. In both contexts, I feel obliged and encouraged to experience, and learn about, through the communication process, the logical force of the research system and to facilitate practical and implicative force in my interactions with others. I aspire to coordinating a reflexive pattern whereby the actions that are privileged are that of cooperation and collaboration in making sense of and evaluating how my own and others interpersonal logics of meaning and action are constructing the *system*.

However, within this particular *system* of meaning and action, there is a contractual complexity in that the therapy team were engaging in couple work when it could be said that the couple were not entirely accepting of that collaborative space. The couple's troubled interaction had reactive and paradoxical dimensions and the offering of a different (reflexive) pattern could be felt, on their part, to be an imposition unless there is a third space negotiated which enables meta-communication.

In taking a research position to my participation in the therapy process, considering the impact of the therapy team on the communication of the couple, it is useful to note that, within the process, my inner talk was troubled, yet probably not enough heed was given to this emotional struggle when contracting with the couple. During the therapy process described above, I experienced what might be called a systemic 'counter-transference' in feeling positioned as an abuser. I am using the term 'counter-transference' to refer to my own state of mind, within the interactions, both emotional and cognitive, imagining that my state of mind is reflective of a *system* dynamic. I experienced such a sense of systemic fragility that any action of inquiry or feedback was felt to be abusive. This became clearer when Jack was able to say in session 4 that he found the therapeutic process humiliating. The team were able to take this feedback seriously and, in the process Jack felt he had been heard and the team were able to negotiate a more collaborative coordination.

Considering how the team (of which I was a part) constructed the social reality of the therapeutic process, we could say that had the team paid more reflexive attention to their own 'states of mind' in initial sessions, the definition of relationship and task of therapy could have had greater potential for coordinated collaboration at an earlier stage. In writing about the process, I am conscious of my valuing and inquiring into such inner experience, emotional and cognitive, for informing what might be systemically unspoken (and possibly forbidden) but important, and thus, facilitating of reflexivity.

Figure 7. summary of CMM analytic structure

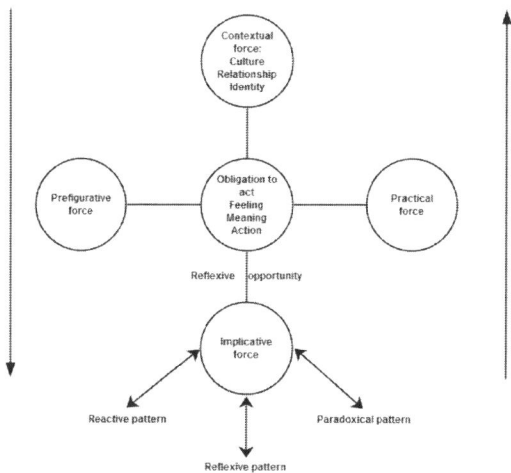

Reflections on CMM as a research tool

CMM has been offered in this chapter as a research framework enabling researcher orientation, hypothesis and interpretation within a *system of coordinated interpersonal logics*. A CMM approach is grounded in the complex detail of communicative interaction patterns, offering a research narrative that links micro and macro details through identifying researchable features of the system such as *interpersonal logics, logical force, coordinated patterns and levels of commensurability*. A research frame is thus offered for exploring how contexts are coordinated, sustained and challenged. The gulf described above between academic and practitioner is thus narrowed. One illustration of this narrowing is in the way that both systemic dialogical practice and CMM research practice both offer similar but different opportunities for meta-communication, the value of which has been highlighted by Watzlawick et al (2011 reprint) in articulating and resolving unwanted patterns.

Conclusion

CMM as a systemic and social constructionist framework facilitates meaning making about communication and guides action within the communicative system for researchers and other systemic practitioners. It has had a profound influence on systemic thinking and practice, particularly in its elaboration of the meaning and performance of context. In this account, I have shown how CMM invites us, with *system* participants, to take a third person position to narratives and patterns of communication within collaborative dialogue, enabling us to reflect on the communication process and its consequences, including our own contribution as 'first persons' to communication episodes, and to meta-communicate about such observations where useful in fulfilling research aims. I have offered a tool for research analysis, facilitating insight (interpretation of the local interaction within a therapy episode) and critique of the contexts in which perceptions are made and the contexts *system* participants act into, through an appreciative focus on *interpersonal logics* of *system* participants. This is inevitably a partial narrative of the social realities constructed and represents hypothesis and interpretation, but the aim is that such interpretation guides research activity in such a way that insight, critique and transformation are invited and realised.

Research using CMM has application in a range of communication contexts where the interest is in developing insight, critique and transformation. The focus might be a primary interaction process of which one is a part, for instance, an organisational meeting or series of meetings, part of a therapy episode or episodes over time; or a secondary interaction process where the researcher is engaging in analysis of an interaction they were not a part of, though in the analysis will be a reflexive participant to analysis of an interactive script. Also, different dimensions of CMM might be selected out as relevant and highlighted, for instance paradoxical patterns; logical forces; interpersonal logics. CMM provides opportunities for contextual analysis providing a structure of rich complex detail and for scholar-practitioners can be a tool in a larger process of consultancy, coaching or psychotherapy as well as an activity in its own right.

A commitment to *systemic reflexivity* requires an attitude of openness to what might be reflexively revealed, consciously and unconsciously, in research conversations. The following Victor Frankl quote highlights the value of Pearce's questions: how was that social world made? What social worlds are we making? What social worlds do we want to make?

'Between stimulus and response there is a space. In that space lies our freedom and our power to choose our response. In our response lies our growth and our happiness' (Frankl, 1946).

References

Alvesson, Mats, (2003). Beyond Neopositivists, Romantics and Localists: A Reflexive Approach to Interviews in Organisational Research, *Academy of Management Review*, 28, (1), 13-33.

Alvesson, Mats & Deetz, Stan (2000).*Doing Critical Management Research,* London: Sage.

Barge, J. Kevin (2004). Articulating CMM as a Practical Theory, *Human Systems: the Journal of Systemic Consultation and Management,* 15, 1-3.

Bateson, Gregory (1972). *Steps to an Ecology of Mind*, New York: Ballantine.

Bushe, Gervase & Marshak, Robert (2009). Diagnostic and Dialogic Premises and Patterns of Practice, *Journal of Applied Behavioural Science,* 45, 3, 348-368.

Boscolo, Luigi; Cecchin, Gianfranco; Hoffman, Lynn & Penn, Peggy (1987). *Milan Systemic Family Therapy: Conversations in Theory and Practice,* USA: Basic Books.

Burnham, John (2005), Relational Reflexivity: A Tool for Socially Constructing Therapeutic Relationships, in Flaskas, Carmel, Mason, Barry & Perlesz, Amaryll, (eds.).*The Space Between,* London: Karnac.

Cecchin, Gianfranco (1987). Hypothesising, Circularity and Neutrality Revisited: An Invitation to Curiosity, *Family Process*, 26 (4), 405-414.

Cecchin, Gianfranco; Ray, Wendell A. & Lane, Gerry (1992).Irreverence, a Strategy for Therapists' Survival, in Campbell, David & Draper, Ros (eds.)

Systemic Thinking and Practice, London: Karnac.

Cronen, Vernon; Johnson, Ken & Lannamann, John (1982). Paradoxes, Double Binds and Reflexive Loops, An Alternative Theoretical Perspective, *Family Process,* 21.

Cronen, Vernon & Pearce, W. Barnett (1985). An Explanation of how the Milan Method Works: An Invitation to a Systemic Epistemology and the Evolution of Family Systems, in Campbell, David & Draper, Ros (eds.) *Applications of Systemic Family Therapy: The Milan Approach,* London: Grune & Stratton.

Cunliffe, Ann L. (2002). Reflexive Dialogical Practice in Management Learning, *Management Learning,* 33 (1), 35-61.

Dallos, Rudi & Draper, Ros (2005).*An Introduction to Family Therapy: Systemic Theory and Practice,* McGraw-Hill: UK.

Frosh, Stephen & Barraitser, Lisa (2008). Psychoanalysis and Psycho-social studies, *Psychoanalysis, Culture and Society,* 13, 346-365.

Gergen, Ken J. (1989). *Texts of Identity,* London: Sage.

Marshak, Robert & Bushe, Gervase (2012). An Introduction to Advances in Dialogic Organisation Development, *OD Practitioner: Journal of the Organisation Development Network,* 45, (1),

Mitchell, Stephen (2000). *Relationality: From Attachment to Intersubjectivity,* USA: The Analytic Press.

Harrison, O., (1997), *Open Space Technology,* San Fransisco: Berrett-Koehler/

Kelm,,J. (1998), Introducing the Appreciative Inquiry Philosophy, in (eds.) Hammond, S.A. & Royal, C. (1998) *Lessons from the Field: Applying Appreciative Inquiry,* 158-171, Plano, TX: Practical Press.

Oliver, Christine (1992). A Focus on Moral Story Making in Therapy using Co-ordinated Management of Meaning (CMM), *Human Systems: The Journal of Systemic Consultation and Management,* Vol.3. 217-231.

Oliver, Christine (1996). Systemic Eloquence, *Human Systems: The Journal of Systemic Consultation and Management,* Vol. 7, No. 4.

Oliver, Christine (2004). *Critical Appreciative Inquiry: Reworking a Consultancy Discourse,* paper for the conference on organisational discourse, Kings College; chapter in Peck, E. (2005), *An Introduction to Organisational Development in Health Care,* Oxford: Radcliffe Medical Press.

Oliver, Christine (2005). *Reflexive Inquiry: a Framework for Consultancy,* London: Karnac.

Oliver, Christine (2013). Coordinating Logics of Meaning and Action: Developing a Vocabulary for (Un)consciousness, in Littlejohn, Stephen W. & MacNamee, Sheila (eds.) *The Coordinated Management of Meaning: A Festschrift in Honour of W. Barnett Pearce,* Madison, N.J: Farleigh Dickinson University Press.

Oliver, Christine; Herasymowych, Marilyn & Senko Henry (2003). *Complexity, Relationships and Strange Loops: Reflexive Practice Guide.* Canada: MHA Institute Inc.

Oliver, Christine & Fitzgerald, Stephen (2013). How to Explore Meaning Making Patterns in Dialogic OD and Coaching, *OD Practitioner,* 45, (1), 30-34.

Palazzoli Selvini, Mara; Boscolo, Luigi; Cecchin, Gianfranco & Prata, Guiliana (1978). *Paradox and Counter Paradox: A New Model in the Therapy of the Family in Schizophrenic Transaction,* New York: Jason Aronson.

Using CMM to Define Systemic Reflexivity

Palazzoli Selvini, Mara S.; Boscolo, Luigi; Cecchin, Gianfranco & Prata, Guiliana (1980). Hypothesising-Neutrality-Circularity: Three Guidelines for the Conductor of the Session. *Family Process,* 19, 3-12.

Pearce, W. Barnett (1989). *Communication and the Human Condition,* USA: Southern Illinois University Press.

Pearce, W .Barnett (1997). *Making Social Worlds: A Communication Perspective,* Oxford: Blackwell.

Pearce, W. Barnett (2013). At home in the universe with miracles and horizons: reflections on personal and social evolution. In Littlejohn, Stephen W. & McNamee, Sheila (eds.) *The Coordinated Management of Meaning: A Festschrift in Honour of W. Barnett Pearce,* Madison, N.J: Farleigh Dickinson University Press.

Pearce, W. Barnett & Cronen, Vernon (1980). *Communication, Action and Meaning: The Creation of Social Realities,* New York: Praeger.

Tams, Svenja & Marshall, Judi (2011). Responsible Careers: Systemic Reflexivity in Shifting Landscapes, *Human Relations,* 64 (1), 109-131.

Van der Haar, Dorieke & Hosking, Dian Marie (2004). Evaluating Appreciative Inquiry: A Relational Constructionist Perspective, *Human Relations,* 57 (8), 1017-1036.

Von Bertalanffy, Ludwig (1968). *General Systems Theory: Foundation, Development, Application,* New York: Brazillier.

Watzlawick, Paul; Beavin Bavelas, Janet & Jackson, Don D. (1967). (2011 reprint). *Pragmatics of Human Communication,* New York: Norton.

14 Research as Daily Practice

Dan Wulff and Sally St. George

"In the longer run it is no longer obvious that the disciplines and the research fields of science and social science are appropriate in their present form. It is no longer obvious that a division of labour is desirable, a division of labour that rests on the parcelling out of patches of truth to different specialists who are then divested of the need to practise other goods." John Law (After Method, 2004, p. 156)

Our aim in this chapter is to trouble the distinctions between practice and research with the hope of reconnecting the notion of research to practice by illustrating how they can be understood and performed as one and the same process. We depart from the current initiatives to *translate* research *into* practice because we often find that this retains a dichotomization and a hierarchy that is neither helpful nor accurate with respect to practitioners.

When seen as two activities conducted by different professionals and requiring separate and unique skill sets, research becomes closely allied with academic experts while practice is considered to be the purview of therapists and other "practitioners" who work in communities, agencies, and people's everyday lives; research is seen as detached and scientific while practice is enmeshed and messy. By keeping these two enterprises separate each with a distinct language, there is then a need for "translation," that is, taking the language of research findings and rewording them into the language of practice or everyday living. We think that these steps to translate or re-explain in a more everyday language can make research knowledge usable (*Positive Aging Newsletter* 2012), but are expensive, time-consuming, and acontextual, usually requiring a second level of translation into a practitioner's particular setting.

In response to this unfortunate separation of the fruits of research from their potential usefulness, we propose not conceptualizing research and practice as two different processes in need of two different sets of professionals. We believe that practitioners *are* researchers by virtue of consistently and rigorously using reflexive analytical processes in daily practice moment by moment. Looked at this way, this embeddedness of so-called research and practice processes can make the idea of knowledge *translation* unnecessary. We recognize that research as a unique set of processes has grown into an entire field of its own and for us to suggest that research is fundamentally practice may distress those who have come to see research as a distinct and essential endeavor of its own. But we believe the advantage of seeing the two as one enhances both the goals of research (knowledge-building) and the goals of practice (to provide effective service).

Two purposes have guided our experimenting with seeing practice and research as the same process (just languaged differently). First, we wanted to underscore the importance and role of curiosity as Cecchin (1987) discusses and what occurs when practitioners adopt this stance. Second, we want to emphasize and highlight the spirit of inquiry that is already part of good practice. Coming from a position of curiosity, practitioners question taken-for-granted premises in order to generate alternative understandings, not as truth tellings but rather as polyphonic expressions of events, circumstances, or persons. Effective practitioners are engaged with clients in a steady process of evolving understandings, utilizing new information and events to continuously refine what we think we know, creating fresh possibilities for moving toward what is most desired. As we have been imagining our current understandings of research and of practice to be progressively overlapping circles, the contemporary distinctions between the two seem less and less useful while the non-distinguishing of the two seems more generative.

Our Context

We are practising family therapists as well as academics in a Faculty of Social Work. Actually, our first dean referred to us as "pracademics" to highlight the connections. Notice that she placed the practitioner portion of her new word first. That is because she understood us to use practice as the driver in our academic pursuits. We have both entered the academic world after 20 years in full time practice (Sally was a middle-school teacher in an inner city school and Dan was a family therapist). Even after obtaining our doctoral degrees in family therapy, we have maintained a practice outlook; we have always practiced as famly therapists, teachers, and administrators alongside of our other academic duties. The both/ and position of having an ongoing clinical practice simultaneous with an academic position affords us continuous opportunities to enjoy the mutual and recursive influence of the activities, and to see the intersections of these worlds and the potential for integration rather than separation. Let us add here that, our ways of *doing* our academic roles (teachers, researchers, administrators, supervisors) closely resemble the multiple tasks employed by practitioners so we sense a kinship with the multi-tasking roles of a practitioner moreso than with the more clearly circumscribed role of a researcher.

Our interest in blurring boundaries between traditionally organized professional activities derived from a number of experiences and observations. We directed a graduate program at the University of Louisville that offered a degree in both social work and family therapy simultaneously. As we developed a curriculum that would meet both social work and family therapy professional requirements, we began to see the similarities (as well as the differences) in the two approaches to helping. Both professions focus on the larger systems beyond the individual as key to understanding and helping individuals (Schulz 1984). When we gave ourselves the task of looking for ways to combine various practices into a common curriculum, we were particularly interested in seeing the congruities as places to economize and streamline the program. This provided the impetus to be aware of places of overlap and to be judicious in using the redundancies that were prevalent in the two approaches to helping. In this program we also taught the first combined research/ practice class—it was entitled "The Researching Practitioner."

Examining integration across other professional discourses and activities was cultivated by our experiences of teaching and supervising simultaneously, editing a journal and doing our own research concurrently, and teaching research courses and practice courses at the same time. Our success in seeing the common elements and skills of disciplines thought to be separate and distinct encouraged us to continue to re-imagine these received distinctions for the purpose of working more effectively and efficiently and in line with our social constructionist grounding.

The Current Interface between Research and Practice

Formal traditional research is not always easily accessible to practitioners, primarily because the language used and the processes described are so different from the discourses of practice. Despite the efforts to bridge the fields of research and practice through translation initiatives, we find the chasm between research and practice is seldom lessened by simply recasting research results into more consumable practice strategies or guides. The common discourses of research and practice do not permit easy or complete alternative renderings. Significant elements or meanings are often lost in translation.

Even in the best case scenario when translation efforts make research accessible and usable to practitioners, knowledge is still developed by researchers and applied by practitioners—a nifty division of labor in which practitioners are dependent on researchers to generate knowledge. Consequently, the local knowledge of the practitioner is bypassed and formal scientific research is given the leading role while practitioner knowledge is cast into a second class part (Wilson 2008). Such a view misses the chance to learn the knowledge generated from practice.

Let us examine the process of adoption of expert knowledge from formally published material. In order to apply abstract knowledge or information that has been created by analyzing group data or studying an individual in detail, practitioners have a series of decisions to make in order to take advantage of that received knowledge (specifically knowledge generated from "without," or in contexts other than the practitioner's own). The knowledge likely will not exactly fit the circumstances faced by the practitioner and thus the practitioner will need to make adaptations in order to apply it. One could make the case that *any* adoption of outside expert knowledge will require modification of that knowledge to some degree or another. This alteration of the expert's knowledge may still inform practice in quite useful ways, but perhaps in ways not intended by the knowledge-developer (and possibly the applications may be quite far afield from what the researcher intended or claimed). The process of knowledge utilization inevitably depends upon modifications (perhaps major modifications) from that which is generated in the research arena.

Given the adjustments necessary to import expert knowledge into a local situation and circumstance, the question arises as to how to improve this uneasy partnership. One response could be reconceptualising both research and practice as not distinct from each other. With this alternative approach, what could be the possible outcomes?

A Different Conceptualization

Research is literally "re-search," but not activity to replicate or do something again precisely the same way. It is a process of looking again, looking with new or fresh eyes or from a different vantage point. To our way of thinking, practice is also a process of searching and searching again in an attempt to make a difference with clients.

The chief difference between research and practice is how the activities and steps are languaged. Another glaring difference between those classified as researchers and those classified as practitioners is that researchers reveal their work through writing for publication and practitioners reveal their work through the therapy they provide. With both of these activities centered on inquiring to "make a difference," can their processes really be that far apart?

We live and practice from a social constructionist stance, attending to language and meanings generated through conversation and interacting (Gergen 2009). The ideas in our chapter have been nourished by (a) our frontline practice experiences with families in serious distress, (b) our close affiliations with social constructionist thinkers and practitioners (Gergen 2009; Tomm 1991), and (c) our experiences as qualitative researchers and editors of a qualitative research journal (see *The Qualitative Report,* http://www.nova.edu/ssss/QR/). From these associations and experiences we have become ever-more attentive to the multiplicities and potentials of any situation and the value of fresh ways of making sense of client situations, regardless of the origin of the ideas or how they become known (Shotter 2010).

The drive to find new and better ways to help clients is not trivial—creating new ways of approaching troubles requires that we not be limited by disciplinary borders or traditions. Clients are waiting and hoping for ways to better respond to the troubles in their lives. Developing new and more effective ways to help clients is the focus of both practice *and* research. Given the common purposes, it would be most beneficial if research and clinical practice were as closely allied as possible. In this spirit, we will examine the possibility of research and practice being considered basically one-and-the-same.

In order to discuss the possibilities of conceptualising and working with practice and research as the same basic process, we have chosen to use the phrase *research as daily practice* (RDP). We define research as daily practice as

> *Continuously examining data/information from our own clinical work reflexively in order to better understand what we do and what we could do.*

We see this as a form of evidence-based practice in that evidence comes from a variety of sources (e.g., clients, practitioners, scientific studies) (Gambrill 2005). In RDP, we focus on the knowledge-in-action that can be developed from practice (Schön 1983, 1987)—this process is often referred to as practice-based evidence. Coming from this position of research as daily practice, we are able to examine the data or information from a variety of sources and viewpoints within our own clinical work in order to make sense of what is going on in a number of different ways. Practicing from a position of being deeply curious about our work and its influences and effects allows us to ground inquiry in the "way we do/conduct practice." Inquiry is no longer a process imported from another discipline or paradigm, nor is it the exclusive domain of a researcher—it is the central process of how we, as practitioners, practice every day.

We "do inquiry" in a conscientious and deliberate fashion, according to a specific purpose or to answer a question. This does not imply a rigid adherence to an a priori series of ideas or moves. Rather we advocate "leaning into" (Reynolds 2012) a focus of inquiry that allows the researcher/practitioner to look at "paths to take" while also considering "paths not chosen." Most importantly, it fits within what the practitioner is already doing in the course of ethical practice, rather than being an extra or extraordinary task.

Development of RDP

We developed RDP from frustration and our sense of being "stuck" with some of our clients in our clinical work. It is important to note that the inception of this idea was thoroughly grounded in the practice arena—this initiative came about because of a clinical dilemma of not knowing the best way to work with clients.

Through close examination of our own caseloads, we each began to notice trends in the kinds of problems our families were coming to therapy about and the ways in which they were struggling with those problems. For example, Sally began seeing several families in which the adolescent daughters (ages 14-17) were leaving home earlier than anticipated on very disagreeable terms with their parents. Dan found that several of his families were using aggressive, almost violent means to attempt to bring about change in their families. When we discussed our observations and concerns with our colleagues, we discovered that they shared similar concerns regarding some of their families. From these discussions, we began to raise questions about what was stimulating these types of problematic situations and how we might we respond differently to better address them.

We invited our colleagues to join us in some case conversations about these troubles and how they may have developed in an effort to provoke to some alternative understandings. However, as with busy practitioners, there was no extra time with which to invest in a new and separate enterprise to look into these issues. We asked ourselves, how can we learn more about these specific clinical dilemmas in ways that will be useful *and* efficient? It was critical for us to relate our situation and ideas to the real world of practice. To design a way to handle "stuck" cases in the abstract was not necessarily going to be workable in the daily world of intense and busy practice; therefore we decided that our way of pursuing our investigation of our practices must fit within the typical work parameters of practitioners. It must be pragmatic and "do-able."

It was at this juncture that we recognized that we were turning our feelings of stuckness into an inquisitiveness–rather than becoming frustrated, we were re-examining what we had been doing and what we might otherwise be doing. Our stuckness with these clinical dilemmas became the focus of our curiosity. How might we understand this stuckness in a way that assists us in becoming unstuck? Our curiosities and questions were fueling the search (and the re-search). Our colleagues and students were happy to join us in this curiosity if it would not mean overloading their already full schedules. Again, we heard the importance of building this inquisitiveness into what we as practitioners were already doing.

Comparing Research and Practice

We will outline some ways that practice maps onto research as traditionally conducted today in order to examine the overlap of research and practice. Our descriptions of research protocols are not intended to reify research, but to provide a basis on which to make the comparisons between research and practice. Research (as customarily understood and practiced) can be described as a series of five phases that map onto similar phases in practice (see Table 1 below). In research, there is a primary question of interest to pursue or a hypothesis to test, while in practice there is a client problem or issue that becomes the focus. Each enterprise starts at a place where something is unknown or confusing and there is a desire to provide an answer or explanation. This starting point requires an articulation sufficient to plan the next steps.

In research, data is collected from the designated participants and/or other sources relevant to the issue or question. In practice an assessment is constructed from the information provided by persons involved in the case (clients and other professionals) through oral, written, or observational means. This collected information becomes the raw material that is organized by the researcher or practitioner in order to make sense. The data itself does not create a specific idea or understanding. It is the action of the researcher and the practitioner that transforms the data through various processes into an understanding or viewpoint from which further action can be taken.

In research, the data is analysed to create outcomes or results that allow researchers to explain or inform a situation/condition and will then be published/disseminated. In practice, a treatment plan is developed from the data, which will then be enacted. In research, the final phase is to produce some document that describes what the researcher produced/discovered and then to recommend avenues for further research. In practice, the practitioner utilizes the treatment plan and then evaluates the effectiveness of the treatment (and from there, whether to continue with the plan or adapt it). Both research and practice conclude with an actionable phase—researchers disseminate their analyses and practitioners put their treatment plans into action.

Table 1. Research and Practice Phases

Research	Practice
Question/Hypothesis	Client Problem/Issue
Enlist Participants	Engage with Clients
Collect Data	Create an Assessment
Analyse	Develop a Treatment Plan
Disseminate Findings	Intervene and Evaluate

From a social constructionist perspective, these five phases differentially called "research" and "practice" are processes that could be understood as derivatives of more inclusive concepts. Research and practice are manifestations of the following five processes (see Table 2).

Table 2. Research and Practice Processes from a Social Constructionist Perspective

Holding and Valuing Curiosities
Developing Relationships
Observing/Examining
Making Sense
Reflecting-in-Action

We developed these five processes by looking at the parallel processes in Table 1 and trying to find a single inclusive term that might embrace the pairs on each row (e.g., "Question/Hypothesis" with "Client Problem/Issue"). By constructing words or phrases that could be considered the host ideas from which research and practice derive their "phases," we have developed five what we call "processes" from which spring many endeavors, research and practice being two. (Notice that all five processes can be considered in any order or any combination.)

These five processes spawn other processes we can identify in our lives besides practice and research (e.g., problem-solving, decision-making, learning, inventing, investing, developing relationships, developing communities). It is interesting to think of research and practice as the same and akin to the other seven items listed in the sentence immediately above. They can be considered variations on similar themes. With the basic processes underlying each of these being more-or-less the same, the emphasis can be placed more on what these processes can produce and less on the peculiar articulations of each in their spheres of influence. In addition, when places of stuckness or impasse emerge in any of our practices, referring back to the basic processes may allow the practitioner/inquirer to revise the dilemma and create alternative pathways to move forward.

Already There

It is our view that practitioners routinely do research in our sense of the word (looking again at a situation/issue in detail to learn more about it). To suggest that they do not use research processes is to subscribe to the (excessively, in our view) narrow and rigidified definition of research provided by science and the academy. Our definition of research (RDP) matches with the more academic version (evidence-based practice, EBP) in some respects and fails to match up in other ways. The following are commonalities:

1 The need to be reflective and attentive to our practices;

2 The need to reflexively analyze practices to determine effectiveness and relevance.

Differences include the following:

1 When using EBP, we tend to punctuate the professional (particularly scientific) literature and consequently de-emphasize the other relevant voices;

2 When using RDP, we recognize that we may be working with those who are outside the "confidence intervals" of scientific research interests and as a consequence inquiry must make adjustments accordingly.

By trying out our approach with one practice project per year for the last 4 years, we have developed some "rhythms" of how to utilize RDP that align with the five processes we mentioned above (Holding and Valuing Curiosities, Developing Relationships, Observing/Examining, Making Sense, and Reflecting-in-Action). Although these individual processes may appear deceptively simplistic, we think that they make an important contribution to the conceptualization of practice using reflexive processes in the service of competent ongoing practices.

The Process of RDP

Holding and valuing curiosities
In RDP we identify or specify a problem/question in practice. We started by looking at those things in our clinical work that we found interesting, confusing, or something that had us stalled in therapy. For example, at The Calgary Family Therapy Centre, the most frequent problem we address is parent-child conflict with the conflict becoming more serious, detrimental, and at times, physically dangerous. We wondered what made this so pervasive within our Centre and what was going on in families' lives and in our communities that would contribute to the increasing severity of such conflict.

We urge practitioners to consider this question:

> *What intrigues you about your work that you would like to understand better?*

This could center around a recalcitrant problem, a desire to understand how some moments are therapeutic, alternative ways to achieve similar results, how a different therapeutic modality could work in one's setting, or any other issue that captures one's interest. This issue should provoke genuine curiosity—this is crucial for developing the energy and motivation to reflexively consider our practices. This curiosity holds the possibility of becoming a great learning opportunity that could lead to new ideas or ventures.

Developing relationships
We suggest inquiring with colleagues about their experiences or ideas regarding a curiosity. When we noticed trends in our caseloads or a

consistent dilemma in our clinical progress we turned to our fellow clinicians and asked them if they were experiencing anything similar. We asked our colleagues and students if they were also seeing a considerable number of families who were experiencing extreme parent-child conflict and if they also wondered about what might be contributing to this in our families. To that end we decided as a group of clinicians and practicum students to take one hour per month to reflexively consider the theoretical connections we could make between the societal discourses and the kinds of parent-child conflicts that our families were presenting in therapy. We committed to meeting regularly as a way to assist each of our practices as a form of collective case consultation that enhanced each of our clinical practices. This was change for us; previously each supervisory dyad met, but our entire group had not.

We suggest to practitioners the following query:

Is anyone else in your agency/practice having similar troubles or interests? Actively wonder if you are alone in this or if there are others who experience this issue.

Posing this question can build a "culture of curiosity" and learning within a group or agency. It also fosters connectedness among practitioners and tends to reduce the isolation that comes from individually working apart from others. Collaborating with others can stimulate the practitioner's learning and can open the possibility for new ideas and practices. An agency that establishes a spirit of inquiry and innovation provides a more stimulating environment fostering growth among staff, a fertile site for practicum students, and builds a reputation in the community as an excellent referral source.

Observing/examining

We take the time to reflect on our usual or taken-for-granted ideas about the issue under review. Referring back to our example, we held discussions about the societal discourses we believed were in action that were contributing influences for our families (e.g., technology, a sense of entitlement, pressures to do more than time and money would allow).

To our colleagues we propose the following:

Let us consider the ways that we typically understand this issue.

This introduces the idea that societal discourses may play a role in what one is seeing—this is a process of deconstructing or unpacking current conceptualisations of the issues. We oftentimes operate through our disciplinary lenses without recognizing how those lenses shape what we see (Leavy 2001). This acknowledges that the stuckness we feel may best be alleviated by making adjustments in how *we* are working. Similarly, our clients may be operating within certain implicit understandings that constrain their ability to achieve happiness or change. The following questions may assist in expanding our understandings, conceptualisations, and possibilities:

> *What words, phrases do our clients repeat within their families as they present their troubles and do these words, phrases appear in other families? What words, phrases do we as clinicians repeat when we talk about our clients? What kinds of rules, traditions, and voices do families seem to be loyal to as they try to solve their dilemmas? Who or what influences their preferred patterns or expectations? What kinds of rules, traditions, voices, do we, as helpers, seem to be loyal to in our efforts to be helpful?*

In our own example, we looked to ways in which we were writing about family dilemmas and interactions in our case notes and keeping track of the words practitioners hear families use to describe their troubles. At our monthly meetings we would record these words.

This series of reflexive questions may allow us to re-examine our work from a slightly different position, giving us the opportunity to sense that our stuckness may come from many locations—ours, our clients', the larger community—we are in a position to participate in a serious co-researching process with those around us (including our clients). The process of sorting out what is happening and what we might do more effectively becomes a common project among those with whom we are in conversation. In a sense, we may even refer to our therapy as "co-research" (Epston 1999). To date, our efforts have been to enlarge the conversation about our practices with others who practice with us or who struggle with similar issues. A next development could and should be to expand the conversation to the recipients of practice, the clients. Further, we could include the extended family networks of clients, the adminstrators of programs, the providers of service funding, government policy-makers, and so on. This expansive dialogue will allow us to get ever-closer to the best possible services for clients by engaging all the players, not just a select few.

Additionally, we specifically look for social discourses that are invisibly present in our professional documentation, in the professional literature, and in the world in which we live.

> *What terminology is repeated in the literature? What themes seem to*

be consistent? What scripts has society provided for our disciplinary activities?

In our own case, we went back to themes in the literature, themes of power and control, child and adolescent development, generational divisions and responsibilities within families, interactional patterns, and cultural differences. We looked for the ways in which these were present in our conceptualization and families' descriptions of their troubles.

We are interested in multiple and additional understandings wherever they may be found. This could include any publication, peer-reviewed or not. It could include pop psychology, websites, blogs, journalistic articles, movies, poetry, or music. The goal is to immerse ourselves in other viewpoints and knowledge to become aware of the discourses that influence our families' actions and our therapeutic decisions. Practitioners are particularly impacted by the discourses of our chosen disciplines or fields. We "grew up" in the field to come to know how things work and what we should do. It is sometimes these very "givens" that inhibit our thinking in genuinely new and innovative ways.

These questions imply that the ways we are doing things are not the only possibilities. We recommend being playful with this brainstorming—it may be at this basic level where we might be developing ineffective strategies based on premises that are faulty. We like to think of the image of a cargo net here. Imagine that all of us (*all* players in the clinical situation) are scooped up into a cargo net. Everyone is squirming and equally uncomfortable and there is no firm grounding for anyone to get on top of or ahead of anyone else. The net represents the discourses that have enveloped all of us and which holds influence that we need to examine.

Making sense

We examine how behaviors, thinking, and actions have come to make sense based on the discourses that surround our clients, us, and our work. We continue by re-imagining the possible implications of the discourses we embrace in our clinical work (or new discourses that we have happened upon) by asking

How are our practices moving in sync with existing social discourses or supporting the status quo? What possibilities can arise from alternative ideas to the status quo? What questions do they provoke? What limitations do they present?

For the project that we are describing, we turned to Adele Clarke (2005) and her postmodern version of grounded theory to make sense of the words we had recorded. We used her series of maps to graphically display our ideas (the data/information we were collecting) in order to see the information more holistically. What we saw was surprising! We had expected to see many negative kinds of discourses as central to parent-child conflict. What we found were "neutral" ideas of the influences of tradition, acceptability, responsibility, hierarchy, and expert explanation—hardly negative (St. George, Wulff & Tomm 2012a).

As you can see, we would play out the answers to envision results and fast forward to see anticipated or expected results/outcomes. We might think of the metaphor of a chess game by imagining several moves/actions, or reactions in advance. Creating scenarios of how these ideas could play out is critical for experimenting with new ideas. If they remain as only interesting concoctions in our heads, we may never see them flower. We must work to manifest them in action.

Making sense of new initiatives that may deviate from previous initiatives might be quite challenging—the traditional ideas, even though to some degree unsatisfying, may have become part of the fabric of our thinking. Taking our new noticings and transforming them into new sensibilities may feel like creating something without directions or blueprints—it may be like creating the path by walking (Almeida, Parker & Dolan-Del Vecchio 2007; Seikkula & Arnkil 2006; Waldegrave, Tamasese, Tuhuka & Campbell 2003) .

Reflecting-in-action

We look at what newness/freshness this examination offers in terms of conversation, conceptualising, and intervening with our client families.

> *What new questions can we develop that take into consideration the invisible influences? Can we converse about the social discourses directly? What new courses of action and joining with others are available to us now? What are new avenues to pursue? Where can we go to now? Are there better questions to pose and pursue?*

For us, this process set in motion a new set of actions in our practices along with the creation of new questions that led to new curiosities. We were not able to make the kinds of theoretical connections we had anticipated, but we developed more than 50 questions that we could use to "talk" societal discourses into our daily therapy sessions with client families.

Engaging in new practices is itself energizing and creates potentials for new outcomes with clients. In addition, we may become interested in new unanticipated questions. Getting clear of our routine practices opens the possibility of different questions to surface. In that sense, all initiatives loop back to the others in an ongoing process of feeding back into our set of curiosities.

Further Thoughts and Recommendations

Although it may appear in our presentation as if the RDP process is linear and clear-cut, it is not in practice. More accurately, it is reflexive and involves revisiting the processes regularly as we engage in new information gathering and sense-making. Over the past few years, we have found that how we articulate these processes shift and evolve as we learn and experience more ways to reflexively consider our clinical practices together with our colleagues. As we said at the outset, this process grew out of our practice stuckness and therefore the process must be responsive to our ongoing practice situations. We are not the same people we were at the outset and our ideas undergo constant revising.

We hope that other practitioners and groups of practitioners will try these ideas out in their own practices. Ideally we hope that practitioners may say, "I am already doing that!" We conducted our yearly RDP practice projects (St. George, Wulff & Tomm 2012a; St. George, Wulff & Tomm 2012b; Wulff, St. George & Tomm 2012) with a team of 10-12 practitioners through a monthly one-hour conversation in which we examined our practices. For publication purposes, we (Dan and Sally) took the extra steps of securing ethics approvals and doing the final writing, but the actual practice projects were conducted by our group of practitioners.

We noticed unanticipated benefits along the way. As a consequence of our monthly meetings, the talk generated special attention and new therapeutic conversations with clients. For example, once we began to talk about societal discourses as part of RDP, our team continued to think about these discourses, recording them in their case notes, and even began talking about them in their sessions—long before the project was complete.

Above all, our main message is that practitioners are credible and valuable "re-searchers" of their work—that is what competent practice involves. They have frontline knowledge of what transpires with clients on a daily basis and conducting research as a daily practice is an effective and efficient way for one to be curious. The potential for innovation is unparalleled.

References

Almeida, Rhea V.; Parker, Lynn & Dolan-Del Vecchio, Kenneth (2007). *Transformative family therapy: Just families in a just society*. Don Mills, ON: Pearson.
Clarke, Adele E. (2005). *Situational analysis: Grounded theory after the postmodern turn*. Thousand Oaks, CA: Sage.
Epston, David (1999). Co-research: The making of an alternative knowledge. In *Narrative therapy and community work: A conference collection* (pp. 137-157). Adelaide, South Australia: Dulwich Centre.
Gambrill, Eileen (2005). *Critical thinking in clinical practice: Improving the quality of judgments and decisions* (2nd ed.). Hoboken, NJ: John Wiley & Sons.
Gergen, Kenneth J. (2009). *Relational being: Beyond self and community*. New York, NY: Oxford.
Gergen, Kenneth J., & Gergen, M. M. (Eds.). (2012). *Positive aging newsletter*. Retrieved from http://www.taosinstitute.net/positive-aging-newsletter
Law, John (2004). *After method: Mess in social science research*. London, UK: Routledge.
Leavy, Patricia (2001). *Essentials of transdisciplinary research: Using problem-centered methodologies*. Walnut Creek, CA: Left Coast Press.
Reynolds, Vikki (2012, June). An ethic of justice doing. Keynote at the *Conversations on the Margins: Therapeutic Change, Social Change, Social Justice Conference*, Ottawa, ON, Canada.
Schön, Donald A. (1983). *The reflective practitioner: How professionals think in action*. New York, NY: Basic Books.
Schön, Donald A. (1987). *Educating the reflective practitioner: Toward a new design for teaching and learning in the professions*. San Francisco, CA: Jossey-Bass.
Schultz, Stephen J. (1984). *Family systems therapy: An integration*. New York, NY: Jason Aronson.
Seikkula, Jaakko & Arnkil, Tom E. (2006). *Dialogical meetings in social networks*. New York, NY: Karnac.
Shotter, John (2010). *Social construction on the edge: 'Withness'-thinking and embodiment*. Chagrin Falls, OH: Taos Institute.
St. George, Sally; Wulff, Dan & Tomm, Karl (2012a). *Societal discourses that help in family therapy: A modified situational analysis of the relationships between societal expectations and healing parent-child conflict*. Manuscript in preparation.
St. George, Sally; Wulff, Dan & Tomm, Karl (2012b). *Talking societal discourses into family therapy: A situational analysis of the relationships between societal expectations and parent-child conflict*. Manuscript in preparation.
Tomm, Karl (1991). Beginning of a HIPs & PIPs approach to psychiatric assessment. *The Calgary Participator, 1*(2), 21-22, 24.

Waldegrave, Charles; Tamasese, Taimalieutu Kiwi; Tahuka, Flora & Campbell, Warihi (2003). *Just therapy - A journey: a collection of papers from the Just Therapy Team, New Zealand*. Adelaide, Australia: Dulwich Centre.

Wilson, Shawn (2008). *Research is ceremony: Indigenous research methods*. Halifax, NS, Canada: Fernwood.

Wulff, Dan; St. George, Sally & Tomm, Karl (2012). *Moving from PIPs to HIPs: A narrative analysis*. Manuscript in preparation.

Notes on Contributors

Harlene Anderson

I am interested in the reflexive nature of 'theory' and practice, and research as part of everyday practice. I call myself a "reflective scholar/practitioner." My particular interest is in postmodern philosophy and related perspectives, and the usefulness of these perspectives to help assure practices that keep up with our fast changing world, exemplified by people around the globe who demand a voice in decisions that affect their lives. Partly toward this aim, I founded the founder and editor of the International Journal of Collaborative Practices (http://collaborative-practices.com) and the International Certificate Program in Collaborative Practices (www.collaborativecertificate.org). My recent research projects include "Handmaidens to Power" in which I learned from the voices of women executive assistants about their histories, rise to their current positions, what they do on a daily basis, the influence they perceive they have on the organization and their boss, and what advice they have for "bosses;" and "Mother-Daughter Businesses" in which I learned about the considerations and decisions that went into their joint business adventure, the influence of their personal relationship on their work relationship and the business and vice versa, and what advice they have for other mother-daughter teams considering joint business adventures. To learn more, please visit me at *www.harleneanderson. org* -I would love to hear from you.

Kevin Barge

I am Professor and Head of Communication at Texas A & M University. I have a longstanding interest in developing practical theory and collaborative research that bridges academic-practiioner interests. As a result, I have been a member of the planning team for the Aspen Conference, a community of engaged organizational communication scholars who work in this area, as well as having been involved with supervising several practitioner MSc and doctoral dissertations through my association with the University of Hertfordshire and the Taos Institute. My major research interests center on developing a social constructionist approach to leadership, articulating the connections between appreciative practice and organizational change, as well as exploring the relationship between discourse and public deliberation, specifically practices that facilitate communities working through polarized and polarizing issues. Other research interests include investigating the role of reflexivity in leadership and management practice, examining ways to develop effective academic-practitioner collaborations, and developing practical theory. My research is inspired by interpretive and discursive research approaches and I am keenly interested in how collaborative research methods can be used to generate usable knowledge and forward movement in organizations and communities. My work on leadership, dialogue, and organizational change in The Academy of Management Review, Management Communication Quarterly, Human Relations, Communication Theory, Journal of Applied Communication Research, and Communication Monographs. *kbarge@tamu.edu*

Saliha Bava

I am passionate about designing and implementing play-based and dialogic processes for wellbeing and change which I have done for 20+ years within organizational, community, family, learning and research systems. I am an Associate Professor of Marriage and Family Therapy at Mercy College, Dobbs Ferry, NY. I am a doctoral advisor at the Taos Institute's PhD Program and faculty in their MSc Relational Leading Program. As the Director of Research with the International Trauma Studies Program, affiliated with Columbia University, I research theater, community resiliency and psychosocial practices. I also serve as a faculty for Houston Galveston Institute's International Certificate Program in Collaborative Practices. I'm a Board Member of American Family Therapy Academy (AFTA) and an American Association for Marriage and Family Therapy (AAMFT) approved Supervisor and Clinical Member. I love to present internationally and have published articles and book chapters. In my NYC-based private practice I sees couples and coaches therapists in business and clinical practices. I also specializes in leadership, trauma, cross-cultural relationships, digital life, and teaching/learning. I am currently researching how people play. Originally from India, I live in NYC with my partner and bonus son. Connect with me at *salihabava.com* and/or on Twitter: *@ThinkPlay*

Alex Chard

In the early part of my career I worked within the voluntary and statutory sectors with young people in trouble. I then began to work independently. I now work as a systemic organisational consultant, a role which includes inquiry into organisational functioning, culture and practice. Over the last twenty three years my consultancy practice has included working within a wide range of public sector contexts including work within children's social care, education, youth work, criminal justice and within the voluntary sector. My experience of assisting organisations manage change has included working with statutory boards, with management teams helping them to improve their services and on occasion managing services or critical projects. I also assist organisations with inquiring into their future and developing their strategies and plans. My current organisational inquiry and research contexts include conducting inter-agency case reviews where significant harm has been caused and in that context developing reflexive approaches to creating pan-organisational learning. In my MSc. dissertation I conducted a systemic inquiry into the impact of government inspection on the management of a service. My professional doctoral thesis *The Art of Organisational Development* was on creating systemic change and development in public sector management with a particular focus on the development work I undertake with services and their management teams. I am also a visiting senior lecturer to the Professional Doctorate in Systemic Practice at the University of Bedfordshire. My work at the University has also included contributing to the development of a systemic module for a Social Work Masters Programme. I am passionate about co-creating professional knowledge from practice based inquiry and research. *alex@ systemicpractice.com*

Rebecca Gill

I am a Senior Lecturer in the School of Management at Massey University (Albany) in New Zealand, as well as the co-curriculum coordinator for entrepreneurship in the College of Business. I studied for my PhD at the University of Utah. My research examines organising and identity and considers how gender and other differences (such as class, religion, and whiteness) shape organising processes and relationships. In particular, I focus

on entrepreneurship and enterprise as informed by contemporary and historical cultural and place-based norms, and my work around these issues has been published in *Human Relations, Organization, Management Communication Quarterly, Communication Monographs, Journal of Applied Communication Research*, and elsewhere. My additional interests include localism, community enterprise, social justice, and co-working, as well as attention to emerging organisational methods. *r.gill@massey.ac.nz*

Carsten Hornstrup

I work as an independent consultant and researcher primarily with social service and health care organizations. I'm on a continuing journey towards expanding our knowledge about systemic – relational approaches to leadership and organizational development. Coming with a very mixed background as electrician, a MSc in Political Science and my doctoral dissertation on Relational Leadership and Change, the practice-theory connection lie at the heart of my work. *caho@hornstrup-partners.dk*

Andreas Granhof Juhl

I help organisations become "knowledge producing" by creating a position, where the organisation is researching into its own practice. At an organisational level it creates a rich and detailed language about how to create success, for example in working with people with sclerosis. At a team level it creates an experimental attitude from the team trying out new approaches to old situations. And at a personal level it re-defines identity for the employee that starts talking about him- or herself as "researcher" into their own organisational practices. The positive impact on job satisfaction is clear.

This fascinating approach to organisational research, where knowledge is creating from within organisational practices and dialogues, is a major shift. Previously the organisational had based their work on knowledge created by external agents. Now the organisations are themselves developing the knowledge needed to succeed. To me personally this kind of work began at the doctoral programme at the University of Bedfordshire where I designed a research approach to look at my own work as organisational consultant. Having felt the impact of systematically looking more closely on my own practice, this approach developed into a full approach to organisational research that is described in the chapter 'Pragmatic Inquiry'. *andreas@granhofjuhl.dk*

Lisen Kebbe

Movement, transformation, emerging, or emergent movements that creates transformations..... it is hard to find the words for what engages me the most, especially when not writing with the words of my mother tongue, Swedish. I wrote my dissertation at the University of Bedfordshire on conversations during succession in business families, an important part of lifecycles. I see succession as an infinite process that rolls on within business families over the generations. But sometimes it can be very useful to have a helper from the outside to support a safe space and enhance dialogue. That is the work I do and it helps family members to co-create new ways of living and working which are built into succession. I am a psychologist within the domains of management and clinical work and I am now starting up a new career at the University of Uppsala, Campus Gotland. Whatever work I do it is the transformational processes that interests me the most and how to best support them whether with individuals, in families, in working groups or with students. I wrote my doctoral dissertation in essay form to be able to explore a multitude of aspects of my practice and I used the writing process in itself as my analytical tool. That is what you can read about in my chapter "Writing essays as dialogical inquiry". Please contact me if you want to "keep up the conversation". *lisen@kebbe.se*

Sheila McNamee

I have been a member of the University of New Hampshire faculty since 1982. I am a founder of the Taos Institute and serve as its Vice President. My scholarly program centers on exploring the ways in which language and social action construct the social worlds in which we live. I analyze the implications of these constructions for cultural life and am interested in how knowledge in general, and forms of action in particular, are embedded within historical and cultural contexts and engendered within ongoing dialogue. Since my graduate school days, I have been occupied by the distinction drawn between practitioners and researchers (or, alternatively described, practitioners and scholars). In my own case for tenure and promotion, my evaluating committee decided that they need four "scholars" and four "practitioners" to review my work. My thought at that time – same as it is today – was, "Scholars *should be* practitioners and practitioners are surely scholars." This focus on blurring the boundaries between professional practice and academic work has been my commitment as someone whose primary place of work is academia. My book, *Research and Social Change: A Relational Constructionist Approach* (with Dian Marie Hoskings, Routledge, 2012) is my most recent articulation of the need to recognize that scholars *must be* practitioners and practitioners *must be* recognized as forging new scholarly understandings. It is vitally important that we remove the veil of superiority from the position of "researcher" and acknowledge the innovative and transformational work of practitioners. *sheila.mcnamee@unh.edu*

Christine Oliver

My research journey began with an MSc dissertation in Social Policy at LSE, exploring the contexts and consequences of compulsory admission into psychiatric hospital. I became attached to KCC Foundation from its inception, but intervened in my training trajectory as a Systemic Psychotherapist to go and spend a year with Barnett Pearce at UMASS, Amherst, contributing to a research project he led on the workings of mediation from a CMM point of view. I returned to KCC

Foundation to finish off my training, armed with CMM. On return to the UK I developed two strands of interest – organisational and therapeutic practice, which I have sustained and for many years taught systemic leadership and therapy Masters courses where I attempted to develop a systemic approach to research, much assisted by the trainees. I now co-lead the MSc in Systemic Leadership and Organisational Development with Martin Miksits for the University of Bedfordshire. I also work as Consultant Family Therapist and Group Analyst at East London Foundation Trust and am an independent psychotherapist and organisational consultant. I provide systemic leadership and management training and consultancy locally and globally. A primary interest is in consultancy methodologies for structuring dialogue to engender reflexive practice in the work place. In my writing I have contributed to the development of systemic theory and practice through published papers and through her recent books: Reflexive Inquiry, published by Karnac, London (2005) and Complexity, Relationships and Strange Loops, published by the MHA Institute, Canada (2003). *www.systemicdevelopment.eu*

Ann-Margreth Olsson

A thread in my life has been to work hard for the dreams I have while being awake. I wanted family, I wanted to work, longed for dialogue and I valued solidarity. In that respect I guess I am a typical Swede of my generation. Becoming a social worker was perhaps a step towards standing out. In Sweden, a country that has been one of the pinnacles of welfare states, strange as it may seem social workers never really were in high esteem. But I saw it as a way of making a difference and reaching towards the dreams. Change and growth both as a person and on a society level has been my enduring concern. I managed to reach a top level in social care management and during that I became involved in systemic practice. This brought me back to education and I managed my way to become a Professional Doctor in Systemic Practice at the University of Bedfordshire. Sport, especially cycling and handball, have always been at the centre of my life. I have trained, I have coached and more recently I have crewed for my eldest son at Triathlon events. I brought coaching into social work and formed a company AMOVE AB with my husband for this and other change work that did not easily fit into our university positions as lecturers. Lately I have however found new openings and acquired funding for action research on Barnahus (Children's Advocacy Center) and on support of military families. *a@amove.se*

Vikki Reynolds

I am an activist/therapist and primarily I aim to shoulder up teams of folks working in the margins alongside minoritized and marginalized people. This work involves bridging the worlds of social justice activism with community work & therapy. I have supervised and worked as a therapist with refugees and survivors of torture, anti-violence counsellors, mental health and substance misuse counsellors, housing and shelter workers, activists and alongside gender and sexually diverse communities. I am Adjunct Professor, City University of Seattle, Vancouver Canada and have been an Instructor with VCC, UBC at City University of Seattle in the Masters' Program where I received the Dean's award for Distinguished Instruction. I have written and presented internationally on the subjects of resistance to 'trauma', ally work, justice-doing, a supervision of solidarity, ethics, and innovative group work. My writing has been translated into 4 languages. My book, entitled *Doing Justice as a Path to Sustainability in Community Work*, is available for free download along with interviews, keynotes, and articles on my website: *www.vikkireynolds.ca*.

John Shotter

Central to my whole approach is a focus on the *spontaneous, bodily responsiveness* of growing and living beings, both to each other and to the other-nesses in their surroundings, and on the *expressive-ness* of *their* own particular and unique ways of coming-into-Being — *spontaneous* (because it is not pre-meditated), *living* (because it involves con-tinuos open exchange with surroundings), *bodily*

(because it is not hidden in prior thought), *expressive* (because it moves others to respond), and *responsive* (because it is responsive to other's expressiveness, to events occurring in one's surroundings).

If we begin like this, to take our living bodily activities as our basic focus, then new possibilities of a quite novel and surprising kind are opened up. And especially surprising, is *the extra-ordinary nature of our ordinary everyday social activities*, and hitherto unnoticed ways within them that come to an understanding of each other's unique judgments and evaluations, and gradually, to an understanding of our *ways* or *styles* of relating ourselves to both the others and othernesses in our surroundings.

Sometimes I am known as one of the originators of the movement in psychology and social theory known as Social Constructionism. However, I have to say that for me, social constructionism as been a way-station on the way to somewhere else. I have always been concerned with the larger social conditions of our lives together, and with our unresponsiveness to the obvious misery and injustices occurring all around us. Once I made my first forays into the social and behavioral sciences, with the aim of becoming more responsive to such troubles and injustices, it thus came as something of a shock to me to realize that the very activity of pursuing good aims with a good will could still (unintentionally) result in the production of social and moral disasters (Scott 1989; Shotter 2004).

Indeed, the very activity of becoming an 'expert', a 'scholar', an 'academic', an 'intellectual', can lead us so very easily into a contempt for ordinary people, and into ignoring of the fact that all our claims to special knowledge — which we want to 'give back' to 'them' through *our* special plans for *their* betterment — in fact have their origins in *their* activities, and in those of their predecessors. Without the benefit of *their* participation in *our* endeavors, our claims as experts would be completely unintelligible. For beginning with the ancient Greek notion of *ideal forms* hidden behind appearances, we can only too easily think of our research task as that of discovering and naming these *forms* or *patterns* as the *content* of people's expressions. Whereas, in fact, the opposite is the case: It is the context that people's expressions *are contained in* that gives them their *meaning*, their way of influencing our lives (Shotter 1993).

In an earlier book, *Social Accountability and Selfhood* (Shotter 1984), in an effort to overcome the dead-hand of the mechanistic approach to human affairs, I called my approach a *social ecological* one, and it is to that approach that I feel I have now returned (Shotter, 2011). It gives rise to a concern with what we might call *before-the-fact* inquiries into possibilities for the future, rather than the current *after-the-fact* inquiries of the traditional Social Sciences aimed at *explaining* existing forms of social life. *jds@hypatia.unh.edu*

Gail Simon

My early career was in therapeutic work with
children and families in statutory and third
sector settings. I came to systemic practice
through social work in the early 1980s when
I trained in family therapy using structural,
strategic and early Milan approaches. I
undertook further training at the Kensington
Consultation Centre (KCC) in London in the
early 1990s. In 1990, Gwyn Whitfield and I
co-founded The Pink Practice as a response to
oppressive psychotherapeutic practices against
the lesbian, gay and queer communities.
Systemic thinking was a real help in the
fight against pathologising theory and social
constructionism helped further in critically situating theory in ideological
contexts. I have been teaching and supervising therapy for many years and
then embraced practitioner research which I find absolutely inspiring! Lots
of people think research is dull until they find out how many forms of inquiry
there are which echo the values and activities of their own practice. My doctoral
research was on "Writing (as) Systemic Practice" in which I experimented with
dialogical writing styles to reflect my conversational and ethical practice in
therapy, supervision and education. Now I lead the Professional Doctorate in
Systemic Practice at the University of Bedfordshire and enjoy researching the
extraordinariness that is involved in human systems and writing and editing
for professional journals and for the new systemic practice publishing tent,
Everything is Connected Press. *gail.simon@beds.ac.uk*

Karina Solsø

I work as an organizational and leadership
consultant in Ramboll Attractor, Denmark
while at the same time doing a PhD at the
University of Hertfordshire. I am exploring
the role of reflexivity in management consulting and its relationship to ethics. I have
an MSc in Psychology and am studying for
a PhD at the University of Hertfordshire.
As a consultant and a researcher I am interested in the potentials of paying close
attention to and reflect on the interesting
and easily ignored details in the situations we find ourselves. So many interesting and fascinating small movement occur right in front us and in us. What if

we started taking more seriously these small movements and took these rather than abstracted and rational ideas as the starting point of our inquiries? My empirical material emerges from experience with clients and I am continuously trying to integrate insights from my research into practice. Having the opportunity to find myself in the identity and position as a researcher and a practitioner is highly satisfactory and fruitful for me. *karinasolsoe@gmail.com*

Sally St George

By day, I am an Associate Professor in the Faculty of Social Work at the University of Calgary, and a Family Therapist and Clinical Supervisor at the Calgary Family Therapy Centre. A former junior high school teacher, I have been practicing marriage and family therapy for the last 20 years, and am dedicated to creating and utilizing social constructionist principles in my teaching and clinical practice. I also serve on the Boards of Directors for the Taos Institute and Global Partnership for Transformative Social Work. On weekends I work as the Senior Editor of *The Qualitative Report*, an open-access online interdisciplinary journal which is committed to creating a learning community of writers and reviewers to present solid, interesting, and novel works of qualitative inquiry. I credit my learning qualitative research to Ron Chenail (Editor-in-Chief for *The Qualitative Report*) who has helped me learn ways to review and edit manuscripts submitted for publication. He did this by reviewing my reviews and suggesting readings I might use to help authors. Now I have the opportunity to repay the favor by helping reviewers learn ways to encourage qualitative researchers to present their work more rigorously. And in between I take as many ballroom dance lessons as possible with my husband and colleague, Dan Wulff. We especially love, the waltz and west coast swing, and find now that we are falling in love with country dancing. We also take advantage of being near the Canadian Rockies by hiking and snow-shoeing. The beauty is breathtaking! *calgary_home@shaw.ca*

Jacob Storch

I hold a Professional Doctorate in Systemic Practice, and have worked as the founder and managing partner of the largest systemic consultancy in the Nordic countries for 15 years. My new consultancy, joint action a/s, works at the intersection of consulting and research. I teach at Aarhus University and have authored or co-authored five books, including

Leadership Based Coaching (2006 in Danish), A Systemic Community (2012, in Danish), and numerous articles on discursive approaches to management and change. *jacob@joint-action.dk*

Dan Wulff

My professional career began as an in-home social worker in the United States, trying to help families successfully stay together through extremely hard times. This practice grounding shaped my approach to doctoral research and beyond (teaching at the Universities of Oklahoma, Louisville, and now Calgary). I continue to do family therapy and supervise graduate therapists while teaching practice and research courses as a faculty member of the Faculty of Social Work. My simultaneous involvement in practice and in teaching has resulted in my dean referring to me as a "pracademic." I believe that research endeavors are much enriched by researchers who have a solid ongoing appreciation for the vicissitudes of frontline practice. The field of social work is embedded in an interdisciplinary world that approaches clients and communities as complex wholes. Breaking systems down into component parts or variables distorts that which is the focus of our curiosities. Relegating research to experts who are specialists in research backgrounds the participants in ways that deny the contributions that they could offer. The chapter for this book that I wrote with my wife, Sally St. George, articulates the value of changing research practices to complement frontline practice rather than the other way around. My practice/research interests have been nourished by my involvement in co-editing the all-online journal, *The Qualitative Report,* and serving on the Board of the Taos Institute, a global virtual organization supporting social constructionist ideas and applications. *calgary_home@shaw.ca*

9378473R00186

Printed in Great Britain
by Amazon.co.uk, Ltd.,
Marston Gate.